"Professor Hoven has presented us with a detailed textbook on significant parts of the history of post-war Canadian hockey. He has also provided us with a carefully crafted, detailed, and finely balanced insight to the unique role played by Father Bauer as well as his hockey philosophy and his formative influence on the lives of a number of young players, both on and off the ice."

— *Dr. H. Ian Macdonald, president emeritus,*
York University, and former chair of Hockey Canada

"In *Hockey Priest*, Matt Hoven makes a persuasive case for the compatibility of sports and religion, in this case Canadian hockey and the Catholic tradition exemplified by Priest-Coach David Bauer. The perils and pleasures of Bauer's lifelong commitment to infuse spirituality into this sport are lovingly chronicled in this compelling biography."

— *Rebecca T. Alpert,*
professor of religion emerita, Temple University

"Father Bauer came to Japan at the invitation of Mr. Yoshiaki Tsutsumi, president of the Japanese Ice Hockey Federation. Father Bauer gave us an abundance of advice and introduced excellent Canadian players to Japanese hockey to raise our game to an international level. Thanks to his guidance I served as a director and vice president of the IIHF for 34 years."

— *Shoichi Tomita,*
former vice president of the International Ice Hockey Federation

"An excellent book on the life of Father David Bauer, a Basilian priest, who had a positive and lasting influence on the development of Canadian ice hockey. The book chronicles Bauer's success as a manager and hockey coach at St. Michael's College School in Toronto, who moved on to found and develop the Canadian National Team program. His emphasis on skill and technique, as well as the development of the whole person, had a profound effect on hockey at the amateur and elite levels. Father Bauer had a positive influence on all those fortunate enough to be involved under his guidance."

— *Dave Chambers,*
retired professor, School of Kinesiology and Health Science,
York University, Toronto Former University,
Junior A, Team Canada Junior, NHL head and assistant coach

Hockey Priest

HOCKEY PRIEST

Father David Bauer

and the

Spirit of the Canadian Game

Matt Hoven

The Catholic University of America Press
Washington, D.C.

Cataloging-in-Publication Data is available from the Library of Congress

ISBN: 978-0-8132-3787-9 (paperback)

eISBN: 978-0-8132-3810-4 (ebook)

For Hannah, Felicity, & Caleb

"The spirit must predominate over the technical.

Use technique, but let the spirit prevail."

CONTENTS

FIGURES

Front Cover: Bauer coaching a game at Maple Leaf Gardens between the National Team and NHL Old Timers on Februrary 28, 1965 (Courtesy of D.K. (Doc) Seaman Hockey Resource Centre, Hockey Hall of Fame.)

CHAPTER ONE

Bauer the Hockey Philosopher

THE MOST POWERFUL MEN IN CANADIAN HOCKEY wanted David Bauer removed from the game. They did not allow exhibition games between his National Team and their Toronto Maple Leafs and Montreal Canadiens. Despite Bauer being one of Canada's leading authorities in international hockey, they did not want him involved in the establishment of Hockey Canada. Their strong dislike of Bauer surprised a lawyer who had arrived at Montreal's historic Queen Elizabeth Hotel to discuss hockey matters in June of 1968.[1] The attorney defended Bauer against the complaints of NHL President Clarence Campbell and the Canadian NHL team executives. He outlined Bauer's dedication to Canadian hockey and his longtime service to the nation's first-ever National Team in hockey. The lawyer concluded with a warning, "... the publicity which might arise from [Bauer] being side-tracked could be most disadvantageous to Mr. Campbell's office and the Canadien

---

1   W. J. Hopwood Jr., Letter to Gordon Juckes, June 12, 1968, MG28 I 263 18, 300-6-11, Canadian Amateur Hockey Association, 1968–1974, LAC.

and Maple Leaf organizations."[2] President Campbell agreed with the lawyer's assessment: Bauer could not be eliminated. The professional hockey leaders would instead maneuver to limit his influence on the Canadian hockey system.

Many misjudged Bauer as simply an idealist or a "do-gooder." His work with the National Team was not just an "experiment." Neither was it a "one-off" chance to rival the corporate game. Misinterpreting his aims were common. One longtime sports journalist stated at Bauer's passing, "Right to the very end, hardly anybody understood what he was really up to."[3]

Bauer wanted to create a Canadian hockey alternative. Born in 1924, David William Bauer grew up in a prominent family in Waterloo, Ontario. He won a Memorial Cup national championship as a player and a coach. Instead of becoming enamored by hyper-commercialized hockey, he joined the Congregation of St. Basil and became one of their priest-coaches. They supported long-held "muscular Christian"[4] ideals like character development, education, and community spirit, upon which Canadian sport was founded. With these values, they forged plans for a way to break through and restructure hockey.

It is difficult to explain Bauer's vision for the sport. It requires knowledge of ice hockey and its history in Canada. It demands an understanding of Bauer's beliefs about the meaning of sport and its role in educating young Canadians. His thought was forged by different books he read and discussed with those in the hockey world and his religious community. This dialogue produced speeches and written documents about a values-inspired, pragmatic response to issues in hockey felt by coaches and players.[5] Even Bauer found

2   Hopwood, Letter to Juckes. The other executives at the meeting were Hartland Molson, David Molson, Sam Pollock, and Stafford Smythe.

3   Jim Proudfoot, "Père Bauer Was a Lot More Than a Hockey Coach," *Toronto Star*, November 11, 1988, Basilian Archives, Box 2, last file, Bauer fonds.

4   The term "muscular Christianity," according to historian Hugh McLeod, is used "to denote those Christians who have seen moral and religious value in sports and other forms of physical recreation, and have argued that churches can and should promote its place." Hugh McLeod, "Muscular Christianity: American and European," in *Secularization and Religious Innovation in the North Atlantic World*, eds. Hugh McLeod and David Hempton (Oxford, UK: Oxford Scholarship Online, 2017), 2. See also Clifford Putney, *Muscular Christianity: Manhood and Sports in Protestant America, 1880–1920* (Cambridge, MA: Harvard University Press, 2003).

5   His perspective was endorsed by other prominent coaches like Roger Neilson, Fred Shero, Clare Drake, Tom Watt, Dave King, and Tom Renney, among others.

it difficult to convey the depth of his message. To a reporter asking about the purpose of the National Team in 1983, Bauer flinched: "We'd really have to sit down for two days to talk about it."[6] He offered a different way to think about the game.

Bauer was a hockey philosopher, but what do we mean by this phrase? Classically, a philosopher is someone who is a friend or lover of wisdom.[7] By thinking deeply on difficult problems in human living, a person becomes more wise. In this sense, anyone who thinks profoundly about a problem, like how to increase youth participation in ice hockey, is a hockey philosopher. More than that, however, ancient Greeks like Aristotle sought to know past responses to a problem so as to understand the historical development of thought. Building upon the insight of others, they determined a more indispensable viewpoint.[8] For a hockey philosopher, then, it is important to understand the workings of the game, its organization, and its historical evolution. A hockey philosopher must also determine why we play the game and to whose benefit it is played. Thus, a hockey philosopher wrestles with the ultimate problems in the sport. He or she can stand outside of the hockey world—while maintaining insider knowledge of it—and critique its institutions and thus challenge the status quo.[9] A philosopher's personal commitment to an ideal provides the motivation to continually raise concerns about issues.

There are only a few well-known hockey philosophers in Canada. Ken Dryden, a Cornell University law graduate who became a goaltender on several Stanley Cup championship teams, has written many hockey books that grapple with the game's meanings and its social issues, most recently *Game Change*.[10] The most popular philosopher has been Don Cherry, who

6   Clancy Loranger, "Finally, Father Bauer...," *The Province*, November 30, 1983, Box 2, last file, Bauer fonds, Basilian Archives, 59.

7   Jacques Maritain, *An Introduction to Philosophy*, trans. by E. I. Watkin (New York: Sheed & Ward, 2005), xix.

8   Maritain, *An Introduction to Philosophy*, xx.

9   This insight is taken from a contemporary understanding of a related term, a public intellectual. Alan Lightman, "The Role of the Public Intellectual," MIT, https://web.mit.edu/comm-forum/legacy/papers/lightman.html.

10   Ken Dryden, *Game Change: The Life and Death of Steve Montador and the Future of Hockey* (Toronto: McClelland & Stewart, 2017), 1. He also wrote arguably the finest hockey book ever, *The Game* (New York: Wiley & Sons, 1983).

promoted his nationalistic agenda and a rough-and-tough brand of hockey from his "Coach's Corner" spot on *Hockey Night in Canada*. We may also include Lloyd Percival. He was an ingenious fitness guru in the mid-twentieth century who, with his edgy style, promoted advanced coaching tactics and player strategies on his *Sports College* radio show.[11] There are also lesser-known hockey philosophers,[12] and others, like child advocate Sheldon Kennedy, who speak out about a particular issue plaguing sport.[13] Thinkers like Dryden, Cherry, and Bauer hold (or held) prominent public roles and engaged everyday Canadians with their broad vision through mass media. In a team sport that emphasizes group dynamics and frowns upon individual attention given to a teammate, widely known hockey philosophers are as rare as superstars named Gretzky or Lemieux.

Bauer witnessed how a for-profit hockey system exploited young people and betrayed the ideals of Canadian sport. Providing a counterpoint to the Goliaths who ran the hockey system, David Bauer planned an alternative form of hockey built around young amateur players. He did not want to define *amateur* according to the Latin *amator* for "lover," i.e., a person who plays for the love of the game and not for finanical reward. Instead, Bauer's spin on *amateur* was a combination of *a* (a Latin prefix meaning "not") and *maturus* (meaning "timely" or "ripe"), thus stating that the amateur athlete was "not mature" enough to handle the demands of preparing for a professional career.[14] In altering the meaning, Bauer underlined how a young player should be seen first as a human person in need of development and education.

---

11   Gary Mossman, *Lloyd Percival: Coach and Visionary* (Woodstock, ON: Seraphim Editions, 2013), 46–48.

12   Such as classics professor W. G. Hardy, who taught at the University of Alberta. Terry Jones, "Coronary Prevented Hardy from Opposing Hockey Czar," *Edmonton Journal*, December 20, 1969, 17, University of Alberta, RCRF, 83-48-378. Another lesser-known philosopher was British-born Alexander Meiklejohn, who became dean of Brown University, where he was an early advocate of the new game. Stephen Hardy and Andrew C. Holman, *Hockey: A Global History* (Champaign: University of Illinois Press, 2018), 97. Other hockey writings by the likes of Roch Carrier or Peter Gzowski have been impactful.

13   Sheldon Kennedy and James Grainger, *Why I Didn't Say Anything: The Sheldon Kennedy Story* (Toronto: Insomniac Press, 2006), 1.

14   Terry O'Malley, "Father David Bauer CSB (1924–1988)—A Life in 'Quotations'," Terry O'Malley Collection.

Understanding Bauer in Hockey and Its History

Bauer's story is particularly significant because it spans major periods in the historical development of hockey, as depicted in four stages by historians Stephen Hardy and Andrew Holman in *Hockey: A Global History*.[15] Stage 1 marks the origins of the sport, when it consisted of diverse, traditional ball and stick ice games. These converged in the Montreal game in the last half of the 1870s, initiating Stage 2, where the general rules and purpose of hockey became accepted, and a game had become *the* game. From 1920 to 1972, Stage 3, there was a divergence globally of hockey's rules, equipment, etc., which offered a diversity within hockey and how it was played by different nations. Stage 4, from 1972 to 2010, marked the dominance of corporate hockey, in which the NHL has become the overriding, global brand of the sport.

Bauer's life in hockey spans the final three stages. His religious community, the Basilian Fathers, became involved in the convergence of the sport (Stage 2) early in the twentieth century when its St. Michael's College Majors won national championships. Bauer, who played for the school in the 1940s, became the Majors' coach and won a national junior championship in 1961. Up to that point, Bauer personally experienced divergence in the Canadian game (Stage 3) as he promoted amateur play against the backdrop of professional demands within the sport. Bauer's founding of Canada's Olympic hockey team established a divergent path for elite hockey in the country, in part supported by hockey insights learned from other nations. However, as the St. Michael's Majors and National Teams experienced, the dominant NHL game squeezed out variant forms of hockey and took control of the sport (Stage 4). The bulk of Bauer's time in hockey was spent fighting against the trends within the final stage, that is, hockey's corporatization, where all roads led to the NHL. Bauer countered that the sport should first serve the needs of persons playing the game. This required holding ideals above profit margins and gratuitous violence.

In forging a National Team program, Bauer established a platform to challenge mainstream assumptions about Canadian hockey determined by a corporate mentality. He argued that producing professional players should not be the concern of a youth hockey system. Thus, he wanted Canadians to talk about the purpose of the sport: How does hockey impact communities

15 Hardy and Holman, *Hockey: A Global History*, 12–13.

and the people who play the game? How could hockey improve so that more people could benefit from it?

To realize Bauer's plans to reform Canadian hockey, it is necessary to understand the hockey system itself. In its own way, this book outlines major trends within Canadian hockey history as seen through Bauer's life. For now, it is helpful to describe the Canadian hockey system as it exists today, with an eye toward Bauer and his criticisms. Knowing the direction hockey took in Canada provides the context for Bauer's concerns.

The Canadian hockey system is organized by player age and ability, beginning with its community hockey organizations and then advancing to club hockey organizations (for teenagers), junior organizations (for young adults), university and college hockey, and professional hockey. For players up to the age of twelve, leagues and teams are run by community hockey organizations, also known as "house league hockey." These local organizations are grouped into geographic zones, creating a non-competitive recruitment system for young players.[16] Players are organized into teams and leagues based upon skill level.[17] For U7 (Under-seven) and U9 (Under-nine) categories, indoor ice-time for a game and a practice per week are shared by multiple teams made up of boys and girls. At the U11 and U13 levels, games are played on a full sheet of ice and time commitment can vary, with higher calibre teams usually completing up to two practices and two games per week.[18] By the end of house league hockey, players are expected to skate, shoot, and play their position. As girls age, they typically play on all-female teams yet can compete against similarly tiered all-boy teams.[19]

16   Hockey Canada, "Answers to Questions Asked by Hockey Parents," https://www.hockeycanada.ca/en-ca/hockey-programs/parents/faq.

17   Jonathon Edwards, "Recruiting and Retaining Canadian Minor Hockey Players by Local Youth Club Hockey Organizations, Canada's Governing Hockey Organizations, Major Junior, and Intercollegiate Hockey Organizations: Exploring Canada's Elite Level Hockey Development System" (doctoral thesis, University of Alberta, Faculty of Physical Education and Recreation, 2012), 6.

18   Hockey Canada, "Answers to Questions." At the upper tiers of community hockey, children may also have several tournaments throughout the year and travel outside of their area.

19   In past decades, Canadians have slowly adapted to European and American advancements to the game, with increased emphasis on scientific measuring and testing instead of merely effort and grit. For instance, U7 and U9 teams today play games cross-wise or "cross-ice" instead of on a full-length sheet of ice, enabling more

At the U15 level, players begin to body check and can compete to play in local club hockey or stay with their community hockey program.[20] At the club hockey level, the most elite level is AAA (Triple A).[21] This level provides the best chance for male players to progress to the NHL via one of two paths: the Canadian Hockey League (CHL or Major Junior), or National Collegiate Athletic Association (NCAA) hockey at a US college (via Canadian Junior A).

The quickest path to the NHL is potentially the CHL or Major Junior hockey (U21). The CHL is the world's largest development league for professional hockey. Its sixty teams—fifty-two of which are based in Canada—vie for the Memorial Cup each spring. When players advance to U18 hockey, their playing rights are drafted by a CHL team (either in Western Canada, Ontario, or Quebec/Atlantic Canada).[22] Top players typically begin Major Junior hockey at age sixteen or seventeen, and as young as eighteen to play in the NHL.[23] The NHL is the premier hockey league in the world, with thirty-two North American teams and a pre-pandemic annual revenue of five billion USD.[24]

"puck-touches" and maximizing artificial ice usage. Some hockey parents disagreed with this change; see Spencer Riehl, Ryan Snelgrove, and Jonathon Edwards, "Mechanisms of Institutional Maintenance in Minor Hockey," *Journal of Sport Management* 33, no. 2 (2019): 100.

20   Hockey Canada, "Answers to Questions"; Hockey Canada, "Hockey Canada Playing Rules, 2020–2021," May 2020, http://rulebook.hockeycanada.ca/english/introduction/. There are some leagues at lower levels of U15 and U18 that offer a non-body-checking option.

21   Edwards, "Recruiting and Retaining Canadian Minor Hockey Players," 7.

22   These leagues are the Western Hockey League, the Ontario Hockey League, and the Quebec Major Junior Hockey League. In 2018–19, CHL teams hosted more than nine million fans in league and post-season play. Canadian Hockey League, "About the CHL," https://chl.ca/aboutthechl. It is also possible for boys as young as fourteen years old to be drafted by a CHL team. See Joe Todd and Jonathan Edwards, "Understanding Parental Support in Elite Sport: A Phenomenological Approach to Exploring Midget Triple A Hockey in the Canadian Maritimes," *Sport in Society* 24, no. 9 (2021): 1591.

23   There are exceptions in the CHL for a limited number of over-aged twenty-one-year-old players.

24   Mike Ozanian and Kurt Badenhausen, "NHL Team Values 2020: Hockey's First Decline in Two Decades," *Forbes*, December 9, 2020, https://www.forbes.com/sites/mikeozanian/2020/12/09/nhl-team-values-2020-hockeys-first-decline-in-two-decades/?sh=594ab17370dd.

The other hockey career path for Canadian males runs through the NCAA. Players who choose to play US collegiate hockey cannot play in the CHL because the league does not meet the NCAA's definition of amateurism.[25] These players advance to the U21 level of Junior A hockey, which is a step below the CHL, but meets the NCAA's eligibility standards of amateurism. After earning their collegiate degree, players may advance toward professional leagues in Europe, the US, or Canada.

During much of Bauer's life, the Canadian hockey system made playing junior hockey and earning a high school or college degree very difficult. Along with many others, he found it shameful that hundreds of Canadians left for a US college to earn a hockey scholarship.[26] More recently, the CHL began offering Canadian university or U SPORTS scholarships to its former players. Former CHL players can earn a university degree while playing in Canada.[27]

Female hockey has grown since Bauer's time. Top players seek advancement in their local hockey clubs toward a chance for a U SPORTS or NCAA hockey scholarship.[28] There are also possibilities of playing at one of a few dozen Canadian sports high schools that are sanctioned by Hockey Canada.[29] While few women can earn a living playing professional hockey, a new league established in 2023 offers improved possibilities.[30] The business model for women's hockey is much smaller than the NHL, which does not

25 CHL players receive a modest, weekly stipend and may receive other monetized perks that break the NCAA's amateur standards of eligibility (even in the midst of the NCAA's acceptance of name, image, and likeness [NIL] rights in 2021). Dan Murphy, "Everything You Need to Know About the NCAA's NIL Debate," *ESPN*, September 1, 2021, https://www.espn.com/college-sports/story/_/id/31086019/everything-need-know-ncaa-nil-debate.

26 Andrew Holman, "The Canadian Hockey Player Problem: Cultural Reckoning and National Identities in American Collegiate Sport, 1947–80," *Canadian Historical Review* 88, no. 3 (2007): 439–68.

27 Today the CHL develops more Canadian university players than Junior A hockey does. Canadian Hockey League, "About the CHL." Also, Jonathon Edwards, interview with author, December 8, 2021.

28 Hockey Canada, "Guide to Female Hockey in Canada," 2018, 4–5, https://cdn.hockeycanada.ca/hockey-canada/Hockey-Programs/Female/Downloads/female_hockey_guide_e.pdf.

29 Hockey Canada, "Guide to Female Hockey," 17.

30 Alex Azzi, "The Current State of Professional Women's Hockey, Explained," *NBC Sports*, January 19, 2021, https://onherturf.nbcsports.com/2021/01/19/the-current-state-of-professional-womens-hockey-explained/.

directly finance the women's game. The best female hockey players also seek to earn a seasonal spot playing for Canada's National Women's Team, which competes at the Olympics and World Championships. Nearly 100,000 girls and women play hockey in organized Canadian leagues annually; male hockey participants number around half a million.[31]

School-based hockey has not been prominent over the past century. Historically, there has been a patchwork of regions that hosted high school hockey leagues, including a small number of preparatory schools.[32] More recently, Hockey Canada has started to sanction these school programs, and now sanctions over 150 hockey schools nationally.[33] These schools allow more players to train during the day when indoor arena availability is high. Some schools merely provide technical training in a publicly-funded setting, whereas others include diverse training methods, organized contests, and residences in a privately-funded setting.[34] While the number of hockey schools grows as a means to respond to increased interest in elite sport training, the great majority of players continue training outside the school setting.

Decades ago, Bauer believed that youth hockey was increasingly mirroring hockey systems that placed high demands on players, promoted violence, and engaged in overly scientific coaching. Today it is easy to see how a win-at-all-costs approach can easily grip a youth hockey team, where team strategies win out over individual skills and personal development.[35] Youth

---

31   Hockey Canada, "Answers to Questions." During the first full season of the pandemic, there was a 5% drop in hockey participation numbers, falling to a total of 605,963. By comparison, USA Hockey reported a smaller drop and had a total registration of 561,700 players—a gap of 44,000 players that has been shrinking over the past decade. Sean Fitz-Gerald, "Hockey Canada Faces Uncertainty as Registration Numbers Plummet," *The Athletic*, November 27, 2020, https://theathletic. com/2222532/2020/11/27/hockey-canada-faces-uncertainty-as-registration-numbers-plummet/. Prior to the pandemic, participation rates among boys had flatlined.

32   Edwards, interview.

33   Hockey Canada, "History of the Hockey Canada Skills Academy (HCSA) Program," https://www.hockeycanada.ca/en-ca/hockey-programs/schools/hcsa. Without sanctioning these programs, Hockey Canada runs the risk of losing control of growing segments of Canadian hockey.

34   Canadian Sport School Hockey League, "National Leaders in Education Based Hockey," http://www.csshl.ca/wp-content/uploads/sites/2/2021/07/csshl-flatsheet-2021-22.pdf. This league is sanctioned by Hockey Canada, and from 2009 to 2021 has grown from eight to ninety-four teams nationally.

35   See further details about this problem in Josh Ogden and Jonathon R.

sport has become a billion dollar industry, where hockey features expensive equipment, private instruction, and showcase tournaments.[36] While youth coaches are typically volunteers working for community organizations, those at the most elite levels can receive salaries.[37] Many parents want their child to graduate into higher levels of the sport, but enrolling a child in a six-month season no longer seems enough. Rising demands on families disrupt other human values. Further, budget-conscious Canadians are left excluded from an increasingly expensive sport.[38]

Another problem tied to Bauer's concern about the management of the hockey system is specifically tied to junior hockey, where the CHL today is mired in court challenges and public dismay over pay-for-play, safe-work spaces, and health risks (e.g., concussions and sexual misconduct).[39] An antiquated mentality trickles down from professional and junior hockey into club and community league systems, where agents look for talent among players as young as age ten in extreme cases and junior players receive preferential treatment in the face of sexual assault allegations.[40] In this vein, several elite hockey programs have arisen that exist outside of Hockey Canada's minor hockey system of community league hockey.[41] These unsanctioned super-leagues typically focus on creating elite hockey players out of even elementary school-aged children, where they offer more ice time,

---

Edwards, "Are Canadian Stakeholders Resting on Their Laurels? A Comparative Study of the Athlete Pathway Through the Swedish and Canadian Male Ice Hockey Systems," *Journal of Sport Management* 30 (2016): 320.

36 Edwards, interview. See also Ken Campbell and Jim Parcels, *Selling the Dream: How Hockey Parents and Their Kids Are Paying the Price for Our National Obsession* (Toronto, ON: Viking, 2013), 1–25.

37 Edwards, interview. Edwards knew of a U15 coach earning $40,000 per year, while many club coaches receive reimbursement of expenses. Some coaches might earn money by charging players for special skills sessions or for spring league coaching.

38 Todd and Edwards, "Understanding Parental Support," 1591.

39 Ken Campbell, "Shocking Allegations in CHL Lawsuit Detail Sexual Abuse and 'A Deviant Culture,'" *The Hockey News*, December 9, 2020, https://www.si.com/hockey/news/shocking-allegations-in-chl-lawsuit-detail-sexual-abuse-and-a-deviant-culture. Rick Westhead, "Former Player Taught 'Craft' of Fighting at 16 Wants WHL Held Accountable, Affidavit Says," *TSN*, May 18, 2021, https://www.tsn.ca/westhead-former-player-taught-craft-of-fighting-at-16-wants-whl-held-accountable-affidavit-says-1.1641818.

40 Edwards, interview; Edwards, "Recruiting and Retaining Canadian Minor Hockey Players," 90–91.

41 Hockey Canada, "Answers to Questions."

high cost coaching, and even air travel to games—and dilute the established community-club system.[42]

Today Bauer would question why fighting remains at the junior and professional levels, despite a drop in hockey violence in past decades.[43] Problems with fighting came into focus after three deaths of former NHL hockey enforcers in 2011. Their passing revealed the impact of concussions, the fragility of young adults, and the need for improved off-ice care.[44]

Issues of racism have also delivered major headlines in recent years— something that runs contrary to Bauer's hockey philosophy of fostering human development. Fingers can be pointed at hardnosed coaches, racist incidents on the ice, and a lack of diversity at the top levels of the sport.[45] An expensive, foreign game played on ice remains a harder sell to many new immigrant Canadian families, despite efforts to introduce newcomers to the sport.

In spite of positive changes in hockey—like scholarships for CHL players, higher participation among females, decreased fighting, outreach to a more diverse audience, improved coaching standards, and better awareness about player mental health—Bauer's underlying philosophical concern about the hockey system remains: Why does a hyper-commercialized hockey mindset direct and maintain control over many choices in the sport? Further to Bauer's primary concern, why does organized hockey not better engage educational institutions so as to make education a higher priority in the sport? Ultimately, Bauer's concern focused on core values: What matters most to Canadians and their youth? What kind of people should hockey create? He was not siding

---

42   These leagues also allow parents to choose the team their child plays for. This is more common, for instance, in the Greater Toronto Hockey League. See Colleen Underwood, "Alberta's Hockey Super League Gains Momentum from Players Looking for Elite Stream," *CBC News*, February 26, 2019, https://www.cbc.ca/news/canada/calgary/alberta-hockey-super-league-1.5033314; Edwards, interview.

43   For instance, see The Canadian Press, "15 for Fighting: QMJHL Announces Stiffer Penalties for Players who Drop the Gloves," *CBC*, October 1, 2020, https://www.cbc.ca/sports/hockey/qmjhl-new-fighting-penalties-1.5745501.

44   Derek Boogaard, Rick Rypien, and Wade Belak died in the Summer of 2011. Tom Cohen, "Three Hockey Enforcers Die Young in Four Months, Raising Questions," *CNN*, September 1, 2011, http://www.cnn.com/2011/SPORT/09/01/nhl.enforcers.deaths/index.html?hpt=hp_c1. See also Dryden, *Game Change*, 433–94.

45   Steve Simmons, "Racism in Hockey—the Story that Never Ends," *Toronto Sun*, January 24, 2022, https://torontosun.com/sports/hockey/simmons-racism-in-hockey-the-story-that-never-ends.

with either hockey purists or progressives. He demanded a rational discussion toward pragmatic solutions of hockey's social issues.

At this moment, when the sport is centrifuged around the NHL and youth hockey often mirrors a hypercompetitive model, it is vital to reflect on major sources, important thinkers, and first principles in hockey. A return to the sources means reflecting on key figures in hockey's past who proposed reforms for the sport. A clear example of recalling hockey's roots is *A Hotly Contested Affair: Hockey in Canada* by Andrew Holman.[46] Reviewing major hockey documents on the occasion of the sport's sesquicentennial, including two pieces written by Bauer, enables a renewed look at both new and perennial problems. It is not the case that past figures have all the answers. Understanding historically-contingent decisions and considering alternative paths from those moments can reimagine tensions in the polarization of Canadian hockey. Past traditions can stir new ideas. This is the pragmatic value of Bauer and other thinkers.

Bauer is not the lone idealist who took up the idea of sport as educational and values-forming. Early feminists, middle-class educators, and Protestant organizations, along with the modern Olympic movement and many Canadian university sporting programs, have all made moral claims within sport and legitimized it as a place of struggle over values and politics.[47] Many emphasized social commitments promoted by the Christian gospel, believing that improving the social environment within the nation allowed for the advancement of Christian values.[48] Throughout the late nineteenth and early twentieth centuries, they promoted a social gospel in sporting programs at public schools, YMCAs, and elsewhere to advance the educational benefits of sport participation.[49]

---

46   Andrew Holman, *A Hotly Contested Affair: Hockey in Canada* (Toronto, ON: University of Toronto Press, 2020), 340–43. Another important scholarly work on the international game is Bruce Berglund, *The Fastest Game in the World: Hockey and the Globalization of Sports* (Oakland: University of California Press, 2021).

47   Bruce Kidd, "Muscular Christianity and Value-Centred Sport: The Legacy of Tom Brown in Canada," *Sport in Society* 16, no. 4 (2013): 409.

48   Although they promoted a narrow anglophile Canadian nationalism, which often excluded French (predominantly Catholic) Canadians, girls and women, and immigrants and Indigenous Peoples, their influence countered commercialized sport into the 1950s. Kidd, "Muscular Christianity," 410. Those who succeeded them in the movement eventually secularized it, and often became more associated with Marxism and socialism than with a Christian denomination.

49   Kidd, "Muscular Christianity," 410.

Bauer's criticisms of the status quo were rooted not in the progressive thought that bloomed in the 1960s, but in philosophers, the Basilian Fathers, and his family. His thought offered reforms according to his faith-inspired values and pragmatic realism. One reporter noted at his passing: "He fascinated me with some of his ideals and philosophies. Most of them offered even the biggest cynic food for thought. They admired him in Russia and loved him in Japan. They called him the Hockey Father and kept inviting him back … for his hockey knowledge … [and] for his beneficial influence on young people."[50] His catchphrases, like "combining hockey and education," or "use technique, but let the spirit prevail," reveal his counterposition to a dominant, corporate model as he cooperated with many in Canada's social and sport reforms.

Understanding Bauer as a Basilian Father and a Priest-Coach

While Bauer gained allies for his approach to hockey, he relied foundationally on the mentorship and institutional framework of his religious community.

The Basilian Fathers began as a group of teachers in the aftermath of the French Revolution. A group of ten priests taught in a few different schools in the early 1800s, as they remained loosely organized out of fear of political leaders who dissolved religious communities that rejected the Revolution.[51] In 1822, they became an official association of teaching and preaching priests in France's southeastern diocese of Viviers; they began taking vows of poverty, chastity, obedience, and stability in 1852.[52] They remained a less formally organized community than many in the Catholic world, not following a strict, singular way of life. Basilian historians note: "Each member retained his individual personality and particular idiosyncrasies, and innate peculiarities were accepted in a spirit of tolerance."[53] The group grew to twenty-two men in 1850, 100 in 1875, and 155 in 1900.

The Basilian Fathers arrived in Canada in 1850 when the Bishop of Toronto, a former Basilian student in France, asked for help teaching an

---

50   George Gross, "Father Dave, Friend to All," *Toronto Sun*, November 11, 1988, 12.

51   Ron Griffin and Michael Hayden, "Transformations and Consequences: The Basilians in France and North America," *Historical Studies* 82 (2016): 7–8.

52   Griffin and Hayden, "Transformations and Consequences," 9. They mitigated their vow of poverty so members could retain some control of their personal income.

53   Griffin and Hayden, "Transformations and Consequences," 9.

impoverished Irish immigrant population.[54] In North America, governments were more neutral on matters of religion. This openness in turn meant that the religious community promoted a secular education for its educator-priests and was not so antagonistic to local governments.[55] The Basilians tried to give their students an education comparable to that in public high schools and colleges, and over time became well-educated high school and university teachers, parish priests, and advocates for social justice.[56]

Based out of Toronto, the religious community eventually became more numerous than the community in France. They established their mother house near St. Michael's Cathedral, and founded a College namesake in 1852.[57] They added Assumption College in Windsor, Ontario in 1870, and worked in several parish churches in southern Ontario.[58] As membership in the community grew, they opened colleges in Texas (Waco and Houston) along with a nearby seminary around the turn of the century.[59] In the late

54 James Hanrahan, *The Basilian Fathers (1822–1972)* (Toronto, ON: The Basilian Press, 1973), 32. The Toronto bishop was Armand Francois Marie de Charbonnel.

55 Griffin and Hayden, "Transformations and Consequences," 12.

56 Hanrahan, *The Basilian Fathers*, 234. Tensions between the two Basilian groups resulted in a split between the French and North American Basilians in 1922. They reunited in 1955.

57 Wallace P. Platt, *Dictionary of Basilian Biography: Lives of Members of the Congregation of Priests of Saint Basil from its Origins in 1822 to 2002*, 2nd ed. (Toronto: University of Toronto Press, 2005), xvii.

58 Hanrahan, *The Basilian Fathers*, 75. This included Toronto, Windsor, Chatham, and Owen Sound.

59 Hanrahan, *The Basilian Fathers*, 132. Here is a list of the Basilian-run high schools and colleges, many of which continue as educational institutions yet not under Basilian leadership: St. Michael's College, Toronto, 1852–1958; Assumption College, Windsor, Ontario, 1870–1957; St. Basil's College, Waco, TX, 1899–1915; St. Thomas High School, Houston, 1900–; Detroit Catholic Central High School, 1928–; St. Mary's Boys' High School, Calgary, Alberta, 1933–1968; St. Thomas More College, Saskatoon, SK, 1936–2010; Aquinas Institute, Rochester, New York, 1937–2000; St. Michael's College School, Toronto, 1950–; St. Charles College, Sudbury, Ontario, 1951–1993; St. Paul's High School, Saskatoon, 1952–1965; St. Francis High School, Lethbridge, Alberta, 1957–2000; St. Mary's College, Sault Ste. Marie, Ontario, 1956–1986; St. Mark's College, Vancouver, 1956–2005; Assumption College School, Windsor, 1957–1994; Michael Power High School, Toronto, Ontario, 1957–1998; St. Joseph's High School, Ottawa, 1958–1962; University of St. Michael's College, 1958–90; Andrean High School, Gary, Indiana, 1959–2012; St. Joseph's College, Edmonton, 1963–2020; St. Pius X High School, Albuquerque, New Mexico, 1968–2000; Bishop O'Dowd High School,

1920s, they sent priests to help with colleges in Rochester, New York, and Detroit.[60] In Western Canada, the community took over a Calgary high school and opened a college in Saskatoon in the 1930s.[61] Athletics began to play a significant role in the schools, especially under the enthused leadership of Father Henry Carr. The community's overall mission had become focused on education; by the start of World War Two, nearly half of the 173 Basilian members worked in high schools. The postwar period was a boom time for the community, as new colleges and high schools were opened in New York, Texas, and across Canada. The North American community soon ran a network of fourteen high schools and universities with its some seven hundred active members, most of whom came from Canada.[62]

By 1947, when Bauer joined the community, many of the Basilian schools promoted sports. This tradition sought to engage sport in the complete education of young men. Through sporting mentorship, the priest-coaches promoted the unity of body and soul, the development of character, a communal spirit, and good citizenship. While reflecting ideals set out by other Christian groups, the Basilian sporting tradition was organized by a religious community of celibate men offering mentorship within schools for boys and which gave greater social prominence to local Catholics.[63] These developments reflected greater interest in sport by Catholic groups around the globe.

Oakland, California, 1978–2001; Holy Redeemer, Detroit, 1999–2005. See Michelle Sawyers, Archivist at Basilian Archives, Email message to author, April 1, 2019. The Basilians also had a short-lived expansion to Louisville, Ohio, from 1867 to 1873, ran colleges in Blida, Algeria, 1868–1903, and Nuestra Señora de la Asuncion College in Cali, Colombia, 1986–2019, and continue to run Cristo Rey High School in Detroit, 2008–. Basilian Fathers, "Apostolate Timeline," Basilian Fathers Bicentennial—2022, https://www.basilianbicentennial.com/. Although Father Tom Mohan, CSB, founded and led Henry Carr High School in Toronto, the school was understood as a "special apostolate" (1973–1990) because it was operated by the Metropolitan Separate (Catholic) School Board. Sawyers, email.

60   Hanrahan, *The Basilian Fathers*, 221.
61   Hanrahan, *The Basilian Fathers*, 224–25.
62   Platt, *Dictionary of Basilian Biography*, xix.
63   A focused review of Bauer's approach to sport-coach mentorship was originally published in Matt Hoven, "Practices for Sport-Coach Mentorship: A Historical Case Study for Coaches in Catholic Schools Today," *E-journal of Catholic Education in Australasia*, 2024, available online at: https://researchonline.nd.edu.au/ecea/

Hockey and Religion

How can we understand the interplay between hockey and religion today in a secularized Canada? A religious voice like Bauer's can offer a larger perspective about the purpose of a sport. It can identify spiritual elements within hockey and interpret their influence as a deep social force.[64] Here, we move past journalistic connections to religion, such as when Mark Messier was dubbed "the Messiah" for a championship New York Rangers team in 1994, or when superstar Connor McDavid was nicknamed "McJesus."[65] Attempting to argue that hockey acts as Canada's national religion—for instance, "In a land so inescapably and inhospitably cold, hockey is the dance of life, an affirmation that despite the deathly chill of winter we are alive"[66]—places larger meanings and nationalistic sentiment upon hockey. This is most distinctly done in traditionally Catholic Quebec, where the Montreal Canadiens are forever known as "Les Glorieux," and their jersey as "La Sainte-Flanelle," even amidst the province's Quiet Revolution and decline in church attendance.[67] For Bauer, the above phrases underline the social significance of sport, but the hyperbole risks idolatry. Hockey players need not be revered as saints or

64   We want to avoid assuming that religious institutions and persons have little to contribute to wider sporting discussions, because to do so would minimize sport's social significance. Tracy Trothen, "Hockey: A Divine Sport?—Canada's National Sport in Relation to Embodiment, Community and Hope," *Studies in Religion* 35, no. 2 (2006): 291. For further theoretical support, see William A. Barbieri, Jr., "The Post-Secular Problematic," in *At the Limits of the Secular: Reflections on Faith and Public Life*, ed. William A. Barbieri, Jr. (Grand Rapids, MI: Eerdmans, 2014), 139; C. Shilling and P. A. Mellor, "Re-Conceptualizing Sport as a Sacred Phenomenon," *Sociology of Sport Journal* 31, no. 3 (2014): 351; and Tom Gibbons, "Challenging the Secular Bias in the Sociology of Sport," in *Global Perspectives on Sports and Christianity*, ed. Afe Adogame, Nick J. Watson, and Andrew Parker (Abingdon: Routledge, 2018), 13–17.

65   J. Scholes and R. Sassower, *Religion and Sports in American Culture* (New York: Routledge, 2014), 134–40; Paula Simons, "The Oilers and the City that Loves Them Gear Up for Glory," *Edmonton Journal*, April 12, 2017, https://edmontonjournal.com/sports/hockey/nhl/edmonton-oilers/paula-simons-8.

66   Bruce Kidd and John MacFarlane, *The Death of Hockey* (Toronto: New Press, 1972), 4.

67   Olivier Bauer, *Hockey as Religion: The Montreal Canadiens* (Champaign, IL: Common Ground Publishing, 2011), 27–30. See also Carrier, *The Hockey Sweater* (Toronto: Tundra Books, 1984); John Valentine and Brandon Toal, "The Rocket, the Riot, and the Revolution: Hockey in French Canada," *Canadian Ethnic Studies Journal* 53, no. 3 (2021): 241.

saviors, and making everything sacred renders religious meanings useless.[68] However, these religious engagements in hockey affirm that participation is neither merely entertainment nor without substance.

To understand how religion works in society and within hockey, some thinkers argue for a more complex approach that weighs historical and contextual realities.[69] Among them are Zachary Taylor Smith and Steven Waller, theorists in sport and religion, who argue that greater contextualization of these instances of sport and religion require interdisciplinary research that makes more accurate accounts of reality.[70] Wrestling with historical accounts, uncovering stories of faith adherents participating in sports, and searching for a spiritual dimension within games assist in advancing understandings of faith in society.[71] Analyzing more carefully the context and interplay between hockey and religion is most helpful for understanding Bauer. Ignoring his religiousness would be a mistake, as would viewing him as a sporting savior.

We see a truer picture of Bauer and the sport through examining prominent historical events, sporting institutions, and his role as a priest in English-speaking Canada. His work is only one of many examples. The Flying Fathers, a group of priests playing exhibition hockey games for local charities nationally and internationally, was co-founded by Father Les Costello, who played at St. Michael's and later for the Toronto Maple Leafs.[72] Costello knew Bauer, as did his brother Murray Costello, who became the head of the Canadian Amateur Hockey Association, later Hockey Canada. Other historical connections lie in a hockey boarding school, Athol Murray College of Notre Dame in Wilcox, Saskatchewan, which Bauer became affiliated

68   Bauer, *Hockey as Religion*, 65–66; Cavanaugh, "Religious-Secular Distinction," 110.

69   Willian Cavanaugh, "The Invention of the Religious-Secular Distinction," in Barbieri, ed., *At the Limits of the Secular*, 110.

70   Zachary Taylor Smith and Steven Waller, "Surveying the Landscape of Theories and Frameworks Used in the Study of Sport and Religion: An Interdisciplinary Approach," *Journal of the Christian Society for Kinesiology, Leisure and Sports Studies* 6, no. 1 (2018): 11–12.

71   Rebecca Alpert and Arthur Remillard, "Introduction," in *Gods, Games and Globalization: New Perspectives on Religion and Sport*, ed. Rebecca Alpert and Arthur Remillard (Macon, GA: Mercer University Press, 2019), 7.

72   Frank Cosentino, *Holy Hockey! The Story of Canada's Flying Fathers* (Toronto: Burnstown Publishing House, 2018), 9–19. Costello played for the Leafs' 1948 Stanley Cup Championship team.

with because of his friendship with Père Murray. Many Canadians supported the Knights of Columbus, a Catholic men's fraternity that has, among other things, sponsored youth hockey across Canada for decades. Missionaries, like the Catholic priests of the Scarboro Missions, spread the Christian message through hockey in Japan and in so doing inadvertently catapulted Bauer into a longstanding hockey role there. These Anglo-Catholic examples of muscular Catholicism have largely been overlooked in the history of Canadian sport, for two reasons: first, religious examples in a secular world can feel taboo and best left to a religious past; second, priority given to muscular Christianity as a Protestant doctrine or a French incarnation reflects the two solitudes of the English Protestant and French Catholic research divide.

The intermingling of Catholic organizations and hockey also has a shadow side. This is most tellingly portrayed in survivors' stories about federally-funded Indigenous residential schools. Many survivors speak of priests enticing children to their schools through sport; sport would help children survive the abuse received from school leaders.[73] Feel-good publicity of Indigenous players' success at a Canadian game hid the hard reality of these schools.[74] For example, Fred Sasakamoose, the first Indigenous person from a Treaty First Nations to play in the NHL, recalled French hockey-loving priests who encouraged his sporting success.[75] Sasakamoose later recanted: "I didn't want to be a hockey player.... All I wanted was my parents." Although

73 Truth and Reconciliation Commission of Canada (TRC), "Document I: Excerpts from *The Survivors Speak: A Report of the Truth and Reconciliation Commission of Canada* (2015)," 78, 80, 77. For further reading, see Michael A. Robidoux, *Stickhandling Through the Margins: First Nations Hockey in Canada* (Toronto: University of Toronto Press, 2012); Will Cardinal, *First Nations Hockey Players* (Edmonton: Eschia Books, 2008); and Don Marks, *Playing the White Man's Games* (Winnipeg: J. Gordon Shillingford Publishing, 2014).

74 Braden Te Hiwi and Janice Forsyth, "'A Rink at This School Is Almost as Essential as a Classroom': Hockey and Discipline at Pelican Lake Indian Residential School, 1945–1951," *Canadian Journal of History* 52, no. 1 (Spring/Summer 2017): 82; Taylor McKee and Janice Forsyth, "Witnessing Painful Pasts: Understanding Images of Sports at Canadian Indian Residential Schools," *Journal of Sport History* 46, no. 2 (2019): 177.

75 TRC, "Document I: Excerpts," 82. See Fred Sasakamoose, *Call Me Indian* (Toronto: Viking, 2021), 1. Richard Wagamese's related novel and film, *Indian Horse*, tell about a young Ojibway boy who finds salvation through playing hockey at a residential school, only to have the abuse suffered there negatively impact his adulthood. Richard Wagamese, *Indian Horse: A Novel* (Vancouver: Douglas & McIntyre, 2012), 56–71. See also *Indian Horse*, directed by Stephen S. Campanelli (Toronto: Elevation Pictures, 2018).

Bauer and the Basilian Fathers never ran an Indigenous residential school, the 2018 hazing of a St. Michael's football player by teammates made national headlines and resulted in four boys pleading or being found guilty of sexual assault.[76] Some Basilian Fathers have pleaded guilty to sex abuse, reflecting a larger clergy sex abuse scandal within the Catholic Church.[77] Hockey itself has also not been void of sexual abuse, as when members of the 2003 and 2018 men's versions of Hockey Canada's World Junior team allegedly sexually assualted women. Seeing only the positive aspects of religious engagement in sport would be naïve.[78]

Religious ties to hockey should not be swept under the rug. How should we consider sport in today's less formally religious society? German theorist Jurgen Habermas, who early in his philosophical writings dismissed religion, more recently argued that modern society needs the cultural bank and spiritual values of religion to address challenges within modern political societies.[79]

76   Liam Casey, "Teen Guilty of Sex Assault at St. Michael's College School in Toronto Given No Time Behind Bars," *CBC*, November 2, 2021, https://www.cbc.ca/news/canada/toronto/st-michaels-sexual-assault-sentencing-teen-1.6233740.

77   Most significantly, Hodgson Marshall was convicted of abusing boys at several Basilian schools in Ontario during decades of teaching, along with coaching basketball. Dale Molnar, "Supreme Court Denies Basilian Fathers Appeal to Sexual Abuse Lawsuit," *CBC News*, April 30, 2020, https://www.cbc.ca/news/canada/windsor/catholic-church-sex-abuse-father-hodgson-marshall-talach-beckett-macleod-mcma hon-1.5551156. See also Michael Higgins and Peter Kavanagh, *Suffer the Children unto Me: An Open Inquiry into the Clerical Sex Abuse Scandal* (Toronto: Novalis, 2010), 29–62; Nuala Kenny, *Still Unhealed: Treating the Pathology in the Clergy Abuse Crisis* (Toronto: Novalis, 2020), 1–19.

78   Ashley Burke, "Investigator Hired to Look into Group Sexual Assault Allegations Involving 2003 World Junior Players," *CBC*, September 4, 2022, https://www.cbc.ca/news/politics/independent-investigator-hired-investigate-2003-group-sexual-assault-allegations-1.6571631. Noteworthy too was the sex abuse of Sheldon Kennedy and Theo Fleury by their junior hockey coach. Roy MacGregor, "After Decades of Silence, Swift Current and Hockey Community Face Invisible Damage of Child Abuse," *The Globe and Mail*, January 1, 2016, https://www.theglobeandmail.com/news/national/swift-current-faces-the-invisible-damage-of-child-abuse/article27985598/. A former student at Notre Dame in Wilcox, SK, alleges that he was brutally hazed. Rick Westhead, "For One Hockey Family, Impact of Alleged Abuse at a Top Canadian Prep School Lingers," *TSN*, December 22, 2021, https://www.tsn.ca/for-one-hockey-family-impact-of-alleged-abuse-at-a-top-canadian-prep-school-lingers-1.1738106.

79   Michele Dillon, *Postsecular Catholicism* (New York: Oxford University Press, 2018), 2–3.

Modernity's progress cannot remedy all problems. The cultural wealth of religions, according to one sociologist, offers "their long-preserved values and moral and ethical principles ... in helping to remediate contemporary ills and thus to rescue modernity and steer it out of its dead-end."[80] This line of thought does not seek a re-established Christian society, but declares that faith organizations can assist in the life of democratic nations.[81]

An example of this assistance appears in hockey today. In 2017, all major Canadian and American hockey associations, including the NHL and Hockey Canada, formally adopted the "Declaration of Principles," which upheld sportsmanship and a number of values. In a letter from the Vatican, an endorsement of the Declaration came from Pope Francis: "His Holiness trusts that this significant gesture will inspire greater appreciation of the pivotal role played by sports and sportsmanship in training future generations to pursue personal excellence and to promote the spiritual values of teamwork, solidarity and mutual respect so necessary for the building of a more just and fraternal world."[82] The Pope was pleased that the international group of hockey organizations had come together formally; the declaration was in part inspired by a Vatican-hosted event in 2016.[83] Attendees included Pat Lafontaine, a former NHL all-star who became the League's vice president of hockey development and community.[84] He felt encouraged to see his role in sport development dovetailing with the papal initiative: "This is giving me more confidence that the path we're on has been endorsed by the Pope and the world leaders of faith."

80   Dillon, *Postsecular Catholicism*, 4.

81   Barbieri, "The Post-Secular Problematic," 139.

82   Mary Clarke, "Here's Why the Pope Endorsed the NHL's Declaration of Principles Initiative," *SB Nation*, September 7, 2017, https://www.sbnation.com/nhl/2017/9/7/16267474/nhl-pope-endorsement-declaration-of-principles-the-vatican-pat-lafontaine.

83   The global conference brought together faith, business, and sport leaders, including United Nations Secretary-General Ban Ki-moon. Ed Edmonds, "The Vatican View on Sport at the Service of Humanity," *8 Notre Dame J. Int'l & Comp. L. 20* (2018), https://scholarship.law.nd.edu/law_faculty_scholarship/1322.

84   Adam Kimelman, "Pope Francis Extols Declaration of Principles," *National Hockey League*, September 6, 2017, https://www.nhl.com/news/pope-francis-extols-nhl-declaration-of-principles/c-290876704. He was joined by Los Angeles Kings President Luc Robitaille.

In 2019, one of the Declaration's signees, the International Ice Hockey Federation (IIHF), held its congress in Rome and met with Pope Francis.[85] The meeting highlighted how hockey has a social value that can extend beyond the ice rink.[86] Further to a papal endorsement of a new ethics board within the IIHF, the pontiff recognized hockey's ability to promote peace and unity and to foster the development of human persons. The effort demonstrated how a hockey organization can anchor itself in common values shared by world religions. The belief that hockey acts as character education has been a familiar refrain in Canadian hockey, as exemplified in virtue promotion during the nationwide celebration of "Minor Hockey Week" dating back to the 1950s.[87] Exactly what those values are and how they are actualized is not always clear, but the collaboration between the IIHF and a pontiff is a sign of the sport's continued interaction with religion and deeper human principles. A sport supported by faith leaders reveals what a post-Christian Canada may look like in the future.

Bauer's Motto: "Use Technique, but Let the Spirit Prevail"

An examination of religious influences on hockey must include Bauer. This hockey philosopher summed up his thought in sport through his motto: "Use technique, but let the spirit prevail." This phrase, first written by Bauer in 1961, comes from Pope Pius XII's 1955 speech given to Italian sports leaders, in which the pontiff argued that the spiritual traditions of the Church can free sport from obsessions over technical aspects of athletics.[88] Pius XII, who

85   The Holy See, "Address of His Holiness Pope Francis to Participants in the International Ice Hockey Federation," September 27, 2019, http://www. laityfamilylife.va/content/dam/laityfamilylife/Documenti/sport/eng/magisterium/ Francis/Address%20of%20His%20Holiness%20Pope%20Francis%20to%20the%20 Participants%20in%20the%20International%20Ice%20Hockey%20Federation%20 -%20Clementine%20Hall%2027.

86   Adam Steiss, "IIHF Meets the Pope," International Ice Hockey Federation, September 27, 2019, https://www.iihf.com/en/news/14971/iihf-meets-the-pope.

87   Holman, *A Hotly Contested Affair*, 67–72.

88   St. Michael's College School, *Hockey Yearbook 1961*, St. Michael's College School Online Archives, https://archive.org/details/stmcshockeyyearbook00testuoft/ mode/2up?view=theater&q=hockey+yearbook+1961. Here, Bauer incorrectly attributed the phrase to Pope Pius XII's October 24, 1956, speech to Olympic athletes departing for the Melbourne Summer Olympic Games. The phrase is only suggested

gave several sports-themed speeches, explained: "Technique, in sport, as in the arts, should not be an impediment to the unfolding of spiritual forces, such as intuition, will, sensitivity, courage, tenacity, which are, after all, the true secret of every success."[89] He concluded: "The spirit must predominate over the technical. Use technique, but let the spirit prevail."[90]

Bauer said that he learned the motto from Joe Primeau, who worked alongside him with the St. Michael's Majors.[91] Bauer wrote: "What then is the essence of greatness ... ? When applied to the game of hockey it is ... to have served to the maximum the ideal ... : 'Make use of technique, but let the spirit prevail.'"[92] A Basilian confrere explained that Bauer believed that his teams could learn and grow from any experience in sport; he set hockey within a broader reality where God could work through relationships in the game.[93] Learning skills remained vital, but this work was set within a larger background of life's meaning and purpose.

"Make use of technique, but let the spirit prevail" underlined a spiritual understanding of the human being: a person of both body and spirit. Bauer questioned why overly commercialized hockey disproportionately put material

---

in this address. The Holy See, "Message of His Holiness Pope Pius XII to Catholic Athletes Participating in the Melbourne Olympic Games," October 24, 1956, https://w2.vatican.va/content/pius-xii/fr/messages/pont-messages/documents/hf_p-xii_mes_19561024_atleti-olimpiadi.html. Kevin Lixey, "Sport in the Magisterium of Pius XII," in *Sport and Christianity: A Sign of the Times in the Light of Faith*, ed. Kevin Lixey, Christoph Huenthal, Dietmar Mieth, and Norbert Muller (Washington, DC: Catholic University of American Press, 2012), 104–120. Pius XII also posthumously received criticism for his silence on the Jewish holocaust during World War II. Harriet Sherwood, "Unsealing of Vatican Archives Will Finally Reveal Truth about 'Hitler's Pope'," *The Guardian*, March 1, 2020, https://www.theguardian.com/world/2020/mar/01/unsealing-vatican-archive-reveal-hitler-truth-pope-pius-xii.

89 The Holy See, "Discorso Di Sua Santità Pio PP. XII Ai Dirigenti E Agli Associati Del Centro Sportivo Italiano," October 9, 1955, https://www.vatican.va/content/pius-xii/it/speeches/1955/documents/hf_p-xii_spe_19551009_centro-sportivo-italiano.html.

90 The Holy See, "Discorso Di Sua Santità."

91 Rick Noonan, interview with author, May 27, 2019.

92 St. Michael's College School, *Hockey Yearbook 1961*, St. Michael's College School Online Archives, https://archive.org/details/stmcshockeyyearbook00testuoft/mode/2up?view=theater&q=hockey+yearbook+1961.

93 Don McLeod, interview with author, June 4, 2018.

concerns above spiritual values. He wanted to make a better society or, in his words, create "a more spiritual world."[94] In this way, Bauer, who could throw a football with either his left or right arm as the quarterback of the St. Michael's team, was likewise ambidextrous in his professional life. He moved between the religious and hockey worlds as a priest and hockey man, experiencing the fluidity and tensions with a religious life on and off the ice. This image of Bauer captures the coming together of both worlds and how, in engaging both, we find his philosophical purpose in the sport. One Basilian explained that Bauer "knew that sports were very important in people's lives, but that their lives were much more important than sports."[95] Bauer put hockey into a larger, transcendent perspective.

Even after his passing, Bauer's motto lived on at the 2002 Salt Lake City Winter Olympic Games. Head coach Pat Quinn explained his plans for the Olympic tournament and added: "I borrowed something from Father Bauer … which was the statement that basically became our motto: Pay attention to detail but let the spirit prevail.… [L]et the athlete do the job he has been given to do and let him use the skills that he has."[96] Quinn's use of Bauer's motto set free the well-trained players for a high-speed game on ice. The players and management of that gold medal team marked their victory with commemorative team rings engraved with Bauer's motto.

Research Sources and Order of Book Chapters

There already exists a scattered yet significant public record about Bauer in books and newspaper articles. Hockey research since the 1970s assists in framing the Basilian sporting tradition and situates Bauer within the evolving hockey landscape. National and local newspapers, as well as scholarly and professional sources, provide much information about the 1961 Majors team and the three Olympic teams that he led. The teams' games and players' personalities are well documented, especially in Greg Oliver's *Father Bauer*

---

94 Carmelite Sisters of St. Joseph, email message to author, November 9, 2018.

95 Mike Mastromatteo, "Fr. Bauer Believed in Fair Play," *Catholic Register*, November 26, 1988, Basilian Archives. Box 2, last file, Bauer fonds.

96 Alan Watson, *Catch On and Run with It: The Sporting Life and Times of Dr. Bob Hindmarch* (Vancouver: AJW Books, 2012), 519. Quinn had attended St. Michael's briefly when Bauer coached the Majors.

and the Great Experiment: The Genesis of Canadian Olympic Hockey.[97] This book also provides a helpful biography of Bauer the hockey coach and manager; however, the text has shortcomings that limit its capacity to explain Bauer's larger vision for a Canadian hockey alternative.[98]

A more complete account of Bauer is necessary. A fuller grasp of his fundamental motivations, his theoretical and strategic ideas about hockey, and his biographical story requires examination of archival records found across Canada.[99] Especially important in these archives are hockey documents that Bauer authored or co-authored for the federal government, CAHA, and Hockey Canada. A thorough analysis of these documents enables a deeper depiction of Bauer's thought, which also finds support in letters to family and friends along with personal notes of his inner thoughts—including those written on dinner napkins.[100] Together, these capture his views about hockey, including its purpose in Canadian society, and his attempts to create alliances within the hockey world. Phone and in-person interviews with family members, religious acquaintances, and hockey people provide further insights about Bauer. Finally, also helpful were Catholic newspaper articles that focused keenly on his motivations.

Drawing from the above sources, an image of Bauer and his thought emerges. Phrases like, "Let the spirit prevail" or "Motivated by a habitual vision of greatness" make more sense when taking into account Bauer's background and his historical context. Hockey documents that he wrote require a historical understanding of professional and amateur hockey, shifts in coaching philosophies, the influence of the federal government, and

---

97   Greg Oliver, *Father Bauer and the Great Experiment: The Genesis of Canadian Olympic Hockey* (Toronto: ECW Press, 2017), 1.

98   The book's list of interviewees does not include the Bauer family and the Basilian Fathers. Some important archives and collections were not accessed, like the General Archives of the Basilian Fathers. Without a fuller framing of Bauer's perspective on hockey issues, the book is unable to explain his full vision. The book still remains valuable, especially when chronicling National Team players and their games played.

99   These included archive collections at: The General Archives of the Basilian Fathers, St. Mark's College at the University of British Columbia, St. Michael's College School, University of Toronto, University of Alberta, Hockey Canada, the Library and Archives of Canada, the Hockey Hall of Fame, Notre Dame Collegiate, Canada's Sports Hall of Fame, Waterloo Public Library, and personal records of family and friends.

100   Noonan, interview.

major hockey events that shaped Bauer's world. Bauer's complex hockey life can only be understood by reciprocally investigating his philosophical and religious influences.[101] This book undertakes that task.

Following this introduction, the remaining eight chapters are divided into significant time periods in Bauer's hockey life. Chapter 2 presents the historical backdrop for Bauer's sporting heritage. He was the product of a tradition cultivated by Basilian priest-coaches and supported by educational institutions, amateur organizations, and a formidable family in the Bauers of Waterloo. Chapter 3 traces the tensions within the Basilian hockey tradition at St. Michael's College in the face of pressures arising from a professionalizing Junior A hockey. Changes in sport and education made the task of actualizing higher ideals in hockey increasingly difficult. Chapter 4 reviews Bauer's establishment of Canada's men's Olympic hockey team program—the first truly nationally represented hockey team in Canada's history. With it, Bauer helped move Canadian hockey into the Cold War era with a team that was as much a throwback to early days in hockey as it was avant-garde in the sport. Chapter 5 details Bauer's efforts to expand his National Team program, which began to challenge the very structures of Canadian hockey. His work forced a reluctant NHL to become part of the newly established Hockey Canada, but left his National Team program exposed to external powers.

Chapter 6 reviews Bauer's lengthy involvement in Japanese hockey and his continued work as a member of the board of directors at Hockey Canada. There, he sought an integrated vision of domestic and international hockey. Chapter 7 explains the resurfacing of the National Team with Bauer as its managing director for the 1980 Lake Placid Games. Chapter 8 recounts political moves within Hockey Canada that left Bauer bewildered and dismissed from the National Team. He remained on the board of Hockey Canada, however, and promoted person-centered values to guide the global brand known as Hockey Canada. Chapter 9 reviews the final decade of Bauer's life and articulates the lasting impact of this hockey philosopher. The book's epilogue captures the success of Bauer's National Team program as measured by the impact of its players as people and citizens.

101   Researching both sport and faith—an area of international research that has rapidly grown over the past two decades—bears fruit in this monograph. Afe Adogame, Nick J. Watson, and Andrew Parker, eds., *Global Perspectives on Sports and Christianity* (Abingdon, Oxfordshire: Routledge, 2018).

At David Bauer's memorial Mass held at St. Basil's Church in Toronto, a telegram from Canadian Prime Minister Brian Mulroney declared: "Perhaps more than anyone in the history of modern hockey, Father Bauer imbued in us sportsmanship, internationalism and the spirit of friendly competition. Most of all he taught us that character was at the root of success.... His gentle spirit hid the fierce competitor he was."[102] A religious hockey coach may seem like an oxymoron, but Bauer's bold determinedness to break through old-school hockey thinking reveals a deeper purpose for Canadian hockey.

---

102 Isobel Lawson, "Father David Bauer," *Waterloo Chronicle*, November 30, 1988 (Seaman Hockey Resource Centre. Rev. Bauer File), A10.

The Roots of Bauer's Sporting Heritage

THE ROOTS OF BAUER'S SPORTING HERITAGE lie in the Basilian Fathers and the Bauers of Waterloo. In the former, we find a successful character-based hockey tradition that led historian Bruce Kidd to declare, "there has been a powerful sporting tradition among Canadian Basilians, the order to which Father Bauer belongs."[1] In the latter, we note a family of means and mentorship that coached and managed local and national sporting teams and organizations.

Father Henry Carr as Architect of the Basilian Sporting Tradition

Father Henry Carr established a strong sporting tradition first at St. Michael's College in Toronto. Many players graduated to become priest-coaches, both there and at other Basilian educational institutions throughout North

---

1   Bruce Kidd and John MacFarlane, *The Death of Hockey* (Toronto: New Press, 1972), 80. Much of the first ten pages of this second chapter were originally published in "'A Powerful Sporting Tradition among Canadian Basilians': Early Twentieth-Century Catholic Priest-Coaches at St. Michael's College," *International Journal of the History of Sport* 39, no. 4 (2022): 366–84, available online at https://www.tandfonline.com/doi/full/10.1080/09523367.2022.2066079.

America. Carr, who held several leadership positions within the community and in post-secondary institutions, was arguably Bauer's most significant mentor despite a forty-four-year age gap. The two of them lived near each other during two periods. First, near the end of Carr's career, in 1949–51, he taught at St. Basil's when Bauer was a scholastic studying theology prior to his priestly ordination. Second, they both lived at St. Mark's College in Vancouver from 1961 until Carr's death in late 1963. The originator Carr would give his approval to the tradition's most daring endeavor with Bauer at the helm.

Born in Oshawa, Ontario, in 1880, Carr was raised in an Irish family of modest means. He entered the Basilian religious community in 1900 and taught at St. Michael's College prior to his ordination in 1905. At that time, the Basilian Fathers ran three boarding schools.[2] St. Michael's College was the flagship institution of the religious community. The college followed a curriculum that was better suited for seminarians than professionals, and it neglected athletics, unlike the Protestant boys' boarding schools in Canada and the US with their growing sports programs.

Carr was a bright student and had attained an Honours Classics degree at the University of Toronto. Upon his arrival as a teacher at St. Michael's, which offered prep school, high school, and university level courses, he aimed to move the college from a position of isolation into the mainstream of Canadian university life and align the college with the Ontario provincial curriculum at the high school level.[3] Thus, he quickly broadened the curriculum to qualify high school graduates for admission at university and, in 1906, he arranged for St. Michael's College to become a federated arts college of the University of Toronto.[4] These two reforms dramatically altered educational opportunities for the local English-speaking Catholic population—which was heavily Irish, worked typically as unskilled laborers—and thus helped it become better assimilated into Protestant-dominated, mainstream Toronto society.[5]

---

2 Michelle Sawyers, archivist at Basilian Archives, email message to author, April 1, 2019.

3 Kevin Shea, Larry Colle, and Paul Patskou, *St. Michael's College: 100 Years of Pucks and Prayers* (Bolton, ON: Fenn Publishing Company Limited, 2008), 13.

4 P. Wallace Platt, *Dictionary of Basilian Biography: Lives of Member of the Congregation of Priests of Saint Basil from its Origins in 1822 to 2002, 2nd ed.* (Toronto: University of Toronto Press, 2005), 86.

5 Mark McGowan, *The Waning of the Green: Catholics, the Irish, and Identity in Toronto, 1887–1922* (Montreal: McGill-Queen's University Press, 1999), 32.

While educational reforms at St. Michael's improved the integration of Catholics in early twentieth-century Ontario, Carr saw similar value in his school's participation in extra-curricular athletic programming, especially in hockey.[6] He believed that competitive sports could help as a physical outlet for boys in a boarding school, while acting as a place of moral formation and garnering public attention for the schools. It would also bring further contact between the Catholic community and other predominantly British and Protestant parts of the city. But this was not without controversy. While international Catholic organizations in sport had received endorsement from the Holy See, Catholic support of sport was not settled. Some Catholic clergy continued to view sport as incompatible with Christian moral doctrines, while others were suspicious of sports that were closely linked with Anglo-Protestant nationalism, including football and hockey.[7]

Expanding St. Michael's College through Hockey

Carr's educational interest in hockey was not uncommon in his day. Many schools and colleges played a vital role in the early development of the sport. They promoted amateur sporting ideals forged by Protestant Christian hegemony in English-speaking Canadian society.[8] The Montreal-form of the sport, which captured the game's first articulated rules in 1877, stemmed from vernacular forms of ball-and-stick ice games and was drawn from sports like rugby, lacrosse, and field hockey. This basis was coupled with advancements in ice skates and indoor skating rinks made with natural ice.[9]

Hockey became seen as an important part of a Canadian boy's education, with exhibition and challenge matches played at schools across the country.[10] Colleges made up many of the first teams in the Toronto Junior Hockey

---

6 Edmund J. McCorkell, *Henry Carr—Revolutionary* (Toronto: Griffin House, 1969), 27.

7 Jean Harvey, "Sport and the Quebec Clergy, 1930–1960," in *Not Just a Game: Essays in Canadian Sport Sociology* (Ottawa: University of Ottawa Press, 1988), 85.

8 Bruce Kidd, "Muscular Christianity and Value-Centred Sport: The Legacy of Tom Brown in Canada," *Sport in Society* 16, no. 4 (2013): 408, https://doi.org/10.1080/17430437.2013.785752.

9 Stephen Hardy and Andrew C. Holman, *Hockey: A Global History* (Champaign, IL: University of Illinois Press, 2018), 70 and 73. See also Alan Metcalfe, *Canada Learns to Play* (Toronto: McClelland and Stewart, 1987), 63.

10 Metcalfe, *Canada Learns to Play*, 65 and 68.

League, which formed in 1893.[11] By 1905, schools, churches, and the YMCA in many larger Canadian urban centers organized the sport as one with amateur ideals, while businesses and other groups also organized games.[12] Schools and colleges played an important role in the early growth of the game, during which they challenged the game's violent tendencies that stemmed from a rugged, new Canadian nationalism, which liked rough-and-tumble play that countered British Victorian ideals.[13]

Highly organized hockey arrived in Toronto in 1888 and, by 1895, produced well-ordered leagues supported by various clubs.[14] Carr wanted the boys at St. Michael's to play in the Ontario Hockey Association (OHA), formed in 1890 by six Toronto clubs. This association included universities and private schools and promoted bourgeois ideals of gentlemanly play.[15] Carr wanted to spring St. Michael's into this circle of influence. While he managed to squeeze enough money out of the school to fund its entry into the OHA, in 1906 he co-created an OHA prep school group.[16] At this time, the Canadian Intercollegiate Athletic Union (CIAU) began to further organize university sport.[17] With the assistance of Jimmy Murphy, who became a longstanding coach at St. Michael's, interest began to grow.[18] Carr's biographer noted, "There was general excitement through the city. The Catholic Church had found a champion."[19]

On the ice, the game changed from nine to seven players by 1900 and dropped another player by the end of World War I.[20] Incidents of violence, despite increased room for players, caused tensions for organizers.

11 Shea, Colle, and Patskou, *St. Michael's College*, 16.

12 Metcalfe, *Canada Learns to Play*, 65.

13 Michael A. Robidoux, "Imagining a Canadian Identity through Sport: A Historical Interpretation of Lacrosse and Hockey," *Journal of American Folklore* 115, no. 456 (Spring 2002): 209–26.

14 Hardy and Holman, *Hockey: A Global History*, 70 and 73.

15 Hardy and Holman, *Hockey: A Global History*, 76–77.

16 McCorkell, *Henry Carr—Revolutionary*, 27. See also John Wallner, "Athletics and Academics: St. Michael's College Withdrawal from Ontario Hockey Association Junior A Competition" (master's thesis, Carleton University, Ottawa, 1990), 11.

17 Don Morrow, "Sport and Physical Education in Schools and Universities," in *A Concise History of Sport in Canada*, ed. Don Morrow, Mary Keyes, Wayne Simpson, Frank Cosentino, and Ron Lappage (Toronto: Oxford University Press Canada, 1989), 83–84.

18 Stephen Harper, *A Great Game* (Toronto: Simon & Schuster, 2013), 246.

19 McCorkell, *Henry Carr—Revolutionary*, 28.

20 Hardy and Holman, *Hockey: A Global History*, 66–69.

St. Michael's sided with those who promoted what social historian Colin Howell describes as "the manly athlete" instead of "the violent brute."[21] This stance encouraged gentlemanly play with speed and respect for opponents; the brutish game featured those "without proper breeding" who liked the free rein of hacking and maiming.[22] For instance, there were eight on-ice episodes of violence that resulted in formal charges of assault in Canada between 1905 and 1918; two stick swinging incidents led to players' deaths and initial charges of murder in 1905 and 1907.[23] In contrast, the gentlemanly form of hockey was captured in a 1911 St. Michael's Yearbook: "By their clean tactics, their wonderful team play and never-say-die spirit," a St. Michael's junior team's success reportedly "won a place in the heart of every supporter of good, clean sport in Toronto, yes, in Canada. Wherever hockey was played … St. Michael's were mentioned as one of the fastest and cleverest teams."[24]

The school found great sporting success in both its junior and senior teams. Once the boys at the junior level were old enough, Carr entered a team at the senior level of the OHA and immediately won two consecutive provincial titles. In 1910, he successfully led a St. Michael's team to the Allan Cup, given to the Canadian champions of senior amateur hockey.[25] In its first national championship, Carr's fast-playing team—dubbed the "seven little men of iron"[26]—faced off against a challenge team in Kingston: "the players differed so widely in physique that at first glance the cause of the

21 Colin Howell, *Blood, Sweat, and Cheers: Sport and the Making of Modern Canada* (Toronto: University of Toronto Press, 2001), 45.

22 Howell, *Blood, Sweat, and Cheers,* 45. Alex Bundgaard, *Muscle and Manliness: The Rise of Sport in American Boarding Schools* (Syracuse, NY: Syracuse University Press, 2005), 192.

23 Andrew Holman, *A Hotly Contested Affair: Hockey in Canada* (Toronto: University of Toronto Press, 2020), 160; Stacy Lorenz and Geraint B. Osborne, "'Talk About Strenuous Hockey': Violence, Manhood, and the 1907 Ottawa Silver Seven-Montreal Wanderer Rivalry," *Journal of Canadian Studies* 40, no. 1 (2006): 126.

24 St. Michael's College School, *Yearbook of St. Michael's College 1911*, St. Michael's College School Online Archives, 53, https://archive.org/details/ stmyearbookofstmich1911testuoft/mode/2up?view=theater&q=yearbook+1911.

25 Dennis Mills, "Hockey at St. Michael's," in *Toronto St. Michael's Majors: The Tradition Lives On*, ed. Dennis Mills (publisher unknown, 1997), 43.

26 St. Michael's College School, *Yearbook of St. Michael's College 1921*, St. Michael's College School Online Archives, 109, https://archive.org/details/ stmyearbookofstmich1921stmiuoft/mode/2up?view=theater&q=yearbook+1921.

College septette seemed hopeless."[27] However, "the little Blue Shirts, by head and hand, with endurance almost superhuman.... [their] superiority of skill and courage was not to go unrewarded."[28] The victory won by the speedy, clever Irish players undoubtedly won recognition for the College.[29] As the OHA senior champions in 1909 and 1910, they made victory tours playing games in New York and Boston. One American paper noted that "never once were they penalized" and another that "they were fast and tricky, while their checking was hard, sure and clean."[30] This recognition later landed a spot for St. Michael's junior team in the University of Toronto Inter-Faculty League in 1915–16.[31] By this time, Carr focused his talents solely on football, coaching successful teams that included the first Grey Cup Championship team.[32] He became known as "one of the best authorities on Canadian rugby."[33]

The expansion of St. Michael's and its hockey program enabled intellectual growth on campus, where serious thinking could be wedded to a values-driven sport. Carr co-found the Pontifical Institute of Medieval Studies (PIMS) in 1929, which connected him with notable philosophers like Étienne Gilson and Jacques Maritain. Together they forged an institute that was, according to philosophers Armour and Trott, "a cool-headed intelligent community of men who could be devout without being narrow-minded, faithful without being suspicious, tolerant without being soft-head."[34]

27 St. Michael's College School, *Yearbook of St. Michael's College 1910*, St. Michael's College School Online Archives, 57, https://archive.org/details/stmyearbookofstmich1910testuoft/mode/2up?view=theater&q=yearbook+1910.

28 St. Michael's College School, *Yearbook 1910*, 58.

29 St. Michael's College School, *Yearbook of St. Michael's College 1915*, St. Michael's College School Online Archives, 98, https://archive.org/details/stmyearbookofstmich1915testuoft/page/n4/mode/2up?view=theater&q=yearbook+1915.

30 St. Michael's College School, *Yearbook 1911*, 62.

31 Dennis P. Ryan and Kevin B. Wamsley, "The Fighting Irish of Toronto: Sport and Irish Catholic Identity at St. Michael's College, 1906–1916," in *Emigrant Players: Sport and the Irish Diaspora*, eds. P. Darby and D. Hassan, 163–81 (Abingdon, Oxfordshire: Routledge, 2008), 174.

32 St. Michael's College School, *Yearbook 1910*, 32.

33 St. Michael's College School, *Yearbook 1910*, 29.

34 Leslie Armour and Elizabeth Anne Trott, *The Faces of Reason: An Essay on Philosophy and Culture in English Canada 1850–1950* (Waterloo, ON: Wilfrid Laurier University Press, 1981), 505.

Maritain, in particular, put the thought of thirteenth century philosopher Thomas Aquinas into dialogue with modern society—a dialogue that could include sport.

Carr's Ideals

Carr believed in sport's ability to build virtue in St. Michael's students. In a 1911 Yearbook, he described the importance of athletics for the school: "No other force can do so much for the happiness and contentment of the boy.... [Athletics] must not be ill-regulated. They must be educated to prize victory, but to submit gracefully to defeat."[35] He believed that sport could foster virtue, balance, relaxation, and bodily development for youth.[36] Manly sporting values could mix with traditional Catholic virtues, giving a new twist to Catholicism in English Canada. While manly ideals of athletics were popular at the time, a Catholic school also promoted more feminine features found in religious practices and spiritualities. For instance, two New York Jesuit colleges around the turn of the century used spirituality, novels, lives of the saints, and scholarship as the means to balance masculine ideals of "athletic prowess, emotional restraint, and military bearing" derived from Protestant influences.[37] More feminine ideals of artistry, devotional sensibility, and modesty—those promoted in the lives of saints and the Virgin Mary— were intertwined with Protestant muscular Christian ideals.

Carr and others at St. Michael's College sought a way forward that maintained Catholic devotional practices and followed an athletic ideology put forward by Protestant Christians. Manly ideals of self-discipline and athletic prowess met the promotion of virtues in a medieval Thomistic framework that was undergoing a renaissance within Catholic thought and popular imagination, reflected in Carr's medieval PIMS institute. Within this philosophical framework, Carr could endorse sport as a real possibility for finding what was true and good in human living.

35 St. Michael's College School, *Yearbook 1911*, 41.

36 St. Michael's College School, *Yearbook of St. Michael's College 1914*, St. Michael's College School Online Archives, https://archive.org/details/ stmyearbookofstmich1914testuoft/mode/2up?view=theater&q=yearbook+1914.

37 Christa Klein, "The Jesuits and Catholic Boyhood in Nineteenth-Century New York City: A Study of St. John's College and the College of St. Francis Xavier, 1846–1912" (PhD diss., University of Pennsylvania, Philadelphia, 1976), 311 and 315.

Carr believed balance between the mind/soul and body was necessary in sport.[38] Both Aristotle and Aquinas sought the golden mean between deficiencies and excesses in one's character, and sought a harmony within the human person.[39] This intellectual, yet earthy, synthesis in Aquinas explained revealed truths of faith (e.g., biblical teachings) as compatible with truths discovered by one's senses or thinking.[40] By understanding what was true in nature, one could cultivate a deeper knowledge of God. Thus, through one's body and soul, a person comes to know God, rather than by otherworldly measures. Carr followed this "balanced humanism" that did not reject the body, the sciences, or the arts, and also did not deem humankind as above the Creator.[41] Sport could be a valued, spirited path to find God and develop virtue.

The school celebrated reverence for religion, intellectual accomplishment, and skill in athletic feats in its logo and Greek motto. The ideal St. Michael's boys who were "worthy stalwarts" of the college were given the now-famous Ms to wear, a varsity letter with the school's logo. It consisted of St. Michael the Archangel's wings and sword, along with a shield of four figures: "the cross and the missal, signify moral and religious training, and the lower two of which, the tree of knowledge, and the olive wreath of victory, signify intellectual and physical culture respectively."[42] The gifting of the school's logo celebrated its ideals in students.

Changing Perspectives on Amateurism and the Church's View on Sport

Central to Carr's experiment with sport was the ideology of amateurism. Prior to World War I, the Canadian Amateur Athletic Union (CAAU) governed Canadian sport according to the ideals of amateurism and against pay-for-play sport that was believed to create cheating, frenzied bidding for players, and general instability in sport.[43] Amateur sporting leaders placed restrictions on

---

38 Wallner, "Athletics and Academics," 26.

39 Wallner, "Athletics and Academics," 27.

40 Armour and Trott, *The Faces of Reason*, 489–94.

41 Wallner, "Athletics and Academics," 28.

42 St. Michael's College School, *Yearbook 1921*, 109.

43 Bruce Kidd, *The Struggle for Canadian Sport* (Toronto, ON: University of Toronto Press, 1996), 35–37.

sport, including the passing of the Lord's Day Act in 1906, which prohibited Sunday competition in the amateur code across Canada.[44] Catholics generally followed the less restrictive tradition of Continental Sundays; in fact, Carr was seen as the perfect advertisement for Sunday golf because he played early Sunday mornings.[45]

Between 1902 and 1907, debates raged about the amateur status of hockey players and the possibility of amateurs competing against professional players. A compromise position arose in 1908–9, when the newly formed Amateur Athletic Union of Canada (AAUC) became the adjudicating body for amateur-professional disputes.[46] It took a more lenient stance toward professionalism in Canadian hockey: it allowed reimbursement of amateur players' lost wages due to travel and it allowed competition with professionals.[47] This enabled the public to more readily enjoy professional play and the beginnings of different professional leagues. Amateur leaders found it difficult to define and give direction to amateurism in an increasingly industrialized society, especially in a Canadian society that was not so clearly class-based.[48] The capitalistic expectation was to maximize profits and attain victory at any cost, which ran counter to much of hockey's organizational framework in educational institutions.

The AAUC offered only functional definitions of amateurism focused on work and money—not on the ideals of amateurism that Carr promoted.[49] He was not concerned about keeping aristocratic social norms when the college housed sons from working class, Catholic homes. The college chose what suited it best from British Victorian and Canadian nationalist value systems, but this path would be increasingly difficult to take as professionalism began to dominate sport by the 1930s and '40s.

For Carr and St. Michael's, changes to the dominance of amateurism in hockey on a national level were balanced with greater openness to sport

44   Kidd, *Struggle for Canadian Sport*, 35–37.

45   Carmelite Sisters of St. Joseph, interview with author, January 17, 2019.

46   Wayne Simpson, "Hockey," in *A Concise History of Sport in Canada*, eds. Don Morrow, Mary Keyes, Wayne Simpson, Frank Cosentino, and Ron Lappage (Toronto: Oxford University Press, 1989), 181.

47   Simpson, "Hockey," 182.

48   Metcalfe, *Canada Learns to Play*, 123.

49   Metcalfe, *Canada Learns to Play*, 123.

by the Catholic Church.[50] Its official teaching body held a more suspicious view of sport in the mid- and late nineteenth century. Clergy interpreted the long-held teaching on the unity of the body and soul more conservatively, emphasizing the primacy of the soul, and they refuted modernity's questioning of age-old values. However, on the heels of Pope Leo XIII's social teaching on work and leisure in *Rerum novarum* in 1891, several Catholic sporting organizations appeared in the early twentieth century. For instance, French and Italian sport and gymnastics federations blossomed. The reign of Pope Pius X (1903–1914) was marked by the Holy See's support of Catholic sport organizations and papal discussions with Pierre de Coubertin about Rome as a possible site for the 1908 Olympics.

Sporting Disciples of Carr

Carr's sporting tradition spread throughout North America and fashioned priests who included extracurricular sport as part of their teaching duties. Along with academically-strong students who might be mentored to become priests, many student-athletes were guided to become priest-coaches.[51] Academics and athletics were major sources of new Basilian recruits.

Fathers Bellisle and Spratt were early disciples of Carr. Mentee Henry Bellisle became a priest in 1915 and endorsed higher ideals in sport, like loyalty and self-sacrifice.[52] "[T]raining the student to hold his temper and keep steady under fire, training him in his resourcefulness and leadership and cooperation with others in a common cause" underlined the important educational and moral role in a Basilian athletics program.[53] Jack Spratt was a superb athlete who played on a St. Michael's senior hockey team that toured the US Northeast. A newspaper reported that Spratt "toyed with the rubber that it seemed like mere play to him to get it away from the New York skaters."[54] Spratt, ordained a priest in 1920, later coached and captained a

---

50 Dries Vanysacker, "The Attitude of the Holy See toward Sport during the Interwar Period (1919–39)," *Catholic Historical Review* 101, no. 4 (2015): 797–98.

51 Jack Gallagher, interview with author, January 15, 2019.

52 E. J. McCorkell, "In Memoriam H. S. Bellisle," in *Yearbook of St. Michael's College 1939*, St. Michael's College School Online Archives, 21, https://www.stmichaelscollegeschool.com/about-us/history-and-archives/archives.

53 Platt, *Dictionary of Basilian Biography*, 37.

54 Shea, Colle, and Patskou, *St. Michael's College*, 23.

Basilian college team in Windsor to victory over the University of Michigan.[55] Soon after, he coached a junior team in Owen Sound, Ontario, to the 1927 national championship.

On occasion, this priest-coach mentorship needed to coax boys to play sport. For example, standout defensive lineman Bernie Holland determined that he could not play the game without swearing and so decided to quit the sport. His pious attitude did not please Carr, who saw the many benefits of sport and saw great talent in Holland. The coach took advantage of a moment when Holland damaged a wall in the residence. McCorkell explains: Carr gave him "an option to commute his sentence—if he played football again. Two years later Holland was acclaimed the greatest defensive lineman in Canadian football."[56] Carr surely smirked when he learned that Holland became a Carthusian Monk in Providence, Rhode Island.[57]

Carr served as the rector of the Basilian scholasticate when the 1925 team won the Intermediate Intercollegiate Football championship. Several players on that team became priests, including Eugene LeBel, "Sham" O'Brien, and Robert Lowrey. The three were ordained Basilian priests one week after the season-ending loss in the Canadian championship game.[58] LeBel was superior and principal at St. Mark's in Vancouver from 1964 to 1971, when he lived with David Bauer and supported his leadership with the National Team.[59] Father O'Brien worked alongside many athletic-minded Basilians in several cities.[60] The third future priest on that football team was Robert Lowrey who, like David Bauer, joined the Canadian Army during World War II and took hockey to new destinations.

Before ordination in 1925, Lowrey and his six brothers played a hockey game versus the senior men's Ottawa Shamrocks.[61] Soon after ordination, he

55 Platt, *Dictionary of Basilian Biography*, 636.

56 McCorkell, *Henry Carr—Revolutionary*, 26–27.

57 St. Michael's College School, *Yearbook of St. Michael's College 1930*, St. Michael's College School Online Archives, 125, https://archive.org/stream/stmyearbookofstmich1930testuoft/stmyearbookofstmich1930testuoft_djvu.txt.

58 McCorkell, *Henry Carr—Revolutionary*, 31.

59 Platt, *Dictionary of Basilian Biography*, 346–48. Lebel earned his MA in English from the University of Chicago and later became president of Assumption College in Windsor.

60 Platt, *Dictionary of Basilian Biography*, 484.

61 "Capt. 'Bob' Lowrey Wins M.C.," Box 1, File 6, Lowrey fonds, Basilian Archives. Bill Roberts, "'More Room for Our Boys,' Asks Father Lowrey of New Year," 1941, Lowrey Box 1, File 6, Basilian Archives. Three of the brothers played

was appointed to St. Thomas High School in Houston, where an indoor ice rink had opened the year prior, and he started playing senior hockey under an alias, Bob Emmett. According to a local report, Lowrey was the best player in the Texas senior league in the 1930s, and he avoided wearing clerical clothing in the locker room so as to not startle his teammates.[62] Lowrey began teaching the sport to his students at St. Thomas and created a secondary school league in the city.[63] His school team won multiple championships during the first years of the league, and Lowrey mentored young men: "Boys love Father Lowrey. They use him as an ideal, and pattern their lives after him."[64]

Lowrey later consented to Carr's request that he become a chaplain in the Canadian Army.[65] During his five years of military service, he spent the summer of 1944 in Normandy and wrote about his front-line chaplaincy role: "[War] really is hell on earth. All our worries about getting the men to the sacraments have disappeared and all are glad to see me come along. It is remarkable what a few mortars and 88 mm shells do to our men."[66] After the war, Lowrey reflected on the sorrows and consolations of his experience, and longed for a brighter future for all nations.[67] Hon. Capt. Lowrey was awarded a Military Cross for distinguished gallantry in the field during the campaign on the Western Front.[68]

---

professionally in the 1930s: Jerry played for the Chicago Black Hawks, Fred played for the Montreal Maroons, and Eddie coached several seasons at the University of Michigan. Lowrey's three sisters were notable skaters. "Lowrey—That's a Hockey Name," *Detroit News*, December 24, 1934, Box 1, File 6, Lowrey fonds, Basilian Archives.

62 Andy Anderson, "Sidelights by Andy," *The Houston Press*, April 12, 1944, Lowrey Box 1, File 6, Basilian Archives. The reporter recalled: "I got a shirt and a tie—the loudest, most striped shirt I could find and the very reddest necktie. But Bob was game and wore it."

63 "Father Robert Emmett Lowrey," 1941, Box 1, File 6, Lowrey fonds, Basilian Archives.

64 Roberts, "Room for Our Boys."

65 Bill Kaplan, "Boys at St. Thomas Bid Farewell to Father Lowrey—He's Off to the War," *Houston Press*, November 11, 1941, Box 1, File 6, Lowrey fonds, Basilian Archives. Honorary Captain Lowrey served with the 4th Canadian Armored Division and the 4th Canadian Armored Brigade from 1941 to 1946 in Canada, the UK, France, Belgium, Holland, and Germany.

66 Robert Lowrey, letter to McCorkell, August 29, 1944, Box 1, File 1, Lowrey fonds, Basilian Archives.

67 Robert Lowrey, letter to Robert Scollard for *Basilian Annals*, April 25, 1945, Box 1, File 1, Lowrey fonds, Basilian Archives.

68 "Military Cross Awarded to Canadian Catholic Chaplain," November 10,

Although he did not return to the classroom in Houston (or elsewhere), he had made a contribution to hockey in Texas. A sports editor of the *Houston Post* "compared his contribution to hockey in Houston in the late 1920s and early 1930s to Gordie Howe's efforts to revitalize Houston hockey in the 1970s."[69]

Carr's other prominent football team was a 1928 team that included two future priests of note: James Whelihan and George Flahiff. Born in Lucan, Ontario, Whelihan graduated from Assumption University in Windsor and fine-tuned his football prowess in Toronto and later in Houston as a priest-coach.[70] When he became a teacher-coach at St. Mary's Boys school in Calgary, Whelihan used unheard-of football formations and strategies taken from a fraternity of coaches at Basilian colleges across the continent. He found success quickly and for decades. One prominent Calgary high school football coach called him "the dean of all coaches ever in Calgary," who was able to win championships for a small school.[71] He collaborated well with others, minimizing tensions between Catholic and Protestant schooling while helping the Calgary Inter-scholastic Football League become one of the most successful of its kind in Canada.[72]

Whelihan had a fun-loving, compassionate personality. He took boxing teams to a veterans hospital in the city where, apparently, not all the nurses appreciated the scene of boys boxing one another in a care-giving facility.[73] His status became legendary as many of his former players took on prominent roles

1945, Box 1, File 6, Lowrey fonds, Basilian Archives. The official citation from Defense Headquarters in Ottawa included: "In the battle outside Sonsbeck when warned by an officer that the Germans were only a few hundred yards forward his reply was 'but we have wounded men there also.' Going forward he brought back to safety three wounded men."

69   Platt, *Dictionary of Basilian Biography*, 359.

70   Dick Schuler, "Veteran Team Builder Sees Solution for the Stamps," *Calgary Herald*, 1985, Box 1, File 2, Whelihan fonds, Basilian Archives.

71   Daryl Slade, "'Dean' of City Coaches Dies in Toronto at 84," *Calgary Herald*, 1986, Box 1, File 1, Whelihan fonds, Basilian Archives.

72   "Special Honours to Lucan Native," *Time-Advocate*, December 18, 1985, Box 1, File 1, Whelihan fonds, Basilian Archives. The man known affectionately as "Wheels" also steered the careers of track athletes to US colleges and the Olympics. Denny Layzell, "Personality of the Week: Father Jim Whelihan," Box 1, File 2, Whelihan fonds, Basilian Archives.

73   Cathy McLaughlin, "Father Whelihan Gets Order of Canada," *Western Catholic Reporter*, January 6, 1986, Box 1, File 1, Whelihan fonds, Basilian Archives.

in society, while he later held a position on the City Planning Commission and received national awards for his service.[74] He lived in Vancouver from 1971 to 1984, and resided there with Bauer and other Basilians. At a recognition dinner at a downtown Calgary hotel, Bauer spoke about his longtime confrere's humor, openness to people of other faiths, and loyal service to the church.[75]

George Flahiff, who also played on Carr's 1928 football team, eventually became the Cardinal Archbishop of Winnipeg. Flahiff was raised with eight Irish siblings in Paris, Ontario, where the family could assemble an entire hockey or baseball team.[76] When he entered St. Michael's College at the age of sixteen, he was more interested in sports than academics.[77] Despite his large stature, he was known for his artful stickhandling and skating rather than for his body-checking.[78] Instead of becoming a priest-coach after ordination, however, he became a historian lecturing at PIMS in Toronto. This led to advancement as the superior general of the Basilian community, as bishop, and then as cardinal in 1969.[79] Flahiff had a compassionate heart, reflected in his involvement in Catholic social action, and openly discussed issues like the role of women in ministry and relations with other Christians.[80]

As superior general in 1955, Flahiff gave a notable lecture on a theology of sport at a Basilian gathering. He affirmed that Christian education must include care for both body and soul because Christ had taken on a human body.[81] He criticized educators who de-emphasized sport and physical education and subsequently viewed sport merely as entertainment

74   A former player with the West End Tornadoes, Peter Lougheed, became Premier of Alberta, and another former player, Frank Quigley, went on to become a Justice on the Court of Queen's Bench of Alberta. Several oil executives, like Bill Mooney, were influenced by their friendship with Whelihan. "James Austin Whelihan," *The Basilian Newsletter*, no. 19, November 28, 1986, Box 1, File 1, Whelihan fonds, Basilian Archives.

75   David Bauer, speech notes, October 22, 1973, Box 3, File 3, Bauer fonds, Basilian Archives.

76   P. Wallace Platt, *Gentle Eminence: A Life of Cardinal Flahiff* (Montreal: McGill-Queen's University Press, 1999), 14.

77   Platt, *Gentle Eminence*, 19.

78   Platt, *Gentle Eminence*, 20.

79   After ordination at 25, he pursued graduate studies in medieval history in Strasbourg and then Paris. Platt, *Dictionary of Basilian Biography*, 217.

80   McCorkell, *Henry Carr—Revolutionary*, 31. Flahiff was named Companion of the Order of Canada in 1974.

81   George Flahiff, "Toward a Theology of Sport," *The Basilian Teacher* 4, no. 5 (February 1960): 22.

or spectacle.[82] Flahiff countered that sport should be treated as a universal human activity for the integrated development of persons.

Flahiff's speech included a review of a 1952 Pius XII speech on the moral and religious aspects of sport.[83] For Flahiff and the pontiff, sport needed to serve the soul, rather than vice versa. The human will was to direct and develop the body, leading to the "development of spiritual faculties" and "cultivation of virtue."[84] In this way, they prioritized the soul more than the body despite their unity together in human persons.[85] Flahiff concluded that victory in sport should not be the only marker of athletic achievement; Basilian coaches were to keep the higher ends of sport in sight.[86]

From those coached directly by Carr, others followed in his sporting tradition. As the Basilian religious community increased in numbers, they administered, taught, and coached at more schools. The Basilian sporting movement spread, becoming prominent elsewhere: Detroit, Windsor, and Rochester, New York.

After reigniting hockey at Catholic Central in Detroit throughout the 1940s, Father Ron Cullen was appointed to Assumption in 1948, where he served the Windsor sports community for half a century and became an iconic coach in the region.[87] Cullen was more hard-nosed than most coaches. His philosophy and tactics were born out of his priestly spirituality and

---

82   Flahiff, "Theology of Sport," 22.

83   The Holy See, "Address to the National Scientific Congress on Italian Sport," November 8, 1952, https://w2.vatican.va/content/pius-xii/it/speeches/1952/documents/hf_p-xii_spe_19521108_gran-cuore.html. This speech was given at an Italian conference on sport science. Pius XII gave more than twenty sport speeches during his pontificate. Kevin Lixey, "Sport in the Magisterium of Pius XII," in *Sport and Christianity: A Sign of the Times in the Light of Faith*, ed. Kevin Lixey, Christoph Huenthal, Dietmar Mieth, and Norbert Muller (Washington, DC: Catholic University of American Press, 2012), 104.

84   Flahiff, "Theology of Sport," 25.

85   Raymond Kardas, "The Popes on Sport" (master's thesis, McGill University, Montreal, May 1992), 66–67.

86   Flahiff, "Theology of Sport," 25.

87   Hockey at Central was started by Father Lowrey and others in 1934–35. Many helped Cullen coach later teams, including Mr. Matthew Sheedy, who became the principal at St. Michael's. James Enright, "Hockey—Its History at C. C.," *The Basilian Teacher* 3, no. 3 (Dec 1958): 62; and "Ronald Cullen," Inductees 1996, The Canadian Baseball Hall of Fame and Museum, accessed May 19, 2021, http://baseballhalloffame.ca/blog/2009/09/17/ronald-cullen/.

intense no-nonsense mentality, having been raised during the Depression in a rough Toronto neighborhood. His teams frequently competed for local, provincial, and national championships, as reported by Marty Beneteau in an account in the *Windsor Star*: "Any player who didn't hit the ice on time or who goofed off during a drill quickly felt [Cullen's] thunderous wrath. He wasn't averse to whacking a player's backside with his stick or cuffing him on the helmet."[88] One former player described Cullen: "He's the kind of guy who just hated to lose and insisted—insisted—in a very demanding way that everybody perform to their potential.... The bottom line was, he wanted people to recognize their potential and settle for nothing less than that."[89] His drive for discipline led to creative goaltending training techniques that in part inspired one goalie to write a doctoral dissertation on imagery rehearsal for goaltenders, leading to a career as a sport psychologist in the NHL.[90]

However tough Cullen was, he remained a strong advocate against fighting or using goon-players in hockey. On one occasion, one of his players started a brawl when he quickly came to the defense of a comrade who had been speared: "I was swinging away [with my fists] when I heard this noise, like a 'chink'.... It was the dressing room key bouncing off my helmet. Cullen had thrown it all the way from the bench and hit me in the head. Immediately you're powerless."[91] There was a gentler and intensely spiritual side to Cullen, who also taught English. Former players said he treated no one alike. As a student of psychology, he pushed or encouraged when needed, and benched star players who broke the team rules.[92]

At a Basilian Christmas conference on extra-curricular activities in 1955, Cullen defended the value of sport in the schools despite changes

---

88 Marty Beneteau, "The Great White Elk: A Profile of Rev. Ronald Cullen," *The Windsor Star*, November 8, 1986, D1. In his later years, Cullen regretted his abusive approach with players. Gallagher, interview.

89 Beneteau, "The Great White Elk," D1.

90 Beneteau, "The Great White Elk," D1; and Scot McFadden, "An Investigation of the Relative Effectiveness of Two Types of Imagery Rehearsal Applied to Enhance Skilled Athletic Performance" (PhD thesis, University of Toronto, Toronto, 1982).

91 Beneteau, "The Great White Elk," D1.

92 He ordered one student to return home for a week out of concern of a lapse into depression. Gary Lamphier, "Values that Sustained Influential Educator Worth Remembering Today," *Edmonton Journal*, July 10, 2010, E1.

occurring in sport (e.g., player specialization and the arrival of televised sport). He retorted:

> I want to make a speech. (Loud applause!) We can and should use all extra-curricular activities to make the boys holier. I explain this to the boys every year. The kids accept it. They don't argue with the referees, because that is against justice; they make the first tackle, because they are trying to exercise fortitude. They don't start fights in games, because that is against patience.... Extra-curricular activities can be part of the boys' spiritual life.... Once we fail in this, we should get out, and hire a layman.[93]

Cullen's rough approach was unorthodox among leading Basilian coaches, yet he remained focused on developing persons—and in the process produced championship calibre teams and several NHL players.[94] He was recognized as "one of the best amateur baseball coaches in Canadian history" by the Canadian Baseball Hall of Fame, at his induction in 1996.[95]

Other priests spread the Basilian sporting tradition to Rochester. Jack Spratt, one of Carr's early sporting disciples, served at the Aquinas Institute for decades. Even in retirement, he introduced a hockey program to the institute and to the nearby St. John Fisher College.[96] Spratt's zeal for the sport inspired David Bauer, who visited the retired confrere on trips to Toronto prior to Spratt's passing in 1981.[97] Teaching and coaching alongside Spratt at Aquinas into the 1960s and 70s was Father Cyril Carter, who helped push the college into the national levels of sport.[98] Based on a framework of character development, he described sport as a means to cultivate natural and theological virtues and paraphrased the ancient Latin claim, *mens sana in*

93   Ron Cullen, "Discussion," *The Basilian Teacher* 1, no. 8 (January 1957): 19.

94   The Canadian Baseball Hall of Fame, "Ronald Cullen." Thirteen of his high school hockey teams advanced to the All-Ontario championships, and he coached future NHLers Marc Reaume, Mike Eaves, Murray Eaves, and Eddie Mio. His ability to form teenage players gained great admiration from the coach and general manager of the Detroit Red Wings, Jack Adams. Beneteau, "The Great White Elk," D1.

95   The Canadian Baseball Hall of Fame, "Ronald Cullen." Big league players Reno Bertoia, Joe Siddall, Stubby Clapp, and John Upham are among his most successful ball players.

96   Platt, *Dictionary of Basilian Biography*, 636.

97   Lisa Bauer-Leahy, interview with author, January 17, 2019.

98   Platt, *Dictionary of Basilian Biography*, 90.

corpore sano (i.e., "a healthy mind in a healthy body"). His main motive—to bring youth closer to God—was explained in an athletics statement shared with the religious community.[99]

The Bauer Family Sporting Tradition

It is noteworthy that many of the Basilian Fathers who carried on their community's sporting tradition were raised in large Catholic, often Irish, sport-loving families. The Lowrey, Whelihan, and Flahiff families promoted sport to develop their children, as did the Bauer family.

Edgar Jacob Bauer and Alice Bertha Hayes married on September 12, 1912, at St. Louis Church in Waterloo, Ontario, approximately one hundred kilometers west of Toronto. The best man was cousin Alfred Wintermeyer, whose son John would work closely with his cousin David Bauer on the funding of the National Team program.[100] According to a local report, Edgar, born (1888) and raised in Waterloo, became a prominent businessman in the town, having taken over his father's cotton felt and batting manufacturing business.[101] Its products were used for padding in horse buggies and automobiles, and later expanded into thermal and soundproofing materials. His wife went by her middle name, Bertha. She was born in 1889 to Irish-Canadian immigrants on a farm north of Waterloo. After attending the same school as Edgar, St. Louis Catholic, she went on to business school and became the secretary to the president of a furniture company in Waterloo.

The couple were prominent Catholics in town, residing closely to the parish and school. Bertha served on the executive of the Catholic Women's League, and Edgar served in many capacities and was later knighted by Pope Pius XII.[102] Edgar was community-minded and involved in local politics.

---

99 Cyril Carter, "Principles for an Athletic Program," *The Basilian Teacher* 2, no. 2 (November 1957): 24 and 23.

100 Bauer Family, *Bauer (A Family History of Edgar and Bertha's Family)* (Waterloo, ON: Self-published, 2003), under "Edgar Jacob Bauer." Private Bauer family records owned by Paul Schmaltz.

101 Karl Kessler, *Three Storeys High, A Hundred Stories Deep: 189 Mary Street* (Kitchener, ON: Pandora Printshop, 2005), 15.

102 Bauer Family, *Bauer (A Family History)*, under "Alice Bertha Hayes"; Bauer Family, *Bauer (A Family History)*, under "Edgar Jacob Bauer." He became a knight commander in the Order of St. Sylvester in 1957. Later, a school in Waterloo was

The German-Irish Catholic family followed traditional devotional practices: reciting the Rosary during the season of Lent, abstaining from red meat on Fridays, and attending daily Mass frequently.[103]

Figure 2.1 Bauer family portrait taken in 1937. Front row *(left to right)*: Edgar, Margaret, Therese, Bertha. Second row: David. Third row: Mary, Frank, Eugene, Alice, Rita. Back row: Jerome, Robert, Raymond.

Courtesy of Stephen Freiburger

The Bauer Family had sports in their DNA. For years they flooded an outdoor ice rink beside their home at the corner of King and Allen Streets. The Bauer children fussed painstakingly over its condition, so much so that Edgar installed full-sized tennis courts to allow for easier ice-making in the winter. Many neighborhood children skated with them. Immediately across King Street sat a modern two-storey brick building that held the offices and factory of the family business. Edgar's corner office had a view of the family

---

named after him; Sir Edgar Bauer Catholic Elementary School was the first "separate" (that is, Catholic) school in Ontario named after a layman.

103   Margaret Laudenbach, interview with author, January 18, 2019.

home, and one can imagine him peering through the window to see his children playing hockey or tennis after school.

Edgar and Bertha had twelve children: seven boys and five girls. All the boys played hockey. The eldest, Frank, along with his Hockey Hall of Fame brother, Bobby, played for the St. Michael's College Junior A Majors and won the 1933–34 Memorial Cup Championship. Next oldest Eugene played for an OHA Junior A champion Kitchener Juniors team and was recruited by three NHL teams.[104] Brothers Jerry and Ray played for a local Junior B championship team in 1940.[105] The brothers were also skilled at baseball, with youngest David known as a standout pitcher locally. Four brothers, playing together, won a local senior softball championship in 1940.[106] Their mother was kept busy attending many hockey or ball games per week.[107]

The skating rink was not only for the boys, as many of the Bauer girls excelled on blades. Rita, the third eldest daughter, won skating titles at the Kitchener-Waterloo Skating Club.[108] While earning her BA at the University of Toronto, she played many intra-varsity sports at St. Michael's: tennis, basketball, badminton, softball, and hockey, becoming captain of the teams in the latter two, and the St. Michael's Women's Athletic president in 1947–48.[109] Next youngest Therese also played hockey and softball with St. Michael's while studying for a BA. Eldest sister Mary was a championship badminton player, diver, and swimmer, although her father prohibited the girls from some sports like bicycling. Later Mary dreamt of becoming a physical education teacher; however, due to limited career choices of that era, she became a successful secretary. Her feisty demeanor led to her tongue in cheek motto: "I like to play, but I play to win."[110] Alice, the second eldest girl, was an excellent long-distance swimmer and provincial champion

---

104 Bauer Family, *Bauer (A Family History)*, under "Eugene Regis Bauer."

105 Bauer Family, *Bauer (A Family History)*, under "Edgar Jacob Bauer."

106 Bauer Family, *Bauer (A Family History)*, under "Eugene Regis Bauer." The youngest, Paul, died at birth in 1927.

107 Bauer Family, *Bauer (A Family History)*, under "Alice Bertha Hayes."

108 Bauer Family, *Bauer (A Family History)*, under "Rita Eleanor (Bauer) Huck."

109 Women's hockey in southern Ontario was dominated in the 1930s by the Preston Rivulettes, located south of Waterloo. Carly Adams, "'Queens of the Ice Lanes': The Preston Rivulettes and Women's Hockey in Canada, 1931–1940," *Sport History Review* 39, no. 1 (2008).

110 Bauer Family, *Bauer (A Family History)*, under "Mary Wilfreda (Bauer) Freiburger."

at badminton.[111] David introduced her to a linemate, Cecil Schmalz, who she married in 1944. David's youngest sister Margaret became president of the Upper Canada Figure Skating Club.

The heavy sporting involvement of the Bauer children in the Waterloo region coincided with the growth of recreational services and support for sporting activities.[112] Many communities throughout North America promoted physical activity in increasingly urban and factory-based work environments. For instance, lawn bowling leagues in Waterloo grew rapidly, and by 1920 as many as 500 bowlers played in various tournaments. Businesses like Bauers Ltd. and Kuntz Brewery (owned by Edgar's uncle) financially supported this sport, along with hockey and baseball. Edgar himself served in many executive capacities in sporting organizations in Waterloo.[113] Many Anglican, Lutheran, and Catholic churches, and the Kitchener-Waterloo YMCA, also actively supported sports during the 1920s and 1930s, and Waterloo had large church leagues in basketball, hockey, baseball, and soccer.[114]

It was brother Bobby whose great success in hockey allowed David to dream large. Bobby left for St. Michael's at the age of 15, playing three of four seasons with the Majors.[115] During the 1933–34 St. Michael's championship season, Bobby was guided in the Basilian spirit of sport. Father M. Stan Lynch, the school's athletics director at the time, wrote that sport should not glorify the body but act as a valuable education.[116] Lynch praised the centrality of dedicated priest-coaches who purposefully shaped players in virtue. For instance, he argued for curtailing body checking at younger levels of hockey:

111   Bauer Family, *Bauer (A Family History)*, under "Alice Magdalena Bauer."

112   Kenneth McLaughlin and Sharon Jaeger, *Waterloo: An Illustrated History, 1857–2007* (Waterloo, ON: City of Waterloo, 2007), 129.

113   Bauer Family, *Bauer (A Family History)*, under "Edgar Jacob Bauer."

114   McLaughlin and Jaeger, *Waterloo*, 130.

115   With Bobby and Frank Bauer on the 1933–34 Majors team, St. Michael's were crowned the Memorial Cup Champions. Dr. W. J. "Jerry" Laflamme coached the team; he had captained Carr's Allan Cup Senior Championship team in 1910. Bobby also played a Junior A season for the Toronto National Sea Fleas, who were coached by the sport innovator Lloyd Percival. Gary Mossman, *Lloyd Percival: Coach and Visionary* (Woodstock, ON: Seraphim Editions, 2013), 34. Bobby claimed Percival was the best teacher of the game he had.

116   M. S. Lynch, "The Place of Athletics in Our Schools." *The Basilian* 1, no. 1 (March 1935): 14.

"Instead of adjusting the boy to the game, the game should be adjusted to the boy!"[117] This gentlemanly spirit was embraced by Bobby.

Bobby Bauer returned to Kitchener-Waterloo area and helped a local team win the Ontario Junior A championship.[118] He next played in the Bruins farm system for the Providence Reds, where the combination of Bauer, Milt Schmidt and Woody Dumart were dubbed "the Sauerkrauts," or, for short, "the Kraut Line."[119] According to local history, the line had skill, athleticism, and a mutual chemistry aided by their common German heritage.[120] They made an impact when they joined the Bruins: the team won four straight league titles and two Stanley Cup Championships in 1939 and 1941. They became one of the greatest lines in NHL history. In 1939–40, they were the first line in NHL to be atop the scoring leaders. When Bauer was posthumously inducted into the Hockey Hall of Fame in 1996, linemate Dumart praised him for his ability to control the puck along the boards and deftly find open spaces.[121] Bauer was small, only 5 foot, 6 inches, and weighed a mere 150 pounds. Following in the lineage of Carr, Bobby Bauer won three Lady Byng awards, acknowledgement of his great skill and gentlemanly play. He amassed only 36 penalty minutes in his seven-year NHL career.[122]

Bobby Bauer's career was cut short by three years because he and his linemates joined the Royal Canadian Air Force in Spring 1942.[123] After his retirement from hockey in 1947, Bobby worked for his father-in-law Roy Charles Bauer at the Western Shoe Company, which in 1933 had been the first to develop a skate permanently attached to a boot.[124] This business became the Bauer Skate

117 Scott Young, *100 Years of Dropping the Puck: History of the OHA* (Toronto: McClelland & Stewart, 1989), 237.

118 Waterloo Public Library, *Waterloo 150: Profiles from the Past, Faces of the Future* (Waterloo, ON: Waterloo Public Library, 2007), 118.

119 Greg Oliver, *Father Bauer and the Great Experiment: The Genesis of Canadian Olympic Hockey* (Toronto: ECW Press, 2017), 16.

120 Waterloo Public Library, *Waterloo 150*, 64.

121 Waterloo Public Library, *Waterloo 150*, 64.

122 Bauer Family, *Bauer (A Family History)*, under "Robert Theodore Bauer."

123 They won the Allan Cup with the RCAF team that year and played in exhibition games for the RCAF Benevolent fund. Oliver, *Father Bauer*, 21. NHL President Clarence Campbell later praised the Kraut line as great citizens in times of war and peace. Oliver, *Father Bauer*, 17.

124 Bobby had married Marguerite Bauer, who was a championship figure skater in the region but of no relation. "Bauer, Robert Theodore Joseph," A73-0026/022(21), Alumni Filed Records, University of Toronto Archives.

Company, which was located in nearby Kitchener, and in 1949 promoted a pair of skates called the Bobby Bauer Special, endorsed by its namesake.[125]

Bobby's influence remained with his youngest brother David. He credited Bobby with ingraining in him hockey's fundamentals: "never give the puck away" and "never take your eyes off the eyes of your opponent."[126] It's hockey advice that David Bauer carried with him on and off the ice.

Qualities of the Basilian and Bauer Family Sporting Heritage

Years after Bauer had established himself as a hockey coach, he reflected on Carr's sporting tradition as continued by priest-coaches and laymen.[127] This tradition reflects the passion and values of sport promoted by the Waterloo-based Bauer family.

The Basilian mix of sport, education, and faith was common at the time for churches and para-church organizations in Canada. For Catholics generally, priests often encouraged local Catholic Youth Organization (CYO) or parish events with a sport theme. Basilian influence furthered this because of their leadership in an expanding number of secondary and post-secondary schools and colleges in English-speaking Canada.[128] Of particular note is the use of hockey by these priest-coaches. From early on, the game was part of the nation's identity and shaped by churches' and lay Christians' sporting organizations.

To conclude, five qualities of this sporting tradition stand out. First, it understood sport as a way to cultivate the unity of body and soul. Through strengthening the body, youth could develop inner character. This tradition objected to an overly violent form of play that threatened the body's health and the soul's purpose. Second, this heritage underscored sport as mentorship. Instead of Basilian schools acting only as places of academic learning, sport enabled a broader education. The coaches were to pay close attention to

---

125   Oliver, *Father Bauer*, 23–24.

126   Oliver, *Father Bauer*, 24.

127   Father McLean highlighted several leaders: "Sheehan, McGahey, Cerre, Sheedy, the McNamaras, Mallon, Flanagan, Whelan, Joe Primeau and others." "In Memoriam: Father David W. Bauer." Majors' player Ray Hannigan became a priest in Montana; see Shea, Colle, and Patskou, *St. Michael's College*, 54.

128   Lay control of sport was delayed in Quebec, as French clergy who endorsed sport did not take firm control until the end of the Second World War. For details, see Jason Blake and Andrew C. Holman, eds., *The Same but Different: Hockey in Quebec* (Montreal: McGill-Queen's University Press, 2017), 7–8.

each player's character and psychology. Third, this tradition promoted sport's capacity to foster personal virtue. Because sport was understood as a serious matter under the guidance of the school, it affirmed the ideals of amateur sport and promoted virtue and shunned vice. Moral toughness was to trump despair for victory. Fourth, this tradition held that sport must endorse good citizenship. Connections between sport and (military) service abound. If sport supported Basilian educational institutions, then they could serve the needs of the country. Finally, this heritage showed that sport should exemplify joy and celebration. Sport ought to be enjoyed by sporting participants and induce community spirit that reaches beyond the hockey rink.

Beginning in the 1930s, however, hockey slowly became less associated with schools, education, and churches as the commercialized game predominated over the amateur.[129]

---

129 This was certainly the case in Toronto. See Alan Metcalfe, "The Role of Religious Institutions in the Growth of Organized Sport in Toronto, Canada, 1919–1939," in *Proceedings of the IX International HISP Congress: Sport and Religion*, ed. Instituto Nacional Dos Desportos (Lisboa, Portugal: Instituto Nacional Dos Desportos, 1981), 227–31.

The Finale of the Great
College-School Hockey Dynasty

BORN IN WATERLOO, ONTARIO, ON NOVEMBER 2, 1924, David William Bauer felt destined for a life in hockey from early on: "From the time I was ten years old until the age of sixteen I only had one desire and that was to become a professional hockey player."[1] At 16, as the family legend goes, the young man lowered his hockey bag out of his bedroom window and snuck off to Hershey, Pennsylvania, for a Boston Bruins training camp. The certain truth in the story is that he made a real impression on the professional hockey men: "At the end of that camp, I was invited to join the Boston Olympics, one of Boston's farm teams. Naturally my father was concerned. A phone call from him reminded me that he would be on the next train to meet me."[2]

His father Edgar viewed hockey, in his son's words, "as a means for the development of my personality, contributing to the growth of the physical and emotional side of my life within the framework of formal education." This

---

1   Donald Boyle, "Promoting Hockey in Japan," *Catholic Week*, December 8, 1973, 4a.

2   David Bauer, *Report to Munro*, 1971, Marc Bauer-Maison Collection, 2.

educational approach was discussed by father and son during many late-night conversations in the Bauer home.[3] The well-educated Bauer children attended textile, business, and secretarial schools, or earned their undergraduate degrees. But young Dave saw "hockey as a commercial enterprise, a way of making a good living. The strong pull exerted by the image-makers, even then [in 1941], had so powerful an influence on me that I knowingly and willingly opted out of schoolwork in order to defeat the goals of my father so that I could be left to pursue my will in peace."[4] His father was uncompromising; he believed in his son's academic abilities, despite teachers who did not.[5] "He told me time and time again that I must try to view the game of hockey within some larger context."[6]

David Bauer at St. Michael's College School

Instead of inspiring Bauer, the Bruins training camp left him disillusioned about professional hockey. He explained, "I saw an empty life.... it was traumatic indeed because for years I had been thinking of my own future almost exclusively in terms of playing in the NHL and now suddenly I had seen that as insufficient."[7] He accepted his father's wisdom, as he typically did, and agreed to attend St. Michael's College School like his brothers Frank and Bobby.[8]

In 1942, Bauer started Grade 11 at the college, attending its original location on the campus of the University of Toronto near Bay Street. He became the captain of both the hockey and football teams. Comparisons were overtly made between Bauer's 1944 hockey team and Carr's 1910 Allan Cup championship team. A yearbook article explains, "[Coach] Paul McNamara produced that spirited hard-fighting, sensational team of this year of 1944 which time and again brought back sweet memories of the skill, the grace, the speed, and the spirit of the Champs of 1910."[9] Father Hugh Mallon, the

---

3   Maureen Bauer-McGahey, interview with author, June 4, 2019.

4   Bauer, *Report to Munro*, 2.

5   Rita Huck, "Dear Dad," in *Bauer (A Family History of Edgar and Bertha's Family)* (Waterloo, ON: Self-published, 2003). Private Bauer family records owned by Paul Schmaltz.

6   Boyle, "Promoting Hockey in Japan," 4a.

7   Bauer, *Report to Munro*, 3.

8   Margaret Laudenbach, interview with author, January 18, 2019.

9   St. Michael's College School, *The Thurible 1944*, St. Michael's College

college's athletics director at the time, often insisted that the young Bauer was the best player ever at St. Michael's—even better than future Hockey Hall of Fame players like Ted Lindsay and Dave Keon.[10]

Figure 3.1 Bauer in Majors uniform. *From left to right:* Bauer, Father F. Boland, Cece Schmalz.

Courtesy of St. Michael's College School

The St. Michael's Majors of 1943–44 was the better of the two teams young Dave Bauer played for, despite it losing out in the Ontario Hockey Association (OHA) Championship Finals. In a summary that appeared in the 1944 yearbook, a glowing endorsement was given to the team's captain:

School Online Archives, 88, https://archive.org/details/stmcsthurible1944testuoft/mode/2up?view=theater&q=thurible+1944. That 1910 team had Jerry Laflamme as its captain. He later coached Paul McNamara for three years with the Junior A Majors.

10   Jim Proudfoot, "Père Bauer Was a Lot More Than a Hockey Coach," *Toronto Star*, November 11, 1988, Box 12, last file, Bauer fonds, Basilian Archives. Mallon later became the Superior of the Basilian Community.

"In all the long history of St. Michael's none have borne the title of captain more worthily than Dave. Friendly, considerate, unselfish, studious, he didn't know how to quit. A constant inspiration and a model, Dave is modest and unassuming." On the ice, he was a skilled left-winger, who skated hard, battled along the boards and played with Bobby's finesse and talent.[11] When he carried the puck in his skates, opponents found it difficult to take the puck from him.[12] The yearbook article ended with: "He had a way of drawing out a goalie and a deadly accurate shot that made opponents squirm when he got in close."[13]

An apparent shoulder injury in his youth made Bauer master how to play sports left-handed. In hockey, he shocked both a goaltender and a reporter by switching from a left to a right-handed shot, producing an unimaginable goal.[14] Switch-hitting Bauer used his ambidexterity on the football field in two undefeated seasons; defenses were bewildered by a quarterback who could throw the ball with his left or right arm.[15] Later, as a priest, when students argued about the size of a strike zone in baseball, the thirty-something priest wearing his cassock began throwing curveballs and sliders for strikes with either arm. Students were stunned.[16]

After the Majors lost in the 1944 OHA Finals, the victorious Oshawa Generals were allowed to add players to their roster due to soldier deployments during World War II. The Generals' pick-ups included Dave Bauer and future NHL icon Ted Lindsay. At one point, however, Bauer threatened to quit the team if the swearing on the ice and in the dressing room did not stop. The players accepted Bauer's challenge and the team went on to win the national championship.[17] Bauer totalled four goals and three assists in an 11–4 final game victory.[18]

11   Kevin Shea, Larry Colle, and Paul Patskou, *St. Michael's College: 100 Years of Pucks and Prayers* (Bolton, ON: Fenn Publishing Company Limited, 2008), 257.

12   James Christie, "Father Bauer Honored," *The Globe and Mail*, 1988, Bauer Fr. David box, SMCS Memorial file, St. Michael's College School Archives.

13   St. Michael's College School, *The Thurible 1944*, 103–4.

14   St. Michael's College School, *The Thurible 1944*, 150.

15   William O'Brien, "St. Mike's Alumni Inducted into the Hockey Hall of Fame: Father David Bauer, CSB," August 1996, Bauer Fr. David box, SMCS Memorial file, St. Michael's College School Archives.

16   Terry O'Malley, interview with author, June 26, 2018.

17   Tom Conaway, "Bauer Remembered as Feisty, Caring," *Record Newspaper*, November 15, 1988, Bauer Fr. David box, Obit file, St. Michael's College School Archives.

18   Greg Oliver, *Father Bauer and the Great Experiment: The Genesis of Canadian*

Figure 3.2 Bauer and the 1944 Oshawa Generals celebrate winning the Memorial Cup. Bauer is front row, second from the left. Ted Lindsay is back row, far right.

Courtesy of D.K. (Doc) Seaman Hockey Resource Centre, Hockey Hall of Fame

Decision to Become a Basilian Father

Dave Bauer enlisted with the military in November 1944.[19] He joined the Canadian Army and was assigned to the Number 12 Basic Training Centre in Chatham, Ontario.[20] His patriotism was largely influenced by his family,

---

Olympic Hockey (Toronto: ECW Press, 2017), 42. Lindsay helped organize the NHL Players Association in the 1950s and subsequently had the "players-voted" MVP trophy named after him. He recalled years later that Bauer acted like a priest and leader even at that time. Oliver, *Father Bauer*, 38.

   19   Shea, Colle, and Patskou, *St. Michael's College*, 256. Subsequently, he played only one game with the Majors that season.

   20   O'Brien, "St. Mike's Alumni Inducted." Bauer played briefly in the Windsor City Hockey League as well as the Ottawa Canadian Postal Corps of the Ottawa National Defence Hockey League.

with all six brothers serving in the air force, navy, army, or reserves.[21] His father's business also contributed its manufacturing facilities to the national effort.[22] Bauer ended up in Chilliwack, British Columbia, at a Canadian Army training center for a six-week summer training program prior to his planned deployment in the Pacific.[23]

He was a religious person, and during this time had been taken by a book about Our Lady of Fatima and her messages given to three Portuguese children in 1917. The book promoted the belief that a special grace was given to priests because they acted like a bridge between heaven and earth. He internally wrestled with God about whether he should become a priest and, according to a fellow soldier, fervently recited his rosary even in the midst of crowded military quarters.[24] After some time, as reported by Carmelite sisters whom Bauer confided in, "I threw the book at the pillow and I said, 'Okay, Our Lady, if you want me to be a priest, get me out of the army by the 8th of September.'"[25] Entering the war at twenty was the honorable thing to do, but Bauer was not unlike other soldiers who made divine appeals for their discharge.

A peace treaty was signed between Japan and the Allies on September 2, 1945. On the return train ride to Chatham, Bauer and other soldiers talked about their war-time experiences and the need for world peace: "We soldiers talked anxiously on what kind of world lay ahead. Then and there, I decided there must be something more meaningful I can do with my life than chase a puck around."[26] Before returning home to Waterloo, he stopped to meet

21   Bob and Ray served in the Royal Canadian Air Force; Jerry in the Canadian Navy; Gene and David in the Canadian Army; and Frank in the reserves. Stacey McLennan, "Region of Waterloo Hall of Fame Induction Report on Father David Bauer," private email attachment to author.

22   Raymond Stanton, "Bauer's Plant Grows Tenfold in 40 Years," *Kitchener-Waterloo Record*, July 27, 1957, 24.

23   Paul Burns, interview with author, August 15, 2018. Another interviewee was certain that he was stationed in Vernon. Carmelite Sisters of St. Joseph, interview with author, January 17, 2019.

24   Douglas J. St. Louis, "In Remembrance," *Catholic Register*, June 10, 1996, Fr. David Bauer box, St. Michael's College School Archives.

25   Carmelite Sisters of St. Joseph, interview.

26   Terry O'Malley, "Father David Bauer CSB (1924–1988)—A Life in 'Quotations,'" Terry O'Malley Collection, 7. This story and many others about Bauer's promotion of a nonviolent form of sport were originally published in "Nonviolence and Catholic School Sport: Recommendations for Supporting Mission as Drawn from

one of his aunts, a Sister of St. Joseph, who told him to be faithful to his promise since God had saved him from combat. But Bauer was not ready to become a priest. He returned to Toronto and enrolled at St. Michael's College to continue his Bachelor of Arts degree with a major in philosophy.

Bauer had not dreamt about becoming a priest. In a 1985 speech to educators, he stated outrightly, "The last thing in the world I personally desired was to be a priest—and certainly I did not desire to be a teacher or educator."[27] He explained that he had other plans: "My personal desire from early childhood was to found a Christian family."[28] His desire would not have surprised the Bauer family. Those alive today said that he had an easy way around people that made women feel comfortable with him. He was handsome, fun, had an easy smile, and listened attentively. Different stories are told about him dating girls in his youth.[29] He was engaged to be married to one woman, but she broke it off. One story is that her father did not think much of uneducated, professional hockey players with no future after hockey.[30] Another is that she found that Dave talked too much about the Blessed Virgin Mary.[31] No matter, the point is that Bauer did not become a priest because he was pressured, lonely, or otherwise.

Instead, in that 1985 speech, he wrote: "Probably I'm here to-day because I have always believed profoundly in Catholic Christian Education. That is why I joined the Basilian Fathers, like so many others." He saw this religious community offering a way to make sense of the world, a means to influence society, through education.[32] Through education, he wanted "to play a role

a Historical Case Study," in *International Studies in Catholic Education*, published online (February 1, 2023): 1–13, available online at https://www.tandfonline.com/eprint/ ETMJRWVQHNI7EJ6EYHSC/full?target=10.1080/19422539.2022.2162908.

27 David Bauer, Speech Notes, 1985, Box 3, File 6, Bauer fonds, Basilian Archives.

28 Bauer, Speech Notes, 1985.

29 His sister Rita's poetry tells of one incident: "And then there was [his brother] Jerry, Dave's best pal; Until Dave was caught kissing Jer's best gal," see: Huck, "Dear Dad."

30 O'Malley, "A Life in 'Quotations,'" 5.

31 Some Basilians also thought his "tremendous pious attachment to Our Lady" needed softening. Neil Hibbert, interview with author, January 16, 2019.

32 Around this time, nearly half of all Basilians were involved in education. John Wallner, "Athletics and Academics: St. Michael's College Withdrawal from Ontario Hockey Association Junior A Competition" (master's thesis, Carleton University, Ottawa, 1990), 10.

in the reconstruction of society—first by bringing a Christian influence to the sporting world." This reconstruction was a prominent ultramontane theme taught in papal social doctrines beginning with Pope Leo XIII's *Rerum novarum*.[33] Bauer, who with many other future Basilians took up this vision with a missionary zeal, believed that Christians in English-speaking Canada should take on leading cultural positions in society—including in sport—similar to the rise of Catholic sporting organizations in Europe and Quebec around the turn of the century.

Bauer turned down a 1946 contract offer from the Boston Bruins "because when the world is in turmoil, the mind wants to know why.... I wanted to get an education ... because it was important for me to see what one could learn about truth."[34] In a *Time Magazine* article, he recalled his father's question about choosing to play professional hockey: "Is there enough of a life in it for you?"[35] The combination of his military experience, the limitations of professional hockey, his love of knowledge and love received from others, and an interior conversion enabled him to stop struggling with God. The hockey player decided to become a priest: "Okay, Lord, you win out," the Carmelite Sisters recalled him saying.

That June, Bauer announced his plans to join the Basilian Fathers. He was playing summer baseball, and his trainer gave him no response. At the season's end, in his heavy German accent, in a tone often repeated by Bauer, the trainer finally responded, "I've been thinkin' about your enterin' the priesthood. Yeah, why the hell should ya have to work for a living."[36] A *Globe and Mail* reporter saw the evidence of Bauer's unusual path to his priesthood: "A cleric with a quick step and a quick smile plus the smashed nose and the spidery lines of scar tissue usually associated with a life more strenuous than that found in a rectory."[37]

---

33   Staf Hellemans, "Is There a Future for Catholic Social Teaching after the Waning of Ultramontane Mass Catholicism?" in *Catholic Social Thought: Twilight or Renaissance?*, ed. Jonathan S. Boswell, Francis P. McHugh, and Johan Verstraeten (Leuven, Belgium: Peeters Publishers, 2000), 18–19.

34   Bruce Kidd and John MacFarlane, *The Death of Hockey* (Toronto: New Press, 1972), 80.

35   "Hockey—Second Bauer," *Time Magazine*, December 27, 1963, File 44, David Bauer fonds, Canada's Sports Hall of Fame Archives, 7.

36   O'Malley, interview.

37   Trent Frayne, "It's How You Played the Game that Mattered to Father Bauer," *The Globe and Mail*, November 10, 1988, Box 4, File 9, Bauer fonds, Basilian Archives.

The Roots of Bauer's Coaching Philosophy

Bauer entered St. Basil's Novitiate, Richmond Hill, Ontario, in September 1946. He made his first profession of vows to the community in 1947 and earned his Bachelor of Arts from the University of Toronto in 1949, majoring in philosophy and showing great interest also in psychology and history.[38] During his studies, Bauer was gripped by a course called True Humanism—known as "TruHu" by the Basilian scholastics—which introduced the philosophy of Jacques Maritain.[39] No other thinker had influenced Carr or the Basilian order like this French philosopher. Maritain challenged the secular humanist assumption that peeling back religion from Western society gave a more accurate picture of human nature. Instead, he argued that to understand the human person authentically—i.e., true humanism—its transcendent dimension must be accounted for. To arrive at a comprehensive understanding, the human person inevitably must realize his or her communion with God. While Maritain wrote nothing about sport, he emphasized how different aspects of modern culture—art, poetry, science, etc.—could activate human self-awareness, a *prise de conscience*, that is, the human person's general movement toward freedom and toward a deeper understanding of his or her identity.[40] Because all parts of culture could speak to a deeper reality forged by a Creator, the human person could discover and know God through this world.

"Tru-Hu" was offered by a young Basilian, Father Ralph MacDonald.[41] Although he was abstract in thought, he had a great enthusiasm for the subject and through lively discussions was able to connect the content personally and academically to ordinary undergraduate students like Bauer. Human freedom, for Maritain, was to be used to develop the whole person, whose moral and spiritual perfection could then help build the common

---

38 P. Wallace Platt, *Dictionary of Basilian Biography: Lives of Members of the Congregation of Priests of Saint Basil from its Origins in 1822 to 2022, 2nd ed.* (Toronto: University of Toronto Press, 2005), 33.

39 Around 1980, Bauer named vital books in Maritain's corpus: *Introduction to Philosophy, The Person and the Common Good, True Humanism,* and Evans and Ward's *The Social and Political Philosophy of Jacques Maritain.* See David Bauer, Letter to Barbara Bauer, Box 3, File 3, Bauer fonds, Basilian Archives.

40 D. A. Gallagher, J. W. Evans, and W. Sweet, "Maritain, Jacques," in *The New Catholic Encyclopedia,* 2nd ed. (Detroit, MI: Gale, 2003), 178.

41 Gallagher, interview; Platt, *Dictionary of Basilian Biography,* 364–65.

good.[42] Human persons, because they are a part of the spiritual order, have an inherent dignity that makes them an end in themselves—and makes possible a transcendent destiny.[43] Inspired by this vision of the human person, Bauer began reflecting more deeply about its implications for how he treated others and how the hockey world treated its players.[44]

Bauer was also attracted to the work of historian Christopher Dawson. This British thinker argued that violent forces threatened to destroy societies because people's spiritual nature was starved and frustrated in a modern world.[45] Without religion's influence, Dawson claimed that Western society was undercut by a predominant sense of nihilism.[46] A technological revolution and the growth of materialism affected human nature, leading to minimizing religious traditions and ignoring their ability to connect societies through a common humanism.[47] Dawson's analysis helped make sense of Bauer's world.

Life at St. Basil's, with over one hundred men studying and preparing for religious priesthood, was a good fit for Bauer. He enjoyed spirited conversations.[48] For instance, when he received a haircut in the barbershop at St. Basil's on a Saturday, Bauer reveled in the discussion and was a catalyst for imagining the future of education and Basilian schools.[49] His passion and care for others attracted people to him.[50] Later, as a theology student, Bauer instigated theological conferences, in part to spread the word about Our Lady of Fatima at a time when her messages were not part of theological training.[51]

---

42 Gallagher, Evans, and Sweet, "Maritain, Jacques," 179.

43 Gallagher, Evans, and Sweet, "Maritain, Jacques," 179. This is part of Maritain's doctrine of personalism.

44 Bauer joined the Young Christian Student movement during this time. Burns, interview.

45 Christopher Dawson, *Understanding Europe* (Washington, DC: Catholic University of America Press, 1952), 229.

46 Dawson, *Understanding Europe*, 206. He argued that world religions had a certain spiritual autonomy despite being shaped by social influences and environment. Ambrose J. Raftis, "Christopher Dawson, Pioneer Historian of Unity," *The Basilian Teacher* 6, no. 1 (October 1961): 13–14.

47 Dawson, *Understanding Europe*, 208. See also, Raftis, "Christopher Dawson," 16–17.

48 Gallagher, interview.

49 Gallagher, interview.

50 Mike Mastromatteo, "Fr. Bauer Believed in Fair Play," *Catholic Register*, June 10, 1996, Box 2, last file, Bauer fonds, Basilian Archives.

51 Carmelite Sisters of St. Joseph, interview.

Conversations with others came easily to him because he had partaken in lively, even volatile, Bauer family discussions.[52]

In 1949, he began theological studies at St. Basil's Seminary while also working toward teacher certification. He was ordained to the priesthood in 1953 at St. Basil's Church, Toronto. But even before his ordination, Bauer began teaching religion and history at St. Michael's College School, which now resided in its new building at Bathurst Street and St. Clair Avenue.[53] In Bauer's classroom, he loved to teach about true humanism, whether the subject of the course was religion or history; he did not let the formal curriculum dictate the direction of the course.[54] One former student, Paul Burns, who later became a Basilian, recalled that the courses were about developing the whole person in a community. For the religion teacher Bauer, being a Catholic meant living out faith in daily life: "Whether, when you're playing a bad game of hockey and getting booted all over the ice, you understand yourself better doing it in the name of Christ. You can be bagging groceries in a supermarket and be very much at ease with yourself, if you're living with Christ."[55] Connecting to God was to make students more like themselves.

Many students liked Bauer's classes, but others found thinned-down courses about Maritain's philosophy difficult to grasp.[56] The ideas could be dense and too much for some students.[57] To clarify things, Bauer placed posters up in his classroom to provoke self-reflection. He wrote money, fame, or reputation at the center of a circle with the corresponding fruit of a life based upon that source. For instance, a life based on a love of money eventually becomes corrupted. A life centered on spiritual values produces virtues. The graphics simplified philosophical concepts and even inspired some students.[58]

---

52   O'Malley, interview. His roots in small town Ontario and rural folksiness put people at ease.

53   The four-kilometer move to the north allowed for growth of the high school and the University of St. Michael's College.

54   Hibbert, interview.

55   Thomas O'Brien, "Father David Bauer, CSB," 1999, "Bauer, Fr. David—Coach" box, St. Michael's College School Archives, 2–3.

56   Ted Schmidt, "Fr. David Bauer Untouched by Perils of Sports World," *Catholic New Times*, December 18, 1988, 16. Bauer received assistance from priests like Father David Belyea to refine his thought and direction, see: Ted Schmidt, interview with author, November 2020.

57   Hibbert, interview.

58   Hibbert, interview. Neil Hibbert was inspired by Bauer and eventually became a Basilian priest.

Later in his tenure at St. Michael's, Bauer became an assistant principal, and on one occasion, he caught wind of student dishonesty. During a winter snowfall, students would step into a coffee house across the street and then later blame the weather for their tardiness. One morning vice-principal Bauer walked over to the full coffee house and began writing down names of the late students with a smile on his face. There was no need to react to the situation, and he returned to the College awaiting the arrival of the students.[59] Another time he disciplined students for hypnotising peers before they entered exams—which some students, oddly, believed would improve performance on tests. Bauer stated that their punishment was to return to school on Saturday. After debating the severity of the discipline, the cassock-wearing Bauer offered them a way out: "I'll take you to the football field and you kick the ball to me and I'll run through you. If anyone lays a hand on me, then no punishment. But if I can get through to the end, you've got to come in."[60] The students could not touch him, and accepted their punishment.

Almost all the teachers at St. Michael's were Basilian Fathers by the late 1950s. Priestly mentorship throughout their North American colleges supplied the novitiate with 60 new members in 1958 alone.[61] The order was gaining momentum, which allowed it to expand educational operations in several cities. There were ample priests who could play hockey at St. Michael's—many of whom played with their cassocks on, hanging down to their ankles.[62] Mixing the sport's rough-and-tumble nature with religious life felt natural for the young priests and revealed their human side.[63] It certainly did for Bauer, who was known to settle a disagreement with a wrestling match.[64]

Over an eight-year period at St. Michael's, Bauer integrated the teachings of Maritain and Dawson into his re-imagining of sport. His personalist coaching philosophy is evident throughout four coaching articles in a hockey magazine produced by the Canadian Amateur Hockey Association (CAHA).[65]

---

59   Burns, interview.

60   Burns, interview.

61   Hibbert, interview.

62   Oliver, *Father Bauer*, 39.

63   Frank Cosentino, *Holy Hockey! The Story of Canada's Flying Fathers* (Toronto: Burnstown Publishing House, 2018), 31.

64   O'Malley, "A Life in 'Quotations,'" 10.

65   David Bauer, "Teams Must Play to Win, But Not at Any Price," *Hockey Canada Magazine*, October 1962, 21.

First, Bauer placed the human person—the hockey player—at the center of his philosophy. He believed that young people's development was the real goal of the sport. He described the development of virtues, such as courage, prudence, teamwork, and fair play. Bauer wanted hockey to produce responsible citizens: "If we can master ourselves and teach our players to discipline themselves in one area, they ought to be able to master themselves in other fields." Players were to be treated with love and respect and not manipulated.[66] Second, instead of using tactics that seek victory at any cost, he reminded coaches that players are human beings. Long schedules, boring practices, and overly rough play should be eliminated; instead make "the game of hockey a game of skill and joy rather than brute force." Knowing a child's temperament, surely a nod to Maritain's emphasis on knowing individual differences, enabled coaches to shape their players' development.

Figure 3.3 Bauer in St. Michael's hockey jacket in 1956.

Courtesy of St. Michael's College School

In another coaching article, Bauer explained why he emphasized checking and a defense-first approach: "I believe so strongly that the offense should roll off a strong defense ... even if you gave me the fifteen greatest offensive

66 Connections between Bauer and Maritain are supported in an article by a colleague at St. Michael's: see Michael Lavelle, "Values in Coaching," *The Basilian Teacher* 8, no. 5 (February 1964): 251.

hockey players in the world I would begin by training them in defensive tactics."[67] Ultimately, he endeavored to form every player into a "a defensive artist" because it ensured that every player had confidence: if a player knows he can recover when he loses the puck to an opponent, he will feel self-assured about trying "more daring offensive maneuvers."[68] His quiet disciplinary style meant he rarely became angry with players and preferred, when issues arose, to use them as opportunities to educate.[69] This was to give players a greater sense of freedom, both on the ice and away from it—and reflected Maritain's personalist thought.

Bauer's calm demeanor enabled different game strategies. He moved players to and from different positions, even placing his goaltender Gerry Cheevers on a forward line, to produce more adaptable players and better students of the game.[70] He was also known for killing penalties with four defensemen.[71] His techniques encouraged experimentation and creativity and kept the opposition coaches guessing, while ensuring players excelled at checking and skating. One reporter called Bauer the "Casey Stengel of Canadian Hockey," after the legendary New York Yankees baseball manager who rotated players in the infield.[72]

Connections between Bauer and a Basilian sporting tradition are obvious: priority on character, a de-emphasis on winning, a focus on the potential and limits of the person, belief in the joy and artistry of the game, and coaching with the whole person in mind. Bauer also thought violent play was offside. In a recollection of a lecture that he gave to a religion class at St. Michael's, Bauer made a careful distinction, however: "Gentlemen, the game of hockey is a good legitimate sport and if a maneuver, such as a clean check, ends up with someone getting hurt, don't blame the game. Real hockey players play lively, clean hockey, and that includes clean, solid body-checks, along the boards or

---

67   David Bauer, "Defensive Skill First Essential to Be Winner," *Hockey Canada Magazine*, November 1962, 21.

68   David Bauer, "Puck Control is the Key to Offensive Success," *Hockey Canada Magazine*, October 1962, 11.

69   Oliver, *Father Bauer*, 61.

70   Bunny Morganson, "Hang on to Your Seats," *Evening Telegram*, March 14, 1945, Bauer Fr. David box, St. Michael's College School Archives. Cheevers thought the change would also help his chances of earning a US college scholarship after high school. See Shea, *St. Michael's College*, 129.

71   Shea, Colle, and Patskou, *St. Michael's College*, 55.

72   Morganson, "Hang on to Your Seats."

at centre-ice."[73] He'd teach how to give and take a hit properly. But he stood in contrast to those who promoted violence in hockey, stoking the fires further by playing up religious differences when the Catholic Majors—those "papist bastards"—arrived for a game.[74]

The on-ice product often turned violent, and were recounted as "bloodbaths."[75] Player Frank Mahovlich, who came from the small town of Timmins, was shocked by the Catholic-versus-Protestant rivalry in Toronto. Such was not the case in northern Ontario, with its greater mix of European immigrants. In one brawl-filled game for St. Michael's, the referees lost control of the situation. Fighting continued while they played the national anthem over the loudspeaker system, and soon wives and girlfriends of the players joined in the melee. The brawl ended when officials turned out the lights in the arena. The director of athletics asserted a Basilian fiat: "No more fighting."[76] Taming aggression in hockey meant drawing a fine line. One former Major told the story of losing badly to the Toronto Marlies at the Maple Leaf Gardens.[77] During the second intermission, the fiery Irish manager, Father Flanagan, went around the dressing room to each player, angrily staring him in the eyes and yelling at him to push back. The coach closed by asking the group to take a knee and recite three Hail Marys. The player felt strange about the coaching tactics.

Bauer's defensively-responsible, nonviolent style of play was especially helpful for smaller players like himself and Dave Keon. Even though Keon was second in league scoring, Bauer benched him in one game because Keon would not play strong defense.[78] Without becoming an effective two-way player, Bauer thought, Keon's smaller stature limited his scoring upside. Keon's brother reported that the two Davids "had physical fights ... rolling around in a room wrestling ... it wasn't easy." Coach Bauer's philosophy won out, and Keon became a two-way player considered by many as the greatest Maple Leaf ever.[79]

73   O'Brien, "Bauer, Fr. David—Coach," 3.

74   Derek Holmes, interview with author, October 16, 2020.

75   Don McLeod, interview with author, June 4, 2018.

76   Ted Mahovlich, *The Big M: The Frank Mahovlich Story* (Toronto: HarperCollins Publishers, 1999), 28.

77   Murray Costello, interview with author, June 3, 2019.

78   Jim Keon, interview with author, November 12, 2020.

79   Oliver, *Father Bauer*, 60. Cheevers thought Bauer's greatest player was Keon, who played a Bauer style of game. Keon also credited other coaches at St. Michael's.

Bauer as a Hockey Leader at St. Michael's

Hockey was important at St. Michael's, and Bauer was one of many hockey leaders at the school.

"Gentleman Joe" Primeau took over as coach of the Majors after Bauer's final season of playing and then led the team to the 1944–45 Memorial Cup championship. He had briefly played for the Majors in 1923–24, and then played in the Toronto Maple Leafs' first Stanley Cup championship in 1931–32. He was part of the famed Kid Line for the Leafs: Primeau was seen as the brains behind the strength and speed of his teammates, and broke into the league at the time when the forward pass was introduced into play.[80] This opened up opportunities for Primeau to show his artistry and his ability to handle and pass the puck. For example, in one game he apparently controlled the puck for a full two minutes with New York Rangers chasing him, to the delight of Leafs fans.[81] He was inducted as a player into the Hockey Hall of Fame and, in 1998, made *The Hockey News*'s list of the 100 Greatest Hockey Players.

Both as a player and a coach, "Gentleman Joe" lived up to his name. In his eight seasons of NHL play, he amassed only 105 minutes of penalties and won the league's Lady Byng Trophy in 1931–32.[82] The award, which was donated in 1925 by Lady (Marie Evelyn Moreton) Byng, is the only NHL award named after a woman. She and her Governor General husband were very fond of hockey, but were dismayed by the poor behavior displayed by some hockey fans and players.[83] The award goes to players showing good sportsmanship and artful play. Between 1932 and 1963, St. Michael's alumni won the award ten times: Primeau (once), Bobby Bauer (three times), Red Kelly (four times) and Dave Keon (twice).

As a coach, Primeau was calm and soft-spoken, with a keen knowledge of the game and an ability to communicate well to players.[84] The St. Michael's Majors standout Frank Mahovlich called Primeau the best coach he ever

---

80 Ed Fitkin, *The Gashouse Gang of Hockey* (Toronto: W. M. Baxter Publishing Company, 1951), 20.

81 Fitkin, *Gashouse Gang of Hockey*, 47–48.

82 NHL.com, "NHL Lady Byng Memorial Trophy Winners," *National Hockey League*, September 11, 2020. http://www.nhl.com/ice/page.htm?id=24938.

83 Evelyn Moreton Byng, *Up the Stream of Time* (Toronto: Macmillan, 1945), 140–41. She was the wife of Lord Julian Byng, the 12th Governor General of Canada.

84 Fitkin, *Gashouse Gang of Hockey*, 105.

had.[85] Primeau coached and managed periodically at St. Michael's College over a near twenty-year span, which included coaching two Memorial Cup teams and being president of the 1960–61 championship team with Bauer. He is the only hockey coach to have won the Stanley Cup, Allan Cup, and Memorial Cup championships.[86] When Primeau returned to St. Michael's in the mid-1950s to run practices for the Majors, he built a relationship with Bauer that lasted their lifetimes. Primeau came from a devout Catholic family and he actively helped CYOs in Toronto.[87] Bauer publicly declared the hockey genius of Primeau and how he learned the phrase, "Use technique, but let the spirit prevail," from him.

Also influential in continuing the hockey tradition at St. Michael's were several priest-coaches in the program. Father Ted Flanagan, who played with the Majors' junior squad in 1931, spent most of his career coaching hockey and football at St. Michael's, where he generously gave of himself and was known for his quick wit.[88] He was proud to tell others that defenseman Tim Horton was the best Catholic player he coached. Horton, who later founded Canada's popular coffee and donut chain, regularly caught an early Sunday morning service at Metropolitan United Church.[89] Brian Higgins was coached by the intense Flanagan, and after ordination remained friends with Bauer and his Waterloo family.[90] Father Higgins was a strict disciplinarian who became so well-known as a football coach and educator in Sault Ste. Marie that its football stadium is now named after him.[91] In an interview, he described several methods used to make boys think about others and the team.[92] To stop their pouting, he would challenge them, accept them, cry with them, or

85   Mahovlich, *The Big M*, 29. Mahovlich entered the Hockey Hall of Fame as a player.

86   He also coached the Toronto Marlboros' senior team to an Allan Cup Championship in 1950 and, in the 1950–51 season, led the Toronto Maple Leafs to a Stanley Cup.

87   Todd Denault, interview with author, June 13, 2019.

88   Shea, Colle, and Patskou, *St. Michael's College*, 54.

89   Lori Horton and Tim Griggs, *In Loving Memory: A Tribute to Tim Horton* (Toronto: ECW Press, 1997), 11.

90   Platt, *Dictionary of Basilian Biography*, 219.

91   Kenneth Armstrong, "Father Higgins Lends Name to St. Mary's Sports Field (6 Photos)," *SooToday*, October 30, 2015, https://www.sootoday.com/local-news/father-higgins-lends-name-to-st-marys-sports-field-6-photos-184196.

92   Albert Lee Higgins, "Hold That Line," *The Basilian Teacher* 2, no. 1(October 1957): 20–21.

show them how ridiculous they were acting. When exasperated, he would tell them to act as if they cared about others; they might sense the good feelings that come from helping others. Through his coaching, Higgins tried to build relationships, listen to concerns, offer advice, and support growth in virtue.[93]

Father Bill Conway was ordained in 1951 and coached the Junior B Buzzers hockey team to the 1961 Ontario championship.[94] This friend of Bauer influenced many students with his warm personality and spirited teaching and coaching. Like others, Conway, too, was fueled by a strong desire for greatness. A description of him explains how he saw "goodness and 'guts'" in each player and "prods them so prodigiously": "To do less would be to break faith with them."[95]

Increased Demands from Junior A Hockey

Educator-coaches at St. Michael's tried to balance the cultivation of character with the competitive element of sport, but sport was changing at its elite levels. The growing acceptance of commercial hockey into the 1930s increasingly challenged amateur ideals. Amateur leaders had allowed pay-to-play athletes rather than risk losing players and public interest.[96] Local entrepreneurs and businessmen, who were rink managers or team financiers, functioned as special event coordinators and used hockey as a form of civic boosterism—where small-town hockey engaged commercial sport to a small but significant degree for the good of civic interests and within the existing amateur structures. In the early 1930s, when the NHL did not yet control the sport, the CAHA overruled its earlier position and eliminated pay-to-play competition. Senior amateur hockey thrived in local communities, where few risked jumping to professional ranks since salaries were low and players feared losing their amateur status, which promised a steady non-hockey job during an economic downturn.[97] Amateur hockey held the upper hand.

---

93   Higgins, "Hold That Line," 22.

94   Platt, *Dictionary of Basilian Biography*, 122. Conway died shortly after the Buzzers' championship.

95   St. Michael's College School, *Hockey Yearbook 1961*, 9.

96   Julie Stevens, "The Canadian Hockey Association Merger: An Analysis of Institutional Change" (PhD thesis, University of Alberta, Edmonton, 2001), ProQuest Dissertations Publishing, 44.

97   Bruce Kidd, *The Struggle for Canadian Sport* (Toronto: University of Toronto Press, 1996), 226.

The CAHA's strict adherence to amateurism effectively disassociated it from hockey's business and civic booster supporters.[98] Instead of controlling the game, the CAHA eventually fell prey to an increasingly stronger NHL, which had been under the thumb of amateur influences since its establishment in 1917.[99] In 1936, the CAHA's community-based organizations agreed to have players learn NHL rules and respect the league's reserve lists, so long as NHL clubs not sign junior-age players.[100] By 1941, the CAHA made further concessions in exchange for $500 for every junior player from the CAHA who played in the pro ranks.[101] The CAHA's negotiator said he wished that "feigned amateurism" would end because elite sport now had sizable ticket revenues, heavy travel expenses, and serious pressure on players.[102] Soldier mobilization for the Second World War caused further disruptions for most senior teams. With the arrival of television and *Hockey Night in Canada* in 1952, the NHL forged a dominant image of commercialized hockey that the idealism and politics of the CAHA could no longer control.[103]

The earlier strict divide between professional and amateur sport created a strict separation between the commercial and amateur/Olympic sectors. Professionals and amateurs had distinctly different labor processes: the NHL was concerned more with corporate hockey on the continent, while Canadian amateur hockey was a national sport produced at the local community level— and also engaged women.[104] This capitalistic shift reinvented male dominance in sport, that, according to Robidoux, emphasized the role of men and the accumulation of profit to promote national pride and unity.[105] Women and girls were increasingly discouraged from participating in sport.[106] For instance,

---

98   Stevens, "Canadian Hockey Association Merger," 48.

99   Stephen Harper, *A Great Game* (Toronto: Simon & Schuster, 2013), 199.

100   Kidd, *Struggle for Canadian Sport*, 226.

101   "New Agreement Is Reached; N.H.L. Gets Under Way Nov. 2," September 13, 1941, 83-48-377, University of Alberta RCRF. The revenues were shared among the teams and associations.

102   Al Parsley, "Dr. Hardy Forthright in Ideas of Changing Trends in Hockey Set-Up," 1940, 83-48-377, University of Alberta RCRF. The CAHA's negotiator was its former president, W. G. Hardy, an English professor at the University of Alberta.

103   Stevens, "Canadian Hockey Association Merger," 48.

104   Kidd, *Struggle for Canadian Sport*, 266–67.

105   Michael A. Robidoux, "Imagining a Canadian Identity through Sport: A Historical Interpretation of Lacrosse and Hockey," *Journal of American Folklore* 115, no. 456 (Spring 2002): 222.

106   Kidd, *Struggle for Canadian Sport*, 94–145.

the St. Michael's College entered a women's team in interfaculty competition at the University of Toronto in 1924, but the team disbanded in the 1940s as it faced chauvinistic pressures.[107]

After the Second World War, the NHL began to dominate the CAHA. Amateur hockey became a vast network of teams and leagues acting as an NHL-controlled feeder system.[108] The league sponsored Junior A amateur teams, which had the best talent of young men under 21. These Junior A teams had Junior B teams, which in turn sponsored midget and bantam teams. The NHL effectively had control of players from a very early age, and every good Canadian player over the age of 10 was connected to an NHL team.[109] CAHA became increasingly dependent, as professional teams donated a combined $800,000 a year to the CAHA for administrative costs from 1958 to 1966.[110] CAHA executive Gordon Juckes bitterly summarized what had happened by the 1960s: "The money barons of the NHL have relegated Canada to the role of a gigantic hockey slave farm.... We have become the Gold Coast of hockey."[111]

By the late 1950s, the NHL's influence affected Bauer and the Majors team for good and ill. St. Michael's continued its Junior A hockey in the spirit of Carr, as it brought publicity, community spirit, and even fiscal benefits. Through its agreement with the Maple Leafs, St. Michael's received funds from the NHL club to cover educational and room and board costs.[112] However, as Junior A hockey became increasingly commercialized, professional hockey had control. Junior hockey's goals of civic boosterism and support of amateur ideals appeared to diminish. For NHL owners, Junior A hockey was a de facto farm system of upcoming talent. Profits were to be made, and the game's violence could tantalize spectators. Bauer's vision of hardnosed hockey without unnecessary violence stood counter to the trends

---

107 Shea, Colle, and Patskou, *St. Michael's College*, 25.

108 Kidd, *Struggle for Canadian Sport*, 226.

109 Paul Conlin, "The Cold War and Canadian Nationalism on Ice: Federal Government Involvement in International Hockey during the 1960's," *Sports History Review* 25, no. 2 (1994): 57.

110 Conlin, "The Cold War," 57.

111 Kidd, *Struggle for Canadian Sport*, 226.

112 Alexandra Mountain, "A Battle for Sanity: An Examination of the 1961 Withdrawal from the Ontario Hockey Association by the St. Michael's Majors," *Boyhood Studies* 10, no. 1 (March 2017): 105. In 1954, the Leafs paid St. Michael's upwards of $10,000, plus additional gate receipts paid by Smythe to the school.

of 1950s professional hockey. His emphasis on puck possession, finesse, and speed contradicted an increase in slam-bang hockey that began from the loss of skilled players who were recruited into military service for the Second World War.[113] More dump and chase hockey resulted, where players shot the puck into the offensive end of the rink and hit opponents into the boards in a blitzkrieg of bodies. More money and more violence were making it harder to rationalize the Majors place in Junior A hockey.

The life of the Majors' Frank Mahovlich, who went on to six Stanley Cup championships, is instructive.[114] Mahovlich's family was from the mining town of Timmins, Ontario. He wanted to play in the NHL; his parents also wanted him to get a good education. Several teams courted Mahovlich, but the Maple Leafs had an advantage: St. Michael's Majors were the Leafs' second junior farm team and the only OHA team sponsored by a high school. When a scout or priest visited the Catholic Mahovlich family, they emphasized the strict, academic learning environment at St. Michael's. But Mahovlich later questioned if academic success was possible alongside the time demands of Junior A hockey. Also, more regular season games were added to the schedule to cover the increasing costs of artificial ice surfaces, equipment, etc. While players in the mid-1940s played approximately 30 games a year, a 1960 team played more than 80.[115] Mahovlich added that he was given $60 per week to play for the Majors in the mid-1950s, while Leafs owner Conn Smythe filled Maple Leaf Gardens with 15,000 people to watch games between his two junior farm teams, the Toronto Marlboros and St. Michael's. The changing economics of hockey were altering its functioning, where growing profit margins placed increased pressures on young players. Demanding that the players devote themselves entirely to their Junior A team demeaned the value of a formal education—which Smythe called "the nonsense of going to college"—and made it nearly impossible to attain.[116]

Conn Smythe became the primary owner of the Toronto NHL team in 1927, and was characterized as bombastic, intimidating, and without tact or forgiveness.[117]

113   Ken Dryden, *The Game* (New York: John Wiley & Sons, 1983), 218–21.

114   Mahovlich, *The Big M*, 21.

115   O'Malley, interview.

116   Kidd, *Struggle for Canadian Sport*, 228–29. Smythe was a graduate of the University of Toronto.

117   Kelly McParland, *The Lives of Conn Smythe* (Toronto: McClelland & Stewart, 2011), ix.

He was a stark contrast to Bauer, despite both men's competitiveness. Raised in a home with strong anti-Catholic and anti-French biases, Smythe grew up fearful of priests.[118] His father promoted theosophy, a movement founded in 1875 that was highly critical of orthodox Christianity and drew upon Eastern and New Age ideals.[119] When he was nearly killed several times in his wartime experience, Smythe emerged with a great deal of confidence. His favorite axiom was, "As ye sow, so shall ye reap," which he strictly interpreted and thus became unrelenting in his drive to expand professional hockey in Toronto.[120] He ambitiously built the Maple Leaf Gardens during the Depression in 1931 and became the NHL's dominant figure, enabling the league's control over the sport.[121] He stood as a major rival to Bauer.

At the heart of Bauer's animosity toward professional hockey was its maligned "C" form. It put NHL owners like Smythe in charge of a player's rights, since its introduction in 1947. Once an 18-year-old signed this form, or had his parents sign it at an earlier age, the club had the option to renew the contract when it expired. Thus, the contract put the club in control of the player's future. Even worse, players could not choose to play for another junior team because each junior organization was in reality a sponsored NHL farm team. Future NHLers like Bobby Hull and Reggie Fleming became the property of club teams before their fifteenth birthdays.[122]

Bauer was not alone in his animosity toward the "C" form contract, as many viewed it as outright oppressive. League leaders believed that the tight-fisted contracts ensured that amateur clubs did not steal players. However, people from outside of hockey, including Quebec Premier Maurice Duplessis and R. L. Seaborn, Anglican Dean of Quebec, rebuked its use. The president of the University of Western Ontario, G. E. Hall, decried, "Schoolboy hockey players are being exploited 'with the viciousness of the mill-owners of the early 1800s.'"[123] Bauer fiercely defended players like

---

118 McParland, *The Lives of Conn Smythe*, 8–9 and 41–42.

119 Annie Besant, *The Origins of Theosophy*, Routledge Revivals (New York: Routledge, 2015), 1.

120 McParland, *The Lives of Conn Smythe*, 41.

121 Julie Stevens, "Conn Smythe: The Complexity and Contradiction of a Hockey Entrepreneur," *Sport in Society* 23, no. 9 (2020): 1476.

122 Stephen Hardy and Andrew C. Holman, *Hockey: A Global History* (Champaign: University of Illinois Press, 2018), 302.

123 Hardy and Holman, *Hockey*, 302.

Dave Keon, Caesar Maniego, Gerry Cheevers, and Arnie Brown, who were pressured early to sign "C" forms. He even negotiated players' professional contracts.[124] Bauer told his players to wait until all their options were on the table, including a US college scholarship, for better leverage in negotiations. Leafs General Manager Punch Imlach famously remarked, "That man should no more be a priest than me."[125]

Because St. Michael's could offer young men an education while playing top-notch hockey, the college had a significant advantage over the other seven OHA Junior A teams. Detroit Red Wings coach and manager Jack Adams argued that the Majors-Leafs' arrangement made nearly every Catholic priest west of Quebec an unofficial scout for St. Michael's and the Maple Leafs.[126] For instance, the Metz brothers, Nick and Don, were from Wilcox, Saskatchewan, and were scouted and sent to St. Michael's as young teens. The boys were quickly signed by the Leafs and became important cogs in the Leafs' championship teams of the 1940s.[127] Smythe created a working relationship with the school despite his philosophical differences: "St. Mike's runs its own business.... I also respect the school's recognition of the fact that if you try to make a doctor out of a hockey player you'll likely end up with a lousy doctor."[128] The relationship was good for business.

The system maintained by the Leafs and Majors produced a steady stream of high-quality hockey players, but by 1958, it was becoming increasingly obvious that schooling and Junior A hockey were incompatible. As the OHA introduced more games to its playing schedule, the College began to complain, as Primeau declared: "St. Mike's is an educational organization and hockey is treated as something not merely to be played but to be taught."[129] Further, in contrast to the scrambly professional game—which Smythe labeled as

---

124   Hardy and Holman, *Hockey*, 302. This included possible US hockey scholarships.

125   Terry O'Malley, email message to author, March 6, 2023. Bauer negotiated "one-way" contracts that guaranteed an NHL level salary for the above players.

126   Mountain, "A Battle for Sanity," 106.

127   Andrew King, *Athol Murray, Recordings of Murray* (Wilcox, SK: Athol Murray College of Notre Dame, 2004), 4–5.

128   Andy O'Brien, "Toronto's St. Michael's Has Sent 40 to the National Hockey League," *Weekend Magazine* 8, no. 52 (1958), Bauer Fr. David box, 1965 and success of SMCS file, St. Michael's College School Archives, 18–19.

129   O'Brien, "Toronto's St. Michael's," 18.

"total war" on ice—Bauer explained that the school promoted knowledge of fundamental skills and the benefits of playing fewer games, which made for keener competition.[130] Could St. Michael's maintain the Majors hockey team in this commercializing environment?

Increased Demands from Schooling

Hockey was not the only social institution undergoing change. Schooling was experiencing its own upheavals in the 1950s and '60s. Earlier, in the interwar period, progressive education methods came into more regular use in Canada. These emphasized weighing the needs of individual children instead of teaching subject areas. Subject areas became integrated, while discovery methods made learning more relevant.[131] However, this utilitarian orientation came under attack in the 1950s by traditional schooling supporters who believed in a liberal education. This traditional perspective prioritized subject content and organized knowledge in step with university research and courses. Further, in response to the successful launch of the Soviet satellite Sputnik in 1957, educational leaders crammed more content into high school math, science, and language courses.[132] Students and parents felt pressured by increased demands. Conn Smythe's son, Stafford, blamed the Ontario Board of Education in 1960 for "putting so much stress on education that the very existence of Junior hockey was threatened."[133] This now comical-sounding critique captured the tensions of the time, in which educational standards and sporting expansion collided.[134] For his part, Bauer gave the senior Smythe a copy of Maritain's *True Humanism* to show a person-centered approach to education and sport.[135]

130   Conn Smythe, *If You Can't Beat 'Em in the Alley* (Toronto: McClelland & Steward, 1981), 128. Andy O'Brien, "How College Hockey Can Come Back," *Weekend Magazine* 12, no. 3 (1962): 35.

131   Henry F. Johnson, *A Brief History of Canadian Education* (Toronto: McGraw-Hill, 1968), 137–40.

132   Johnson, *Canadian Education*, 139 and 148.

133   Mountain, "A Battle for Sanity," 108.

134   E. Brian Titley and Kas Mazurek, "Back to the Basics? Forward to the Fundamentals?" in *Canadian Education: Historical Themes and Contemporary Issues*, ed. E. Brian Titley (Calgary: Detselig Enterprises, 1990), 115. High school graduation rates rose from 35% in 1961 to three-quarters of Canadian students in 1976.

135   Shea, Colle, and Patskou, *St. Michael's College*, 55.

When Basilian superior general Flahiff spoke at the 1955 Christmas conference about extracurricular activities, there were not only concerns about Junior A hockey at St. Michael's, but also a feeling that academic standards at every Basilian school should increase. Catholic educational philosophy, which was led then by the teachings of Jacques Maritain, was staunchly traditional and promoted a liberal arts education. In his address, Flahiff advocated for a recreational model of sport that would not interfere with a traditional model of education, but could assist in the integrated development of human persons. Higher costs and the influence of sport had come under increased scrutiny at Basilian colleges since the 1930s.[136] For instance, in 1936, one Houston-based Basilian priest endorsed the academic benefits of physical exercise, but complained that when sport is no longer a means to an end—but an end in itself—it distorts the harmony of right order.[137] Flahiff's concern was a traditional position within the community.

The 1955 conference on extracurricular activity revealed two opposing sides within the religious community. Because Basilian priestly vocations primarily came from academic students mentored by Basilian teachers or athletic students mentored by priest-coaches, the "brains" were pitted against the "sweat socks." The "brains" bunch were not against extracurricular sports, but, like Flahiff, had serious reservations about the proper balancing of academic and sporting demands. One priest, who later earned his PhD in English Literature, argued that extracurricular activities sacrificed students' growth in "intellectual virtues" and distracted teachers from their primary concern.[138] He was concerned especially when Basilian schools were labeled as "hockey schools" or "football schools."[139] Another Basilian, who became

---

136   Wallner, "Athletics and Academics," 10.

137   Albert Lee Higgins, "Restoring Right Order in Athletics," *The Basilian Teacher* 2, no. 3 (March 1936): 49. One young philosopher warned about the dangers of "surreptitious suppression by physical culture" following a Spartan model. Stanley Murphy, "The Assumption Lecture League," *The Basilian* 1, no. 2 (April 1935): 27–28.

138   J. F. Madden, "Are Extra-Curricular Activities Compatible with the Basic Aim of Education? [Con]," *The Basilian Teacher* 1, no. 7 (December 1956): 13.

139   Madden, "Extra-Curricular Activities [Con]," 15. St. Michael's was seen as a hockey school. In its 1958–59 yearbook, prominent NHL persons "King" Clancy, Maurice "the Rocket" Richard, and Frank Mahovlich visited a school pep rally. St. Michael's College School, *The Tower 1959*, St. Michael's College School Online Archives, 94–97, https://archive.org/details/stmcstower1959testuoft/mode/2up?-view=theater&q=tower+yearbook+1959.

a professor in physics, complained that too often their schools were earning publicity through sports headlines instead of newspaper acknowledgements for outstanding student scholarship.[140] What kind of students were their colleges attracting?[141] "Brains" priests also questioned those who emphasized the personal morality of students more than academic learning. Their concern was clear: focusing on sports was limiting academic learning and the future lineage of Basilian scholars.

At St. Michael's in particular, part of the senior faculty believed a Junior A team should not be in a Catholic high school.[142] Father Patrick Gorman, an English teacher, is said to have "led that charge" at the school. For one, some Majors players only took a partial schedule of courses and had a higher status at the school because of fan interest in hockey. Athletes in other sports felt envious of the Majors' players, hurting the school spirit.[143] Also, working at St. Michael's required round-the-clock dedication by the priests. Along with teaching and coaching demands, they cared for on-site boarders and said Masses. The grind of this all-encompassing life affected the health of the priests and educators.[144] The "brains" had strong academic and workplace concerns about losing a fundamental work-life balance.

A story about Bauer as an assistant principal illustrates this concern.[145] A French teacher complained that one of his hockey-playing students was failing the course. Bauer reponded that the boy focused on hockey because his family agreed that he could be a professional player. The school was to do what it could to support the boy academically, but he would not be one of the stronger students in the course. The French teacher was exasperated. The student in question was Frank Mahovlich's brother Peter, the "Little M." Bauer's pragmatism tried to realistically set educational standards for hockey students and in turn sent a clear message about the school's academic standards to the "brains" group. They felt compromised.

---

140   Ruth Norbert, "Academic Standards in Our High Schools," *The Basilian Teacher* 3, no. 1 (October 1958): 10.

141   Gerald Phelan, "The End of Education and Extra-Curricular Activities," *The Basilian Teacher* 1, no. 8 (January 1957): 4–5.

142   Burns, interview.

143   Hibbert, interview.

144   Hibbert, interview.

145   O'Brien, "St. Mike's Alumni Inducted."

The "sweat sock" types saw things differently. At that Christmas conference, defense of elite athletics was less punchy and more diffuse. Presentations asked rhetorical, abstract questions about the purpose of education or what made quality teaching. One priest, an expert in pedagogy, believed extracurricular activities expanded educational horizons and produced better Christians and citizens because students gave of themselves.[146] Leadership and creative abilities could be further developed, enabling a happier, more successful life. These less measurable, softer outcomes were not the priority of the "brains." The pedagogue continued: by working with students outside of the formal classroom, educators could exert the greatest influence on student lives.[147] Another priest specified his support: sports built school spirit, and schools have a civic responsibility to participate in extracurricular sports.[148]

The most thorough rebuff to the "brains" position came in the form of a theoretical article written by Father Edward Garvey, who later lived in Vancouver with Bauer and shared a lifelong passion for sport and Maritain. In Garvey's "Philosophy of Sport," he affirmed that the proper end of education was a "well-rounded personality" and not simply the development of intellect.[149] Just as a person's relationship with God is dependent upon both seen and unseen realities, education was an intellectual pursuit that should incorporate the bodily life.[150] From this perspective, "sweat sock" supporters coordinated the students' natural faculties with those of the supernatural order. One former principal of St. Michael's earlier claimed that narrowly conceptualizing a student as a "tool-using animal" reduces educators to "machinists of the mind" who constantly "measure and [mistakenly] circumscribe his spiritual faculties."[151] The unity of body, mind, and soul were to be realized through religious sensibilities intertwined with an education in the arts and sciences, and with leisure pursuits.

146   A. R. Looby, "Are Extra-Curricular Activities Compatible with the Basic Aim of Education? [Pro]," *The Basilian Teacher* 1, no. 7 (December 1956): 12 and 14.

147   Looby, "Extra-Curricular Activities [Pro]," 14. Also noted was how poor planning and communication by the school administration could exacerbate concerns with extracurricular activities.

148   D. McCarthy, "Discussion," *The Basilian Teacher* 1, no. 8 (January 1957): 6.

149   Edward Garvey, "Philosophy of Sport," *The Basilian Teacher* 3, no. 7 (April 1959): 184.

150   Wallner, "Athletics and Academics," 2.

151   Wallner, "Athletics and Academics," 3.

For Garvey, athletics were the place to round out a complete, liberal education.[152] Given that some academically-driven Basilians equated sports with "frill activities," Garvey explained how manual work promoted ingenuity and accuracy of mind and stirred artistic activity.[153] He argued that a broader educational approach also confronts modern acceptance of Rene Descartes' reduction of human emotions and embodiment. Despite Garvey's argument that supported "sweat sock" supporters, elite hockey at St. Michael's remained on thin ice.

An Unavoidable Face-Off Between Hockey and Education

The hockey-priests at St. Michael's desired to win their games, but were determined to avoid a winning-at-all-costs approach. A recreational form of sport, or even a purely intramural system, was insufficient for their drive and coaching aptitude, however. To alleviate pressures on their junior players, Bauer carried extra players so that boys did not have to play every game, giving them extra time to catch up on school work. He also held fewer practices. Both moves helped, but the number of games was unfathomable to him. After the 1961 championship season, Bauer complained to Smythe how a hockey season of ninety-eight games put undue stress on players.[154] Games were even scheduled on Christmas Day, Bauer protested.

Because St. Michael's was the only college-based team in the OHA Junior A league, their academic concerns and demands for a shortened season went largely unheard. In fact, the other teams felt that the Majors were given special status in the league because they had an advantageous relationship with the Maple Leafs. The Majors were given a reprieve for the 1960–61 regular season. They played 48 of the 54 regular season games that the other teams played; six of their games counted for double the points.[155] Playing fewer games, practicing less frequently, and carrying extra players did not appease the "brains" group. Bauer complained to Conn Smythe: "What the Junior 'A' council doesn't appreciate is there has been a tremendous revolution taking place in the academic world. I can't see how any school in Canada

152   Garvey, "Philosophy of Sport," 187.
153   Garvey, "Philosophy of Sport," 185.
154   Mountain, "A Battle for Sanity," 109.
155   Oliver, *Father Bauer*, 69.

could enter the OHA Junior 'A' league."[156] In another letter to Smythe, Bauer summarized that Junior A hockey's "growing professionalism ... so often results in unfavorable publicity [that it is] difficult for an educational institution to handle gracefully."[157]

For Flahiff and other critics, the problem was simple: the demands of professional hockey should not be allowed to conflict with the academic goals of a school. Flahiff's biographer explained that the General Council, the administrative body of the religious community, consulted with the school's principal and many hockey-priests over a two-year period and determined a list of factors that predicted the demise of the Majors.[158] With the writing on the wall, the priest-coaches were allowed to keep the Majors and, one can assume, try to work out further concessions with the OHA and Smythe. When Flahiff received word that the General Council's strong recommendation was not to be exercised immediately, he "expressed his disappointment" and decided "not to take any action"—at least for the moment.

St. Michael's Majors, 1961 Memorial Cup Champions

As pressure mounted on the "sweat sock" coaches at St. Michael's, Bauer managed the Junior A Majors from 1957 to 1961, including becoming interim head coach in 1960.[159] During this period, he taught religion and was an assistant principal and guidance counselor. Because of his interest in theology, he took summer school courses at the University of Notre Dame in South Bend, Indiana, from 1955 to 1957, and later in 1962.[160]

The 1960–61 Memorial Cup championship team was talented but generally had less star power than previous champions. Goaltender Gerry Cheevers went on to a Hall of Fame NHL career, winning two Stanley Cups with the Boston Bruins. Others on the team had NHL careers: Larry

---

156   Mountain, "A Battle for Sanity," 109.

157   Mountain, "A Battle for Sanity," 110.

158   Platt, *Gentle Eminence*, 61.

159   Shea, Colle, and Patskou, *St. Michael's College*, 128. Apparently, Bauer could not find a replacement.

160   This was determined by two emails: Angela Kindig, email message to author, March 2019, and Michelle Sawyers, email message to author, April 2019. Ironically, demands arising from the National Team hockey program restricted his time and he never finished his graduate degree.

Keenan, Arnie Brown, Billy MacMillan, Terry Clancy, Dave Dryden, and Barry MacKenzie. Some became key pieces in Bauer's National Team: captain Terry O'Malley, Paul Conlin, Gary Dineen, and MacKenzie.[161] Assistant manager and trainer Jim Gregory, with Bauer's support, became the Maple Leafs' general manager and a longtime executive with the NHL. Bauer believed that the team's strength laid in their heart for one another, a drive to win, and a never-say-die spirit.[162] Like many previous St. Michael's coaches, Bauer endorsed a defensive style of hockey that kept the game score close at all times.[163]

The team defeated a talented Guelph group to win the OHA championship, and then the Moncton Beavers to advance to the Memorial Cup Championship series held in Edmonton. Against the Oil Kings, the Majors—nicknamed the "Fighting Irish of Bay Street"—played a strong checking game and relied on the goaltending by Cheevers. Bauer the strategist found decisive lineup matches.[164] The team, along with alumni, attended Mass each morning in the hotel, with Bauer presiding at a portable altar on loan from the Archbishop of Edmonton.[165]

The Majors won the first three games of the best-of-seven series, followed by two loses to the Edmonton team. Reporters gathered around Bauer after the fifth game to hear his reaction to the Oil Kings' victory and the series' reversal of momentum. Was Coach Bauer worried? "Yes, I'm very worried, but, what I'm really worried about is the situation in Russia, Cuba, Vietnam, Cambodia and all the other troubled spots. Now I think that hockey ... [is] a very important part of life but if I'm going to be worried about something in a very serious way, I'm going to concern myself with the really important issues, because all these lesser things will eventually fall into place."[166] Years later Bauer explained that the team had earlier discussed different global issues and that his response enabled players to look at each

161   Shea, Colle, and Patskou, *St. Michael's College*, 129. Several players had fathers who played in the NHL.

162   St. Michael's College School, *Hockey Yearbook 1961*.

163   Shea, Colle, and Patskou, *St. Michael's College*, 128. O'Malley, interview.

164   Oliver, *Father Bauer*, 64–67.

165   Shea, Colle, and Patskou, *St. Michael's College*, 135. This practice echoes a longstanding tradition from Notre Dame football began during the tenure of Knute Rockne in the 1920s. See William J. Baker, *Playing with God: Religion and Modern Sport* (Cambridge, MA: Harvard University Press, 2007), 139.

166   David Bauer, "The Role of Hockey," 1979, Terry O'Malley Collection.

other and gain perspective on the loss. Bauer played the part of a master psychologist, even moving the team to the historic Hotel MacDonald and spending time at a nearby lake swimming and playing baseball.[167] The move took the pressure off the players; they won the next game 4–2.

The Majors were crowned Memorial Cup Champions of Junior A hockey. The victory must have been particularly sweet for Bauer. He had proven to detractors in hockey circles that a group of young men could play hockey and earn an education at the same time. In a rebuke to Conn Smythe, who had said that an education ruined hockey players—giving them a "jellyfish handshake"—Bauer had juggled hockey and schooling to make the best team in the country.[168] In the 1961 school yearbook, Bauer reiterated the value of each player and support staff member. He then opined, "What then is the essence of greatness ... ? When applied to the game of hockey it is, in my opinion, to have served to the maximum the ideal" given by Pope Pius XII: "Make use of technique, but let the spirit prevail."[169] He concluded that this team had done it nobly.

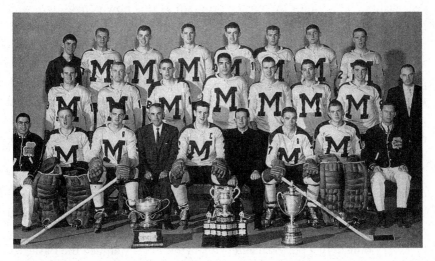

Figure 3.4 1961 St. Michael's Majors Memorial Cup Champions.

Courtesy of St. Michael's College School

167 Oliver, *Father Bauer*, 68.
168 Kidd and MacFarlane, *The Death of Hockey*, 80.
169 St. Michael's College School, *Hockey Yearbook 1961*.

A parade and Toronto City Hall celebration happened shortly afterwards, which included toasting the Buzzers' victory in the Junior B OHA championship. An estimated one thousand people, mostly teenagers, set off firecrackers and threw confetti. Bauer's mother hosted a team reception in Waterloo. The victory gave the Majors its fourth Memorial Cup, the most of any team at that time. The only damper on the celebrations was that Bauer had admitted to reporters in Edmonton that there was "substance to the rumours" that the Majors could withdraw from Junior A hockey.[170]

St. Michael's Withdrawal from Junior A Hockey

Undeterred by the school's two championships, Basilian superiors ended the business of Junior A hockey at St. Michael's. On Tuesday, June 6, 1961, Principal Father Matthew Sheedy made the announcement: "It is with the feeling of profound regret that we announce the withdrawal of the Saint Michael's Majors from the Junior 'A' Series of the Ontario Hockey Association. The Junior 'A' hockey program as it is now constituted, with its long and demanding schedule, with its lengthy and drawn-out playoff arrangements, militates against effective school work.... Efforts to bring about an appreciable change seem to have met with no success."[171] Bauer put it simply a decade later: Junior A hockey, which was sponsored by NHL teams, "was really professional hockey without the real dignity of recognized professionalism."[172] One Basilian Father claimed that the decision had been made earlier, giving the OHA one year's notice and Dave Bauer the chance to coach "our swan song."[173]

Sheedy, a talented basketball coach in his own right, made the difficult choice because he believed the "inescapable association" between hockey and big business went against the mission of the school.[174] Despite Smythe's and the OHA's concessions, Bauer's juggling act was not enough to appease the General Council. In a personal letter to Smythe, Sheedy argued the Basilians'

170   Oliver, *Father Bauer*, 68–69.

171   St. Michael's College School, *Hockey Yearbook 1961*.

172   Bauer, *Report to Munro*, 7.

173   Cyril Doherty, email message to author, September 2020.

174   "Father Matthew P. Sheedy, CSB," Fr. Sheedy file, St. Michael's College School Archives.

position forcefully: "We feel that we are fighting a battle for sanity in sports. Does St. Michael's stand alone in this battle for reasonableness?"[175] Sheedy's announcement made headlines in the media and he "took a lot of heat" from many at St. Michael's. According to one Basilian, a couple of hockey-priests "never forgave" Sheedy and "did their best to undermine anything he ever tried to do."[176]

Conn Smythe urged the school to stay, offering to increase the annual $13,000 junior payment to $20,000. He argued that St. Michael's had "allowed some of the sharper annoyances to blot out the larger picture in which your College has contributed more to Canada than any other College.... [It is] a sad thing to see an institution which has achieved something glorious, fold and leave such a void in ... all Canadians who respect and honor good sportsmanship."[177] Smythe lost much with the team's folding. In 1958, for example, the team played 35 games at his Gardens and accounted for roughly 10% of his profits.[178] For Sheedy and Bauer, the problem was not monetary, but a philosophical difference that increasingly became intolerable.

The Impact on Bauer and the Basilian Hockey Tradition

Throughout the first half of the twentieth century, elite youth sports in North America were increasingly formed into adult-led organizations that grew in popularity.[179] Groups like the Basilian Fathers began asking questions about the ethics of these athletic organizations. Exploitation became noted because young athletes generated revenue that they were unpaid for. Serious sport could limit their childhood experiences and restrict their future options. Identifying the exploitation of youth in sport is complicated because of assumptions that sport is play rather than work and that competitive sport is good for young people.[180] Many at St. Michael's recognized that the professionalized standards of the OHA were exploiting youth.[181]

---

175   Mountain, "A Battle for Sanity," 113.
176   McLeod, interview.
177   Mountain, "A Battle for Sanity," 112.
178   Mountain, "A Battle for Sanity," 112.
179   Mountain, "A Battle for Sanity," 103.
180   Mountain, "A Battle for Sanity," 103.
181   In fact, Father Gorman used the word "exploit" in his questioning of the sports' place within a school.

The withdrawal left Bauer seriously wounded, especially when winning a championship did not salvage the team. In a 1987 interview, he argued that hockey was poorer as an institution without St. Michael's involvement as "a major recreational institution in this country."[182] But Bauer recognized the reality of commercialized sport, adding: "The entire world has become a marketplace. That spirit seems to be pervading everything." Bauer was uncertain whether a permanent Majors' presence in Junior A hockey could have been a moderating influence on the sport—but he wished the possibility had been tried. He explained privately to a former student why his agreeing to the Majors' departure was the worst decision he had ever made: "Because we're trying to teach the motto of our school, 'Teach me goodness, discipline, and knowledge'—the Basilian credo. . . . Nothing exemplified that better than twenty teenagers with the St. Mike's blazers walking downtown Toronto into the Gardens . . . we've never been able to duplicate that."[183] Disbanding the team only solved a short-term problem at St. Michael's and with the OHA, Bauer believed. Both parties turned their backs on a larger complication: the exploitation of youth and the professionalization of the Canadian hockey system.

Could the Basilian sporting tradition find a place in the changing landscape of elite sport? Basilian priest-coaches were faced with the corporatization of hockey and its costs of indoor artificial ice, better equipment, further travel, greater overhead, and increased media coverage. This new reality was possible because of the growing affluence in postwar North American society. The St. Michael's approach to Junior A hockey became structurally out of step with the demands of commercialized sports leagues and organizations. Other priest-coaches followed Bauer in the sporting tradition, nonetheless. They still made an impact, even if to a smaller degree. For example, Father John Redmond, who was a hockey player, ran a nationally-recognized track and field program at Michael Power School in Etobicoke until his early death in 1981. Father Patrick Gallagher was a prominent track coach. He was a field judge for the 1976 Montreal Olympics.[184]

However, along with growing societal affluence came the professionalization of many societal roles, like teaching and counseling, and the drastic drop of

---

182 Oliver, *Father Bauer*, 70–71. Bauer confirmed that the General Council had discussed early on the potential termination of the Majors.

183 Costello, interview.

184 Hibbert, interview.

religious priests and sisters in Canada.[185] Fewer priests available overall meant fewer priest-coaches. Their numbers likely shrank further because sport was seen as a lower form of priestly ministry and because sectarian sport, like a Catholic sport program, was viewed as passé and not at all progressive or ecumenical.[186] Higher coaching standards in the 1970s and '80s, a sign of adult-organized sport and increased sport specialization, intensified focus on building elite athletes.

Because of the falling-out between St. Michael's and the OHA, the country lost its greatest college-school hockey dynasty. The team's luster was relegated to the history books. The Majors did play in a new metro league, but a year later dropped down to the Junior B level. Of its 14 enshrined members in the Hockey Hall of Fame, Cheevers is the youngest of the group.[187] In 1985, he asked his mentor, David Bauer, to speak at his Hall of Fame induction ceremony.

185   Hugh McLeod, *The Religious Crisis of the 1960s* (Oxford, UK: Oxford University Press, 2010), 115.

186   Hugh McLeod, "Muscular Christianity: American and European," in *Secularization and Religious Innovation in the North Atlantic World*, ed. Hugh McLeod and David Hempton (Oxford, UK: Oxford Scholarship Online, 2017), 9.

187   Dennis Gibbons, "St. Mike's 1961 Memorial Cup Champs Honoured 50 Years Later," May 29, 2011, The Majors 1960–61 file, St. Michael's College School Archives. The college's player inductees are Frank Rankin, Reg Noble, Joe Primeau, Turk Broda, Ted Lindsay, Red Kelly, Tim Horton, Frank Mahovlich, Dave Keon, Bobby Bauer, Dick Duff, and Gerry Cheevers. David Bauer and Murray Costello entered in the builder's category.

The Establishment of the
National Team Program

WITH THE SUPPORT OF THE CANADIAN AMATEUR HOCKEY ASSOCIATION, Bauer established a National Team program that promoted the education of hockey players and sought to inspire global peace through Canada's national sport. Three factors were decisive in the establishment of the program: the Bauer family, the rise of Soviet hockey, and his arrival at St Mark's College in Vancouver.

The Bauer Family

The Bauer family inspired David's interest in international hockey and global affairs. In his *Report* to Minister John Munro in 1971, he succinctly explained his nationalistic fervor: "[I cannot separate] my concerns with Canada and with world peace. I was brought up in a strongly patriotic family. This patriotism was not of the 'My country, right or wrong' sort; however, it was marked by a fierce determination to see that my country chooses the right.

And from my youth this has been united in my mind with world peace and Canada's role in developing it."[1]

David Bauer's paternal great-grandfather, Karl Bauer, emigrated from Bavaria, Germany, in 1848, to Buffalo, New York. There he met and married another newly arrived German immigrant, Sophia Kuehlerbert, in 1853. Two years later, the pair moved northwest less than two hundred kilometers to Waterloo, Ontario, an agricultural village heavily populated with German immigrants.[2] Aloyes Bauer, David's grandfather, was born there in 1861. Waterloo and its nearby sister town of Berlin proudly celebrated their German roots, and were distinct from English-settled Ontario towns and cities like Toronto and London. Pride in the homelands of Germany and England were at a high in 1871, when residents of Waterloo and Berlin celebrated the end of the Franco-Prussian War, which reunited German states and forged a united country.[3] Kaiser Wilheim I ruled a united Germany, while Prince Albert, the German husband of Queen Victoria, was part of the British monarchy.[4] Eighty percent of the residents of Waterloo were of German origin and, along with their fellow citizens of English descent, celebrated shared ideals that marked both nations: liberty, observance of law and order, the dignity of constituted authority, and acceptance of truth, religion, and morality. These liberal roots enabled healthy Anglo-German communities living in Canada.[5]

In 1888, Aloyes Bauer married Magdalena Kuntz, and established a cotton felt and batting manufacturing business in downtown Waterloo.[6] These manufactured products were used for furniture, mattresses, and horse-and-buggy cushions, and later for thermal insulation and soundproofing in automobile manufacturing in the early twentieth century. Family history says that Aloyes personally had contact with the R. S. McLaughlin Carriage Works, now General Motors, and with the Ford Motor

---

1 David Bauer, *Report to Munro*, 1971, Marc Bauer-Maison Collection, 52.

2 Private Bauer Family Records, Paul Schmalz Collection.

3 Kenneth McLaughlin and Sharon Jaeger, *Waterloo: An Illustrated History, 1857–2007* (Waterloo, ON: City of Waterloo, 2007), 74.

4 McLaughlin and Jaeger, *Waterloo*, 74.

5 McLaughlin and Jaeger, *Waterloo*, 74.

6 Paul Schmalz and Steve Freiburger, interview with author, January 18, 2019. The land was purchased from Aloyes's brother-in-law Louis Kuntz, whose Kuntz Brewery was situated nearby.

Company when Henry Ford I ran it.[7] Most German speakers in Waterloo belonged to the local Lutheran Church at the turn of the century; however, German-speaking Catholics increased to more than nine hundred by 1911. That there was little sectarian strife in Waterloo is reflected in the fact that many Lutherans supported the building of the St. Louis Roman Catholic Church, hoping to draw potential Catholic residents to town.[8] In 1912, David Bauer's parents' marriage took place in the church. David Bauer was baptized in the same building.

Canada's declaration of war against Germany in 1914 made many suspicious toward the strongly German towns. German flags and the use of the German language in public were seen as signs of disloyalty to Canada.[9] Counterarguments were made that it was possible for proud German-speaking Canadians to be loyal to Canada; in fact, many left Germany to flee from militarism in their former lands. In the face of mounting anti-German prejudice, the town of Berlin voted to change its name to "Kitchener" after Britain's secretary of state for war.[10] Overcoming the shame of their German heritage, Waterloo had the highest per-capita contribution to support the war in all of the Dominion.[11] The town's determined effort to identify as Canadian continued into the Second World War.[12]

Bauers Ltd. was incorporated in 1917 and Edgar became its chairperson in 1925, the year following the birth of his son David. The interwar years were boom times for the Bauers' acoustical and thermal automotive products, and the growth continued after World War II. By 1957, the factory had grown substantially and included yarn, twine, foam rubber, and felt departments. Edgar also became president of Globe Furniture Company and Waterloo Mutual Fire Insurance Company. Waterloo had become a thriving manufacturing town, with smokestacks lining the horizon, and was home to several insurance companies. Prohibition in the US and Ontario overlapped for much of the 1920s and spurred a growing bootlegging industry; Seagram's distillery was located near

7 Henry Koch, "R. A. Bauer Buys All Bauer Stock," *Kitchener-Waterloo Record*, June 6, 1972, Business Binder, Bauer Ltd. file, Waterloo Public Library, 1 and 3.

8 McLaughlin and Jaeger, *Waterloo*, 83.

9 McLaughlin and Jaeger, *Waterloo*, 88.

10 McLaughlin and Jaeger, *Waterloo*, 74. Lord Horatio Herbert Kitchener had recently died on a sank battleship.

11 McLaughlin and Jaeger, *Waterloo*, 93.

12 McLaughlin and Jaeger, *Waterloo*, 136.

the Bauer factory.[13] More money could be made bootlegging than playing hockey at the time. The Bauer clan were one of many German industrialist families well-connected through the Kitchener-Waterloo business community. Edgar also became a Waterloo alderman and served on several local Catholic boards.[14] This civic-mindedness inspired Edgar and Bertha's children. Eldest son Frank served as an alderman and mayor of Waterloo for several terms,[15] while Jerry served on the separate school board in Waterloo. He and older sister Alice assisted in several organizations helping the mentally disabled.[16] Siblings Marg and Frank also aided on figure skating, baseball, and hockey associations.[17]

The Bauer family's participation in local civics led to involvement in international hockey. Brother Ray represented the nation with the Sudbury Wolves senior men's hockey team at the 1949 World Championships in Stockholm, Sweden.[18] The brothers continued to play hockey, skating together on Sunday mornings after Mass, into the 1960s.[19] After his retirement from the NHL, Bobby played senior men's hockey as a reinstated amateur for the Kitchener-Waterloo Dutchmen. A good communicator, he naturally stepped into coaching a Guelph junior team and the Dutchmen. As coach and president of the K-W Dutchmen, he won Allan Cup Senior Hockey Championships in 1953 and 1955, which meant they could represent Canada at the next Winter Olympics in Cortina, Italy (1956). Only the best amateur team went to the Olympics because "play for pay" athletes were disallowed. That Dutchmen team lost to both American and Soviet teams, and settled for a bronze medal. Although the president of the CAHA praised the team

---

13   Marg Rowell, Ed Devitt, and Pat McKegney, *Welcome to Waterloo* (Waterloo, ON: Waterloo Printing, 1982), 63.

14   "Edgar J. Bauer, Industrialist, Dies," 1959, Paul Schmalz Collection. He served on the boards of Waterloo separate schools, St. Mary's Hospital, St. Jerome's College, and the Carmel of St. Joseph, Kitchener.

15   Bauer Family, *Bauer (A Family History of Edgar and Bertha's Family)* (Waterloo, ON: Self-published, 2003), under "Francis Norbert Bauer," private Bauer family records owned by Paul Schmaltz.

16   Bauer Family, *Bauer (A Family History)*, under "Alice Magdalena Bauer." Alice was also president of the Catholic Women's League in Cambridge, Ontario.

17   Bauer Family, *Bauer (A Family History)*, under "Margaret Angela Bauer."

18   Bauer Family, *Bauer (A Family History)*, under "Raymond Aloysius Bauer." Despite a disappointing second place finish, Ray scored a record eight goals and added an assist in a 47–0 trouncing of Denmark. Ray's gregarious personality embellished the record, including stories of summersaults on the ice.

19   Bob Bauer, Jr., interview with author, June 6, 2019.

as "wonderful ambassadors for Canada at all times," that kind of sentiment, according to sports author Scott Young, is "never precisely what most Canadians have in mind when it comes to international hockey."[20]

Bobby took over as Dutchmen coach prior to the 1960 Squaw Valley Olympics. Only four players from across the country accepted the team's invitation to join their expanded roster, but their participation revealed that hockey officials had begun to mobilize talent nationally before players signed a professional contract.[21] The team went undefeated in pre-tournament games played across Canada, but lost a lopsided 3–2 affair to the Americans and their standout goalie Jack McCartan in Squaw Valley. The Canadians settled for silver—and a telegram from an alderman from Kingston was anything but congratulatory: "From the birthplace of hockey, I'm going to call for an official day of mourning, and ask that our flag be hung at half-mast."[22]

For Bobby Bauer, the loss was difficult to take. He had reluctantly taken the coaching position because he could not resist the challenge, but the disruption to his business career resulted in his departure from Bauer Skates.[23] Much was asked of amateur senior men's coaches and players representing Canada internationally. For instance, among the 1956 team members were men whose day jobs were schoolteacher, logging trucker, and gas attendant.[24] Improved quality of play globally made it doubly difficult to win gold. By the late 1940s, Czechoslovakia and Sweden had become serious contenders for gold. In 1954, the Soviets stunned a Canadian team, the East York Lyndhursts, 7–2, and the public reaction was vociferous. Conn Smythe called the loss "a national humiliation" and offered the Leafs' services to give the Reds "a lesson in shinny."[25] Brother Ray Bauer publicly demanded a full national effort.[26]

---

20   Scott Young, *War on Ice: Canada in International Hockey* (Toronto: McClelland & Stewart, 1976), 54.

21   Young, *War on Ice*, 84.

22   Young, *War on Ice*, 92. George Webb was the alderman.

23   Bauer Family, *Bauer (A Family History)*, under "Robert Theodore Bauer;" and Bob Bauer, Jr., interview. He then took on a startup hockey stick factory with former linemate Woody Dumart.

24   "Flying Dutchmen Play Hockey for Canada," *CBC Sports*, CBC Sports Digital Archives, January 5, 1956, https://www.cbc.ca/player/play/1466890691.

25   Ainsley B. Rose, "An Historical Account of Canada's Participation in International Ice Hockey, 1948–1970" (master's thesis, University of Western Ontario, London, 1976), 74.

26   Young, *War on Ice*, 94.

The Rise of Soviet Hockey

The modern game of hockey conformed increasingly to its Montreal prototype over several decades. Changes in organizational structures—e.g., amateur and professional ties, financial operations of indoor rinks, impact of hockey organizations and national bodies—influenced how the game was played in each nation, whether Canada, Russia, Sweden, America, etc.[27]

The Montreal game had become Canada's game, where it played a role in national unity. In Russia, the cultural ice game was the sport of bandy. Resembling field hockey more than ice hockey, it used a much larger ice surface with more players and a ball instead of a puck. Yet bandy was not an Olympic sport, and could not be exploited for political purposes during the Cold War. In 1949, the Central Committee of the Communist Party declared that its socialist sports system could prove its cultural superiority, and many top bandy players converted to Montreal-rules hockey.[28] Instrumental were coaches Arkadi Chernyshev and Anatoli Tarasov, who later was dubbed the father of Russian hockey.

Tarasov was passionate, and relentlessly sought to improve the top Russian players.[29] He believed that differences between Soviet and Canadian teams were not a by-product of the influences of European soccer and bigger ice surfaces, but rather style dissimilarities stemming from cultural differences. He believed that Soviet players passed the puck more often because they were not individualistic like their Canadian counterparts. A collectivist way of life cultivated teamwork and comradeship.[30] Whereas Canadian players were more likely to drive to the net, Tarasov wanted better passing and puck possession in the international form of the game—especially when it was played on a larger ice surface and placed restrictions on checking in the offensive and neutral zones. While Tarasov credited cultural differences in play, others noted how an authoritatian system of training gave coaches total control over full-time athletes in a socialist state.[31]

27 Stephen Hardy and Andrew Holman, "Periodizing Hockey History: One Approach," in *Now is the Winter: Thinking About Hockey*, ed. Jamie Dopp and Richard Harrison (Hamilton, ON: Wolsak and Wynn Publishers Limited, 2009), 24–32.

28 Stephen Hardy and Andrew C. Holman, *Hockey: A Global History* (Champaign: University of Illinois Press, 2018), 328.

29 Hardy and Holman, *Hockey: A Global History*, 329. He coached the Central Red Army team and co-coached the country's national team at international tournaments.

30 Hardy and Holman, *Hockey: A Global History*, 342–43.

31 Hardy and Holman, *Hockey: A Global History*, 343.

Instead of copying Canadian professional play in the 1950s, Tarasov tried different techniques: "To copy somebody else is to be always second best."[32] Given limited finances and time on artificial ice, his teams paid great attention to off-ice training and conditioning. He searched for literature about Canadian hockey and was surprised to find hardly anything of use, except for *The Hockey Handbook* by Lloyd Percival. It was Percival who had coached Bobby Bauer and offered sessions at St. Michael's College School.[33] Percival's alternative, scientific perspective on the sport fit well with Tarasov's demands for hockey perfection. By 1969, Tarasov offered a stern critique about Canadian hockey and the NHL: "You play only for the spectacle [instead of improving play or teamwork]. Of course, each Canadian team strives for victory, but your brand of hockey as a whole is directed only secondarily toward success and creative growth."[34]

North American Cold War propaganda depicted Canadians as creative, capitalistic, and supportive of freedom, while the communists destroyed sport in their thirst to prove themselves.[35] Soviets were cool and not driven by passion to win. They were unwilling to fight to defend themselves in hockey. Yet their talent, physical conditioning, style of play, and focused system caused Bauer to forecast future problems for Canadian hockey.[36] For instance, poorer conditioning meant that Canadians "whacked and slashed" faster Russian players—and were penalized for it.[37] The rough Canadians created a poor image internationally, leaving diplomats from Canadian embassies in Europe asking for better teams to be sent abroad.[38] A Swedish national official in

---

32 Paul Quarrington, *Hometown Heroes: On the Road with Canada's National Hockey Team* (Toronto: Collings, 1988), 150.

33 Kevin Shea, Larry Colle, and Paul Patskou, *St. Michael's College: 100 Years of Pucks and Prayers* (Bolton, ON: Fenn Publishing Company Limited, 2008), 105. This was through Majors' coach Charlie Cerre.

34 Anatoly Tarasov, *Road to Olympus* (Glendale, CA: Griffin Publishing, 1969), 170.

35 Brian Kennedy, "Confronting a Compelling Other: The Summit Series and the Nostalgic (Trans)Formation of Canadian Identity," in *Canada's Game: Hockey and Identity*, ed. Andrew C. Holman (Montreal: McGill-Queen's University Press, 2009), 53.

36 Murray Dryden, *Playing the Shots at Both Ends* (Toronto: McGraw-Hill Ryerson, 1972), 75; and Greg Oliver, *Father Bauer and the Great Experiment: The Genesis of Canadian Olympic Hockey* (Toronto: ECW Press, 2017), ix.

37 Matthew Fisher, "Hockey History," *The Sunday Sun*, May 13, 2001, Bauer Fr. David box, SMCS Memorial file, St. Michael's College School Archives.

38 John Soares, "Our Way of Life against Theirs: Ice Hockey and the Cold War,"

1960 reportedly scolded coach Bobby Bauer because "the noble Swedes" participated as hockey players and "not as murderers." Bauer was directed to "take his Canadian thugs and go home."[39]

Bauer Sent to St. Mark's College in Vancouver

Bauer publicly put a positive spin on the Basilian decision to remove him from St. Michael's College. As he recalled in his *Report to Munro* in 1971: "We could no longer justify ourselves in bringing boys into a situation which had become inimical to their own best interests."[40] He told his Basilian superiors that he wanted a different kind of ministry. Some Basilians believed he should take a sabbatical to finish his graduate studies at Notre Dame, especially because of his love of football.[41] Instead, he was appointed to St. Mark's College at the University of British Columbia (UBC). Bauer was "pleasantly surprised" to hear of his appointment, despite the fact that "Vancouver was hardly a hockey hotbed."[42]

In reality, however, Bauer was downcast about his dismissal from St. Michael's. According to his sister Margaret, he was unusually upset.[43] Bauer felt shame instead of only accomplishment from the Majors' championship. One former Majors player recalled that Bauer told him, "It's about as far as they could move me from Toronto." His removal from St. Michael's would make room for a new hockey project, however.

St. Mark's was a vastly different place from St. Michael's. It was on the campus of a much newer Canadian university, located at the western tip of the Point Grey Peninsula overlooking the Pacific Ocean. Bauer was chaplain and dean of residence for undergraduate and graduate men and women. He also taught ethics and philosophy courses to undergraduate nursing students for St. Paul's Hospital, located in downtown Vancouver. St. Mark's was a much newer and smaller institution than St. Michael's, and had no athletics program. It was a fresh start for the Basilians, who went on to found or

in *Diplomatic Games: Sport, Statecraft, and International Relations Since 1945*, ed. Heather L. Dichter and Andrew L. Johns (Lexington: University Press of Kentucky, 2014), 272.

39   Young, *War on Ice*, 87.

40   Bauer, *Report to Munro*, 8.

41   Cyril Doherty, email message to author, September 17, 2020.

42   Bauer, *Report to Munro*, 8.

43   She spoke to him the day he was transferred. Margaret Laudenbach, interview with author, January 18, 2019.

take over nine new educational institutions in the late 1950s. St. Mark's was founded in 1956 through discussions heavily influenced by Carr, who was teaching in the UBC's classics and philosophy departments. Carr maneuvered boldly to make the Basilians stick at UBC; many of the Basilian's top priests were sent there to teach in other departments. His new chaplain and lecturer was another way to break through at UBC.

The spirited push at UBC meant that Bauer lived with many academics at St. Mark's, who probably agreed with curtailing hockey's influence at St. Michael's. However, given the new circumstances, what Bauer found was a community by-and-large supportive of his hockey talents. While other hockey men had familial obligations, Bauer lived communally with university priest-professors. Coupled with his family's patriotism and the rise of Soviet hockey, the Basilian support in Vancouver made possible a re-visioning of a hockey tradition under the leadership of Bauer.

The Beginning of the National Team Program

Prior to Bauer's arrival at St. Mark's, the UBC athletics department—in need of a hockey coach for their beleaguered team—sent a letter asking if he would coach the varsity team. Bauer declined, saying he would help as assistant coach. By Christmas 1961, he took over as head coach on the condition that he would have assistance from one of the department's coaches, Bob Hindmarch.[44] Hiring the most recent Memorial Cup-winning coach was a boost for UBC athletics and their hockey team, who, as Bauer was informed, "had never won a game in intercollegiate competition."[45] The campus was without an ice rink, and the city was not hockey-mad like Toronto.[46]

Bauer used the remainder of the 1961–62 season to solidify his UBC Thunderbird team. Despite losing his first three games by a combined score of 34–6, Bauer remained positive, especially when the team hung on for a 4–2 loss to the Golden Bears of Alberta. Speaking with local Vancouver media, Bauer's emphasis on spirit and education came through: "We're just getting started.... I shuffled the boys around all the time and now they have

---

44 Bauer, *Report to Munro*, 8. See also Bob Hindmarch, interview with author, August 17, 2018.

45 Bauer, *Report to Munro*, 8.

46 Robert F. Osborne, "Letter to Father Garvey," December 4, 1962, Box 7, Carr—Correspondence and Misc. file, St. Mark's College Archives.

found themselves. I was extremely proud of the fighting spirit the boys had."[47] He added that he was "calling practices off for next week" and playing fewer exhibition games "to keep the players' academic standing high." With help of four former St. Michael's players who sought to play hockey and get a university education, the team made it to their first national university championship in the 1962–63 season. Their silver medal is the hockey team's best ever finish to date.

Figure 4.1 Bauer leading UBC practice in 1962.

Courtesy of Corpus Christi-St. Mark's College

The Bauer family dream of a reconfigured National Team took shape soon after, as detailed in Bauer's *Report*.[48] Brother Ray persuaded the charismatic Basilian coach from Calgary, Father Whelihan, and Bauer to fly to Colorado Springs, Colorado, to scout games at the 1962 World Championships.[49] While

47   Alan Watson, *Catch On and Run with It: The Sporting Life and Times of Dr. Bob Hindmarch* (Vancouver: AJW Books, 2012), 135.

48   Bauer, *Report to Munro*, 9.

49   It was brothers Dave and Ray who had persuaded Bob to take the Dutchmen

talking there, Bauer recalled, "It began to dawn on me that perhaps it would be possible to apply, with an Olympic Team, the philosophy of sport that it had not been possible to apply adequately in Junior A hockey."[50] Also attending were CAHA President Jack Roxburgh and Secretary Gordon Juckes. Whelihan and the two Bauers made a pitch to them: icing a team of amateur, junior-aged players to represent the country at the 1964 Olympics. The CAHA chose the team that would represent Canada in international play, because it held Canada's seat on the International Ice Hockey Federation (IIHF) board. The group of men departed Colorado Springs to take the idea back to the CAHA executive and to Bauer's Basilian superiors at St. Mark's.

Either before or after that meeting at Colorado Springs, David and Ray met Bobby at his cottage to discuss possible solutions to Canada's participation in international play—and many scotches were involved.[51] The brothers agreed that the American sporting development system was superior.[52] It sent the best athletes to university. Establishing a National Team would create greater fan interest in Canadian university hockey, attracting better players to universities who then would have a chance to join the National Team for the Olympics. Bauer had further reason to be encouraged: some former players from his Majors team asked how to continue their education while playing hockey. He would need to get student loans for future players. Thus, during his return to studies at Notre Dame in the summer of 1962, he dreamed of the formation of an Olympic team as a visible reality that people could support and raise funds for.[53] Superiors at St. Mark's were supportive of the plan, including Carr: "He saw at once what was at stake with regard to the proposed Olympic Team and encouraged me to go ahead with it."[54]

to the 1960 Olympic Games, where Ray was secretary (having been president for the 1956 team).

50   Bauer, *Report to Munro*, 10.

51   Bob Bauer, Jr., interview.

52   As US college hockey expanded postwar, coaches recruited from a seemingly unlimited Canadian talent pool. By 1967, four hundred Canadians were playing at US colleges. Andrew Holman, "The Canadian Hockey Player Problem: Cultural Reckoning and National Identities in American Collegiate Sport, 1947–80," *Canadian Historical Review* 88, no. 3 (2007): 444–47.

53   Trent Frayne, "It's How You Played the Game that Mattered to Father Bauer," *The Globe and Mail*, November 10, 1988, Box 4, File 9, Bauer fonds, Basilian Archives.

54   Bauer, *Report to Munro*, 11.

Carr was the oldest living Basilian at 81—forty-four years older than Bauer—and offered counsel to him. The two men had a natural affinity for one another because of their sporting interests. Both were physically smaller men and gifted storytellers. Carr was academically trained, while Bauer took graduate studies. Bauer filled a key role as a chaplain at UBC.[55] Carr, realizing the newness of St. Mark's, discussed how Basilian ministry might change in a public university setting. He and other leaders were not looking to restore Christendom, but sought a new Christian order within a pluralistic society.[56] Christian thought and activism could shape a better world. Bauer's ability to connect with those outside the Catholic fold reflected Carr's own gifts and enabled a larger vision for chaplaincy—and hockey—on campus.[57]

Carr's engagement with a public university fit with Bauer's intellectual and social curiosity. Carr knew that Bauer had a difficult role because many young adults left their Catholic upbringing at university.[58] Yet Carr did not want the younger Bauer to become defensive or ideologically entrenched. Carr's approach over decades of postsecondary work rejected retreating into a sectarian cocoon. Bauer needed to build goodwill at Point Grey: reach out to students, teach ethics courses through St. Paul's Hospital, and work cooperatively with the UBC athletics. Instead of seeing Bauer's hockey talents as a stumbling block to ministry—as had happened at St. Michael's—Carr saw them creating an opportunity far beyond a confessional setting. Carr criticized the Church's inability to produce national leaders that could influence major areas of society. He saw Bauer's potential for leadership in Canadian hockey.[59]

Bauer and Carr also had a craving for the spiritual life. Both were profoundly influenced by the renewal of Carmelite spirituality in the early twentieth century. This spirituality aligned with Thomistic thought and its openness to human experience, where deeper union with God is possible through acts of love. According to theologian McMahon, union with

55 Edmund J. McCorkell, *Henry Carr—Revolutionary* (Toronto: Griffin House, 1969), 146.

56 Ron Griffin and Michael Hayden, "Transformations and Consequences: The Basilians in France and North America," *Historical Studies* 82 (2016): 16.

57 Henry Carr, "Teaching the Catholic Religion at a Secular University," *The Basilian Teacher* 5, no. 1 (October 1960): 11.

58 Carr, "Teaching the Catholic Religion," 11.

59 Henry Carr, "Speech at the Inaugural Dinner, the Blessing and Official Opening," September 9, 1958, Vancouver, BC, Box 7, Henry Carr—Heart of the Matter file, St. Mark's College Archives.

God, then, was not something abstract, but began with an examination of embodied thoughts and feelings.[60] Careful introspection by one's will, in a sense, fires up "supernatural metabolism" and enables growth in holiness.[61] Thus, reflecting upon sport's purpose in Canadian life, and feeling what uplifts the spirit in sport, could cultivate the spiritual life. Hockey could be engaged on a spiritual plane.

Father Edward Garvey, whose 1959 article had supported Bauer in his views on the value of sport, arrived at St. Mark's in 1961, assuming leadership roles as the superior and principal. He encouraged the idea of a National Team. As a philosopher, he sought to apply philosophical principles from medievalist Thomas Aquinas to contemporary life. Garvey showed how Christian humanism could guide modern life, through his earlier work with labor leaders in Windsor, where he founded the Pius XI Labour School at Assumption University.[62] He believed that social action movements need not be driven by socialist thought, but were actually organic developments within democracy.[63] Christian social responsibility required just relations among individuals and institutions in order to promote the moral freedom of each person.[64]

Bauer, who had been active in the Young Christian Student Association at St. Michael's, followed Garvey's thought. This Catholic social action had an ultramontane sense of mission, where likeminded organizations faithfully looked to Rome for direction in creating a more just society through restructuring of it along Christian lines.[65] This was not a rejection of Edgar

60 P. T. McMahon, "Carmelite Spirituality," in *The New Catholic Encyclopedia*, vol. 3, 2nd ed. (Detroit: Gale, 2003), 136.

61 McMahon, "Carmelite Spirituality," 135.

62 Brian Hogan, "Ivory Tower and Grass Roots: The Intellectual Life and Social Action of Congregation of St. Basil, Archdiocese of Toronto, 1930–60," in *Catholics at the "Gathering Place": Historical Essays on the Archdiocese of Toronto, 1841–1991*, ed. Mark George McGowan and Brian P. Clarke (Toronto: Canadian Catholic Historical Association, 1993), 255–74.

63 P. Wallace Platt, *Dictionary of Basilian Biography: Lives of Members of the Congregation of Priests of Saint Basil from its Origins in 1822 to 2022, 2nd ed.* (Toronto: University of Toronto Press, 2005), 243.

64 Hogan, "Ivory Tower," 259.

65 Staf Hellemans, "Is There a Future for Catholic Social Teaching after the Waning of Ultramontane Mass Catholicism?" in *Catholic Social Thought: Twilight or Renaissance?*, ed. Jonathan S. Boswell, Francis P. McHugh, and Johan Verstraeten (Leuven: Peeters Publishers, 2000), 18.

Bauer's conservative or business-minded perspective.[66] Instead, it could support a nationalistic viewpoint that promoted the principles of democracy, freedom, and justice, and also labor opportunities for Canadian hockey players.

In August 1962, Bauer went before the executive of the CAHA in Toronto. It knew that sending the best senior amateur team from the previous season was ill-fated, especially when reinstated professionals on those teams were disallowed from playing the international game. Other plans were hatched. For instance, one proposal called for an all-star team of graduated junior players who would be financed by exhibition games across Canada—however, the NHL was not about to let the top young players play outside their league.[67] Bauer's plan was to collect the best graduating juniors and US and Canadian college players, assemble them at UBC, and let them earn an education while playing hockey. His plan leveraged a university infrastructure, yet the real advantage was in the Bauer name. The family was dedicated to the international game, while the priest-coach had scouted many top young players from behind the Majors' bench. The CAHA executive, which believed that Bauer could avoid an international hockey incident and possibly win a tournament, deliberated only briefly. Years later, Bauer recalled: "To my horror, in a way, it was accepted. We would begin in the fall of 1963.... It was just crazy. We had no uniforms, no ice, no schedule, no base, no money, nothing.... I'm tempted to say it was a giant act of faith."[68]

The CAHA's decision revealed what little choice the amateur association had in the face of the growing dominance of the NHL game. A rebuttal came from the University of Alberta's Dr. Maury Van Vliet, who called Bauer's new standalone team "an absolute farce": "Surely someone must have confused this entire request with the grass hockey team. UBC fields good teams of Asiatics in this sport."[69] He complained that Bauer's team would work out of "a university that does not own a hockey rink, located in an area that has never produced a hockey player with a team that has

66 Paul Schmalz, email message to author, April 2019.

67 Bruce Kidd and John MacFarlane, *The Death of Hockey* (Toronto: New Press, 1972), 78. This was put forth by Saskatchewan's Frank Boucher, who coincidentally won the Lady Byng trophy a record seven times.

68 Jim Proudfoot, "Father Bauer Recalls 'Giant Act of Faith,'" *Toronto Star*, 1987 or 1988, Box 4, File 9, Bauer fonds, Basilian Archives.

69 "Van Vliet Still Upset," 1964, Rev. Bauer file, Seaman Hockey Resource Centre. Van Vliet had previously worked at UBC.

never beaten anyone." But the CAHA believed in Bauer's abilities. President Roxburgh retorted that "David Bauer is the best hockey coach in Canada."[70] Fact of the matter was that the team was a major triumph for the university hockey system and amateurism overall—and that it was not possible without Bauer's efforts.[71]

Bauer's Vision for the National Team

Bauer wanted to alter Canada's blueprint for hockey through the National Team program. In a 1962 interview, he commented that in the postwar period "too much board-thumping hockey" came into prominence while new changes were arising in the game: puck possession was becoming a "key factor" and gave an advantage to "a team of artists."[72] He set out to reverse trends of unbridled commercialization and artless play and to renew the game with a spirit of internationalism.[73]

Most Canadians in the 1950s and '60s showed little interest in the international game. Televised, professional play became dominant and cast a shadow on amateur sport as sub-par or novice.[74] Bauer discounted criticisms that international, amateur competition was "just the carefree mixing of youth of all nations" or, more cynically, "a sort of irrelevant extension of the Cold War."[75] He argued:

> Within the context of the world struggles for power in which our freedom was and is at stake, Canada cannot play a decisive role but it can make real contributions of its own. It can do so, however, only if our leaders have seriously faced and thought out our aims and our capabilities. In the same context one can locate the role of our sports in the development of the human person who would one day be called upon to lead wisely in a turbulent world.... [International

---

70   Frayne, "How You Played." This endorsement caused Bauer to howl even years later.

71   Osborne, Letter to Father Garvey.

72   Andy O'Brien, "How College Hockey Can Come Back," *Weekend Magazine* 12, no. 3 (1962): 35.

73   Bauer, *Report to Munro*, 51.

74   Rose, *Historical Account*, 11 and 13.

75   Bauer, *Report to Munro*, 9–10.

sport] is an opportunity to apply on a higher level that same principle I spoke of before: Make use of technique, but let the spirit prevail. It is a chance to show the world the true character of our people—on a secondary level, no doubt, but one which all the world watches and one which can "capture the fleeting idealism of our youth."[76]

Despite the limits of a sparsely populated Canada or its moderate sporting successes, Bauer believed the National Team could reveal the nation's spirit coming out of the postwar era, relying less on its British roots yet engaging traditional ideals of sport. Central to his idealized vision was "the fleeting idealism of our youth," which reflected optimism present in youth culture in the twentieth century's first decades. Different waves of idealism in youth movements continued until after the Second World War; they often started on university campuses, as a youthful Dave had experienced.[77] In his coaching and teaching of young people, as mentored by Basilians, Bauer had found an enthusiasm and playful spirit that could reinvigorate people of all ages.[78] Something as simple as a game of hockey could be "profoundly important" if not understood cynically or materialistically.

With the Cold War becoming more polarized around the time of the Cuban Missile Crisis in 1962, Bauer argued in his *Report to Munro* that international sport risked becoming a means instead of an end. Canadians had two visions of life to choose from: "between democracy, which is ultimately founded upon the Christian concept of individual freedom, and a materialistic conception of the world in which the freedom of the individual is subordinated to a collective world."[79] He thought that sports should support a liberal way of life. While setting democracy clearly against collectivism appears simplistic, Bauer feared that Western ideals were insufficiently defended and were fatally threatened in a shrinking world.

In hockey, Bauer saw deeper human meanings of freedom, character, personhood, spirit, and the like. With mentorship and reflection, an individual in sport could find personal development—and even union with God.

76   Bauer, *Report to Munro*, 9–10.

77   Paul Johnson, "The Lost Ideals of Youth," *New York Times*, March 25, 1984, https://www.nytimes.com/1984/03/25/magazine/the-lost-ideals-of-youth.html.

78   Carmelite Sisters of St. Joseph, interview with author, January 17, 2019.

79   Bauer, *Report to Munro*, 52 and 54. Here Bauer cited Chancellor Konrad Adenauer of West Germany.

According to one Basilian, Bauer "was convinced that there was a noble human and even Christian meaning possible for athletics, and that this was being neglected."[80] His new plan was taking shape.

Preparing the National Team

Bauer quickly began preparations for the 1964 Olympic Games. He asked UBC's Bob Hindmarch to be the general manager and assistant coach. Hindmarch noted that Bauer broke ground by creating the role of assistant coach, a role unknown in the NHL.[81] Hindmarch and Bauer developed a strong relationship over many years. He joked: "It was an ecumenical coaching program because he was a Catholic and I was raised a Protestant."[82] Bauer, Hindmarch, and trainer John Owen were the management team for the entire program in 1963.[83]

Players from across the country tried out for the team. The core of the Olympic team were the four players from the Toronto area—Ken Broderick, Barry MacKenzie, Dave Chambers, and Terry O'Malley—who played for the Thunderbirds in the previous season. The four, according to Bauer, were good players "with hearts as big as mountains."[84] Bauer criss-crossed North America that year speaking with young men on his quest for hockey talent and character. With a meager budget, recruiting was made possible by the support of Ian Sinclair, the president of Canadian Pacific, who supplied Bauer with free flights to anywhere, as well as free lodging at the company's hotels. Bauer asked the Carmelite Sisters in Waterloo to pray for the right players for the team. He scouted the World Championships of Hockey in Stockholm, Sweden, in March 1963.

Tryouts were held in August 1963 at the University of Alberta, with the support of hockey coach Clare Drake. Bauer preferred older players studying

---

80   Jack Gallagher, "The Basilian Way of Life & Higher Education," in *Toronto St. Michael's Majors: The Tradition Lives On ... The Official Magazine of the Toronto St. Michael's Majors*, 1997, 56.

81   Watson, *Catch On*, 5.

82   Watson, *Catch On*, 3.

83   Watson, *Catch On*, 10. Hindmarch, the Bauer hockey-student, became the winningest coach with the UBC men's hockey program. He went on to become the vice president of the Canadian Olympic Association for 16 years and the Canadian Chef de Mission at the 1984 Winter Olympics in Sarajevo.

84   Watson, *Catch On*, 139–40.

for graduate degrees because he thought undergraduate students would miss too many classes.[85] He sought players with character, who lived up to the Bauer standard of conduct and would not embarrass the country overseas.[86] It was a challenge to attract French-speaking players to train and attend university in an exclusively English-speaking environment. Bauer took the best twenty-five players at the tryouts and, according to Conacher, ended up with ten centermen playing different forward positions. The players were not under the illusion that they were the best players in Canada; they were simply some of the best players available outside of the professional ranks.[87]

Bauer spent much of the hockey off-season in 1963 winning support of financial backers and government officials.[88] In addition to Sinclair, Calgary newspaperman Max Bell and Winnipeg businessman James Richardson provided much backing.[89] Support also came from brother Ray who, from the beginning, according to one friend, "helped [Dave] a tremendous amount" to get the team up and running. Ray was paid back over time, and benefited from garnering business contacts for Bauer Ltd.[90] Not all money was welcome. In the fall of 1962, Conn Smythe gave Bauer $500 for the National Team, but Bauer flung the money down onto a dormitory room floor and told the players: "I don't want Mr. Smythe's money.... You boys use it for books or something, whatever you want."[91] Knowing how Smythe's professional brand had disregarded amateur hockey, Bauer sought a hockey alternative outside of Smythe's influence.

Another major supporter was Père Athol Murray, the face of Notre Dame Collegiate in Wilcox, Saskatchewan. Born in Toronto, with studies completed at Université Laval in Quebec City, Father Murray was a grand nationalist who eventually moved west to Regina and then to the small town of Wilcox to lead a school already begun by the Sisters of Charity of St. Louis. It was during the Depression, and Murray wanted to educate

85   Watson, *Catch On*, 144.

86   Al Fotheringham, "UBC Coach Works to Restore Classic Ideal," *UBC Alumni Chronicle*, Winter 1963, Box 37, "Research on Fr. Bauer" file, St. Mark's College Archives.

87   Brian Conacher, interview with author, June 5, 2019.

88   Watson, *Catch On*, 137.

89   Oliver, *Father Bauer*, 102–3.

90   Paul Burns, interview with author, August 15, 2018. Ray regularly communicated with Hindmarch, asking how he could help. Hindmarch, interview.

91   Wayne Parrish, "Fr. Bauer's Team Wasn't for Sale," *Toronto Sun*, August 13, 1987, Box 2, last file, Bauer fonds, Basilian Archives.

young boys instead of them working on road-building crews with no future prospects. With a larger-than-life personality, Murray garnered a charter from the University of Ottawa, and Notre Dame was incorporated as a liberal arts college. The educational endeavor was matched by Notre Dame's prowess in ice hockey, connecting future NHL stars like Nick and Don Metz to the St. Michael's Majors.

The fiery Père Murray quickly endorsed Bauer's dream.[92] When the team formed and toured the country for training and financial support, Murray once spoke to them between periods. With speeches often laced with profanities, he began his talk about the importance of representing the nation and inspiring Canada's youth with, "So you're the Canadian bastards who will carry Canada's hockey colours in the next Olympics."[93] Murray, despite his realism, still dreamt of wedding together the power of education and a patriotic hockey program.

Support from the federal government was slow to arrive, especially since the idea of government involvement in Canadian sport was new. It finally came from the National Advisory Council (NAC) on Fitness and Amateur Sport in late 1963. Red Kelly, a former St. Michael's player and then a member of Parliament (while playing for the Maple Leafs), put Bauer in touch with the minister of amateur sport, Judy LaMarsh, which led to a conversation with Lester B. Pearson, the prime minister of Canada.[94] Pearson was a superb sportsman who earlier coached the Varsity Blues hockey and football teams while as a history professor at the University of Toronto.[95] Bauer's program received an NAC grant of $25,000. Minister LaMarsh flew to Vancouver to personally present the cheque. Bauer had his players serve hors d'oeuvres, coffee, and tea at the formal event. Everyone was involved, and the bulky hockey players got into the spirit of things.[96] The cheque was an immense help for the financially strapped program.

92 Jack Gorman, *Père Murray and the Hounds* (Winnipeg, MB: Hignell Printing, 1977), 89.

93 Terry O'Malley, "Father David Bauer and the National Team Hockey Experiment: 1963–1980, A Personal Recollection," 2001, Terry O'Malley Collection. Despite the college's poor finances, Murray donated $1,000.

94 David Bauer, Letter to Red Kelly, MP, June 24, 1963, Box 5, File 1, Bauer fonds, Basilian Archives.

95 University of Toronto Alumni, "Lester B. Pearson," News & Stories, Featured Alumni, November 28, 2013, https://alumni.utoronto.ca/news-and-stories/featured-alumni/lester-b-pearson.

96 Watson, *Catch On*, 180.

Sparse living conditions awaited the players in Vancouver. There was little money to go around after tuition and living costs were covered. But Bauer avoided complaint and was not going to let players feel sorry for themselves.[97] Perhaps the hardy life the players lived mirrored Bauer's own vow of poverty, or a paltry Basilian school making ends meet. The program was an amateur organization, with little infrastructure and modeled on the volunteer workings of the CAHA. This was not high-end, professionally-run hockey.

Bauer envisioned a Canadian hockey model closer to the US collegiate system, where Canadian university athletics would supply the athletes for the 1968 Olympic Games.[98] If the National Team was successful, it could bring better players to Canadian universities and create Canadian university hockey programs that could mirror US college football. University hockey could celebrate connecting travelling experiences with sport, especially travel to the Olympics. Historically, ever since the CAHA sided with the NHL in 1936, Canadian universities remained strict adherents to amateur ideals and consequently had a comparatively low-caliber product. By infusing greater talent into universities, as was the case in hockey's early history, the ancient Greek connection between academic and athletic pursuits was possible. Bauer denied that he wanted to turn hockey players into intellectuals, but sought to reignite ideals in the sporting situation.[99]

There was no hockey rink on the UBC campus, but Bauer used a familial connection to the brewing industry for assistance. His grandfather, Aloyes, had helped manage the Kuntz Brewery for decades; it later joined with Carling Breweries.[100] Bauer approached Hartland Molson, co-owner of the Montreal Canadiens, to contribute money toward a new arena. Molson, a former junior hockey player and known philanthropist, cut a cheque for $125,000. By the time matching funds were amassed by the university and student body, only half a million dollars had been raised. Bauer found a contractor who had finished

---

97   Fisher, "Hockey History." Later, when players were paid $2,000 a year for their tuition and other costs, Marshall Johnston was a teacher who paid his own substitute teacher when he traveled to games with the National Team.

98   Watson, *Catch On*, 139–40.

99   O'Brien, "How College Hockey," 34.

100   His brother-in-law had passed away at a young age. Rowell, Devitt, and McKegney, *Welcome to Waterloo*, 36. The newly merged business dropped the German-sounding "Kuntz" from its name and later was bought out by Labatt's Breweries. Waterloo Public Library, *Waterloo 150: Profiles from the Past, Faces of the Future* (Waterloo, ON: Waterloo Public Library, 2007), 8.

building a rink in Esquimalt, British Columbia, on the same small budget. Former player Mickey McDowell chuckled, "So our rink at UBC was identical to the doors, to the toilets, to everything as that building in Esquimalt."[101] McDowell scored the first goal in what is now known as the Father David Bauer Arena.

Players' accommodations were also orchestrated by Bauer. The residence was located on the UBC campus and was a composite of two buildings: a modest, white stuccoed farmhouse used during the war as a wireless station by the military, and a show-home that was auctioned off at the end of the Pacific National Exhibition.[102] The team painted their new, two-part home, installed new windows, and had a handy player complete work on several rooms. "Hockey House" was home to almost the entire team and "Ma" Byers was their "old school" cook. With a restricted budget, baloney sandwiches were typically served for lunch and bones from sides of beef were ground for soap.[103] Players reminisce fondly about a no-frills experience at Hockey House. It built team spirit and resolve.[104]

Training for the National Team included Bauer's random questions about politics and society; he even suggested readings pertaining to both. He wanted players to see hockey from 35,000 feet—not just ice level. For instance, Bauer wrote to *Sports Illustrated* to get his players copies of an article about the moral force of sport.[105] In it, sporting examples from Thailand, Ghana, Venezuela, and Iran showed how sport could bring about reconciliation and peace.[106] Team members reading this could grasp Bauer's vision for sport as a promotion of values worthy of a nation's devotion, as captured in a hockey team.

---

101   Mickey McDowell, interview with author, August 16, 2018. He added, "only Bauer can do things like that."

102   McDowell, interview. Bauer got the house at a discounted rate, including its free delivery to Point Grey.

103   McDowell, interview.

104   After the 1964 Winter Olympics, Hockey House was home to the rowing pair of Roger Jackson and George Hungerford, who won gold at the 1964 Summer Olympics in Tokyo. Jackson became prominent in Canadian Olympic sport management roles, crossing paths with Bauer into the 1980s.

105   David Bauer, Letter to *Sports Illustrated*, June 28, 1963, Box 5, File 1, Bauer fonds, Basilian Archives.

106   Sargent Shriver, "The Moral Force of Sport," *Sports Illustrated Vault*, June 3, 1963. https://www.si.com/vault/1963/06/03/594230/the-moral-force-of-sport.

Bauer as the Priest-Coach of the National Team

Why did players choose the National Team? Headed by a skilled coach with Bauer's pedigree, young men expected to develop into better players, receive a university education, travel the globe, and represent Canada at the Winter Olympics. It looked more promising than bouncing around the minor leagues of professional hockey; opportunities in the six-team NHL were few.

Players quickly learned that Bauer was more mentor than hardened hockey man. McDowell claimed that Bauer was vastly different from any coach he previously had: "I'd been with all these cigar-chomping, gum-chewing, swearing, old-time hockey players ... a lot of people that society didn't want. My first coach was a pedophile, the second was an alcoholic, the third one was a deadbeat."[107] In terms of coaching style, previous coaches often responded to player mistakes with negativity and threats. But Bauer was thoughtful, holding team meetings in the hotel on the morning of a game so he had the team's undivided attention. When the prepared team hit the ice, his practices had only a few whistles. Russian coach Tarasov observed: "He never raised his voice. But there were many quiet, peaceful and, at times, heartfelt talks. Judging by the faces and gestures of the players one could see that the players were satisfied with that sort of contact with the coach."[108] Bauer directed his competitiveness through his ideals.

Bauer was considered a teacher as much as coach.[109] He focused on fundamental skills and techniques and respected players' responsibilities toward schoolwork. Hindmarch noted two relevant stories about Bauer's person-centered approach.[110] Once, Bauer let a player finish practice early because he lacked the stamina that others had. The player scored three goals at the next day's game. More generally, Bauer did not designate one player as captain. He would sometimes choose a captain for just one game, knowing that it would bring the best out of that player for that game. He combined his knowledge of the game and sport psychology to improve team results.

Player Dave Chambers, who became an NHL coach, commented that Bauer was a master motivator. Because of the way he handled people, players

107   McDowell, interview.
108   Tarasov, *Road to Olympus*, 28.
109   Conacher, interview.
110   Watson, *Catch On*, 183.

showed a mutual respect.[111] McDowell recalled how Bauer inspired the least talented players on the team, giving them a defined goal of stopping opponents: "Bauer had them believing in the team and themselves ... it was a marvel to watch it."[112] He could also be a disciplinarian, telling players to stay onside by imagining that the blueline was a 50-foot cliff if they did not have the puck.[113]

Figure 4.2 Bauer preparing for photo with 1964 National Team players. From left to right: Bauer, Ross Morrison, Jack Wilson, Barry MacKenzie, Henry Akerval, Don Rogers, Terry O'Malley.

Courtesy of Terry O'Malley

Unity of the team was central to Bauer's philosophy of sport, in which adversity endured was their greatest asset.[114] The players bonded together, sharing a household, studying, and receiving the same financial reward for their efforts. Bauer promoted conversations at the dinner table and he

---

111   Oliver, *Father Bauer*, 260.

112   McDowell, interview.

113   Watson, *Catch On*, 200.

114   Proudfoot, "Father Bauer Recalls."

was not averse to guitar-led sing-alongs. His tending to team spirit made "late pick-ups" before a major tournament rare. Even when Bauer could have picked up junior star Yvan Cournoyer shortly before leaving for 1964 pre-tournament games in Europe, he would not drop someone else: "I believed our strength was the players' powerful loyalty to each other. I felt there was an intangible that had to be preserved." He was determined to keep the team's spirit.

Bauer needed a creative strategy for the international game, since overly rough hockey tactics were heavily penalized. For instance, in games prior to the Olympics, Bauer became convinced that soccer strategies of European clubs provided more insights than North American hockey: "It's a combination of a big ice surface and the fact a player can protect the puck merely by turning his back to you. In Canada you just hoist him one from behind. Over here you can't do it."[115] In personal notes, Bauer wrote about the importance of puck possession, discipline, and the ability to learn.[116] Skills and checking were paramount in his system, allowing players to find freedom within the game, to echo the work of Maritain. Skill and speed created space around players and provided for better opportunities, or they could take away space through defensive positioning and checking.[117] Thus, freedom as a moral quality could be displayed on a hockey rink, whether by players' tactical movements or their ethical character.

During early competition in the Fall of 1963, the National Team defeated some American university and professional teams, along with the Czechoslovakia National Team. Perhaps the team had a chance at Olympic gold. Bauer crowed: "This is the start of the proof that it's going to work."[118] Expectations and belief were growing—but they had yet to play the world champion Soviets. The Soviets' conditioning was superior to that of Canadian teams. In a 1968 story, Tarasov proclaimed that the Russians were best at team conditioning, team tactics, and team techniques. But he added, Canada made hockey players who detest losing: "I will never be able to teach my players to hate to lose the way Canadians hate to lose.... Ergo, the thesis of Canadian

---

115   Watson, *Catch On*, 158. Bauer told defensemen to stay out of the corners so they would not get out of position.

116   David Bauer, Notes, Box 3, File 1, Bauer fonds, Basilian Archives.

117   McDowell, interview.

118   "Hockey—Second Bauer," *Time Magazine*, December 27, 1963, File 44, David Bauer fonds, Canada's Sports Hall of Fame Archives.

hockey: 'Try harder.' Canadians play with emotion and passion, and sometimes individual brilliance.... Canadians will die to win."[119] While the Soviets learned from Percival and others—and from the sport of soccer—Bauer tried to control the passing of the circling Soviets through unique defensive techniques garnered from coaches at St. Michael's. According to Tarasov, Bauer may have looked like he was aloof to what was happening on the ice, but his "eyes were lively" and his mind was processing how to slow down the Soviets.[120]

Because of the bash-and-bang reputation of Canadian teams at World Championships, Bauer declared that he "would bend over backward" to reestablish an alternative Canadian hockey identity.[121] Sometimes opponents goaded the National Team, trying to prod them into taking penalties. In an exhibition game, Czechoslovakian players spat and kicked at the Canadians. Bauer leaned over to an enraged player on the bench and said, "Are you going to get that guy?" When the player answered in the affirmative, Bauer bellowed, "Sit down, then; you're not going anywhere."[122] Bauer implored the players to maintain their sense of purpose, especially when many questioned if Canada should send a team to the Olympics.

Bauer the Priest

Putting a priest in charge of a hockey team was not extraordinary. Hindmarch thought it was nonsense that Bauer favored Catholic players; the coaches wanted to ice the best team possible.[123] Player Marshall Johnston quipped, "If you were a Protestant and good enough, you still got on the powerplay."[124] For some players, though, Bauer was first and foremost a priest.[125] Bauer said

---

119   Susan Foster and Carl Brewer, *The Power of Two: Carl Brewer's Battle with Hockey's Power Brokers* (Toronto: Key Porter Books, 2007), 260–62. NHL defenseman Carl Brewer explained that Bauer "is acknowledged as one of hockey's great creators" with "the most adaptable and preferred system I have encountered."

120   Tarasov, *Road to Olympus*, 28.

121   "Editorial—Father David Bauer," *Toronto Star,* November 12, 1988, Rev. Bauer file, Seaman Resource Centre.

122   Paul Hunter, "Wanted Less Mayhem in International Hockey," *Toronto Star,* November 10, 1988, Box 2, last file, Bauer fonds, Basilian Archives. The player was Barry MacKenzie.

123   Watson, *Catch On*, 182.

124   Marshall Johnston, interview with author, August 22, 2019.

125   Paul Conlin, interview with author, June 3, 2019.

daily Mass during hockey trips and regularly said his morning and evening prayers. He once said his evening prayers quietly in the team's shower room before a game. The players were unaware and began talking about their exploits with women, drinking, etc., when suddenly Bauer appeared among them and their tall tales. The embarrassed players fell silent and the priest walked out of the dressing room.[126] Other times, he used humor to deal with awkwardness. When someone on the bench said, "For Christ's sake," Bauer responded, "Now, now, I do the praying around here!"[127] Having a priest-coach ministering in the hockey world made for awkward moments that Bauer tried to overlook or smooth out.

Bauer explained once to Tarasov that he was the head of the National Team in part because it was a divine calling.[128] One can imagine that many Basilian priests rolled their eyes when he established the National Team. Many wondered why he was getting more involved in hockey after his superiors had terminated the Majors.[129] Was Bauer sincere? Was this hostile retribution? And would taking their sporting tradition to the international stage work—and would it support the community's traditional educational ministry? Bauer's chaplaincy position at St Mark's was flexible, and the Basilians could afford to let Bauer chase a sports dream because of the record-breaking number of Basilian recruits. Even with the support and goodwill of Carr and Garvey, Bauer regularly had to "mend fences" with his religious confreres due to his travel schedule.[130]

The 1960s were a time of reforms in the Catholic Church as it adapted to modern life. Many priests enthusiastically embraced the changes, but Bauer was not seeking cutting-edge innovations. He maintained his traditional Marian devotions, yet supported ecumenism. Many religious sisters and priests stopped wearing religious attire; Bauer wore his roman collar consistently until late in life. Wearing a black shirt and pants simplified life for the traveling priest. On one occasion, a nephew of Bauer's arrived at his grandparents to take his uncle to the airport: Bauer stood at the door in boxer shorts and asked if the nephew would pick up his pants at the cleaner. The nephew kidded

126   McDowell, interview.
127   Watson, *Catch On*, 189.
128   Tarasov, *Road to Olympus*, 28.
129   Don McLeod, interview with author, June 4, 2018.
130   Hindmarch, interview.

that surely a vow of poverty allowed for more than one pair of pants.[131] Wearing a collar behind the bench sent a strong message: according to one observer, Bauer was not just another dirty hockey coach.[132] During games, Bauer thumbed through rosary beads in his pant pockets.[133]

1964 Olympics

The National Team practiced and played games in the fall and winter in preparation for the 1964 Winter Olympics in Innsbruck, which began in late January. While other national teams, like the Soviets and Czechoslovakians, were amateurs in name only—"shamateurs" who played hockey full-time and worked minimally away from the rink—Bauer held to his bigger purpose for the team. He promoted a team spirit that aspired to higher ideals: "God gives us all different talents. The nobility ... lies in being a better person than you previously were."[134] His goal remained the same: "If you improve a young man, you improve his ability to play hockey."[135]

The priest-coach was a sensation in Europe. Coach Hindmarch recalled how Bauer spoke to a packed church behind the Iron Curtain.[136] An Italian magazine did a cover spread and full introspective article on Bauer: "Father David Bauer has the healthy face of an open and straightforward athlete, his clear, frank eyes often giving a hint of a good-humored wink, his expression shaped by a spirit that is profoundly good, his bearing erect and agile ... his handshake strong and firm. He is a very good conversationalist, and his thinking flows lucidly with simple diction."[137] Another reporter shared her first impressions: "Father Bauer of the bashed nose in a handsome face to which photographs do no justice walks quickly, smiles quickly, looks you right in the eye, makes you feel good. A big man, you would say, though not physically. He is of medium height and not heavily built—all wire and

131   Bob Bauer, Jr., interview.

132   Chima McLean, "Father Bauer's Reputation Makes Event 'A Natural,'" *Hockey Showcase: Father David Bauer Cup*, March 28–30, 1996, 11.

133   Carmelite Sisters of St. Joseph, interview.

134   Archie McDonald, "Father Bauer Remembered," *Vancouver Sun*, November 10, 1988, Box 2, Bauer fonds, Basilian Archives.

135   Watson, *Catch On*, 200.

136   Hindmarch, interview.

137   Alberto Montagna, "Sparate Goal!" trans. J. Rent, *Citta Nuova* 8, no. 4 (February 25, 1964): 6.

muscle."[138] European newspapers noted that boxing blows of past teams were replaced by artful, nonviolent play.[139]

In the Italian magazine article, Bauer theorized about a united vision of the human person—body and soul—that echoed Thomistic thinking. He affirmed the goodness of sport, declaring it "a universal language, beyond and above politics," that could develop the "psycho-physical composite" of humans. With the help of divine grace, the body/soul unity of a person could find self-control and wrestle with a person's emotions. Despite the rough ways of hockey, the sport should contend with the reality of human persons. To conclude, Bauer turned to his motto, "use technique, but let the spirit prevail," because hockey afforded him the ability to develop spirit and technique in harmony with one another.[140] Maritain's true humanism was being broadcast in full technicolor on the international hockey stage.

Bauer's openness toward whatsoever was good, however, was narrowed toward communism and its extremes. Arriving in the Soviet Union for its pre-Olympic tour, the team encountered very tight security: spotlights shone on them, soldiers carried rifles, and cardboard covered their hotel windows.[141] Bauer was convinced spies and hidden microphones were everywhere.[142] Based on his reading of Dawson and others, he believed that he needed to reject the ethics of communist countries and their totalitarian regimes. He was aware of their denial of human rights and use of mass executions.[143] He felt this evil in off-ice experiences and on-ice goading by Eastern European teams that sought to wear down Western ideals. Bauer saw the Soviets' investment in athletics as "window dressing" that was alien and even oppressive.[144]

Bauer's disdain for communism and socialist workings conflicted with others. As a graduate student who worked alongside Bauer in the late 1960s, Bruce Kidd felt uncomfortable about elements of Bauer's conservative nationalism.[145] Bauer spoke out of a black and white mindset, mirroring

138   Phyllis Griffiths, "Father Bauer: He Molded a Dream," *The Telegram*, February 11, 1964, David Bauer file, Canada's Sports Hall of Fame Archives, 5.

139   Montagna, "Sparate Goal," 4.

140   Montagna, "Sparate Goal," 7.

141   Fisher, "Hockey History."

142   Watson, *Catch On*, 188.

143   Christopher Dawson, *Understanding Europe* (Washington, DC: Catholic University of America Press, 1952), 211.

144   Watson, *Catch On*, 165.

145   Bruce Kidd, interview with author, June 4, 2019.

Dawson and others and seeing political manifestations of Marxism as evil. Kidd found it to be a "one-dimensional polemical account of what was happening" in communist countries, instead of understanding these societies as attempting to create more equitable settings amidst complex and difficult questions. Although other Catholic thinkers like Paulo Freire or Gregory Baum found value in Marxist thought, Bauer did not understand how a revival of Marxism could support humanist thinking. For Kidd and others, simply defeating Soviet communism was not a sure path for making a better world.

Amidst Cold War tensions and a burgeoning sense of its own postwar national identity, Canada as a nation sought new symbols as a step away from the British, colonial roots of the nation.[146] Many nationwide changes came about: the new flag, the combining of the country's military under the "unroyal" name of Canadian Armed Forces, the founding of the Order of Canada, and the National Team. Bauer was not a neo-nationalist who sought to break all ties with traditions from Britain. He was a deeply committed, passionate Canadian nationalist. His nationalism reflected Britishness in that he was raised in an English-speaking home in Waterloo and was part of a mainstream English-speaking Catholic culture in Ontario. Linguistic identification showed loyalty to the nation.[147] Unlike French-Canadian co-religionists and strongly British Anglo-Protestants, Catholics like Bauer followed Anglo-Canadian socioeconomic mores and imagined an independent Canada within a commonwealth of equals.

Bauer supported a vision of Canada that was not centrally-controlled economically and that sought more independence from British rule based on the equality and responsibilities ordained for all. The basis for interdependence among equals, for Bauer, was the ethical ideals and spiritual foundations of the Christian West. The new flag and his new team went hand in hand, and he supported the British rule of law, individual rights, and ancient Greek influences on western thought.[148] The National Team was his means in part

146 Christian Champion, *The Strange Demise of British Canada: The Liberals and Canadian Nationalism, 1964–1968* (Montreal: McGill-Queen's University Press, 2010), 1–20.

147 Mark McGowan, "Toronto's English-Speaking Catholics, Immigration, and the Making of a Canadian Catholic Identity, 1900–1930," in *Creed and Culture: The Place of English-Speaking Catholics in Canadian Society, 1750–1930*, ed. Terrence Murphy and Gerald J. Stortz (Montreal: McGill-Queen's University Press, 1993), 211 and 204.

148 Terry O'Malley, email message to author, March 6, 2023.

to promote his particular nationalistic vision to millions while witnessing to Christian values.[149]

After playing ten pre-tournament games in Europe, the National Team arrived at the Innsbruck Games. They won their first five games, thanks to strong goaltending and tight-checking, including a victory over a favored Swedish team. That game was remembered primarily for an incident that bloodied Bauer. A Swedish player, Carl-Goran Oberg, threw his stick into the players' bench. It struck Bauer and cut him above the right eye. He remained calm and yet forcefully restrained his players from retaliating.[150] The injury was not serious. He met with Oberg the next day as a sign of reconciliation, which further expanded his popularity in Europe.

Two games remained for the tight-checking Canadian team. A close game against the Czechoslovakia team was lost 3–1 after an injury removed goaltender Seth Martin. In the final game against the undefeated Soviet team, Canadian victory would result in a gold medal. The team held two different leads but the game went into the third period tied. The better-conditioned Soviets scored, and won 3–2.[151] Players felt defeated despite accolades about their sportsmanship. They finished behind the undefeated Soviet team and shared identical 5–2 records with Czechoslovakia and Sweden. Because the Canadians believed that the tie-breaking method was goal differential among the top four teams, they went to the medal ceremony anticipating reception of a bronze medal. However, a majority of IIHF member countries voted for a rule change—during the final game of the tournament—and resolved that goal differential was to be determined by all seven games at the Olympics. The Canadian team had throttled back in an early game against Switzerland—which ended in an 8–0 score—instead of tacking on extra goals to buoy its goal differential.[152] That energy-conserving, sportsmanlike decision ended up being decisive, and the National Team was slotted into fourth place.

The team and the country were outraged. Forward Brian Conacher bluntly recalled: "We got screwed."[153] Despite being the models of the amateur ideal,

149 Carmelite Sisters of St. Joseph, interview.

150 The Canadian Press, "Special Gold Medal for Father Bauer; Players Stay Away," February 19, 1964, David Bauer file, Canada's Sports Hall of Fame Archives, 22.

151 Oliver, *Father Bauer*, 117–18.

152 Oliver, *Father Bauer*, 119–20. Hindmarch believed that the rule had not been changed and it was an unnamed CAHA member who had mistakenly informed Bauer about the tie-breaker rule. Hindmarch, interview.

153 Conacher, interview.

the team's disciplined behavior seemed to have been partly the reason for their downfall. Defenseman Marshall Johnston memorably quipped, "The shepherd and his flock have been fleeced."[154] Conacher, like others, said that the changing of the rules at the last moment made the Olympic experience bittersweet.

At an award ceremony on the last day of the Games, Bauer was presented a special gold medal for showing restraint when he was struck in the face with a stick.[155] Bunny Ahearne, president of the IIHF and the man who had orchestrated the last-minute rule change and later denied the occurrence, called Bauer a gentleman who showed the highest standard of ethical behavior.[156] Ahearne stated that it was the first awarded Olympic gold medal for sportsmanship, but Bauer's feelings were surely mixed. It was widely known that Ahearne unscrupulously used his authority to advance his travel agency business.[157] His deceptive behavior often worked to his advantage, where he controlled North American teams internationally and thus had general support from Europeans. Bauer had fallen victim to Ahearne and the IIHF. The medal is on display today at the arena in Wilcox, Saskatchewan.

Although in 2005 the IIHF retroactively awarded that Olympic team with a World Championship bronze medal for their third place showing (the Olympics doubled as the World Championships, and tie-breaking rules were distinct in each), players' efforts to receive Olympic bronze medals proved unsuccessful. Bauer never advocated for such a move, and only complained that the change in policy had occurred during the tournament.[158] While Bauer continued to model sportsmanlike behavior, he also could have stood up firmly and sacrificed some of his public status for his players' glory.[159] Not winning a medal at the Olympic Games was a disappointment, and reflected poorly on his program and the international game.

Before returning to Canada, the team played exhibition games in Germany and Italy, which included an audience with Pope Paul VI at the Vatican. They also received a personal telegram from Prime Minister Lester Pearson. The team had changed the narrative about Canadians internationally. At Bauer's

---

154   Oliver, *Father Bauer*, 120.

155   The Canadian Press, "Special Gold Medal," 22. Players of the National Team boycotted the ceremony, and only the team trainer, John Owen, and the president of CAHA, Art Potter of Edmonton, attended.

156   Oliver, *Father Bauer*, 121. The Canadian Press, "Special Gold Medal," 22.

157   Hardy and Holman, *Hockey: A Global History*, 280.

158   Oliver, *Father Bauer*, 121.

159   Murray Costello, interview with author, June 3, 2019.

passing in 1988, one hockey executive noted: "He was the first who taught us how to play the international game with discipline," where he endorsed the Basilian motto, "Teach me goodness, discipline and knowledge."[160]

Figure 4.3 Bauer and the National Team greeted by Pope Paul VI in 1964.

Courtesy of the Canadian Press

Developments Arising from the National Team

It was difficult to articulate the full scope of Bauer's program.[161] For instance, after the National Team was blown out in a game in 1965, forward Conacher left the ice as the winning team's national anthem played. Bauer was livid with Conacher, and threatened to send him back to Canada.[162] Bauer then painstakingly explained what was at stake when players wear the maple leaf in international competition. Conacher remembered Bauer's main point: "In the world of sport today with its ever-growing competitiveness, no one nation is going to be able to win indefinitely.... There has to be something good come out of competitive sport even at a top international level for the loser as well, or nations slowly would withdraw themselves from competing.... [E]ven the

160 McDonald, "Father Bauer Remembered."

161 David Bauer, Letter to Karl Scheibock, October 17, 1963, Box 5, File 13, Bauer fonds, Basilian Archives.

162 Brian Conacher, *Hockey in Canada: The Way It Is!* (New York: Poseidon Press, 1993), 47–48.

losers have something to gain in good, keenly-contested competition." In that moment, Conacher understood that players modeling the character of Canadians and spreading goodwill for the nation were more valued than an ambassador. When the nation's international performace lacked, it could still show how to properly play the game.

Bauer's vision for the National Team led to his involvement in national bodies of Canadian sport. Following the Olympics, he was among fifteen men and women appointed to the National Advisory Council on Fitness and Amateur Sports. This body was composed of leaders of Canadian amateur sport.[163] Government involvement in national sport was limited, but growing. Bauer was positioned at the ground level to influence hockey and other sports. He and Hindmarch were also included among directors of the Garibaldi Development Association, which was preparing a bid to host the 1976 Winter Olympics north of Vancouver.

Another important offshoot of the National Team were its coaching clinics. Prior to this, coaching clinics were sparingly offered in Canadian hockey. The National Team began leading clinics when Bauer heard that a town's mayor and aldermen were upset that the team, much like the circus, left after the game with most of the gate receipts. McDowell thought the team could reciprocate by hosting a hockey clinic for the town's youth. Bauer liked the idea, shared it with local politicians, and set up a clinic for the next morning. After playing a game in the evening and not falling asleep until typically 2 am, McDowell's teammates were unhappy about their 7 am wakeup call. The National Team had begun its longstanding tradition of hosting hockey clinics in towns across the country.

Making of the Hockey Alternative

In Canada's centennial year, Bauer received the Order of Canada, a newly founded national honors system recognizing lifetime achievement and exemplary service to the nation.[164] The Order's motto, *Desiderantes meliorem*

163   The Canadian Press, "Father Bauer on Fitness Council," March 6, 1964, Box 2, last file, Bauer fonds, Basilian Archives. It included leaders in CAHA and university sport, as well as the president of the Canadian Olympic Association. Another priest-coach, Father Marcel de la Sablonniere, a Jesuit from Montreal, was also included.

164   Other recipients included former Prime Minister Louis St. Laurent, Father Georges-Henri Lévesque, and hockey superstar Maurice Richard. The Order of

patriam ("They desire a better country") reflected his passion for hockey as a vehicle to build the country's future. He reflected on the meaning of his appointment: "The Order of Canada is ... a bringing together of all Canadians in a dialogue about what Canada could mean to each of us as individuals and as citizens within a world community. It is meant to build trust and faith in our future."[165] For Bauer, the honor put diverse visions of the nation side by side to spur discussion about the *raison d'être* of Canada.

With the support of brothers Bobby and Ray, Bauer created a values-driven, pan-Canadian team that became a significant symbol of Canadian unity. "He made it happen against all of the skeptics," commented Kidd, "who said it'll never happen, 'This is Canada, this is such a divisive country.' Bauer made it work and found a model to make it work.... [I]n terms of his concrete legacy, we owe him big for that."[166]

Father Carr died two months prior to the Innsbruck Olympics. Bauer later found encouragement meeting Jacques Maritain near Toulouse, France, where Bauer explained the meaning of the National Team program and talked about their mutual friend.[167] Finding further inspiration was necessary, because Bauer's hockey alternative faced large organizational issues that put it in the crosshairs of the NHL. His battle for Canadian hockey had just begun.

Canada, "1967 Creating a National Order," accessed October 4, 2018, https://www.orderofcanada50.ca/1967. Bauer was first awarded a "medal of service" and later appointed "officer" of the Order.

165 Terry O'Malley, "Fr. Bauer Notes and Letters," Terry O'Malley Collection, 11.
166 Kidd, interview.
167 Platt, *Dictionary of Basilian Biography*, 34.

Plans to Change Canadian Hockey

THE NATIONAL TEAM PROGRAM WAS BAUER'S MODEL for the reconfiguration of Canadian hockey. Former chair of Hockey Canada Douglas Fisher succinctly described this alternative: "Bauer [was] after a major change in the organization, style and values of hockey in Canada, and through hockey, a change in the nature of sport participation by young Canadians."[1] To expand the National Team program, Bauer fought to find steady income sources, reliable player development streams, and a more stable system of competition for its players.[2] Its sources of income were fragile, consisting of government grants, individual donations, and portions of ticket sales. Setting up an alternative structure in the hockey world—that could change the nature of youth hockey—would lead to a zero-sum battle against the professional game.

The hockey system found it easiest to have youth focused on playing games. Exceptions to the rule existed outside of St. Michael's, but the system's

---

    1 "Bauer, David," File 45, David Bauer fonds, Canada's Sports Hall of Fame Archives.

    2 Canadian Amateur Hockey Association, "Minutes of Annual Meeting," 1968, Calgary, AB, Minutes file, Hockey Canada Archives, 66.

capacity to seemingly push children away from education was a great evil in the eyes of Bauer and others.[3] Leaving Junior A and professional hockey players without a high school diploma played into the hands of hockey owners. One NHL scout explained this bluntly: "Let's face it. I'd rather deal with the big dumb 195-pounder any time."[4] An alternative to the professional route was US college hockey, which gave players more career options with a degree in hand, including a better negotiating position against professional hockey managers.[5] Conacher wrote that National Team players signed for three times the amount of players straight out of junior hockey.[6] The same NHL scout added: "But now instead of getting the big dumb 17-year-old, we're getting the big smart 21-year-old and half of them have lawyers with them. Things have changed."

Many noted the player drain to US colleges, but it was Bauer who dared to change this reality and splashed it onto the sports pages of Canadian newspapers. Former National Team player Mickey McDowell used an analogy to explain how young men trying to make the NHL was similar to the sacrifice on display in a salmon run. Different species of the fish take a tumultuous spawning journey from the Pacific Ocean to their birthplace in the British Columbia interior. Just as an aging fish drives upriver to return for spawning, young Canadian men, from McDowell's viewpoint, were giving themselves wholeheartedly to get an NHL contract. They were willing to forego an education to become a pro: "Every kid in Canada's yearning to get up to those headwaters, the NHL [team owners] own this lovely fish ladder. 'You're welcome to join and come up that fish ladder. There's just one condition. You have to check your mind at the beginning.'"[7] At the age of 16, a boy had the right to quit school and do whatever he liked. Even if apprenticeship in

3   Paul Conlin, interview with author, June 4, 2019. Other junior teams did occasionally allow a few academically-minded players to attend university—like the Toronto Marlies, in the case of Brian Conacher; and the Edmonton Oil Kings, in the case of Roger Bourbonnais.

4   Murray Dryden, *Playing the Shots at Both Ends* (Toronto: McGraw-Hill Ryerson, 1972), 64.

5   Canadians like Red Berenson (Michigan), National Team player Marshall Johnson, and Jimmy Brown (Denver) left the country to play hockey and get an education—as did Bob Bauer, Jr., the son of Bobby Bauer.

6   Brian Conacher, *Hockey in Canada: The Way It Is!* (New York: Poseidon Press, 1993), 52.

7   Mickey McDowell, interview with author, August 16, 2018.

hockey gave young men the slimmest of chances of making it to the NHL, many were willing to try it.[8] Bauer had seen the problem at St. Michael's and then faced it with the challenge of recruiting players for the National Team. Conacher stated it plainly, "Father Bauer was a renegade: 'These boys don't have to give up everything on the gamble, the high-risk gamble that they may, *may* have a chance to play professional hockey.'"[9]

Bauer was philosophically sympathetic to workers' rights and the development of youth, as highlighted in the work of Basilian associates like Garvey. Drawing from Maritain's thought, many Basilians worked toward a just society that tries to ensure individuals are able to attain their due. As NHL players struggled to forge a players' association in the 1950s and '60s, Bauer sought a path for young hockey players who were particularly vulnerable. To develop persons more completely, widen their opportunities, and ensure a more stable income long term, Bauer's conviction required a revolt against the NHL-driven system. Not everyone had a terrible experience in junior hockey, to be sure.[10] Nonetheless, Bauer theorized that there was a systemic problem in junior hockey no matter the examples to the contrary: young men needed a hockey route inclusive of their full development.

The smallness of a six-team NHL hurt players' chances of making the big league, but it inadvertently enabled Bauer to find quality players for the National Team. Instead of players wasting away in the minor leagues, Bauer's National Team program became a viable path to help young men develop as hockey players and prepare for careers after hockey. The team became leverage for top players, too, giving them a serious option outside of the North American professional leagues. For instance, superstar Bobby Orr considered joining the National Team in the Summer of 1966.[11] Widening opportunities for players was a matter of justice for Bauer and something an increasingly educated public could get behind.

8   Terry O'Malley, interview with author, June 26, 2018.

9   Brian Conacher, interview with author, June 5, 2019.

10   For instance, National Team player Morris Mott had a positive experience playing in Weyburn, Saskatchewan, for Jack Shupe, who later coached the Medicine Hat Tigers in the WHL. Morris Mott, interview with author, July 15, 2020.

11   Orr's agent, Alan Eagleson, recalled: "We talked and talked—and believe me, Father Bauer could talk—about Bobby and other good young players spending a year with the national team." Alan Eagleson and Scott Young, *Powerplay: The Memoirs of Hockey Czar Alan Eagleson* (Toronto: McClelland & Stewart, 1991), 57.

The program's patriotism also spoke to Canadians: Canada was being frozen out of its own game. Most NHL teams and many Junior A teams were owned by Americans. Despite only two Canadian cities having NHL teams, league-announced expansion in 1966 included six additional teams in US cities. In a political cartoon Bauer kept from the early 1960s, an NHL version of the map of Canada had a hockey rink extending from Toronto to Montreal.[12] The rest of the undeveloped nation was depicted as unexplored tundra. A player left this wilderness for the hockey "fortress" in central Canada, where he remained controlled by American interests or left the country for the US. At a time when Canada was trying to foster its own national identity, American commercial interests held sway over Canada's game.

Soon, the two Canadian NHL clubs grew to dislike the National Team, because Bauer tried to expand its program. The Montreal Canadiens' general manager Frank Selke—at one time the coach of Joe Primeau—had earlier offered some financial help to the National Team.[13] But when Sam Pollock became general manager in 1964, his team became increasingly defensive of its talent. Despite a previous working relationship between the Maple Leafs and St. Michael's Majors, owner Conn Smythe had little time for the hockey-priest, and his son, Stafford, "vowed to never sit down at the same table" as Bauer.[14]

Everyday Canadians were led to wonder if the National Team could ever defeat other National Teams without professional players. One French commentator argued that the brutal reality of the Cold War made realizing an Olympic ideal impossible.[15] Because sports were professionalizing, as exemplified by the state-funded Soviet team, playing non-NHLers internationally was foolish. Fans typically wanted to win and prove Canadian hockey supremacy.

For Bauer, the trend toward hyper-commercialized sport produced moral conflicts that required serious discussion. Although he had earlier

---

12   James Reidford, "NHL Map of Canada," Box 1, File 6, Bauer fonds, Basilian Archives.

13   And this despite the fact that the Montreal team remained upset over a Bobby Bauer player choice at Squaw Valley. Alan Watson, *Catch On and Run with It: The Sporting Life and Times of Dr. Bob Hindmarch* (Vancouver: AJW Books, 2012), 182.

14   Paul Conlin, "The Cold War and Canadian Nationalism on Ice: Federal Government Involvement in International Hockey during the 1960's," *Sport History Review* 25, no. 2 (1994): 60.

15   Jacques Lemoyne, "Le Père Bauer Croit que l'Idéal Olympique Doit Nous Inciter à Continuer!" *La Liberté et Le Patriote*, September 4, 1964, 10.

seen promise in US college football as the model for Canada's national sport, he began to realize the imperfections of this system, too. In another *Sports Illustrated* (*SI*) article that Bauer had his National Team read, he pointed out a moral crisis in sport to his players.[16] The article's starting point was NFL quarterback (and former Notre Dame standout) Paul Hornung who was caught gambling on football games while playing for the Green Bay Packers.[17] The article argued that subtle changes in sport were affecting players, coaches, and owners; the excess of success was undoing persons who had an inability to cope with achievement. Drawing on sociological thought, the piece claimed that in a very commercialized sporting environment the athlete "is first turned into a robot, and then sometimes the robot becomes a burglar." Bauer made his point: the excesses of commercialized sport often de-humanized people.

Bauer's vision of the National Team fit with the sporting ideal portrayed in the *SI* article: "Sport will retain its character, its unique quality as sport, only so long as the player and the fan and the kid who stands three hours in the rain to get Willie Mays's name on a crumpled program believe in its sacrosanctity."[18] The article echoed Carr's sporting tradition: "The purpose of sport is to offer recreation, to lift men out of their humdrum experience and offer them an exultation they cannot find in other pursuits. When profits become the only objective, sport dies. The name is retained, but it is a mockery." This stark image—of sport taking control of its players and destroying their humanness—was Bauer's central concern. Knowing that the American college route was not without its pitfalls—and being convinced of professionalized hockey's danger to youth—Bauer sought to protect the sacrosanctity of sport. Hockey has expenses, and Bauer knew that it always had entrepreneurial elements. But he rejected the idea that all hockey paths must lead to the NHL, especially when the professionalism of hockey players was unlike that of other professionals, like doctors and lawyers, who were self-regulated and carried economic clout.[19]

---

16   David Bauer, Letter to *Sports Illustrated*, June 28, 1963, Box 5, File 1, Bauer fonds, Basilian Archives.

17   John Underwood, "The True Crisis," *Sports Illustrated Vault*, May 20, 1963, https://www.si.com/vault/1963/05/20/593620/the-true-crisis.

18   Underwood, "The True Crisis."

19   O'Malley, interview.

Bauer Moves Behind the Scenes

Bauer stepped down as head coach of the National Team—though he remained general manager—when it moved to Winnipeg for the start of the 1964–65 hockey season. Bauer accepted the CAHA's decision to merge his team with one of the best senior teams in the country, the Winnipeg Maroons, creating a permanent venture maintained by the CAHA and a group of backers from Western Canada.[20] While new head coach Gordon Simpson focused on winning the world championships in 1965, Bauer believed the team should build itself toward the 1968 Olympics.[21] Simpson's drive for short-term success clashed with Bauer's aspiration to build a program in four-year cycles, where players could both earn a post-secondary degree and improve their play at the highest amateur level of competition. Nonetheless, Bauer avoided confrontation with Simpson, as he became increasingly aware of those who disapproved of a peace-building approach for Canadian international hockey. Under Simpson's coaching, the team earned a disappointing fourth place at the 1965 World Championships in Finland. Support for the team grew in Winnipeg, however, where the city opened an international-sized rink called the Dutton Rink, named after the fallen sons of "Red" Dutton, a former NHL president who clashed with league owners and eventually resigned his position.[22]

As the general manager, Bauer was concerned about losing National Team players to the professional leagues. Playing for an education, personal and skill development, and joy of the game could only go so far against the lure of a hockey salary.[23] For example, Brian Conacher left the team and joined the Maple Leafs in 1965. Bauer also had difficulty finding adequate competition for the National Team in preparation for world tournaments. Over several years, only five games were played against NHL teams—all American clubs. The professional teams found playing the National Team a near no-win situation,

20 S. F. Wise and Douglas Fisher, *Canada's Sporting Heroes* (Don Mills, ON: General Publishing), 290. This included people like Max Bell and Père Athol Murray, and Manitobans Mervyn "Red" Dutton and James Richardson.

21 Conacher, *Hockey in Canada*, 44–45.

22 Jack Bennett, "Richardson Stresses Importance of Nats," *Winnipeg Free Press*, September 14, 1967, Box 7, Carr—Correspondence and Misc. file, St. Mark's College Archives.

23 Jim Coleman, "Canadian National Team Deserves Some Support," *Edmonton Journal*, October 22, 1965, 12.

according to one hockey executive.[24] He recalled that manager Bauer would beg to play a higher level of competition against Western Hockey League teams in the 1960s. The problem, however, was that Bauer's teams were a defensive juggernaut that checked opponents to a standstill. Low-opportunity matches were not crowd pleasers and losing the game embarrassed a second-tier professional league that struggled for status versus the NHL. The executive called out Bauer: "You're setting us up for failure and you're gaining notoriety at our expense. And you want us to help you to do that?" It felt like the entire hockey system was pushing back against Bauer.

The shift to management and less frequent contact with the media suited Bauer and his religious community. His work in hockey still remained contentious for many religious confreres despite support from some prominent Basilians. Father Neil Hibbert explained that during seminary training, young men were taught to show a Christ-like humility in the face of people's adulation because of their priestly status.[25] It was not about self-hatred, Hibbert recalled, but there was a strong sense that personal status should not become greater than the God served. This minimalist mindset meant that Bauer was positioned better as a manager than as the coach of the team, as far as his confreres were concerned. Yet the prominence of his role disrupted collaborative activities with other Basilians at St. Mark's and ran the risk of negatively impacting the community, according to a long-time associate.[26]

The demand to downplay his personal status as founder of the National Team sometimes required a contortionist act. Bauer was an ardent supporter of amateur sport and knew how to command a room. He spoke powerfully about how the hockey system was exploiting young men; this moved his audiences.[27] Yet his religious training prepared him to take a backseat whenever possible. Bauer told the story about sitting beside a girl on a flight to Saskatoon.[28] He wore his roman collar and, as they struck up a conversation, she asked, "What are you going to Saskatoon for?" He said, "It might sound strange but I'm going to talk on the fundamentals of ice hockey." She responded, "That's not so strange. I see a priest on TV involved in hockey." He said, "Would you like to meet him?" But before she could answer, he said,

24   Murray Costello, interview with author, June 3, 2019.
25   Neil Hibbert, interview with author, January 16, 2019.
26   Chris Lang, interview with author, June 6, 2019.
27   Bruce Kidd, interview with author, June 5, 2019.
28   Carmelite Sisters of St. Joseph, interview with author, January 17, 2019.

"Would it really make any difference if you ever met him?" And she said, "No." At the luggage claim, he introduced himself to her parents and said, "I want to meet the parents of a girl who had enough sense that it wouldn't make any difference if she met me or not."

Bauer's humorous way of dealing with his celebrity deflated his public persona as a hockey leader and helped maintain his priestly humility. This contortionist act is best captured in the image of Bauer Ltd., which produced automotive soundproofing and seat padding. These things were hidden from sight, but were required for a smooth ride. The company made an invaluable product that was best unseen and unheard. This was similar to Bauer's constructed identity. He felt driven to make hockey and sport in Canada better for young people, yet wanted to do so away from media or celebrity status. It was a difficult, if not unrealistic, combination.

As Bauer took on a more behind-the-scenes role, he began writing formal documents about his ideas on hockey. He had at his disposal a number of academically-minded priests at St. Mark's, and it was his friendship with Father James Hanrahan that proved instrumental.[29] Hanrahan taught in UBC's history department while also writing about education and spirituality. "Hanny" could also be the life of any social event. He was a large but unathletic man from Nova Scotia who had a booming voice and a knack for making up songs when needed. His spirit endeared him to the Bauer family on somewhat regular visits. With Bauer, he shared an interest in sport and offered his support through editorial work on Bauer's writing.

Hanrahan would become the Superior General of the Basilian Fathers during the 1970s. His high-profile role further protected Bauer's work on multiple hockey projects when some Basilians questioned Bauer's contribution.[30] Hanrahan was known for his shrewdness when nurturing different men's gifts, even if these were not traditionally cultivated within the religious community.[31] Instead of hemming Bauer in, Hanrahan frequently edited and typed hockey-related documents that Bauer created as a blueprint for re-conceptualizing hockey. Hanrahan the academic provided Bauer with a major intellectual source for the promotion of hockey ideals.

29   Lisa Bauer-Leahy, interview with author, January 17, 2019; Paul Burns, interview with author, August 15, 2018; and Don McLeod, interview with author, June 4, 2018.

30   Burns, interview.

31   McLeod, interview.

"The Polite Revolt Against the Tycoons"

In the 1960s, it was obvious that the structure of Canadian hockey was broken, and many wanted to determine a new direction for it. Prior to this, in 1943, the federal government passed the National Physical Fitness Act to aid in national preparedness of future soldiers. At the time, people were concerned about the state's intervention into something in the private realm—sport—but tolerated this incursion even if it was in conflict with the Victorian ideal of gentlemanly sport and athletes who trained without outside financing.[32] With the 1961 Act to Promote Fitness and Amateur Sport, the government began to intervene in elite amateur sport.[33] It founded the National Advisory Council on Fitness and Amateur Sport (NACFAS) that year—Bauer joined in 1964—and was aware of the professional influence on amateur hockey. Unlike the 1980s or today, the Council had modest budgets for grants, which they gave to provinces for hosting sporting events and coaching clinics—and gave to the National Team.

Members of NACFAS pondered how to reform the structures of Canadian hockey, which had become increasingly dominated by professional interests. A *Globe and Mail* reporter called their unrest against the powerbrokers of the sport, "the polite revolt against the tycoons."[34] As the National Team founder, Bauer was one of many Council reformers wanting to make hockey cleaner, faster, and more skillful rather than penalty-filled and overly rough. The problem, according to the article, was that the amateur leaders were "still vague, disunited and hesitant" in their planning: "There is a feeling of ambiguity, of things hidden. Positive actions seem to be taking shape, then they melt away in a haze of pipe-smoke."[35] The Council met infrequently and had no jurisdictional authority over hockey; the state was uneasy about taking control of a sport.

In April 1966, a Hockey Study Committee was created by the NACFAS, with the cooperation of the CAHA, to report on the status of amateur hockey in Canada.[36] The timing was significant, as the CAHA was

---

32   Conlin, "The Cold War," 51.

33   Conlin, "The Cold War," 56.

34   G. E. Mortimore, "Polite Revolt against the Tycoons," *The Globe and Mail,* March 15, 1963, 7.

35   Mortimore, "Polite Revolt," 7.

36   Canadian Department of National Health and Welfare, *Report on Amateur*

renegotiating the professional-amateur agreement with the NHL. Bauer was a major contributor to the report. The committee was chaired by professor William L'Heureux, who had a deep connection with Bauer.[37] L'Heureux had earned a BA in Classics at the Basilian-run Assumption University, and later played for the University of Toronto Varsity Blues.[38] He remained in touch with the Basilians at St. Michael's then and later in his life.[39] A successful hockey player who turned down tryout offers from the NHL, he chose education over hockey—and later teaching over coaching, as he became a leading physical educator in Canada and Dean of the Faculty of Physical Education at Western.[40] L'Heureux wrote an original instructional book on hockey skills that emphasized sportsmanship and the value of education. The book became an award-winning series of short films titled, "How to Play Hockey," and were reportedly praised by Tarasov.[41] Though L'Heureux's writings focused on hockey, he tried to create a way forward for Canadian amateur sport that was realistic, gritty, and long-lasting.[42]

Hockey in Canada by the Hockey Study Committee of the National Advisory Council on Fitness and Amateur Sport, by William L'Heureux et al., Ottawa: Department of National Health and Welfare, 1967, 1–2.

37   Kidd, interview.

38   L'Heureux earned his graduate degree at the University of Toronto. University of Toronto, Students' Administrative Council, *Torontonensis, 1939*, University of Toronto Archives and Records Management Services, 334, https://archive.org/ details/torontonensis?&sort=date. See also, "L'Heureux, Willard Joseph," Donohue Funeral Home, Obituary, accessed May 19, 2021, https://donohuefuneralhome.ca/ tribute/details/4138/Willard-L-Heureux/obituary.html. He played for the Chatham Maroons, who became the Ontario Hockey League Senior Champions in 1937–38.

39   Bill L'Heureux, Jr., interview with author, September 18, 2019.

40   In 1967, L'Heureux was awarded a Doctor of Laws from the University of New Brunswick for being "the most outstanding figure in Canadian physical education and athletics." University of New Brunswick Libraries, "L'Heureux, Willard Joseph," Pomp and Circumstance, 1967 Fredericton Convocation, accessed September 25, 2019, https://graduations.lib.unb.ca/award/17971. He led discussions with the Canadian Medical Association to form the Canadian Association for Sports Medicine. Devon Elliot, email message to author, September 24, 2019. When he retired from Western in the early 1980s, L'Heureux became the head coach of its women's varsity team. L'Heureux, interview.

41   Bill L'Heureux, *Hockey for Boys* (Chicago: Follett Publishing Company, 1962), 92–94 and 7. L'Heureux, interview.

42   University of New Brunswick Libraries, "L'Heureux, Willard Joseph."

Bauer and L'Heureux agreed on the primary danger facing Canadian hockey: if the interests of amateur hockey went unrecognized, then a two-stream system would fully collapse and leave a monopoly for commercialized sport. Based on this belief, the two led a five-person working committee that released the *Report on Amateur Hockey in Canada* in January 1967.[43] The *Report* dared to speak up for amateur hockey: "from the amateur point of view, what is good for the N.H.L. is not necessarily good for hockey in general."[44] Because each had different sets of objectives and values, it was necessary for amateur hockey to be able to function independently from the professional game. The *Report's* definition of amateur hockey asserted that "we have no wish to turn back the clock to the days of 'Victorian' amateurism" since "salary payments in amateur hockey has existed since 1940, and is here to stay."[45] The amateur could still receive compensation for equipment, travel, and the like, but was expected to have a full-time occupation or be enrolled in full-time studies.[46] The committee promoted re-entrenching a nonprofessional track in Canadian hockey outside of the NHL's control. What may have seemed like a high-flown idea actually was grounded in the reality of the situation, given the *Report's* timely release in the face of the NHL's American expansion, possible increased sporting involvement by the federal government, and increased financial backing of the National Team.

Unsurprisingly, NHL leadership showed apathy toward the *Report*. Spokespeople for the league claimed that many of the recommended changes—like ending NHL sponsorship of individual junior teams—were

43   Other committee members included Bauer's former Majors' teammate Judge Frank Dunlap, Max Bell, Bill Crothers, and Professor John Meagher. Canadian Department of National Health and Welfare, *Final Report: Report on Amateur Hockey in Canada by the Hockey Study Committee of the National Advisory Council on Fitness and Amateur Sport*, by William L'Heureux et al., Ottawa: Department of National Health and Welfare, 1968, MG28 I 263 18, 300-6-6, Federal Government Position on Hockey (2 of 2), LAC.

44   Canadian Department of National Health and Welfare, *Report on Amateur Hockey*, 1967, 10. The study drew from questionnaires from hockey people, junior team officials' questionnaires, a review of magazine and newspaper reports, and interviews with many amateur and pro hockey people—including Athol Murray and Joe Primeau.

45   Canadian Department of National Health and Welfare, *Report on Amateur Hockey*, 1967, 19.

46   Canadian Department of National Health and Welfare, *Report on Amateur Hockey*, 1967, 20.

already going into the then-currently negotiated agreement. Montreal Canadiens' Sam Pollock questioned the makeup of the committee: "If I was put on a committee to investigate swimming or basketball, people would ask 'what do you know?'"[47] Pollock's comment was typical. It showed how professional hockey people usually ridiculed or sarcastically addressed the report. They were unwilling to let educational principles influence their business interests.[48]

At this time, Bauer and Hanrahan submitted a "privately circulated" document to CAHA leadership to assist their negotiations of the revised pro-amateur agreement. It laid out a positive future for the National Team program, which depended on a healthy, more independent amateur system, and thus asked for an examination of the structures of the game.[49] The two priests stated that the National Team required better financing—including scholarships for players and salaries for coaches—and that a clear division from paid-to-pay hockey was needed. They affirmed professional hockey as "admirable" despite its "defects."[50] Amateur hockey, too, should want to produce top-rate players with a desire to win through strong coaching, yet maintain the goal of the development of the individual player—both as a human being and a hockey player.

In the private document, they argued for a firewall between professional hockey and amateur play. They admitted that, in theory, the two should be able to work alongside each other, but that theory "leaves out the fact that the game is run and played by human beings" with varying motives. Thus, when amateur hockey organizations were in financial troubles in the 1930s and they reached out to the NHL for assistance, "the professional sponsorship seemed a heaven-sent remedy." "It turned out," they bluntly stated, "to be a pain-killing drug that led to terrible addiction." The National Team, on the other hand, could be "an alternative to the young players who are at present subjected to intense pressures in the direction of professionalism."[51]

47   The Canadian Press, "Fitness Council Asks for Bill to Protect CAHA from NHL," *The Globe and Mail,* January 26, 1967, 25.

48   "Bauer, David," Canada's Sports Hall of Fame Archives.

49   David Bauer and James Hanrahan, "Canada's Future in World Hockey: A Private and Confidential Survey for the Information of the Recipient Only," 1966, Hockey Canada Library (3), Hockey Canada Archives.

50   Bauer and Hanrahan, "Canada's Future."

51   Bauer and Hanrahan, "Canada's Future."

The Establishment of the Canadian Hockey Foundation

Because the CAHA relied on NHL dollars for administrative support, Bauer found that the amateur association's support of his program was partial and financially inadequate. To avoid living a hand-to-mouth existence, Bauer promoted the establishment of a Canadian Hockey Foundation.[52] This legally incorporated, non-profit organization would "give public backing" to his project, allowing it to voice support for a values-based hockey and ensure the professional game made "a satisfactory arrangement" with amateur sport. As it garnered significant supporters, it resembled amateur hockey's past: it was a throwback to local boosterism from civic and business interests across the country that supported senior men's hockey. The Foundation would promote the National Team's objectives, arrange its financing, and manage these funds.[53] Bauer dreamed large: he envisioned multiple National Teams requiring an annual amount of $250,000 for one hundred player scholarships. Funds were to come from corporations—who could sponsor a player for $2,500 per year—and a nationwide, individual contribution campaign. The federal government would match funds dollar-for-dollar.

The Canadian Hockey Foundation, about which Bauer and others held meetings across the country in the second half of 1966, was formally established in March 1967, just a couple months after the *Report* was released. It began with a meeting of more than twenty persons: CAHA officials, Bauer and new National Team head coach Jackie McLeod, and several interested businessmen from across Canada whom Bauer solicited for aid.[54] John J. Wintermeyer became its president. He was a provincial politician from Kitchener, who was Bauer's cousin and later served as chair of Bauer Industries.[55] Two early supporters of the National Team, Max Bell and James Richardson, became co-chairs of the Foundation. Other Western Canadian,

---

52 Bauer and Hanrahan, "Canada's Future." This too had been promoted in the *Report*.

53 Bauer and Hanrahan, "Canada's Future."

54 Canadian Amateur Hockey Association, "Minutes of Annual Meeting," 1968, 66; and "Canada's National Hockey Team: A History," File 37, David Bauer fonds, Canada's Sports Hall of Fame Archives.

55 Bauer Family, *Bauer (A Family History of Edgar and Bertha's Family)* (Waterloo, ON: Self-published, 2003), under "Edgar Jacob Bauer," private Bauer family records owned by Paul Schmaltz. Wintermeyer's father, Alfred, was groomsman at Dave's father's wedding.

patriotic businessmen with connections to hockey and university learning joined—they were also tired of an Eastern-centric NHL.[56] Their goal of supplying the National Team with players to defeat the communist-bloc hockey teams conflicted with the professional leagues' aim of recruiting players from the same talent pool.[57]

The Foundation proved useful during its short existence. Financially, it provided the National Team with a $40,000 grant to begin a second National Team in Ottawa, coached by Jack Bowness.[58] The expansion to the bilingual city was especially necessary for building a talent pipeline for French Canadian players.[59] By the spring of 1968, Richardson, Bell, and Sinclair had already invested $132,000 in the National Team.[60] Support from prominent Canadian business and civic leaders pushed back against the Americanization of the sport.

The Hockey Foundation also provided political support for an organization whose parent body, the CAHA, was working in step with its major rival, the NHL. The Foundation members "seriously questioned" and tried to intervene in the NHL-CAHA agreement before it was signed in the summer of 1967.[61] The Foundation began discussing the hockey tug-of-war in Canada and possible policies to make the National Team viable. Because the group had, in Bauer's words, an "independent position" in hockey, it began "to study the [hockey] situation and to formulate policies" that could lead to a successful National Team rising up from the shadows of amateur hockey's

---

56 Laurie Artiss, newspaper editorial, August 16, 1967, Box 7, Carr—Correspondence and Misc. file, St. Mark's College Archives, 22. Others were Ian Sinclair, Cyrus McLean of Vancouver, Norm Whitmore and Bud Ramsay of Regina, Culver Riley of Winnipeg, oil executives Charles Hay and Vernon Taylor, and Ray Bauer, Dave's brother.

57 Artiss, newspaper editorial, 22.

58 Canadian Amateur Hockey Association, "Minutes of Annual Meeting," 1968, 66.

59 Denis Messier, "Sport Choc," *La Tribune: Sherbrooke*, May 8, 1967, 11. Bauer's speaking engagements included Quebec cities, as also noted by Marcel Desjardins, "Un Souhait du P. Bauer: Voir le Hockey Fleurir au Canada," *La Presse*, October 4, 1965, 40.

60 Canadian Amateur Hockey Association, "Minutes of Annual Meeting," 1968, 66.

61 File 38, David Bauer fonds, Canada's Sports Hall of Fame Archives, 8; and, Julie Stevens, "The Canadian Hockey Association Merger: An Analysis of Institutional Change" (PhD thesis, University of Alberta, Edmonton, 2001), ProQuest Dissertations Publishing, 53.

past.[62] Developing a more expanded role, the Foundation approached the federal government for a charter that would establish it as a non-profit able to use donations other than for scholarships alone. Its title would be Hockey Canada Corporation.[63] Political unrest and the 1968 federal election delayed the sought-after changes, but the title would be taken as the global brand of Canada's national governing body of hockey decades later.

With the Canadian Hockey Foundation for support, the National Team believed it would start attracting some top Canadian junior hockey players and alter the dominant structures of the sport.[64] Secretary-Manager of the Foundation Jack Hargreaves argued that a united, national effort was required in order to beat the Russians at the Canadian game—and that it might take a decade to accomplish the task.[65] The Foundation would "abide by the new agreement between the NHL and CAHA and won't touch a boy until he hits twenty years of age, but if a boy and his father come to us," Hargreaves admitted, "we could make the odd exception."[66] The willingness to disregard the parameters of player movement in Canadian hockey was a warning shot: the National Team would not simply accept leftover players from the NHL. The move angered professional hockey men and potentially could upset their de facto cartel of control in the sport. Hargreaves added, "We have no intentions of ever giving up on the National Team idea, which was Father David Bauer's brainchild."[67] A revolt had begun.

"The Battle is Far from Over"

Both the *Report* and the private document for CAHA leadership sought to galvanize the CAHA, in Bauer's words, around a "people-first" vision for a new pro-amateur agreement with the NHL.[68] Approved in the summer of 1967, the agreement brought the end of NHL sponsorship of amateur junior teams and introduced a comprehensive national draft to determine

62   David Bauer, *Report to Munro*, 1971, Marc Bauer-Maison Collection, 30.

63   File 38, David Bauer fonds, Canada's Sports Hall of Fame Archives, 8.

64   Jack Hargreaves, Letter to Gordon Juckes, September 11, 1967, MG28 I 151 24, Canadian National Hockey Foundation, CAHA fonds—A18, LAC.

65   Dan Rosenburg, "Roach Joins Ice Nationals," February 1, 1968, MG28 I 151 24, Canadian National Hockey Foundation, CAHA fonds—A18, LAC.

66   Hargreaves, Letter to Gordon Juckes.

67   Rosenburg, "Roach Joins Ice Nationals."

68   Bauer, *Report to Munro*, 14.

which team owned the professional rights of amateur players.[69] Despite these victories, many hockey people protested the trimming of the earlier CAHA-voted calendar date from December to May for the age of the draft.[70] Moving actual professionalism several months earlier helped the NHL fill out six expansion team rosters added for the 1967–68 season. Bauer, L'Heureux, and the rest of the "polite revolt" were upset at other negotiated points.[71] They were disappointed that the CAHA accepted a definition of amateur based on *not* being a professional, instead of on the positive ideals of amateurism. This acceptance made the "polite revolt" look like supporters of naïve Victorian amateurism. As well, NHL payments for players developed by junior teams were not to be distributed through a CAHA Draft Commission but incentivized and delivered to each team. Thus, it was commercially advantageous for individual teams to produce drafted players. In Bauer's words, "the professional mentality continued to dominate."[72]

Bauer complained that junior teams drafted 15- and 16-year olds, like his nephew Bob Jr. playing midget hockey in Kitchener-Waterloo, which often required them to leave home to play for their team. He questioned: "By what right do a group of junior operators, looking only to their own profit, determine that a fifteen year old boy must leave his home in order to play hockey at the level suited to his talents?"[73] In effect, the professionalism of hockey was offloaded on to the junior programs themselves.[74] Bauer added: "If any other group of men in this country undertook to make their fortunes by exploiting sixteen to twenty-year olds while hindering or preventing their proper education public indignation would be overwhelming."[75]

The NHL-CAHA agreement was also detrimental to the National Team. The program could not negotiate with players drafted by NHL teams in May until October 21 of each year. That meant that a player could not enroll in

69 Bauer, *Report to Munro*, 18.

70 "Canadian Amateur Hockey Association's Decision on Age Limits Protested by Group in Toronto," *The Globe and Mail*, January 22, 1968, 18.

71 Hockey Committee, "Final Report to the National Advisory Council on Fitness and Amateur Sport," February 26, 1968, MG28 I 263 18, 300-6-11, Canadian Amateur Hockey Association, 1968–1974, LAC.

72 Bauer, *Report to Munro*, 18.

73 Bauer, *Report to Munro*, 19.

74 Bruce Kidd and John MacFarlane, *The Death of Hockey* (Toronto: New Press, 1972), 56–59.

75 Bauer, *Report to Munro*, 19.

fall-term, post-secondary courses as a National Team player and had few other options to choose from by mid-term. This made recruitment of players even more difficult, or, in Bauer's words, "a constant struggle."[76] Working through the Foundation, however, potentially allowed Bauer to recruit players outside the NHL-CAHA agreement.[77] This move put the National Team program at odds with the NHL, while the agreement explicitly stated that Bauer's program was not to receive NHL monies for player development—unlike junior teams.[78]

After a decade of butting heads with the NHL, Bauer had become increasingly critical of its domination. For instance, in an interview months after the Innsbruck Olympics, he said, "The pros must realize that hockey is obligated to a boy in more ways than the athletic. The human personality must be liberated in every way and developed to the fullest potential in the classroom."[79] Elsewhere, he added that the "pros dominate the game from the cradle to the grave": "We have lost sight of the fact that we must distinguish between the objectives of professional hockey and amateur hockey."[80] Problems encountered with the St. Michael's Majors were now reappearing on the national stage.

Bauer reported the complexities of the hockey situation to his Basilian superior, Father Eugene Lebel, at St. Mark's in Vancouver. Lebel was a former St. Michael's all-star running back in football.[81] In an April 1968 letter, Bauer reviewed meetings set up with the federal government in Ottawa "to discuss the next steps to be taken over the lack of concern shown by the CAHA on the committee report on the pro-amateur agreement."[82] He wrote with disgust that "the CAHA is becoming an appendage of the NHL. In fact, the full time employees of the CAHA receive their payment out of a $75,000 grant from the NHL." The NACFAS, claimed Bauer, is "disturbed" that CAHA appears

---

76 Bauer, *Report to Munro*, 20. See also Kidd and MacFarlane, *The Death of Hockey*, 80 and 84.

77 Bauer, *Report to Munro*, 25.

78 Bauer, *Report to Munro*, 20.

79 Dick Beddoes, "No Nation Is an Island," *The Globe and Mail*, August 31, 1964, File 1, David Bauer fonds, Canada's Sports Hall of Fame Archives, 14.

80 George Lonn, *Faces of Canada* (Toronto: Pitt Publishing, 1976), 265–67.

81 E. C. Lebel, "Overview of Lebel," I, 1986 VIII 11, Box 4, File 1, Lebel, E. C. fonds, Basilian Archives.

82 David Bauer, Letter to Fr. Eugene Lebel, Spring 1968, Box 7, Carr—Correspondence and Misc. file, St. Mark's College Archives.

willing to "go it alone with NHL support financially." Bauer concluded, "the battle is far from over."[83]

When Bauer and L'Heureux released the third and final document of the Hockey Study Committee,[84] they held nothing back. Because NHL player development funds supported junior hockey, Bauer and L'Heureux claimed that the CAHA was no longer an amateur operation and should be ineligible for federal government grants.[85] They encouraged provincial governments to pressure the CAHA by legislating against professional interference in minor hockey. Hockey players, they argued, should effectively choose where they play—including the National Team—without the interference of the NHL. Speaking in May 1968, L'Heureux threatened that if the CAHA did not cut ties with the NHL, the large majority of its members under the age of 15 could band together and begin a new hockey system.[86] Things were reaching a tipping point.

CAHA leadership felt betrayed by Bauer: he was forgetting their past work with the National Team and youth hockey. Dan Johnson, president of CAHA in Newfoundland, handwrote a long letter to Bauer in response to the *Report*. He chided Bauer, writing, "Are you with us or against us in the C.A.H.A.? How can you come amongst us taking an active part and then let your name be party to such a report?"[87] Johnson speculated whether Bauer only supported the CAHA when it was politically advantageous and now sided with the National Advisory Council. Did Bauer simply want to control many of the top junior players for his National Team? Johnson's angry rebuttal led to his claim that the *Report* "is only a joke" and that Bauer should have raised his concerns at a CAHA semi-annual meeting.

The final Hockey Study report also pointed its finger at the NHL for its treatment of the National Team: "That there should be opposition is not surprising. The whole nature of the National team, its purposes, structure

83   Bauer, Letter to Fr. Lebel.

84   D. MacIntosh and M. Hawes, *Sport and Canadian Diplomacy* (Montreal: McGill-Queen's University Press, 1994), 26. The second report focused on minor hockey and was released in October 1967.

85   Hockey Committee, "Final Report."

86   Bob Ferguson, "Federal Intervention in Hockey Needed," *Ottawa Citizen*, May 28, 1968, 28.

87   Dan Johnson, Letter to Fr. Bauer, January 13, 1969, Box 1, File 8, Bauer fonds, Basilian Archives. Johnson's letter piled on his many frustrations, even joking, "Father I am only to page 7 and still going strong. It is a good thing I was not an apostle. It would take a life time to read my gospels."

and character, has from the start run counter to the established pattern of organization of hockey in Canada," which ultimately promoted "the ideal of hockey as a professional career."[88] The NHL had only given "the most nominal co-operation," summarized a different statement.[89] The Maple Leafs and Canadiens had never played against the National Team, while some of Bauer's players feared being ostracized by NHL managers if they refused a professional contract.[90] For Bauer, L'Heureux and others, Canadian hockey needed to escape the trappings of the professional tycoons.

The National Team program and its Canadian Hockey Foundation were at odds with the NHL and the CAHA. The situation was boiling over.

Support for Bauer and the Hockey Alternative

Pressure was mounting on the federal government to take a more active role in sport. For instance, in 1961, Lester Pearson, who was the Leader of the Opposition, responded to a government member's praise for amateur ideals in sport: "[With] all the publicity attached to international sport and the fact that ... communist societies use international sport ... for the advancement of prestige and political purposes, it is a matter of some consequence that we ... develop and regain the prestige we once had ... in international competition."[91]

Pearson, who became Prime Minister of Canada from 1963 to 1968, was an excellent athlete. He played ice hockey for the famous Oxford Canadians, an amateur team of academics studying in the UK. His prowess for stickhandling earned him the nickname, "Herr Zigzag," and he briefly became a member of a Swiss hockey club Davos, making him eligible to play for Switzerland in the European championships.[92] Soon Pearson became a

---

88   Hockey Committee, "Final Report."

89   File 38, David Bauer fonds, Canada's Sports Hall of Fame Archives, 4–5.

90   "Le Père Bauer Doit Bien Se Demander ce qui Lui Arrive," *Le Petit Journal*, June 30, 1968, 48.

91   Canada, *Parliamentary Debates*, House of Commons, September 22, 1961 (Lester Bowles Pearson, Leader of the Official Opposition), https://www.lipad.ca/full/1961/09/22/4/.

92   John English, *Shadow of Heaven: The Life of Lester Pearson, Volume 1: 1897–1948* (London: Random House UK, 1994), 83; Lester B. Pearson, *Mike: The Memoirs of the Rt. Hon. Lester B. Pearson, Volume Two: 1948–57* (Toronto: University of Toronto Press, Scholarly Publishing Division, 2015), 48–49.

lecturer at the University of Toronto, where he coached university football and hockey teams. He recalled: "I loved doing this ... working them hard but keeping the fun in playing, without all the pressures that now have become common in competitive sport."[93]

When Bauer and L'Heureux's *Report* reached the prime minister's desk, there was hope that Pearson the sportsman would increase federal government involvement and implement protections for amateur hockey. Some national and provincial organizations had already endorsed the *Report's* recommendations. However, its exhaustive detailing of NHL interference in amateur hockey, and its demand for an examination of the reserve clause under the Combines Investigation Act, were too bold for Pearson and his Liberal government. Pearson rejected the *Report* and forcefully scolded L'Heureux for trying to undermine the positive influences of the NHL and *Hockey Night in Canada*.[94] Challenging the might of the league was too much, especially for politicians seeking reelection. The dismissal of the *Report* and the committee's frustration led its junior researcher, Bruce Kidd, to write a now classic book on Canadian hockey, *The Death of Hockey*.[95] Without federal government backing, Bauer and his National Team were increasingly vulnerable to the advances of corporate hockey.

Some support remained for Bauer's National Team program. Reporters stayed up late into the night talking with Bauer about hockey and its problems. They gave him and his program a long leash because they realized that Bauer was trying to do the impossible in attempting to change hockey in Canada. Some were intrigued by Bauer, like long-time sports writer Jack Matheson: "I often think that if I had one interview left before being shipwrecked on a desert island I'd probably choose Father Dave."[96] His views intrigued reporters. Following Innsbruck, he spoke with journalist Dick Beddoes about delaying young players' entrance into the NHL so that they could develop educationally and athletically—which would enable the National Team to potentially have top young players.[97] The addition of the Ottawa-based team

93 Pearson, *The Memoirs*, 53–54.

94 Kidd, interview. Today the Lester B. Pearson Award is given to the NHL player voted to be the most outstanding by his peers. The award began in 1971.

95 Kidd and MacFarlane, *The Death of Hockey*, i.

96 Jack Matheson, "Editorial," *Winnipeg Tribune*, September 14, 1967, Box 7, Carr—Correspondence and Misc. file, St. Mark's College Archives. Matheson was also the father of the Hockey Hall of Fame writer Jim Matheson.

97 Beddoes, "No Nation," 14.

found support among French media, as it strengthened the competitive level and skill of the program.[98] Bauer dreamt about an ideal Canadian team for the international game: strong skating forwards like Jean Béliveau, Maurice Richard, and Dave Keon who checked and shot well; puck-moving defensemen like Carl Brewer and Tim Horton who shot the puck hard. Speaking about top junior and NHL players on the National Team program surely irritated NHL ownership.

Changing the organization of hockey was a radical idea, but many could see value in it. By 1967, a Young Nats team began competing in the Metro Toronto Hockey League (MTHL), trying to live up to the ideals of Bauer and the National Program. The team of 12-year-olds were required to show coaches their report cards in order to keep playing and were told that retaliation was cowardly. With three teams in the MTHL, plans were to expand to midget and junior levels by 1969 and provide a separate feeder system for the National Team program.[99] Others did want more of an artful style of play and many National Team players, like Marshall Johnston and Ken Dryden, went on to play (and later become executives) in the NHL.

Support for the National Team required backing from university hockey. The long history of amateur ideals in the collegiate game made for an obvious connection. In a private letter from 1963, Bauer explained a common purpose: "to free amateur hockey from professionalism in order that our national game gain a position of greater respect and prestige."[100] Roots of the game lay in university hockey, where the first recorded indoor game was played by McGill University students in 1875. The students formed the university's first official hockey club that year, and in 1894 played the first international collegiate game versus Harvard.[101] Playing according to the values of amateurism, teams soon formed the Canadian Intercollegiate Hockey Union, around the time that Carr began organizing hockey teams at St. Michael's. The first national

98 Jacques Lemoyne, "L'Équipe Nationale de l'Est Remporte Deux Victoires et Apprend Une Leçon!" *La Liberté et Le Patriote*, December 21, 1967, 4.

99 Bob Pennington, "A National Experiment—On Ice," *Toronto Telegram*, December 29, 1967, "Bauer, David William," Alumni Files Record, University of Toronto Archives, 11.

100 David Bauer, Letter to Duncan McLarty, September 14, 1962, Box 5, File 1, Bauer fonds, Basilian Archives.

101 Steve Knowles, "Canadian College Hockey," in *Total Hockey: The Official Encyclopedia of the National Hockey League*, ed. Dan Diamond et al. (Kansas City, MO: Andrews McMeel Publishing, 1998), 417–24.

championship under the Canadian Intercollegiate Athletic Union (CIAU) took place in 1963. The CIAU was not known as a pipeline for the NHL, but rather a place for university students to play competitive hockey. Universities were leery of the path taken by US colleges in football. University athletics' opposition to professionalism in sports left it rooted in older definitions of amateurism, but their support was necessary for Bauer's project.

Bauer Addresses Violence in Sport

Around this time, Bauer took part in a half-hour documentary on the CBC about violence in sport.[102] This philosopher's earnest yet conversational way of speaking was not ideal for television audiences, but he nonetheless tried to explain how violence promoted by overly commercialized sport threatened the well-being of the players in the game.[103]

Bauer's explanations in the documentary rested on a pillar in Maritain's Thomistic thinking: humans require harmony between the life of the body and life of the mind because human beings are a unity of body and soul. The challenge of life, according to Bauer, is to re-establish these harmonies "in everyday life from morning to night." The danger of a sporting life, Bauer argued, is that emotions can overwhelm or block out reason; then "our lower natures completely dominate" and "the desire to love" is conflicted with the desire to hate. In the case of hockey, money and violence had become central motivators, and Canadian boys left home at 16 to play junior hockey. The situation provoked Bauer to quote seventeenth-century philosopher Blaise Pascal: "Not to know the relative importance of things is to be ever a child or a slave."[104]

Whereas aggressive team sports can exhibit physical violence, Bauer argued that any contest that drives participants to seek victory can cause interior "psychological violence." To combat this mental insecurity, Bauer explained, coaches and managers should "create buffers and create human situations where a player can understand the limits of his potential." Even when a player is demoted, teams are obligated to find value in him, trying to harmonize his abilities, the challenges before him, and his mental health.

---

102   Gary Lautens, "Violence in Sports," Heritage, CBC production, March 12, 1967.
103   "Bauer, David," Canada's Sports Hall of Fame Archives. See also Paul Schmalz and Steve Freiburger, interview with author, January 18, 2019.
104   Lautens, "Violence in Sports."

Bauer remarked that the greatest teams provide the best supports for players' well-being: "Because we are primarily human ... we respond best to human treatment. And wherever we act and think consistently with what we are, I really believe that you will get the finest. [It] will flower in the person, whether he is an amateur or a professional."[105] Pointing out toxic patterns within elite sport is a step toward finding a peaceful harmony between mind and soul; thus, players can understand their limits, cultivate their humanness, and develop rationally so as to sidestep destructive emotions and actions. Too often, he concluded, overt violence like fighting was promoted in hockey: "We elders bear a terrific responsibility for the effect of our actions on the young."[106]

Recruitment and the 1968 Winter Olympics

Bauer travelled endlessly in the late 1960s, seeking out player talent and advocating for the National Team. He often visited his mother, who still lived in the Waterloo area along with many of his siblings. His family owned a cottage beside Lake Huron, west of Waterloo, where his summertime stays allowed him to connect with the hockey community in southern Ontario.[107]

Bauer's never-ending meetings with players in cottage country and across the nation was buoyed by optimism arising from the founding of a second National Team in Ottawa in 1967. Bauer increasingly received letters and phone calls from interested young players, which encouraged his continued efforts.[108] He felt he lacked a couple of goal-scorers and a superior defensemen who could make the difference against top European teams. The most fortunate break the team caught was when all-star defenseman Carl Brewer had a contract dispute with the Maple Leafs. Brewer thought he could find something more to his liking in the National Team. A devout Catholic, he petitioned many confessors for help with his decision to join the team.[109] After much deliberation and effort, he was given his release from the Leafs to play in the 1967 World Championships. A thinker by nature, he was fascinated with the idea of combining education with hockey and thought that

105 Lautens, "Violence in Sports."

106 Stan Obodiac, "Father Bauer Man of the Hour," 1961, Bauer Fr. David file, St. Michael's College School Archives.

107 Schmalz and Freiburger, interview.

108 "Bauer, David," Canada's Sports Hall of Fame Archives.

109 Susan Foster and Carl Brewer, *The Power of Two: Carl Brewer's Battle with Hockey's Power Brokers* (Toronto: Key Porter Books, 2007), 48.

the National Team would be different from professional hockey. He hoped that "working with Father Bauer would help him regain his faith and find his purpose in life."[110] Bauer, however, wanted Brewer the defenseman more than Brewer the soul-searching Catholic who had once aspired to become a priest. Bauer rebuked any Catholic hockey player who praised him for his success as a priest.[111] Thus, Brewer complained that Bauer had not given him the time and attention demanded, leaving the player somewhat discouraged.[112] Nevertheless, Brewer was an incredible addition to the team.

Another notable hockey player with the National Team was Ken Dryden, who played for the team at the 1969 World Championship and stayed on for the 1969–70 season to tend the net while completing his law degree. Dryden, who became one of the most prominent thinkers of the game, knew that making the Montreal Canadiens lineup was unlikely because the team already had two formidable goalies. Dryden the idealist liked the idea of combining hockey and education: "If I turned pro with Montreal, the instant cash would be great ... but who needs it?"[113] The National Team helped produce many lawyers, in fact, and Bauer was pleased to see players taking university studies and challenging the image of "dumb" hockey players.

Jackie McLeod became the head coach during the 1965–66 season. McLeod, a former NHLer, had played some youth hockey at Notre Dame in Wilcox. He received a call to meet Fathers Bauer and Murray. McLeod recalled: "Father Bauer asked me if I would be interested in coaching the national team. I spent two days there, not so much being interviewed as ... he was getting my philosophy on life."[114] Bauer and McLeod worked well together, and enjoyed the team's biggest success at its gold medal victory in the 1967 Centennial Cup in Winnipeg. Bauer found in McLeod a coach dedicated to international hockey and full of integrity.[115]

Bauer promoted the power of team spirit to overcome talent shortcomings. Rick Noonan, a former student at St. Michael's who became a trainer with the National Team, gave the example of the team that played in the 1965 world

110   Foster and Brewer, *The Power of Two*, 52.

111   Bob Hindmarch, interview with author, August 17, 2018.

112   Foster and Brewer, *The Power of Two*, 62.

113   Dryden, *Playing the Shots*, 73.

114   *Hockey Hall of Fame Magazine*. "Bauer." 1989. St. Michael's College School Archives. Bauer Fr. David file, 42

115   Greg Oliver. *Father Bauer and the Great Experiment: The Genesis of Canadian Olympic Hockey* (Toronto: ECW Press, 2017), 216.

tournament in Tampere, Finland. The team was disjointed because it was a mix of previous National Team members and senior men's players from Winnipeg.[116] Bauer was fond of road trips and evenings that included sing-alongs to unite a team. He frowned on watching TV during dinners. For this reason, Bauer phoned a team favorite, George Faulkner, living in Newfoundland, to ask him to join the team in Finland—with his guitar.[117] Bauer wanted hockey players with character, personality, and a sense of humor.

Bauer continued to view that National Team as a national symbol, an ideal for young people to aspire to and to promote the country internationally. In a 1966 World Championships game against Czechoslovakia, poor refereeing gave the National Team eleven penalties and disallowed two goals in a 2–1 loss. The discouraged team and coach debated Bauer about quitting the tournament, long into the evening. After two newspaper reporters failed to change the team's mind, Bauer then brought in the Canadian ambassador for support and argued that "if you quit now, all the players that come after you won't have this opportunity that you had."[118] The players backed down, knowing that their efforts were about more than hockey, and Bauer kept alive the cornerstone of his Canadian hockey alternative.

Going into the 1968 Grenoble Olympics, the National Team was an underdog. Nevertheless, they beat the Czechs, Swedes, and Finns. If they won their final game against the Soviets, they would take home the gold medal. That game was not close, with the Russians winning the gold medal 5–0.[119] Russian dominance was clear. Beating the Russians at the Olympics would have rewritten the National Team story. Bauer kidded that the victory would have elevated him to a cardinal.

Government Intervention and the Task Force on Sport

Bauer's National Team had respectable showings internationally, but did not win a world championship against the best teams in Europe. Their moderate success supported recommendations from the Hockey Study Committee: an unencumbered team that had fair access to the country's top young talent could

---

116   Rick Noonan, interview with author, May 27, 2019.

117   Noonan, interview. Faulkner also participated in the 1967 World Championships in Austria.

118   Oliver, *Father Bauer*, 148–50.

119   Conlin, interview.

probably win a world championship. However, the lack of cooperation from the NHL handcuffed its potential, and positioned the league as the possible savior of Canadian international hockey. The National Team looked incapable to many. One French commentator mocked Bauer as an angel sent down from heaven who mysteriously believed that losing a game meant victory.[120]

The end of the stalemate between the NHL and the National Team began during a campaign stop of Liberal leader Pierre Elliot Trudeau in Spring 1968. He promised to investigate all levels of Canadian sport, especially hockey, because of the country's inability to win international tournaments and matches.[121] Given the American influence on Canadian sport, Trudeau's promised task force won political points for his nationalistic vision and assisted with his election victory.

After winning the election, Trudeau established a three-member Task Force on Sport with three goals: to examine the effects of professional sport on amateur sport; to determine the role of the federal government in sport; and to improve Canadian participation in sport nationally and internationally.[122] All three aims were in part directed at the National Team, giving Bauer hope that the government would mark out room for his program. The three-member Task Force was commissioned by Health and Welfare Minister John Munro, with businessman Harold Rea as chair.[123] The group sought input from across the country.

Bauer and Hanrahan submitted a lengthy paper to the Task Force on Sport in the Summer of 1968.[124] In it, Bauer and Hanrahan reviewed the successes of the National Team—competitive international representation, university degrees earned, promotion of coaching clinics across the country, and diplomatic gains in Europe—versus failures surrounding its win-loss record internationally and lack of financial backing from the government and

120   *La Liberté et Le Patriote*, "Offre-t-on Notre Équipe Nationale de Hockey en Sacrifice?" December 18, 1968, 5. This originally appeared in Montreal's *Le Devoir* on December 12.

121   MacIntosh and Hawes, *Sport and Canadian Diplomacy*, 7.

122   Canadian Federal Government, *Report of the Task Force on Sport for Canadians* (Ottawa: Queen's Printer, 1969).

123   Rea was also the father-in-law of hockey star Carl Brewer. The other two committee members were Olympian Nancy Greene and exercise physiologist Paul DesRuisseaux. Canadian Federal Government, *Task Force on Sport*.

124   David Bauer and James Hanrahan, "Paper Submitted to the Task Force on Sport," Summer 1968, Box 1, File 8, Bauer fonds, Basilian Archives.

the general public.[125] Its inability to "gain total victory" was raised time and again by National Team nay-sayers. Bauer was unsurprised: "The whole nature of the National team ... has from the start run counter to the established pattern of organization of hockey in Canada.... The National team, with its invitation to young players to break out of this [professionally-oriented] system ... issued a challenge that was not likely to be ignored."[126] The priests were not the only churchmen complaining about the sport. In February 1969, the widely distributed United Church *Observer* heavily criticized organized hockey participation for boys. The Synod of the Anglican Church in Canada had earlier condemned the child slavery of the NHL.[127]

Bauer and Hanrahan's written critique of the NHL pointed out "a fundamental weakness" of the CAHA: its inability to "guarantee a reasonable freedom for the team" despite the fact that it ran amateur hockey in the country.[128] Without restricting the NHL's control, Bauer argued that "young boys" would continue to be "lured, under promises of fame and future in hockey careers—promises which for many, if not most, must be illusory." Instead, he believed that improvements to amateur hockey would improve the professionals. A more collaborative relationship between the two included Bauer's boldly proposed "World Amateur Tournament" pitting top professional and amateur team against one another for the Stanley Cup.[129] A more combative solution called for the development of a rival, pan-Canadian professional league that could develop players for international competition and avoid the meddling of the NHL.[130] Radical ideas challenged the status quo and led Bauer to become increasingly defensive about the National Team program.[131] He felt attacked by for-profit hockey from all sides.

In a letter written to Hanrahan later that fall, Bauer stated his belief that their arguments about organizational problems in Canadian hockey and the over-reaching power of the NHL had impacted the committee and its

125   Bauer, *Report to Munro*, 26.

126   Bauer, *Report to Munro*, 27–82.

127   Kidd and MacFarlane, *Death of Hockey*, 53; and *Montreal Star*, "N.H.L. Given 'Bodycheck' By Anglicans," September 11, 1952, 55.

128   Bauer, *Report to Munro*, 28–29.

129   Bauer, *Report to Munro*, 31.

130   "Thoughts for Tuesday Meeting – Task Force," MG28 I 151 25, A19, Canadian National Hockey Foundation, Federal Task Force on Sport for Canadians, CAHA fonds—A18, LAC, 69.

131   McDowell, interview.

direction: "[O]ur article—your article has been the real backbone of Dr. Rea's report as well as for the final proposals of the fitness council's hockey report which was handed in to the government."[132]

Before the Task Force report was completed, representatives from hockey groups met at a Summit Meeting held in December 1968 at the Chateau Laurier in Ottawa. Bauer was not invited. Attendees advocated for open competition, making professionals eligible in international tournaments. They also supported the formation of "a corporation to be known as Hockey Canada Incorporated," with a board made up of representatives from different bodies, including the federal government and the NHL.[133] The National Team would be filled with professional players.

The Summit's direction clashed with Bauer's vision, which questioned why control of both domestic and international hockey should be handed over to professional hockey men. The philosophical differences between Bauer and powerbrokers of the game left him exposed. For example, Conn Smythe declared that the National Team would always be a failure.[134] He mocked Bauer: if the priest-coach could make it work, Smythe would run for prime minister and he would recommend Bauer as pope. Smythe allowed no room for Bauer's broader, educationally-concerned hockey model. Many hockey men sabotaged the National Team at every turn, denying Bauer the best players and slandering his name to potential recruits.[135]

Around this time, a CAHA lawyer went to discuss the league's potential support of the National Team with ownership of the Montreal Canadiens and Toronto Maple Leafs, along with league President Clarence Campbell. According to the lawyer, Hartland and David Molson, Stafford Smythe, and Campbell "did not appear to be particularly pleased" that Bauer remained involved in the administration of the team. As noted in this book's introduction, the lawyer wrote: "I explained that Father Bauer had been devoted to the National team for several years, he was instrumental in helping form the club originally and that he had been most loyal.... I

---

132   David Bauer, Letter to Fr. Hanrahan, 1968, Box 36, "Bauer, Dave 1971–1980" file, St. Mark's College Archives.

133   Lou Lefaive, Letter to Mr. L. A. D. Stephens, January 9, 1969, MG28 I 263 18, 300-6-8, Hockey—General, 1969–1975, LAC.

134   Conn Smythe, *If You Can't Beat 'Em in the Alley* (Toronto: McClelland & Steward, 1981), 233.

135   Kidd, interview.

pointed out that in my opinion the publicity which might arise from his being side-tracked could be most disadvantageous to Mr. Campbell's office and the Canadien and Maple Leaf organizations. Mr. Campbell agreed with this."[136] The men were clearly against the National Team expansion to two teams. The CAHA attorney complained that the executives' attitude hamstrung the National Team, as they demanded that Bauer's every move be approved by the NHL.[137]

When the Task Force findings were released at the end of February 1969, the NHL sat comfortably within Hockey Canada. On one hand, the document echoed Bauer and others who criticized hockey's promotion of violence and its distasteful moral influence.[138] It even stated how Bauer's program's recruiting efforts faced heavy resistance from professional hockey and junior teams. It agreed with the earlier *Report* that the draft age of twenty years old was "too low" and that it was wrong for the NHL to contribute to the administrative expenses of the CAHA. It called for many structural changes to address these and other problems.[139] On the other hand, the Task Force did not strategize exactly how hockey should be organized in Canada, nor make room for a serious hockey-education alternative.[140] It focused on inefficiencies within the administration of Canadian sport, rather than ensuring some independence for amateur hockey and the National Team.[141] Rea and the other members affirmed the creation of national teams in other sports, where athletes could receive an "intensive training programme" in athletics with improved, professionalized structures.[142]

For the Task Force members, hockey on the world stage marked the final battle between amateur and professional sporting interests.[143] Whereas Bauer saw the Task Force as an opportunity for a renewed definition of amateur sport and its meaning for the nation, others thought the demise of

136 W. J. Hopwood Jr., Letter to Gordon Juckes, June 12, 1968, MG28 I 263 18, 300-6-11, Canadian Amateur Hockey Association, 1968–1974, LAC.

137 Hopwood, Letter to Gordon Juckes.

138 Canadian Federal Government, *Report of the Task Force on Sport*, 24 and 27.

139 Canadian Federal Government, *Report of the Task Force on Sport*, 31.

140 Canadian Federal Government, *Report of the Task Force on Sport*, 33.

141 "Canada Backward in Sports, Administration is Pitiful: Rea," *The Globe and Mail*, May 13, 1969, ProQuest Historical Newspapers, 32.

142 Canadian Federal Government, *Report of the Task Force on Sport*, 67; Kidd, interview.

143 Canadian Federal Government, *Report of the Task Force on Sport*, 11.

Bauer's National Team program was inevitable. The Task Force document noted that changes brought about by technological and social revolutions over the previous hundred years had changed the cultural phenomenon of sport. The text even quoted futurist Marshall McLuhan, who claimed that "sport is a magical institution, celebrating by a precise ritual the impulses that seem most necessary to social functioning and survival in any given group."[144] The document's culturally-aware vision for sport accepted the demise of amateur ideals. Even hockey's ability to advance international diplomacy was of little value to the many Canadian hockey fans who were "discouraged, pessimistic, angry, or demanding of a better performance" internationally.[145]

The Task Force's endorsement of open competition in international hockey gave the NHL the upper hand. Professional hockey could dominate the sport and seek immediate gains in international competition.[146] Trudeau's foreign-policy strategy included Canada playing a decisive role in bringing the Soviet Union into the mainstream of international politics.[147] Over and above any criticisms leveled by the Task Force or Bauer, the league still had unrivaled access to the best players in the country, and the federal government saw international victory as a means to improve global relations and bolster national unity.

Hockey Canada and the Neutralizing of the National Team

Although the name "Hockey Canada" originated with the Hockey Foundation, the establishment of an organization under that title by Minister Munro was the brainchild of Rae.[148] With the filing of the articles of incorporation of Hockey Canada on February 24, 1969, the Hockey Foundation was disbanded.[149]

---

144 Canadian Federal Government, *Report of the Task Force on Sport*, 7.

145 Canadian Federal Government, *Report of the Task Force on Sport*, 30; MacIntosh and Hawes, *Sport and Canadian Diplomacy*, 25.

146 Conlin, "The Cold War," 66.

147 MacIntosh and Hawes, *Sport and Canadian Diplomacy*, 31; Gary Smith, *Ice War Diplomat* (Madeira Park, BC: Douglas and McIntyre, 2022), 70–87.

148 Canadian Federal Government, *Report of the Task Force on Sport*, 30; MacIntosh and Hawes, *Sport and Canadian Diplomacy*, 27. Hockey Canada was established prior to the release of the Task Force Report at the end of February. Canadian Amateur Hockey Association, "Minutes of Annual Meeting," 1968, 66.

149 Deidra Clayton, *Eagle: The Life and Times of R. Alan Eagleson* (Toronto: Lester & Orpen Dennys, 1982), 77.

Hockey Canada was given the mandate to organize and support international representation of Canadian hockey, and to assist the development of hockey domestically.[150] But creating a comprehensive vision for Canadian hockey was problematic, because board members represented various organizations: the National Team, the NHL, the NHL's Player Association, the federal government, CAHA, CIAU, and the business community. These organizations each had vested interests that pulled Hockey Canada apart rather than drawing it together in a single vision of the sport.[151] Despite former Hockey Foundation members Max Bell, Ian Sinclair, and Charles Hay taking on leadership roles, the inclusion of the NHL on the board signalled that the league wanted a lead role in the global game.[152] As Young noted: "By agreeing to join Hockey Canada, the NHL moved a step closer to [accessing the international game]. They knew then that they had finally defeated Father Bauer."[153]

Bauer maintained cordial relations with Minister Munro in the hope that things could be salvaged. Munro, seeking to smooth difficulties with Bauer, argued that "the 'Bauer concept' was not dead. Rather it had been put in a larger frame, the hope being that greater co-operation from the NHL representation in Hockey Canada would open up a better player supply for the national team."[154] He wishfully thought that the philosophical and pragmatic divide between parties could be overcome. Munro's big tent approach ensured the NHL's supremacy.[155]

The CAHA handed ownership of the National Team over to the Hockey Canada Corporation, but it still maintained its voting seat on the IIHF and control over any international hockey events for the nation.[156] The National

150   Clayton, *Eagle*, 77–78.

151   Conacher, *Hockey in Canada*, 125. One author remarked, "their diverse interests ultimately created bickering, and several people were caught in the cross-fire." Clayton, *Eagle*, 78.

152   McIntosh and Hawes, *Sport and Canadian Diplomacy*, 27; Morris Kurtz, "A History of the 1972 Canada-USSR Ice Hockey Series" (PhD thesis, The Pennsylvania State University, State College, 1982), ProQuest Dissertations Publishing, 30.

153   Scott Young, *War on Ice: Canada in International Hockey* (Toronto: McClelland & Stewart, 1976), 150.

154   Douglas Fisher, "A Hockey Series That Challenged Canadians' View of Themselves," *International Perspectives* (November/December 1972): 15.

155   O'Malley, interview. See also Hindmarch, interview.

156   Canadian Amateur Hockey Association, "Minutes of Annual Meeting," 1968, 138–40.

Team continued despite an uncertain future. Bauer declared that once Hockey Canada took charge of the program and gave prominent powers to "men with a background in junior and professional hockey," the ideals and generosity of his players were "ridiculed" and had no place "in Hockey Canada's plans."[157] Thus, Bauer summarized, "Salvation, it seemed, would come from the professionals." Bauer chided that in the summer of 1969 fourteen former National Team members, including players who were cut from that year's world championship team, were signed by NHL teams: "Yet these players were not good enough to be considered in Hockey Canada's future plans!" Bauer added that that summer produced no signings of "outstanding junior players" to the National Team. Hockey Canada showed little concern for the team's long-term future.[158]

Bauer's hockey alternative was on life support, yet he was still named a member of the original board of Hockey Canada. In Bauer's words: "The composition of its board had been a delicate and difficult matter. I was included on the board only after a series of complicated meetings, and only with the understanding that I was not to say anything. I was to be seen and not heard.... I agreed to this because I hoped that Hockey Canada might do some good and I did not want to appear to be opposed to it or to hinder it."[159]

Government influence within Hockey Canada did not counterbalance the desires of the NHL.[160] Hockey Canada quickly succumbed to the values of corporatization and professionalization. Bauer, CAHA representatives, and other Hockey Canada board members would be outvoted time and again by NHL supporters.[161] The successes of the National Team program were neutralized.[162]

Hockey Canada Withdraws from the 1970 World Championships

On January 4, 1970, Minister Munro, flanked by CAHA President Earl Dawson and Hockey Canada's Charles Hay, withdrew from the 1970 World Championships—despite the fact that the event was being held in Winnipeg

---

157   Bauer, *Report to Munro*, 39.

158   Bauer, *Report to Munro*, 32.

159   Bauer, *Report to Munro*, 33–34. Bauer added, "Again, I think you will remember this, [Minister] John [Munro], because it was finally decided in your office."

160   Stevens, "Canadian Hockey Association Merger," 55.

161   Scott Young, *100 Years of Dropping the Puck: History of the OHA* (Toronto: McClelland & Stewart, 1989), 249.

162   Young, *War on Ice*, 157.

and Montreal that spring. Munro explained at a news conference: "The day is coming where these imaginary distinctions [between amateurs and professionals] are no longer valid. It goes back to the day when sports were the preserve of the well-to-do."[163] Amateurism was cast as outdated and a form of classism, despite Bauer's attempts to rebrand his traditional ideals as a real hockey alternative. Dawson said bluntly, "We quit. We will not return until ... we can play our best players."[164] Shamateurism frustrated many Canadians. Other nations' players were paid secretly. According to one report at the time, Russians paid their hockey players better than their doctors, the Czechoslovaks received nearly $1000 in monthly wages, and the Swedes were paid discreetly.[165] Many Canadians found this unjust and wanted Canada to compete with its best players.

Bauer believed that the delegation's decision to withdraw from the world championships was shortsighted and wrongheaded, according to his Report to Munro.[166] Hockey Canada's lack of experience in international hockey and geopolitical realities meant they had not taken into account that the IIHF was run by the "wily politician" Bunny Ahearne, who had grown an organization through cooperation with Czechoslovakia, Sweden, and the Soviet Union along with giving "little favors" to minor countries to control IIHF voted-decisions. These countries determined Canada's participation and the eligibility of its top players. Bauer complained: "How often I have watched with amazement as innocent Canadian delegates have approached meetings apparently convinced that their Russian counterparts were just fellow sportsmen who happened to speak a different language! And the Czechs! They are the stalking horse for the Russians ... time and again our delegates have been taken in with the idea that the Czechs were our friends. As for the Swedes, in my experience they have always been unpredictable and unreliable."[167]

Bauer explained his diplomatic path toward expanded player eligibility in his Munro report. Canadian delegates in Crans, Switzerland, in April 1969, negotiated gains toward professional involvement—i.e., Canada would be allowed to use nine professional players from outside the NHL, and also

---

163   John Walker, "Old Rules Labelled 'A Charade,'" *Edmonton Journal*, January 6, 1970, 83-48-378, University of Alberta RCRF.

164   Walker, "Old Rules."

165   Journal News Services, "Swedes Demanding Ahearne's Resignation," *Edmonton Journal*, January 5, 1970, 83-48-378, University of Alberta RCRF.

166   Bauer, *Report to Munro*, 40–41.

167   Bauer, *Report to Munro*, 41.

players reinstated as amateurs by February 10, 1969. While the media made a big deal about the use of nine professional players, Bauer thought the latter concession was more significant.[168] If the "NHL were willing to give the CAHA some autonomy," a number of professional players could have joined the team before the February deadline. Bauer believed "our performance [in Crans] left me wondering about the quality, if any, of our diplomacy. In my opinion we alienated most of our friends and antagonized our enemies beyond repair."[169] Bauer was astounded, arguing that it was foolish "to foist on them in an arrogant manner a sort of power play which no country could seriously hope to bring off in international affairs—not even the might of Russia or the United Sates could do it in the United Nations."[170]

Bauer believed that a cooperative offer to reinstate players' amateur status was still a viable solution. For instance, a National Team had amassed several leading junior scorers from the Ontario Hockey Association who, along with the former professional players, had beaten the Soviets several times on a cross-Canada tour.[171] However, because the Canadian delegation's response to cutting nine professional players from a Canadian team was overblown, an opportunity was missed. Bauer cried, "we huffed and we puffed and blew our own house down. . . . We could have won in 1970. We could have used any players we wanted. All it would have taken was a modicum of imagination from Hockey Canada, and just a bit of cooperation from the NHL and CAHA. Had we done that, we would have been in a very strong [diplomatic]

---

168   Professional and amateur players joined the Canadian team at the annual Izvestia tournament in late 1969.

169   Bauer, *Report to Munro*, 42.

170   Bauer, *Report to Munro*, 42. To Bauer's dismay, the revamped National Team with several former professional players earned a silver medal at the December 1969 Izvestia tournament in Russia. He reported having said to Munro and Hay: "If we wanted the 1970 Tournament in Canada with the use of pros we should take care not to do too well in Russia." He added, "But the desire to teach the Russians a lesson was too strong. The only trouble with teaching the Russians a lesson, however, is that they learn too fast." Bauer, *Report to Munro*, 43. Soon after, at the request of the Russians and Swedes, the IIHF asked the head of the IOC, Avery Brundage, whether a nation's eligibility for the 1972 Olympic Winter Games in Japan would be upset if a national team competed against professional hockey players at an earlier tournament. Bauer quipped that Brundage's rejection of professional hockey players at the Olympics was "predictable" and on January 4, 1970, the IIHF moved to overturn its earlier Crans decision to allow professionals to play in international games.

171   Noonan, interview. See also Bauer, *Report to Munro*, 33.

position in the IIHF. I knew that at the time, but I was being studiously ignored by those who were making the decisions."[172]

Hockey Canada gift-wrapped the situation for the professional hockey men. Bauer ridiculed the CAHA and junior teams who were happy to merely "scramble for the dollars scattered by the NHL."[173] He believed that the National Team had offered a better alternative: it was "the only amateur body which ever seriously rocked the boat of professional dominance of amateur hockey." Bauer felt people had let their unbridled passion for victory blind them.

The End of the National Team

With Canada's withdrawal from international hockey, the National Team lost its main objective and was officially declared dead on a cold February day in Toronto at the Royal York Hotel by Presidents Clarence Campbell (NHL) and Charles Hay (Hockey Canada). Reporter Scott Young wrote that "Campbell admitted that the NHL has always opposed the national team-in-being concept" because it competed for young, Canadian hockey talent.[174] Hay offered a "sort of sad logic," according to Young, that "it was just not reasonable for Hockey Canada to compete with the NHL for players and still have to count on the NHL for general co-operation and support." Both rationales—one admitting that the NHL did not want the competition and the other safeguarding the NHL's claims—protected the status quo. Bauer had lobbied Hockey Canada members to upset the league's business model, but they were unwilling to do so.

Young turned and saw Bauer at the back of the room: "He was staring at the row of big wheels in the front of the room, the professional morticians officiating at the death of the good idea he had borne and nurtured. He said nothing, but his face was not exactly expressionless."[175] In the moment, Bauer saw his aspirations of the past decade and the internationalization of Carr's sporting tradition

---

172   Bauer, *Report to Munro*, 43–44. Prior to the January 4th decision, the Canadian IIHF delegates had already determined that Canada would withdraw from international hockey if the decision to allow nine professionals to play was overturned. Young, *War on Ice*, 155. CAHA leaders Juckes and Dawson had voted against the take-it-or-leave-it approach.

173   Bauer, *Report to Munro*, 44.

174   Scott Young, "Editorial," *Toronto Telegram*, February 20, 1970, 10.

175   Young, "Editorial," 10.

suspended indefinitely. The league had effectively blocked player recruitment and opportunities for compeitition, and now ran Hockey Canada.[176]

Bauer had daringly challenged the NHL's control of hockey. He sought to create, in his words, a "modern and realistic" distinction from professionalism that would protect the development and education of Canadian youth in hockey, where more children would play hockey and receive better coaching and training.[177] His unconventional ideas did not align fully with any national organization, making his authority fragile. Silenced on the Hockey Canada board and lacking authority to make the changes envisioned, his opponents found him a victim to dispose of. Years later, Young shared his opinion on what had transpired: "There were Canadians in NHL offices in the Father Bauer years who must (or at least should) have reflected later with shame on the implacability with which they fought the idea."[178]

In the end, no one not named Bauer had a more consequential role in the founding of Hockey Canada: his National Team was the *raison d'etre* for the organization's establishment. It was unlikely that the professional model promoted by the NHL would have started a National Team. While the league cared little about national team representation, Bauer proved that a pan-Canadian team could be iced and thus contribute to the revival of the nationalist agenda in sport.

Bauer had forced the hand of the NHL to reluctantly get involved with Hockey Canada. Kidd summarized: "if it wasn't for Father Dave, Hockey Canada would never have happened ... he created the environment where that could happen."[179] Bauer cornered the NHL, effectively prompting its membership in Hockey Canada and sparking its role as a supporter of international hockey and, subsequently, the national agenda. Bauer's establishment of the National Team and his work on the National Advisory Council paved the way for an educational tradition for international sport in Canada.[180] It was through Bauer's team-in-being that focused on "excellence, education and values," Kidd wrote, that "his vision set the aspiration for the Canadian sport system to this day."[181]

---

176   Kidd and Macfarlane, *The Death of Hockey*, 89.

177   Bauer, *Report to Munro*, 49; "Bauer, David," Canada's Sports Hall of Fame Archives.

178   Young, *History of the OHA*, 248.

179   Kidd, interview.

180   Kidd, interview.

181   Oliver, *Father Bauer*, book cover.

Overseas in Japan and
Behind the Scenes in Hockey Canada

PRIOR TO THE 1972 SUMMIT SERIES, Soviet head coach Anatoli Tarasov spoke at a coaching conference provocatively titled, "How to Defeat the Russians." Tarasov recalled how Bauer gave the main address, warning that Canadian professional teams would have no easy victories against the Russian National Team.[1] Bauer's advice went unheeded by the coaches, who believed no opponent could upset the best Canadian players. When Tarasov took to the stage, he politely examined differences between the two styles of play. He recalled how it was only Bauer who nodded his head in agreement with his analysis: "All the rest applauded ... the Russian coach who was naïve to believe that Russians were able to keep stride with hockey professionals."[2]

Tarasov pressed more forcefully elsewhere: "We assure you that our boys will be able to knock the eagerness for rough-housing out of anybody

---

1 Anatoly Tarasov, *The Father of Russian Hockey: Tarasov* (Glendale, CA: Griffin Publishing, 1997), 120.
2 Tarasov, *Father of Russian Hockey,* 121.

who tries to play rough against a Soviet hockey team."[3] The approach to hockey, both regimented and scientific, showed its strength in mastery of fundamentals. Yet its capacities were belittled by the Canadian hockey establishment, who believed it was based on rote, mechanical drill.[4] Canadians believed that no other nation could beat its best players at its own game.

Hockey Canada unabashedly promoted open competition in international hockey, as the federal government sought increased political capital associated with the national sport.[5] The organization now charged with promotion of Canada in international hockey decried the sanctions against professional players: "This double standard can result only in humiliation to our team and our country. It's no crime to lose; it's almost one to ice a team that hasn't a chance to win."[6] Even after the demise of the National Team, leaders continued to insult it.[7]

Hockey Canada desperately sought a challenge series with Canada's best players on the ice, even proposing that the Stanley Cup Champion play the IIHF World Champion.[8] A change in Canadian foreign policy toward the Soviet Union made joint sporting competitions more likely. While in the postwar period the nation squarely supported the US and other Western countries, Canada began to soften its position in the 1960s. The government formalized cultural, scientific, and technological exchanges agreements starting in 1966; sport exchanges were formally included in 1971.[9] In early 1972, negotiations among the Soviets, the federal government, Hockey

3   R. Alan Eagleson, "Sport is Big Business and Hockey is a Sport," *The Empire Club of Canada Addresses,* January 29, 1970, 231–47, http://speeches.empireclub.org/61279/data.

4   Brian Kennedy, "Confronting a Compelling Other: The Summit Series and the Nostalgic (Trans)Formation of Canadian Identity," in *Canada's Game: Hockey and Identity,* ed. Andrew C. Holman (Montreal: McGill-Queen's University Press, 2009), 49.

5   Julie Stevens, "The Canadian Hockey Association Merger: An Analysis of Institutional Change" (PhD thesis, University of Alberta, Edmonton, 2001), ProQuest Dissertations Publishing, 56. The CAHA's influence shrank in this new hockey reality.

6   Hockey Canada, "Annual Report, 1969–70," Annual Reports file, Hockey Canada Archives.

7   His credentials listed for his role as director were simply "C.S.B.," the concealed acronym of the Basilian Fathers.

8   Eaton Howitt, "Ahearne: He Must Have Had a Nightmare," *The Toronto Telegram,* October 1, 1970, MG28 I 151 25, A18, Hockey Canada-71, 15.

9   D. MacIntosh and M. Hawes, *Sport and Canadian Diplomacy* (Montreal: McGill-Queen's University Press, 1994), 23.

Canada, the CAHA, and Canadian diplomats at an IIHF meeting in Prague resulted in agreement for an eight-game series between a top Canadian and Soviet team for September. Despite the agreement resulting from the work of several groups, it was Alan Eagleson who grabbed the headlines, since he was the first to phone home with the news.[10]

Eagleson stepped into the void when Hockey Canada's president, Charles Hay, fell ill, and Eagleson thus took on a leading role in the series. The Toronto-based lawyer was known as a fast talker, a natural salesperson, and a hard negotiator.[11] An early biographer of Eagleson stated: "To this day, no one in Hockey Canada likes to admit how quickly it happened, but suddenly Eagleson was zooming past the entire hockey community ... his reward was the power to call the shots in Canada's international hockey."[12] Eagleson was a Director on the Hockey Canada board because he led the NHL Players' Association (NHLPA), but he openly showed disdain for Hockey Canada and wanted to dominate the series according to his wishes.[13]

In a newspaper report a couple of days prior to the series starting, Bauer appeared confident in Team Canada's abilities, but remained frustrated by Canadian arrogance toward international competition.[14] This stemmed from the assumption that the National Team was filled with subpar players. A former National Team player recalled the sentiment: "The NHL is gonna wipe [the Russians] off the map."[15] That changed on a warm night in Montreal on September 2, 1972, when the Soviets took down the NHL's all-star team 7–3. One coach commented that on that night "people were suddenly very aware of the real strength of Father Bauer's student teams."[16] Bauer watched Game 1 on television from Vancouver with Hindmarch: "Father and I shared

10   MacIntosh and Hawes, *Sport and Canadian Diplomacy*, 32–33. See also Gary Smith, *Ice War Diplomat* (Madeira Park, BC: Douglas and McIntyre, 2022), 88–115.

11   Douglas Fisher, "A Hockey Series That Challenged Canadians' View of Themselves," *International Perspectives* (November/December 1972): 18.

12   Deidra Clayton, *Eagle: The Life and Times of R. Alan Eagleson* (Toronto: Lester & Orpen Dennys, 1982), 92.

13   Smith, *Ice War Diplomat*, 118.

14   Rick Prashaw, "Russians' Timing Was a Surprise," *Toronto Star*, September 1, 1972, File 15, David Bauer fonds, Canada's Sports Hall of Fame Archives.

15   Brian Conacher, interview with author, June 5, 2019.

16   Roy MacGregor, "History Appears to be Ready to Repeat Itself—And That's Just Fine," *Unknown* magazine, 1978, Bauer Fr. David file, St. Michael's College School Archives, 47–48.

one of those 'I told you so' moments that gives you absolutely no pleasure."[17] The Bauer family found it hard not to cheer for the Russians, while former National Team players called each other after the game: "We were ecstatic. That game reestablished our self-respect and gave some measure to our accomplishment as a team."[18]

Two years later, Bauer wrote about watching a rebroadcast of that Montreal game and was surprised to hear series hero Paul Henderson describe Team Canada's "shock and dismay" after the first period of the game.[19] Bauer explained: "I was particularly interested in [Henderson's] thoughts as I had had a rather intense debate with Paul ... to tell Paul these truths six years ago about the Soviet players, their individual skills and the team play based on these skills." Neither players like Henderson nor organizers like Eagleson cared to hear from Bauer.[20]

Bauer must have felt further vindication at the end of the Montreal game when the NHL players predictably resorted to rough tactics against the Russians. One writer noted: "The loss to the USSR in Montreal seemed, in the eyes of many beholders, far less of a *national disgrace* ... than the behavior of Team Canada on and off the ice."[21] Author Kennedy summarized this reaction as shamefully felt by all Canadians: "That loss was taken as a national castration."[22]

Bauer attended the remaining three home games played across the country, including in Winnipeg, where he was honored at center ice for his work with the National Team.[23] Team Canada finished with only one victory and a tie in the four home games. When Canadian fans booed the team after the game in Vancouver, they sent a message about the team's poor play on the ice and their belief that Canadian values of individualism and freedom should be greater than the collectivist mentality of the Soviets. Kennedy explained: "It simply was not considered possible that the Russian way of doing things

17   Alan Watson, *Catch On and Run with It: The Sporting Life and Times of Dr. Bob Hindmarch* (Vancouver: AJW Books, 2012), 236.

18   Roy MacSkimming, *Cold War: The Amazing Canada-Soviet Hockey Series of 1972* (Vancouver: Greystone Books, 2012), 66. Others made similar statements, like Herb Pinder.

19   David Bauer, Letter to Allyn, January 29, 1974, Box 1, File 6, Bauer fonds, Basilian Archives.

20   Fisher, "A Hockey Series," 18.

21   Jack Ludwig, *Hockey Night in Moscow* (Toronto: McClelland & Stewart, 1972), 42.

22   Kennedy, "Confronting a Compelling Other," 52.

23   Smith, *Ice War Diplomat*, 181.

could work, whether in a hockey arena, in business, or in government.... [Canadians] could not bring themselves to admit that their identity might need to take into account this other [nation] that was so forcefully asserting itself."[24] One former National Team player described just how successful the Russians had become: "You got to be at ice level, burnin' all your rockets and have one of these cowboys walkin' away from you to really understand what's going on."[25] Better training and conditioning were evident. Canadians needed to rethink the game's future.

The image of Canadian hockey did not improve when Team Canada stirred up ugly on-ice brawls and subsequent public relations disasters during two exhibition games in Sweden before traveling to Moscow.[26] Despite Team Canada losing its first game in Russia, it came back to win the concluding three games, which included Henderson's series-winning goal with 34 seconds left in the deciding game. The viewing audience was estimated at three-quarters of the Canadian population, which more than doubled the viewership of the 1972 Stanley Cup Finals.[27] That moment validated professionally-oriented hockey in many minds. That winning goal is remembered as an iconic moment in national history—with a Canadian's arms raised in the midst of dejected Soviet players. Like many Canadians, Bauer appreciated the spirit of Team Canada—its grittiness and togetherness, like soldiers in battle.

The direction of Team Canada was markedly different from Bauer's approach. Team Canada took on the personality of Eagleson: scrappy, crude, emotional, and bitchy.[28] Their rough-and-ready approach contrasted with a more rational yet spirited model. Bauer was unimpressed with the players' behavior: "Our team acted terribly—and then when I heard about that reception and chartered plane—I just about passed out as did Chris Lang, Douglas Fisher, etc. They admitted to me in Prague that they sold out and that it was just one long nightmare" since Eagleson took over.[29]

24   Kennedy, "Confronting a Compelling Other," 53.

25   Mickey McDowell, interview with author, August 16, 2018.

26   MacIntosh and Hawes, *Sport and Canadian Diplomacy*, 35. Even the Canadian ambassador to Sweden, Margaret Meagher, reprimanded the team in their dressing room.

27   Smith, *Ice War Diplomat*, 237.

28   Fisher, "A Hockey Series," 13 and 20. Canadian Ambassador to the USSR, Robert Ford, detailed the diplomatic difficulties arising from the behaviors of the players. Smith, *Ice War Diplomat*, 240.

29   David Bauer, Letter to Barbara Bauer, October 2, 1972, Terry O'Malley Collection. Team Canada partied afterwards and on the return plane to Canada.

One Montreal evening had vindicated Bauer, yet it was overshadowed by the Summit Series victory. Author Dowbiggin captured this point: "most hockey people quickly abandoned the lessons of Father Bauer as if they were flared lapels and paisley ties.... [The Summit Series win] meant that testing the will of opponents *well* outside the rules was part of the game."[30] Leaders like Sam Pollock noted how Bauer saw the changes coming in international hockey long before others did; however, few acknowledged the importance of naming social issues that were haunting Canadian hockey.[31]

Breaking Ethnic Barriers for Japanese Hockey

As Canada's participation in international hockey changed, Bauer worked on two fronts to recalibrate his hockey alternative. First, he took up a fortuitous hockey opportunity in Japan, where his openness to other ethnicities, determinedness for peace internationally, and a youthful sense of adventure were rewarded. Second, he tried to redirect Hockey Canada.

Bauer knew next to nothing about Japanese hockey until he met Father Bobby Moran.[32] Moran, who had played hockey earlier at St. Michael's College, later became a priest with the Scarboro Missions religious community. In 1964, Moran the missionary packed his hockey skates and boarded a ship for the two-week journey to Japan. The priests' Tokyo headquarters was near one of a few artificial skating rinks owned by the billionaire Tsutsumi Yoshiaki. Moran, who studied Japanese full time upon his arrival, recalled that he often skated late into the evening and, soon enough, joined a local team and then one in Shinagawa. He was able to learn more colloquial Japanese from locals, and accrued publicity for the church through national television and newspaper reports.[33] Later, in a role as player-coach of Seibu Tetsudo, a team owned by Tsutsumi, Moran became the first foreign-born player in Japanese professional ice hockey. The six-team professional league had equivalent abilities to Canadian Junior A and B teams.[34]

---

30   Bruce Dowbiggin, *The Meaning of Puck: How Hockey Explains Modern Canada* (Markham, ON: Red Deer Press), 118–19.

31   Mike Zeisberger, "Fr. David Bauer," *Toronto Sun*, November 10, 1988, Box 2, last file, Bauer fonds, Basilian Archives, 118. Pollock was the famed general manager of the Montreal Canadiens.

32   Bobby Moran, interview with author, July 25, 2020. Moran had played Junior B hockey elsewhere previously.

33   Robert Moran, "Apostolic Hockey," *Scarboro Missions*, 1966, 5–8.

34   Moran, "Apostolic Hockey," 5–8. The Japanese League mimicked national

Tsutsumi was more than a hockey team owner. He was one of the world's wealthiest people, and built up several inherited holdings through the Seibu Corporation. According to Bauer, Seibu "seems to be just about anything and everything. It has stores, ski resorts, skating rinks, hotels, golf courses and recreation centers of all kinds."[35] Tsutsumi devoted resources to develop ice hockey in Japan when Sapporo was awarded the 1972 Winter Olympics.[36] He became the president of the Japanese Ice Hockey Federation and owner of two of the league's teams. Russian coaches were hired by northern teams in Japan, while Finnish, Czech, and Canadian involvement ensured an international flavor and fostered Tsutsumi's business interests (e.g., pulp and paper, an international network of hotels, and specialty products).[37]

At the 1968 Grenoble Olympics, Moran set up a meeting with Bauer at Tsutsumi's request. Bauer agreed to visit Japan that September when, coincidentally, the Soviets were on a tour of the country. Although Tarasov and Bauer negotiated possible games for their teams through translators— no agreements were produced—Bauer also spent time carefully watching practices and sometimes skating with the Seibu team as Moran translated during the two-week trip. Moran recalled feeling that Bauer was purely "a hockey nut," wrapped up in the National Team and hockey organizations. Bauer liked the idea of collaborating with Japanese hockey brokers, instead of surviving hand-to-mouth, as his National Teams had done.[38]

Hockey was the aim of the trip, but Bauer mused about culture. In a letter to Hanrahan during the trip, Bauer wrote of his appreciation of "this amazing country": its beauty, its shrines and temples, the people's willingness to speak

---

baseball rules that stipulated only two foreign born players were allowed on each team. Moran held his position between 1965 and 1968.

35   Donald Boyle, "Promoting Hockey in Japan," *Catholic Week*, December 8, 1973, 4a.

36   Robert T. Moran, Phillip R. Harris, and Sarah V. Morgan, *Managing Cultural Differences: Global Leadership Strategies for the 21st Century*, 7th ed. (Burlington, MA: Butterworth-Heinemann, 2007), 144.

37   Boyle, "Promoting Hockey in Japan," 4a. Terry O'Malley, email message to author, March 6, 2023.

38   David Bauer, *Report to Munro*, 1971, Marc Bauer-Maison Collection, 48. In 1971, after Canada had exited from international play, Bauer told Hockey Canada that he could entice Japanese officials to offer one of two open spots in the tournament to a wild card Canadian team. The offer went nowhere.

with him, and even the promptness of their train system.[39] He marvelled at the "the achievement of the Japanese people." Young people spoke to him about their strong interest in science instead of philosophizing about life's meaning, but he remained impressed how "culture and custom preserve much of the order present."

Christian missionary organizations often assisted in spreading western sports to Japan. Prior to the turn of the century, the YMCA and different Christian schools and colleges introduced sports like track and field and rugby for educational training.[40] Scarboro Mission Fathers arrived in Japan in 1948, after leaving China when Mao Zedong declared a one-party state. Other Catholic religious communities already ministered in the country: the Jesuits established a mission in the sixteenth century and, while many religious communities arrived around the turn of the twentieth century, their work was given greater freedom with the US-imposed democratic constitution in 1946.[41] Yet only a Canadian religious community would have a keen interest in ice hockey, and artificial ice rinks boomed with the backing of the Tsutsumi family.[42] The hockey-minded men built relationships for evangelical purposes at the rink.[43]

There were earlier hockey connections between Japan and Canada. In 1973, Bauer explained that Canada had never sent a touring team to Japan, but there was an early 1936 team made up of Canadians living in Japan.[44] Bauer claimed that Japanese hockey teams had played exhibition games in Canada as far back as 1935; that first team lost its games badly.[45] Other teams

---

39   David Bauer, Letter to Fr. Hanrahan, 1968, Box 36, "Bauer, Dave 1971–1980" file, St. Mark's College Archives.

40   Allen Guttmann and Lee Thompson, *Japanese Sports: A History* (Honolulu: University of Hawai'i Press, 2001).

41   A. Schwade and P. F. O'Donoghue, "The Catholic Church in Japan," in *The New Catholic Encyclopedia*, vol. 7, 2nd ed. (Detroit: Thomson/Gale, 2003), 736–44.

42   Tom O'Toole, interview with author, January 15, 2019. This Scarboro Mission priest also recalled the American army stationed in Japan and their soldiers playing at the Tokyo rinks built by lumber companies, like Seibu.

43   Don Boyle, "Fitsoo-San," *Scarboro Missions*, 1983–1984, 8–10.

44   Boyle, "Promoting Hockey in Japan," 4a. Anne Park Shannon and Lana Okerlund, *Finding Japan: Early Canadian Encounters with Asia* (Vancouver: Heritage, 2012), 167. Players associated with the Canadian embassy were joined by CP and CN representatives.

45   Boyle, "Promoting Hockey in Japan," 4a.

had toured in the 1960s, as international exhibition games were popular around the Christmas season.[46]

With the financial backing of Tsutsumi and support of Canadian coaches, ice hockey was ready to grow in Japan. Bauer immediately accepted the role of advisor to the Seibu team—avoiding an official coaching role and giving him the flexibility to help with a second team—and won Seibu's first championship in 1969–70.[47] The Seibu Bears were based in Tokyo; the Kokudo Bunnies played out of Karuizawa. Teams were owned by companies like Seibu or Oji, the latter of which was a pulp and paper company in northern Japan that sponsored the Oji Eagles. Most players came from the colder, northern island of Hokkaido and became company employees who worked for the business during the off-season and in their post-playing careers.[48] When Bauer arrived in Japan, the professional leagues were new and the total number of players across the country was two to three thousand; by the decade's end, there were about ten thousand players.[49] A well-financed league treated Bauer well. He crowed once that the new Fushimi arena near Kyoto was "more lavish and better than Maple Leaf Gardens—take that Ballard," who owned the Maple Leafs.[50] Bauer invited family members to travel with him to Japan, as he had free dining and accommodation at the Prince Hotel chain owned by Tsutsumi.[51] Scarboro Mission priests joked that it was a difficult way to live out his vow of poverty.[52]

Bauer received support from Basilian leadership for his Japanese exchanges, yet several community members thought he was veering too far from their ministry in education: "C'mon Bauer. Get back into the classroom," one Basilian recalled thinking.[53] Bauer scheduled trips to

---

46 Canadian Amateur Hockey Association, Unsigned Letter to the Czechoslovak Ice Hockey Section, January 7, 1960, MG28 I 151 4, Japanese and European Tours of Canada file, 1959–1960, LAC. Moran, interview. For instance, a Moscow Dynamo team toured Canada in 1957, and the National Team played at an annual Christmas tournament at Colorado Springs. Marshall Johnston, interview with author, August 22, 2019.

47 Boyle, "Promoting Hockey in Japan," 4a. O'Malley, email message to author.

48 J. Simpson, "Stars Fly in Hockey in Japan, Has Flavor of Canada," *The Globe and Mail*, February 26, 1979, S18.

49 Simpson, "Stars Fly."

50 Bauer, Letter to Lisa Bauer, Box 3, File 1, Bauer fonds, Basilian Archives.

51 David Bauer, "Fr. Bauer Notes and Letters," Terry O'Malley Collection, 11.

52 O'Toole, interview.

53 Don McLeod, interview with author, June 4, 2018. Hanrahan was the

Japan between his responsibilies as chaplain at St. Mark's and his teaching philosophy and ethics courses to undergraduate nursing students at St. Paul's Hospital. Often absent from Vancouver, he was understood as "in the air" by his confreres: he was away for his hockey commitments and physically absent from the religious community.[54] His life's work as teacher and mentor fit well with his travel to Japan—even if he was not a pure academic like some priests at St. Mark's.[55]

In Japan, Bauer found a complementary style of hockey. He could persist in his peace-making outreach and bring Canadians and Japanese together through the game. Too often, Canadian hockey fans could be narrowminded and myopic about the international game, where they supported a protective nationalism that cared little about their opponents. Engaging Japanese hockey allowed Bauer to help break down ethnic barriers within the sport.

Bauer needed translators when he coached the Seibu and Kokudo teams, and Moran introduced him to Mel and Herb Wakabayashi.[56] Sons of Japanese immigrants, the two brothers were born in internment camps in British Columbia and Ontario during World War Two.[57] Later raised in Chatham, Ontario, the boys earned hockey scholarships to the University of Michigan and Boston University, respectively, where they became All-Americans. Over time, Mel learned Japanese and translated for Bauer. The elder brother recalled half a century later Bauer's enthusiasm and values when he spoke to the team: "What he really wanted us to learn was the Canadian spirit. The biggest impact he had on me was when he said, 'Mel, hockey's a great sport, but remember to make use of technique but let the spirit prevail.'"[58] Bauer emphasized enjoyment, excellence, and cooperation, and remained positive and open in his demeanor.

The NHL did not scout hockey in Japanese arenas and very few of its players were not white. Japanese hockey was not an upgrade from the National Team, yet in Japan Bauer had ownership's support for a values-driven style

superior general of the entire Basilian community from 1973 to 1981, and worked out difficulties between Bauer and his community. Hindmarch, interview.

54   Neil Hibbert, interview with author, January 16, 2019. Hibbert concluded, "We lost him in a way. We just didn't brush up against him."

55   Paul Burns, interview with author, August 15, 2018.

56   Moran, interview. Moran paid release monies to the Detroit Red Wings in 1968.

57   Mel Wakabayashi, interview with author, July 21, 2020.

58   Wakabayashi, interview.

of game. He disagreed with nativistic or isolationist forms of Canadian nationalism prevalent in hockey. Rather, leaning on the thought of Maritain, Bauer could be openminded. In response to the Vichy regime during the Second World War, Maritain wrote that "racism is ... above all an irrationalist reaction" that rejects wisdom and human individualism, becoming at its worst "a biological inferno."[59] In its quest to restrict and ultimately do away with other races, racism discards the human spirit in its yearning for power. In contrast, Bauer's time in Japan reflects Maritain's integral humanism and its belief in the dignity of each person, both in Bauer's openness to a foreign culture and his opportunity to share values in skating arenas.

Mel Wakabayashi assumed that Bauer did not tell him about his time in the Canadian army in order to protect his image: to avoid causing division or discomfort in Japan. When the Canadian-born Wakabayashi moved to Japan, he recalled facing racism in his parents' homeland, where he was called a foreigner who supported the destruction of Tokyo. Unfortunately, the Wakabayashi family were often viewed as foreigners in Canada as well, despite the boys' citizenship. Mel Wakabayashi heard opponents call out racist phrases on the ice, even as he developed friendships with teammates and classmates.[60] Bauer's time in Japan was against the grain of Canadian hockey culture and in step with Maritain's ideal of "fraternal friendship" amongst all peoples.[61]

Bauer ran practices and set game lineups for the Seibu team. He watched the game from the press box, but gave input to the coaches via a walkie-talkie.[62] Cultural differences between Japan and the West created many impediments when advancing a North American game in Japan. While players might be compliant with a Canadian coach's demands, breaking up a line or grouping of players, for instance, was incompatible with the Japanese social-cultural value of harmony, or *wa*.[63] The Japanese respect for the hierarchical relationship between old and young persons—i.e., *senpai kōhai*—made it difficult to manage a hockey team democratically. For example, it was

59 Jacques Maritain, *The Twilight of Civilization*, trans. Lionel Landry (New York: Sheed & Ward, 1944), 19 and 21.

60 A contemporary examination of Canadian hockey through South Asian voices is offered in Courtney Szto, *Changing on the Fly: Hockey through the Voices of South Asian Canadians* (New Brunswick, NJ: Rutgers University Press, 2020), 1.

61 Maritain, *The Twilight of Civilization*, 59.

62 David Bauer, Letter to Barbara Bauer, February 20, 1974, Terry O'Malley Collection.

63 Moran, interview.

difficult to bench a senior player for missing curfew, which altered disciplining methods and team-building opportunities.[64] The same challenge held true on the ice. An older player often received a return pass immediately from a younger player who sought to honor his senior. An elder player might stand in front of the net in the offensive zone, directing his younger teammate into different corners of the ice.[65]

Japanese cultural practices did not always fit with Bauer's sense of team and the importance of the individual, but he was impressed how the Japanese discouraged violence: "I have yet to see a fight on the ice. If there ever was a brawl, the guilty players would be brought before their families, the company they work for, a press conference, and the hockey league's board of directors. It would be too embarrassing for them."[66] Bauer appreciated how the Japanese system mirrored his ideals: "I'd like to re-establish hockey as an art at all levels. In its true form it is a much faster, cleaner game than we play here in Canada. We don't have to stop body contact, just the needless violence."[67] It was this complementary style that led to Tsutsumi entrusting Bauer with choosing the Japanese National Team in 1974.[68] Other Japanese hockey leaders were pleased with a Canadian tradition that sought the integral development of players.[69]

Japanese hockey in the early 1970s was in its infancy. Its 27 high school teams played only eight games a season, and lacked ice-time for practices.[70] Bauer and others ran hockey camps on fundamentals each spring, to bring players up to Canadian levels of skill development. He explained: "You can teach a young player how to shoot. Most of these boys couldn't fire a backhand or lay down a fast pass when we started but now ... you wouldn't see

---

64   Barry MacKenzie, interview with author, March 12, 2020.

65   Terrence Kennedy, "I Was Warned It Would Be Different," *Scarboro Missions*, 1964, 18–21. Another Scarboro priest noted the decorum in a post-game celebration: players bowed to each other and gave a cheer to the crowd, followed by a bow to it. They concluded with a few tours around the ice.

66   "Back in the Spotlight: Father David Bauer, c.s.b.," Pepsi-Cola International Hockey Classic for the Father David Bauer Cup, December 1–5, 1982, Box 2, Bauer fonds, Basilian Archives.

67   "Back in the Spotlight."

68   David Bauer, Letter to Barbara Bauer, November 12, 1974, Terry O'Malley Collection.

69   Watson, *Catch On*, 11. This was said by Shoichi Tomita, who became the vice president of the IIHF.

70   Boyle, "Promoting Hockey in Japan," 4a.

a whole lot of difference between them and their Canadian counterparts."[71] Bauer's reputation also led to his head coaching the Austrian national team at the 1973 Group B World Championships in Graz.[72]

The experiences of people like Bauer and Moran opened opportunities for people who had played with the National Team and UBC. These players were hockey missionaries, engaging in cultural exchanges through sport. Terry O'Malley and Wakabayashi played and coached for Kokudo, Barry MacKenzie for Seibu.[73] Hockey was played differently in Japan, yet business and language contacts were made. These people were ambassadors of a different Canadian tradition and, in their own way, peace emissaries from the West, carefully handpicked by Bauer to ensure their success and avoid embarrassment. Bill Holowaty, a university player at UBC, adapted well to Japanese society and, in time, helped bring the Muira golf brand to North America.[74] The Japanese sought out the expertise of Canadian players and coaches, and offered benevolent treatment in return.[75] Bauer connected others to hockey in Japan, where he enjoyed time out of the limelight of the hockey world.[76] It afforded him the chance to pray and read widely, and enjoy the accommodations.

After more than a decade of involvement in Japan for Bauer, Tsutsumi ended their relationship. Bauer's south all-star team, representing the main island of Honshu, lost an important tournament against the north island's team of Hokkaido, which determined who should control the country's national team.[77] Tsutsumi was embarrassed by his team's defeat and Bauer was shunned, according to Japanese business customs. Once Bauer agreed

71   Boyle, "Promoting Hockey in Japan," 4a.

72   A newspaper article explained that "he's probably the most sought-after Canadian coach in other parts of the world." *The Globe and Mail*, March 27, 1973, File 27, David Bauer fonds, Canada's Sports Hall of Fame Archives. The team earned a 2–5 win/loss record and allowed twice as many goals as it scored. It was not a good hockey experience for Bauer; he did not coach the Austrians again. Bauer, Letter to Barbara Bauer, February 20, 1974.

73   O'Malley, email. O'Malley stayed for seven years, while others like Dave King, Wally Kozak, and Darryl Sutter were involved in a variety of ways.

74   Bill Holowaty, interview with author, February 1, 2019.

75   MacKenzie, interview. MacKenzie lived there for three seasons and reflected, "I just knew that I was the piece of the puzzle that they wanted, and they'd be quite happy to get rid of me when the time came."

76   Carmelite Sisters of St. Joseph, interview with author, January 17, 2019. MacKenzie, interview.

77   MacKenzie, interview.

to depart from Japanese hockey, he received a large sum of money for his lengthy service, which Bauer used to establish a trust prior to his death.[78] He would return to Japan for a tournament with the 1980 National Team.

Bauer's view of hockey was well suited to Japan. The Japanese sought a faster, passing game with less violence, which also resembled the Russian style. Yet Bauer implemented more hitting and more play up and down the wing in southern Japan than there was in the Soviet-influenced northern game.[79] Bauer's endorsement of a rougher, gentlemanly game was a piece of a larger convergence in the growth of the global game. At a time when Canada had withdrawn from international hockey at the highest levels, Bauer influenced the game globally through his promotion of ideals and philosophies he held central to hockey. With his time spent in Japan—along with hockey tours throughout Europe—he came to understand himself as "a citizen of the world—not only Canada—but Europe, Asia, all over."[80]

Bauer's Influence on Hockey Canada and the Development Committee

Bauer sought to recalibrate his Canadian hockey alternative, despite losing the National Team. He would try to do so as a member of Hockey Canada's board, a position he held for the organization's first two decades.

The Canadian hockey scene remained politically charged.[81] In 1970, three junior leagues based in Ontario, Quebec, and Western Canada split the Junior A ranks and left the CAHA. They later formed the Canadian Major Junior Hockey League in 1975.[82] The World Hockey Association started in 1972, and competed for professional hockey players globally. Amidst this complicated hockey scene, Bauer communicated his hockey philosophy and worked strategically within Hockey Canada. It was a fine line to walk. For instance, he explained how Hockey Canada asked him to speak about advancements in

---

78   Terry O'Malley, interview with author, June 26, 2018. See also, Moran, interview.

79   Greg Oliver, *Father Bauer and the Great Experiment: The Genesis of Canadian Olympic Hockey* (Toronto: ECW Press, 2017), 186.

80   David Bauer, Letter to Barbara Bauer, April 18, 1975, Terry O'Malley Collection.

81   David Bauer, Notes, Box 3, File 1, Bauer fonds, Basilian Archives.

82   Ed Sweeney, "Junior Hockey and the Memorial Cup," in *Total Hockey*, ed. Diamond et al., 407 and 412.

domestic hockey on *Hockey Night in Canada,* between periods on January 30, 1971. Bauer recalled how *Telegram* reporter—and friend of Bauer—George Gross threatened to "attack me in his newspaper if I appeared to support the [Hockey] Canada program—because it would be an endorsement of Canada's action of Jan 4, 1970." Squeezed between competing agendas, Bauer felt exasperated and cried out in his letter, "I know they don't need me Père—but also I don't need them. It will be a fifty-fifty proposition or nothing. They don't have to sell out to me but nor will I sell out to them."[83]

Bauer was an original member of Hockey Canada's domestic hockey committee, which grew in importance with Canada's withdrawal from international play in 1970.[84] Bauer co-authored a 1969 report with Hanrahan that promoted "a program for hockey that will fit the aspirations and needs of this country."[85] The men gave an educational perspective on sport:

A full education must aim not simply at the development of the intellect, but at the development of the complete man, with a well-rounded personality. Physical, emotional and intellectual growth are all involved. That athletics can be of great value in the first two areas and not irrelevant in the third was clear to the Greeks long ago.... The educators of the Renaissance returned to a more balanced ideal [from the Greeks], but were never able to make it effective beyond the circle of a privileged few. From that time on the ideal has never been totally lost sight of.... In practice, however, there has been an oscillation between the dominance of intellectualism—either the theoretical intellectualism stemming from the thought of Descartes or the practical intellectualism coming from Locke—and that of an emotionalism coming from Rousseau and the progressivist approach. There have been instances too of what

83   David Bauer, Letter to Père Murray, February 1971, Athol Murray College of Notre Dame Archives. Frequently, Bauer confided to Père Murray in letters or conversations—and often would later read about it in the newspaper.

84   Ken Martin, "Confidential Letter to CAHA Board," February 25, 1970, MG28 I 151 25, A18, Hockey Canada–70, LAC. This committee was at first called the education committee.

85   David Bauer, James Hanrahan, and Brian Conacher, "The Hockey Canada Corporation and Education," Presentation to the Education Committee of Hockey Canada Corporation, May 14, 1969, MG28 I 151 24, A18, Hockey Canada–70, 1969–1970, LAC. This document is also contained in Bauer, *Report to Munro,* 34–38. They also had the assistance of former National Team member Brian Conacher.

might be called athleticism, an emphasis on sports to the detriment of other educational purposes. In Canada one may say that a reaction to athleticism as seen in some of the football factories of the United States has reinforced an already dominant Lockean tendency in our universities. A better balance is sorely needed.[86]

Their account of two anti-athletics positions within education—followers of Descartes and Locke, emphasizing intellectualism, or Rousseau, a source of progressive education—resembled tensions at St. Michael's College a decade earlier.

The report proposed a way forward, one that avoided athleticism, challenged an overly intellectualized education, and did not settle for a progressivist approach. It included a critique of amateurism overly fixated on excluding money from sport. Those with such a narrow view—idealists who believe "professional sport has grown into a fearsome beast; they naturally fear to touch the tiger even by the tip of his tail"—create a vision of the sport based on "a negative ... mental concept of amateur sport." Instead, Bauer argued for a sporting tradition primarily concerned with the individual's "whole development as a human being." Motivation was found in the fact that "hockey players, as a group, have a lower educational level than any comparable group in North America.... [It] can only be called a national disgrace."[87] The authors' vision required support from Canadian universities and the CIAU. How Hockey Canada addressed this problem, the group predicted, would determine its legacy.

Shortly after their report was presented in May 1969, it was clear that Hockey Canada's understanding of education was narrower than Bauer's.[88] Nonetheless, Health Minister John Munro defended the inclusion of domestic development in Hockey Canada's mandate and affirmed the organization's role in developing hockey in high schools and universities, following an American model.[89] This included a Canadian university hockey tournament, a

86   Bauer, Hanrahan, and Conacher, "Hockey Canada Corporation."

87   Bauer, Hanrahan, and Conacher, "Hockey Canada Corporation."

88   Douglas Fisher and Chris Lang, Memo to Maurice Regimbal, Chair of Education Committee, May 26, 1969, MG28 I 151 24, A18, Hockey Canada–70, 1969–1970, LAC.

89   Journal News Services, "Swedes Demanding Ahearne's Resignation," *Edmonton Journal,* January 5, 1970, 83-48-378, University of Alberta RCRF; Hockey Canada, "Verbatim Minutes of the Board Meeting," Toronto, ON, February 18, 1970,

coaching certification program, and funding for hockey research.[90] A bursary program funded by Sport Canada and managed by Hockey Canada distributed approximately $100,000 per year—in amounts of $400 to $1,200—to university players throughout the 1970s.[91] Bauer, who was on the scholarship selection committee, was pleased that former National Team players, like Morris Mott, earned a bursary.[92] The goals of the development committee included earlier suggestions made by Bauer, but avoided naming a humanistic framework that might be challenged by corporate hockey.

Bauer was critical of the new scholarship program. He saw it as merely a positive gesture rather than a crafted move to make "a decisive difference in the way hockey is being run in Canada."[93] He wondered why the scholarships had not enticed players to stay in Canadian university hockey: "Are the Lafleurs and Dionnes, the top junior players, being as diligently persuaded by Hockey Canada of the advantages of education as they are by Mr. Sam Pollock of the advantages of signing with the Montreal Canadiens? When we had a national team, I could and did argue this with almost every top-flight junior who still had the option."[94] In Bauer's view, Hockey Canada bowed to the interests of the NHL, and its forum-style structure led to forever seeking compromises to its objectives.[95] This disabled it in effecting substantial change, and led to Bauer's admission that "probably I will resign from Hockey Canada."[96]

MG28 I 263 9, LAC. Hockey Canada, "A Summary," February 17, 1970, MG28 I 151 24, A18, Hockey Canada–70, 1969–1970, LAC.

90   Hockey Canada, "Newsletter 1, no. 2," 1970, MG28 I 151 25, A18, Hockey Canada–72, LAC; William A. R. Orban, "Report on the Research and Educational Aspects of Hockey in the USSR and CSSR," December 18, 1969, MG28 I 151 24, A18, Hockey Canada–70, 1969–1970, LAC.

91   Hockey Canada, "Report on Former Bursary Programme," June 1981, MG31 E 72 37, H2 (3), Athletic Assistance Programme 1980–1981, LAC.

92   Hockey Canada, "President's Report: Board of Director's Meeting," June 17, 1971, MG28 I 151 25, A18, Hockey Canada–72, LAC. Hockey Canada, "Newsletter 1, no. 1," 1971, MG28 I 151 24, A15, Fitness and Amateur Sport Directorate–72, LAC. Mott was a graduate student at Queen's University in sport history.

93   Bauer, *Report to Munro*, 44–45.

94   Bauer, *Report to Munro*, 44–45.

95   M & M Systems Research Ltd., "Report: The Organizational Development of Hockey Canada," Hockey Canada Library (11), 1974–75, part I, Hockey Canada Archives, 4.

96   David Bauer, Letter to Barbara Bauer, August 26, 1971, Terry O'Malley Collection.

Coaching Clinics

The development committee was keen to make improvements to hockey coaching. The CAHA had already begun national coaching clinics as early as 1966 in Montreal, but the volunteer organization had limited financing, motivational variances among volunteers, and regional disparities, which produced uneven results.[97] Youth hockey reforms as basic as decreasing body contact or introducing helmets were, according to one executive, "resisted like the devil," as coaches typically followed an adult model of sport.[98] Hockey Canada's development committee rivaled the work of the CAHA and viewed the volunteer-based organization as ineffective.[99] To ameliorate tensions between the two organizations, they formed a Hockey Technical Advisory Committee, where leading Canadian universities assisted with technical and physiological research.[100]

With pressure applied from Hockey Canada and Canada's razor-thin margin of victory in the Summit Series, the CAHA began a more systematic training of youth. Prior to this, no standardized format or coaching certification program was used to develop children's hockey skills in Canada.[101] As chair of CAHA's development council, Hindmarch recalled leading a tour of the Soviet Union's developmental system: "What struck us most was their scientific approach to sport. The Russians were light years ahead of us in that regard. They were studying and implementing all sorts of things—conditioning to name one ... [and] weight-training and nutrition."[102] Soviet coach Tarasov, for instance, told Hindmarch that they knew Carl Brewer

---

97   Oliver, *Father Bauer*, 265.

98   The Canadian Press, "Juckes Reflects on Years in Amateur Hockey," *Lethbridge Herald*, May 27, 1981, 32. CAHA's executive director Gordon Juckes made this point.

99   Martin, "Confidential Letter;" Stevens, "Canadian Hockey Association Merger," 59.

100   M & M Systems Research Ltd., "Report: The Organizational Development," 2. This report's findings were confirmed later that decade, in "Hockey Canada and the Canadian Amateur Hockey Association," circa 1978, Sudbury, Ontario: Laurentian University Press, Hockey Canada Library (2), Hockey Canada Archives.

101   Watson, *Catch On*, 237.

102   Watson, *Catch On*, 263. See also, "Hockey Canada—'The Road Ahead', A Discussion Paper for the Board of Directors," May 12, 1987, private email attachment from Paul Carson, Vice President, Hockey Development of Hockey Canada, January 22, 2019.

skated seven kilometers a game with the National Team; they fed him the puck early and often to wear him down.[103]

Hindmarch led the creation of coach training programs in Canadian hockey.[104] With financial backing from the federal government, he gathered a number of university hockey coaches to run clinics, including Clare Drake, George Kingston, Dave King, Tom Watt, Bauer, and others.[105] Hindmarch wrote the first three levels of the coaching manuals, while the other coaches made revisions. Bauer played an important role in the development of coaching techniques at the national level.[106] For instance, Hindmarch complained to him that some coaches would not publicly explain their strategies. Bauer retorted: "What a bunch of nonsense.... All you have to do is watch it."[107] National Team players like Ken Broderick and Mickey McDowell assisted with the coaching clinics.[108]

Bauer's humanistic approach promoted the development of the full person. Former National Team player Mott recalled Bauer often explaining this relationship: "Many coaches think you can't be friends with players, but I don't believe that. You need to respect the difference in roles, yet coaches need to know their players as people—not just athletes—and the players need to get to know their coaches personally."[109] This strengthened the confidence of players and the spirit of the team, as described in a letter in 1974:

> [The coach must] organize and harmoniously co-ordinate these individual skills within the framework of offensive and defensive team play ... which make possible a learning environment—a joy will be developed for the game itself and team spirit will be such that the players will look forward to games to test their acquired individual and team skill.... [T]eam play is based on the development of individual skills which foster self-confidence and joy at realizing

103   Watson, *Catch On*, 264.

104   Watson, *Catch On*, 236.

105   Bob Hindmarch, interview with author, August 17, 2018. Many of these coaches, along with others like Scotty Bowman, ran the high-level clinics.

106   S. F. Wise and Douglas Fisher, *Canada's Sporting Heroes* (Don Mills, ON: General Publishing, 1974), 290.

107   Hindmarch, interview. Hindmarch named the Vancouver Canucks' coach, Hal Laycoe, in this example.

108   McDowell, interview.

109   Morris Mott, interview with author, July 15, 2020.

one's potential. This self-knowledge forms the basis of a strong and determined individual spirit coming alive and responding to a leadership which co-ordinates these same individual skills into a strong and determined offensive and defensive style of team play.[110]

NHL coaches generally were tepid toward newer coaching strategies, yet Philadelphia Flyers' coach Fred Shero incorporated new developments with his championship team and helped with coaching clinics. While his Broad Street Bullies played the game with intimidation and violence, Shero echoed Bauer in saying that "just winning games is not the most important thing. The most important thing is the complete person.... A coach not only shapes expectations but also influences attitudes toward self and job."[111] Shero and Bauer shared a collaborative mentality about team chemistry and built a strong friendship.[112] When Shero's Flyers team beat the Soviet Red Army team in 1976, a reporter wrote that the National Team concept "finally was vindicated" because the Flyers attacked "with basically the same diligent forechecking barrage Father Bauer used during the years his team was in operation.... [T]he Flyers needed the kind of never-say-die enthusiasm those overmatched Nats used to have.... [I]t must be exhilarating these days for Father Bauer, teaching in Vancouver, to hear the hockey mob saying the very thing he was maintaining—and being ridiculed for—a decade ago."[113] Both men endorsed spirit and togetherness, even if Bauer believed these could not be balanced with intimidation and brutality.

Bauer's person-centered approach within the development committee was at odds with many trends in Canadian sport. The emotional response to the Summit Series showed Trudeau how increased government involvement in sport could further unite Canadians. Sporting organizations were usually kitchen table-like operations run by volunteer officers and unable to execute national goals effectively.[114] A new national body, Sport Canada, formed

---

110   Bauer, Letter to Allyn.

111   Rhoda Rappeport, *Fred Shero: A Kaleidoscopic View of the Philadelphia Flyers' Coach* (New York: St. Martin's Press, 1977), 96. Shero credited these ideas to one of his coaching idols, John Wooden, the legendary UCLA basketball coach and adherent of muscular Christianity.

112   McDowell, interview.

113   Jim Proudfoot, "Editorial," *Toronto Star*, January 21, 1976, C2.

114   John Matthew Amis, "The Internal Dynamics of Strategic Change in Canadian National Sport Organizations" (PhD thesis, University of Alberta,

in 1971, began to oversee the running of National Sport Organizations (NSOs) and offered improved organizational skills and leadership. The government's emphasis on sporting bureaucracies created increased focus on a performance principle and a results orientation, making organizations like the CAHA feel pressured to become professionalized, more efficient, and focused on high-end performance.[115] Progress became performance-oriented. Professional sport was not narrowly understood as paying athletes, but about creating a professionalized, bureaucratic sporting system.[116] The thinking behind this radical shift in national sport conflicted with Bauer's views. Whereas his primary concern lay with the total development of the person, Hockey Canada focused on improving player skills, coaching and refereeing, and its understanding of hockey's social significance.[117] Bauer's educational approach placed human development, rather than performance results, as its chief aim.

Projecting Ideals into Hockey Canada's Domestic Program

Amidst an evolving hockey landscape and uncertainty caused by tensions with the CAHA, the purpose of Hockey Canada was debated. Many directors focused on international competition, especially defeating the Soviets. Bauer's interest remained equally weighted on the organization's early objectives: international success and domestic development. The Summit Series made

Edmonton, 1998), 1, https://doi.org/10.7939/R33R0Q26V. Former National Team members Bourbonnais and Conlin served on committees and worked at the National Sport and Recreation Centre, respectively. Roger Bourbonnais, interview with author, August 26, 2019; Paul Conlin, interview with author, June 4, 2019.

115   Donald MacIntosh and David Whitson, *The Game Planners: Transforming Canada's Sport System* (Montreal: McGill-Queen's University Press, 1990), 9–10; Canadian Department of National Health and Welfare, *Federal Government Hockey Study Report, Amateur Hockey in Canada, a Blueprint for the 70s and Beyond,* by John Meagher, Ottawa: Department of National Health and Welfare, 1971, Hockey Canada Library (3) file, Hockey Canada Archives. Even prior to the founding of Sport Canada, the Department of Health and National Welfare in 1971 hired Dr. John Meagher to write another report trying to determine the future direction for amateur hockey.

116   MacIntosh and Whitson, *The Game Planners,* 13.

117   Hockey Canada, "Planning and Development Committee Report to the Board of Directors," Annual General Meeting, December 7, 1985, Box 3, File 7, Bauer fonds, Basilian Archives.

certain issues apparent, such as sportsmanship and lower skill levels, that required corresponding changes in youth hockey.[118] Bauer thought that Hockey Canada required "a change in the relationship with professional hockey." He added that the organization should continue communications with professional hockey, but it needed to expel the NHL and the NHL Players' Association (NHLPA), along with the World Hockey Association (WHA), from Hockey Canada's board. He wrote that, given the "present complexity of professional hockey and the nature of the tasks facing Hockey Canada [it would be] inappropriate for these interests to continue to be directly represented on the Board of Directors of Hockey Canada."[119] After the political and financial success of the Summit Series, such an eviction would be difficult—but the move was necessary for the rebirth of his hockey alternative.[120] The National Team would "become the focal point of the program for the development and testing of hockey skills," where its annual summer hockey institute would include a coaching symposium and discussions about a philosophy of hockey.[121] Bauer was adamant that players needed a different end point than simply the NHL.[122] He stated plainly that they require "the actual projection of our ideas in practice."

Over the next months, Bauer co-authored a final development committee position paper with Hanrahan and the chair of the committee, Maurice Regimbal. The former president of the CIAU, Regimbal came from a French-Catholic family in northern Ontario and attended St. Peter's Seminary in 1940–1 in London, Ontario.[123] He was a supporter of Bauer, declaring that

118 David Bauer, Mislabeled Introduction of *Report to Munro*, c. 1973, Rev. Bauer file, Seaman Hockey Resource Centre, 3. The introductory pages from 3 to 6 are mistakenly included in the *Report to Munro*, as found at the Seaman Hockey Resource Centre. These pages were written after the 1971 report and the Summit Series.

119 Bauer, Mislabeled Introduction, 3.

120 Bauer, Mislabeled Introduction, 4. He also advocated for postsecondary scholarships, establishment of community club programs, and subsidization of artificial ice by governments.

121 Bauer, Mislabeled Introduction, 5.

122 Bauer, Mislabeled Introduction, 6. He added that the National Team "could inspire our youth to a better understanding of themselves and of their goals in life and the place of hockey in their lives and that of our country."

123 Gisele Regimbal, interview with author, March 4, 2020. Gisele is Maurice Regimbal's daughter. Maurice Regimbal was the first director of athletics at Laurentian

"any steps in the development of coaching in Canada should be structured around the participation of Father David Bauer."[124]

The group's first draft about the role of hockey in Canada understood sport as a "human phenomenon" related to other areas like the arts, education, finance, and international affairs.[125] From this perspective, they critiqued sport science: "We all agree that the emphasis on the technical and on the tactical side of the game will always take second place to our deep pre-occupation about the physical, moral and spiritual welfare and growth of the people involved in the game ... without that basic and ultimate concern, technique and machines can become so engrossing ... that [people are] literally ready to sacrifice everything including man's soul on the altar of progress."[126] To avoid taking this "tunnel approach," the three implored hockey leaders to think more broadly about the role of hockey and establish a Hockey Institute for the study of "our national heritage."[127] Some rejected their thinking. Roger Jackson openly criticized Regimbal and the proposed Hockey Institute. He promoted a program based on preexisting technical ideas that could be sold to coaches for improved skill development.[128] Bauer, Regimbal, and Hanrahan thought that blindly endorsing technique was unwise and risky.

In the second draft of their position paper for the development committee, they stated that, despite the fact that "hockey is not the most

---

University in Sudbury, Ontario. He later produced Franco-Ontarian recreation resources and became director of athletics at St. Michael's College School from 1979 to 1985, where he also taught theology.

124   Hockey Canada, "Minutes of the Development Policy Committee," September 29, 1970, MG28 I 263 6, 400-9 Hockey Canada–1969/70, LAC.

125   Dave Bauer, Maurice Regimbal, and James Hanrahan, "Hockey's Special Position," 1973, Box 36, "Bauer, Dave 1971–1980" file, Accession number 2014-2, St. Mark's College Archives, 1.

126   Bauer, Regimbal, and Hanrahan, "Hockey's Special Position," 6.

127   Bauer, Regimbal, and Hanrahan, "Hockey's Special Position," 11 and 12. They stated: "Other art forms, medical research, contribution of psychological and sociological nature must be gathered so little by little many of the myths created over the years can be replaced by facts supported by competent observation."

128   Roger Jackson to Doug Fisher, "Hockey Institute," April 17, 1973, MG28 I 263 18, 300-6-6, Federal Government Position on Hockey (1 of 2), LAC. Roger Jackson had encountered Bauer's National Team in Vancouver while he was training in rowing for the Tokyo 1964 Summer Olympics. He responded to Fisher about the direction of Hockey Canada.

important thing around ... it might be that it is the most Canadian thing."[129] The draft sought harmony between sport science and humanistic sport:

> The development of hockey skills is not an end in itself. Hockey Canada is, without any doubt whatever, fundamentally directed to act in and through the development of hockey to facilitate the physical, mental and social development of Canadians. Our youth, especially, in the full process of their growth, deserve this concern.... [Hockey Canada's] objective must be to search out and foster programs and structures that serve that aim.... What is at stake is the dignity of the individual person.[130]

To make its point, the document added that the experience of hockey must be something that "opens possibilities for the person rather than closing them. The conditions under which hockey is played should not be such as to narrow a man, but should contribute to a broader range of experiences and to the ability to reflect on these experiences."[131] To enable this broader development through hockey, the document concluded with a plea:

> There must be in the society a body charged with responsibility for the development of sport, and in any particular society this takes on a special urgency in the case of a particular sport that is most expressive of that society. Hockey is such a sport in Canada and Hockey Canada has been established for this purpose. Its task is to see that hockey is so developed in this country and internationally that the true nature of the game is preserved and that the identification of hockey and Canada may be a true and gratifying reality.[132]

Bauer feared that without considering longstanding ideals, hockey's significance would be lost. Without discussing the meaning of hockey, its values would be forgotten.

Bauer was pleased by the committee's response: "Maurice [Regimbal] and I have tried to call [Hanrahan] from time to time (he even called to Houston) to

---

129 David Bauer, Maurice Regimbal, and James Hanrahan, "Position Paper: Hockey Canada Development Committee," 1973, Box 36, "Bauer, Dave 1971–1980" file, Accession number 2014-2, St. Mark's College Archives, 2.

130 Bauer, Regimbal, and Hanrahan, "Position Paper," 3.

131 Bauer, Regimbal, and Hanrahan, "Position Paper," 4.

132 Bauer, Regimbal, and Hanrahan, "Position Paper," 14–15.

tell you of the very positive reaction your paper received at our last meeting."[133] CAHA leaders Jack Devine and Gordon Juckes, along with Charlie Hay, responded favorably. The committee was supporting their ideals. It began to develop the concept of a Hockey Institute and took on Bauer supporters.[134]

The expansion of the committee into domestic hockey was abruptly ended by the CAHA, which had historically organized minor hockey. In May 1974, supported by the minister of sport, the CAHA's Dan Johnson threatened Hockey Canada representatives: "We might have said, 'Well, look boys, you're gone. You're through.' ... [But] Hockey Canada is in existence this morning because as a group of officers ... [we] decided to let them live."[135] Funding for domestic hockey training switched to the CAHA and, by the end of 1974, Hockey Canada had basically become an advisory and policy formulating body for the Federal Government in international hockey.[136] The organization let go many fulltime staff, and the Toronto offices were moved to Ottawa.[137] Fisher later bluntly declared to Regimbal: "the Development Committee of Hockey Canada as it was constituted is over."[138]

Bauer reacted strongly: the "domestic arm of [Hockey] Canada [was] lopped off in an attempt to placate CAHA. This time CAHA went for [Hockey Canada] itself in its overtures to government."[139] Nevertheless, after discussions with CAHA leadership, he determined that the major reason for

133 David Bauer, Letter to James Hanrahan, late October 1973, Box 36, "Bauer, Dave 1971–1980" file, Accession number 2014-2, St. Mark's College Archives.

134 M & M Systems Research Ltd., "Report: The Organizational Development," 3–4. L'Heureux became chair of the "innovative programs committee" and Bourbonnais was named chair of a legal committee.

135 Canadian Amateur Hockey Association, "Annual Meeting 1974 (Meeting of Board of Directors)," May 24, 1974, Winnipeg, MB, Meeting Minutes file, Hockey Canada Archives, 80.

136 M & M Systems Research Ltd., "Report: The Organizational Development," 9. Hockey Canada would only remain involved in domestic hockey on difficult-to-define, pan-Canadian issues like junior and midget ownership and draft rights and how to coordinate provincial legislation against violence in hockey. Doug Fisher to Maurice Regimbal, May 20, 1975, MG28 I 263 19, 300-6-14, Development Committee Hockey (1 of 3) 1974–1975, LAC.

137 M & M Systems Research Ltd., "Report: The Organizational Development," 1. This office was under the umbrella of the Administrative Centre for Sports and Recreation.

138 Fisher to Regimbal. Regimbal was the chair of the committee.

139 Bauer, Notes, Box 3, File 1, Bauer fonds, Basilian Archives.

its demise was "the desire for the quick efficient solution ... won by the bureaucrats and others seeking influence and power."[140] He came to distrust both Hockey Canada and the power wielded by the minister of sport, Marc Lalonde. Bauer had limited influence; others made the final decisions within Hockey Canada.[141] An internal research report from 1975 declared that Hockey Canada had become at risk from personalities from different constituencies who put their interests ahead of those of Hockey Canada.[142] Some board members had ulterior motives: Eagleson sought the financial windfalls from open competition tournaments, while the NHL wanted international hockey without Hockey Canada.[143]

Without a development committee to connect international competition and domestic hockey in practice, Bauer argued, Hockey Canada "becomes just an arena in which special interests compete for government attention and favors, or a political instrument to cover problems over while we hope they will go away."[144] He voiced his concern about a power imbalance within the board, where he bemoaned the increasing influence of bureaucrats at the expense of the private sector—ironically, Bauer was a government appointee to the board.[145] He was unwilling to place his confidence in the federal government again, after it had endorsed an open forum that let corporate hockey interests take charge in Hockey Canada's infancy.

Bauer felt tensions in the hockey world more acutely because of behind-the-scenes issues. Three of his brothers died in the mid-1960s, creating uncertainty for the Bauer family business. With the passing of his father Edgar in 1959, followed by his mother Bertha in 1971, a

140   David Bauer, Letter to James Hanrahan, July 1975, Box 36, "Bauer, Dave 1971–1980" file, Accession number 2014-2, St. Mark's College Archives.

141   Chris Lang, interview with author, June 6, 2019.

142   M & M Systems Research Ltd., "Report: The Organizational Development," 6 and 7–9.

143   Clayton, *Eagle*, 149; Smith, *Ice War Diplomat*, 251–53.

144   Dave Bauer, "Speech to the Board of Hockey Canada," April 26, 1975, Box 36, "Bauer, Dave 1971–1980" file, Accession number 2014-2, St. Mark's College Archives.

145   His cousin Wintermeyer resigned over concerns that the reorganization made "the Government the arbiter of hockey" without a significant role for the business community. John J. Wintermeyer, Letter to Marc Lalonde, Minister of Health and Welfare, April 3, 1975, Box 36, "Bauer, Dave 1971–1980" file, Accession number 2014-2, St. Mark's College Archives.

prominent Waterloo business was at a crossroads despite several decades of growth.[146] Among the remaining siblings, brother Ray acquired all of the shares in the business and became its CEO.[147] Ray's support of Dave and the National Team was significant, and Dave reciprocated by serving on the board of directors of Bauer Ltd. when the company expanded during the 1970s. Whereas Dave was introspective and more cautious, Ray took more risks and expanded the company during the high inflation of the 1970s.[148] The economic uncertainty caused great concern for Dave. On one occasion, he used his connections in Canadian hockey to secure for the company interest-free loans from Hartland MacDougall, an executive at a major national bank.[149] Bauer was troubled by the problems he saw all around him, declaring in a personal letter that "the entire world order is on the verge of a total breakdown, bidding us more to prepare for catastrophe of unimaginable proportions."[150]

In his fifties, Bauer started to gain weight. He tried to stop drinking alcohol—it had provided a release from life's pressures—and lower his sugar

---

146 Private Bauer Family Records, Paul Schmalz Collection, Goderich, ON. He died at St. Mary's Hospital in Kitchener with Dave and many children present. Dave presided at each funeral Mass, with Bishop J. F. Ryan of Hamilton present and who also offered the eulogy at Edgar's Mass. The local newspaper ran a biography claiming that "Bauer's Limited ranks as one of Waterloo's most important industries." J. E. Middleton and Fred Landon, *The Province of Ontario: A History, 1615–1927*, vol. 4 (Toronto: The Dominion Publishing Company, 1927), 490.

147 Henry Koch, "R. A. Bauer Buys All Bauer Stock," *Kitchener-Waterloo Record*, June 6, 1972, Business Binder, Bauer Ltd. file, Waterloo Public Library. This acquisition included the shares owned by his cousin James, who had left the company after serving as secretary and general manager.

148 Ray's busy lifestyle led in part to an episode of cardiac arrest, where off-duty emergency personnel administered lifesaving CPR. Ray later funded an innovative program to provide CPR training for the company's workers. Chris Masterman, "Bauers Limited Made Batting, Twine and Padding," *Waterloo Region Record*, March 1, 2018, W11.

149 David Bauer, Letter to Barbara Bauer, May 1974, Box 3, File 3, Bauer fonds, Basilian Archives; and Bauer, Notes, Box 3, File 1, Bauer fonds, Basilian Archives. Bauer promised MacDougall that he would remain on the Bauer Ltd. board until the company was out of financial trouble.

150 Bauer, Notes, Box 3, File 1, Bauer fonds, Basilian Archives. The company survived for many decades, expanding to North Carolina and employing more than 300 people by the late 1990s. It closed its doors in 2008. Chuck Howitt, "Bauer Seeks Bankruptcy Protection," *Waterloo Region Record*, February 24, 2009, C1.

intake. He continued to smoke cigars.[151] A lifestyle filled with high-level meetings, travel, player negotiations, and managing a public persona made it difficult to quit these pleasures.[152] He skated for his exercise—either before or after hockey practice—and felt that he was in good physical condition for his age. But he feared that he might be destined to an early death because of his brothers' passings from congenital heart issues.[153] A mood of doubt and discouragement festered within him because of these family, personal, and hockey matters.

"Another Chance Would Come His Way"

Bauer's influence in Canadian hockey had shrunk. In a 1974 letter, he compared himself to Aleksandr Solzhenitsyn, the Russian dissident who was sentenced to eight years in Soviet work camps for his criticisms of Josef Stalin following the Second World War.[154] Solzhenitsyn's exposing of the Gulag labor camp system and critique of Soviet communism led to his exile in 1974, at which time he also criticized the West's consumeristic materialism and lack of ideals. In Solzhenitsyn, Bauer found consolation. Both men had lived by their ideals and stood up to government figures—and suffered the consequences of their stances. In a private letter, Bauer lamented the "killing" of the National Team but drew a hopeful comparison between his life and Solzhenitsyn's: "he realized when he was first taken prisoner years ago that another chance would come his way—which did happen. That's the way I felt in 1970 and still feel to-day."[155]

With the help of Regimbal and Hanrahan, Bauer composed a paper about Canada's international hockey program. The three wanted to promote human understanding and interdependence in the face of nuclear proliferation.[156] For instance, because of the expansion of artificial ice rinks globally, Canadians

---

151 David Bauer, Letter to Barbara Bauer, January 10–17, 1975, Terry O'Malley Collection.

152 O'Malley, interview.

153 Bauer, Letter to Barbara Bauer, February 20, 1974.

154 Joseph Pearce, *Solzhenitsyn: A Soul in Exile* (Grand Rapids, MI: Baker Books, 2001).

155 David Bauer, Letter to Barbara Bauer, February 19, 1974, Terry O'Malley Collection.

156 Maurice Regimbal to James Hanrahan, February 28, 1974, MG28 I 263 19, 300-6-14, Development Committee Hockey.

needed to accept that they could never be assured of victory in hockey—just as the English had accepted the international character of soccer.[157] Qualities of speed, teamwork, and variety in players' sizes made the game more inclusive and, for the authors, were the "true values" of the game that developed persons and communities.[158] Further, international play offered impactful, broadening experiences through encounters and friendships.[159] Olympic hockey could invigorate and inspire hope for victory and "serve as the apex of amateur development in this country."[160]

Bauer's vision for international hockey stood in contrast to Eagleson's. Despite his poor behavior in Moscow at the Summit Series, he managed to convince the government to appoint him as the organizer of the first major-league World Cup of Hockey (i.e., the 1976 Canada Cup).[161] As head of the NHLPA, and its member on the board of Hockey Canada, he directed Hockey Canada's policy decisions about international play, enabling it to assist in American expansion of the NHL and producing a financial windfall for Hockey Canada.[162]

In alignment with Hockey Canada's mixing of professional and amateur hockey, Eagleson and Bauer were named co-chairs of its International Committee at the end of 1974.[163] The two men could not have been more different in their approach to sport. Whereas Eagleson brought a win-at-all-costs, Trump-like manner to negotiations, Bauer built diplomatic relations and believed hockey to be an important path to positive outcomes in international affairs. Bauer soothed troubled waters between other nations and Canada; Eagleson agitated others to get what he wanted.[164] The partnership caused a great deal of stress for Bauer. However, because he thought there

---

157   "Hockey Canada and International Play," July 1974, Box 36, "Bauer, Dave 1971–1980" file, Accession number 2014-2, St. Mark's College Archives, 1.

158   "Hockey Canada and International Play," 15–16.

159   "Hockey Canada and International Play," 5.

160   "Hockey Canada and International Play," 10.

161   Clayton, *Eagle*, 155. According to columnist Jim Coleman, "'Czar' is a word with unfortunate tyrannical connotations but, Eagleson would be a singularly wise and enlightened autocrat." Jim Coleman, "Editorial," *The Whig-Standard*, June 3, 1975, 14.

162   Clayton, *Eagle*, 146. Eagleson was also the agent of more than 100 NHL players. Clayton, *Eagle*, 171.

163   Canadian Amateur Hockey Association, "Minutes of Board of Directors Meeting," January 26–27, 1975, Toronto, ON, Minutes File, Hockey Canada Archives.

164   Mott, interview.

was little value in international hockey driven primarily by Eagleson's interests in profits and notoriety, he believed that his focus on human development would be helpful.[165]

Bauer's co-chairing of the International Committee was the beginning of his second chance. After assisting with the formation of the Japanese National Team for the 1975 World Championships, Bauer traveled to Dusseldorf, West Germany, with Eagleson, for the Group A tournament and noted how "it seemed that everyone wanted to talk with me" about the proposed Canada Cup 1976.[166] Despite the enthusiasm for the anticipated event, conflicting jurisdictional issues between several professional and amateur associations and leagues made the tournament nearly "an impossibility," from his viewpoint. Bauer believed that the motivating factor for Eagleson and the Americans was "gold at the end of this rainbow": "popularizing the game in the U.S. for future gates domestically and internationally."[167] Canadians at the event showed little interest in the Olympics compared to other countries—to the dismay of Bauer.

Bauer added, "Canada had better wake up or else the U.S. will sophisticate the game of hockey beyond our ability of possibly keeping up with them."[168] The US hockey system was growing at the high school and collegiate level, mirroring American excellence in basketball and football, and "expanding their facilities at a surprising rate." Improving players' conditioning and fundamental skills, along with adopting European tactics and strategy, the Americans, explained Bauer, "will propel [themselves] beyond us very quickly unless we restructure our existing organization of the game." Bauer believed that "we might be able to reorganize amateur hockey" if the CAHA and its amateur programs build towards "a competitive Olympic Team for 1980." Building the hockey alternative would mean having "to upgrade high school and university hockey" so that minor and junior hockey players would favor a route through "community, college, university and senior hockey."[169] This

165   Bauer, "Speech to the Board." Hockey Canada, "Directors Meeting," April 28, 1975, MG28 I 263 19, 300-6-24, Hockey Canada Annual Meeting 1975, LAC.

166   Bauer, "Bauer Notes and Letters," 12.

167   Bauer, "Bauer Notes and Letters," 12.

168   Bauer, "Bauer Notes and Letters," 12.

169   Bauer, "Bauer Notes and Letters," 12. Bauer lamented: "We will live and learn to regret the extinction of the H. C. development committee just as we lived to regret the dismantling of our National Team a few years ago."

major shift would upset the CHL; in short, "something would have to happen with the junior situation." Without the switch, Bauer foretold Canadian hockey stalling while other nations would surpass it.

The violence of the 1970s professional game increased the public's appetite for a reborn National Team. A thinner talent pool for two competing professional leagues (i.e., the NHL and WHA) caused an increase in violent play; less skilled players resorted to intimidation and goonism. Public weariness over the glorified violence led to reports by provincial and federal governments.[170] Research showed that children imitated their goon heroes, and that parents and coaches were reinforcing these violent acts. The hope was that overzealous, hard-nosed coaches would gradually be replaced with better-trained coaches who had played college hockey.[171]

Public frustration peaked during the 1977 World Championships in Vienna, when Canada returned to the tournament with a roster of professional players whose teams had not made the NHL playoffs. In a final round game against the Soviet Union, the Canadians lost 8–1 and resorted to goon-play to slow down the Russians.[172] The Canadian Embassy in Vienna stated that the team produced "lurid publicity" and shattered "the image of the invincibility of Canadian professionals."[173] It explained that "it is presumably difficult to train a young man to fight for his professional life, and then to convince him in a short time that … he must for a few weeks be *sans peur et sans reproche.*" An opportunistic whiskey advertisement made an eye-catching poster of a hockey player with the caption: "We Are Hard on the Ice, but Soft on the Taste." The country's disgust was palpable.

The new federal minister of sport, Iona Campagnolo, had attended the game and called for a parliamentary committee to report on international

---

170   For instance, in Ontario, a task force committee to investigate "Violence in Amateur Hockey" was created by Hon. René Brunelle, Minister of Community and Social Services in 1974.

171   Wayne Simpson, "Hockey," in *A Concise History of Sport in Canada,* ed. Don Morrow et al. (Toronto: Oxford University Press, 1989), 179.

172   Donald Ramsay, "Team Canada Loses on the Ice—and Then off It," *The Globe and Mail,* May 7, 1977, 1. The Finnish referee called most of the game's twenty penalties against the Canadians.

173   Department of External Affairs to the Parliamentary Committee on International Hockey, "Appendix D, A Report by the Canadian Embassy in Vienna," in Brief submitted to the Parliamentary Committee on International Hockey, by the Department, Senator S. L. Buckwold, September 22, 1977, RG29 2077, LAC.

hockey.[174] The committee's report echoed Bauer's past criticisms. It spoke out against programs single-mindedly geared toward for-profit hockey.[175] In response, the committee called for the integration of international and youth development programs, the renewal of the National Team, and a study into the feasibility of a national university league. The document called Major Junior hockey "exploitive."[176] Campagnolo wanted to expand her review of hockey and its myths with the help of several university studies. She would thus carve out a pathway for a hockey alternative.[177] One reporter commented: "[Campagnolo] is shooting for North American hockey reform and the pros are going to have to jump. Father Bauer must be smiling."[178]

In an earlier private letter to a niece, Bauer candidly commented, "Patience has had its reward in my steady rise to power."[179] Eagleson's push for hosting Canada Cup 1976 came with a promise to send a team to the 1980 Winter Olympic Games. Bauer was quickly put in charge of Hockey Canada's Olympic Committee and, in a collaborative effort with the CAHA in 1977, announced preparations for a National Team at the 1980 Lake Placid

174   Government of Canada, *Report by the Committee on International Hockey to Iona Campagnolo*, by S. L. Buckwold, et al., Ottawa, ON: Government of Canada, 1977. The report was based on hundreds of surveys and dozens of interviews, including ones with Bauer, former players (Conacher, Conlin, Dryden, Ellis, Mott, and O'Malley), and others like Hindmarch, Noonan, and Regimbal. Former player Derek Holmes was the advisor for the committee.

175   Government of Canada, *Iona Campagnolo*, 3, 5–6.

176   Government of Canada, *Iona Campagnolo*, 6. It stated: "Examples of bad conduct and poor sportsmanship do not occur in a vacuum and the minor and junior hockey training systems must accept its share of responsibility."

177   "Hockey in Deep Trouble, Government Report Says," *Toronto Star*, May 9, 1979, RG29 2074, LAC. Campagnolo also released *Toward a National Policy on Amateur Sport: A Working Paper*, which also challenged in part the influence of the professionalized interests in hockey. MacIntosh and Whitson, *The Game Planners*, 22. Government of Canada, *A Status Report on the Canadian Hockey Review*, by J. J. Urie and L. E. Began, Ottawa, ON: Government of Canada, 1979, 7. For instance, the principal reasons for youth dropping out of hockey remained: too competitive, too violent, and too much guided by a professional orientation.

178   John Dulmage, "Noble and Renewed," *Windsor Star*, February 24, 1978, Box 36, "Bauer, Dave, 1971–1980" file, St. Mark's College Archives. When Campagnolo's Liberal Party lost the federal election in May 1979, the Progressive Conservative Party set aside Campagnolo's plans for restructuring the sport.

179   Dave Bauer, Letter to Barbara Bauer, late June 1971, Terry O'Malley Collection.

Games.[180] Bauer had come full circle, having led the Olympic program, seen it dismantled, and now began putting it together again. His hockey alternative was taking shape: "My interest remains in a program not an event by itself. I'm interested in the upgrading of the game itself and the youth of the players who participate in the games. I'm also interested in technical development, sports science, etc., too, but not to the detriment of the growth of the individual hockey player."[181]

In a 1987 discussion paper presented to the board of Hockey Canada, its author noted that "it was not until the 1980s that the relationship between development at the youth levels and success at elite international levels was recognized and fully accepted as an integral component of success and quality."[182] Bauer was among those who made this connection more than a decade earlier. Hockey played in distant Asian and European cities could no longer be seen as exotic, but was part of the sport's future. Ice rinks in Tokyo were connected to those in Truro and Toronto. A recalibrated National Team could help guide the future of the global game.

180   Hockey Canada Olympic Committee, Untitled, Summer 1977, Box 3, File 1, Bauer fonds, Basilian Archives.

181   David Bauer, "To State My Position," Box 1, File 6, Bauer fonds, Basilian Archives, 1. Bauer's notes defined his understanding of amateur: "Development of human person and persons—increases options—one which is excellent playing hockey, i.e., development of attitude, skills, consistent with the finest aspiration of the human person."

182   "Hockey Canada—'The Road Ahead.'"

The Reemergence of the
National Team Program

TO OBTAIN THE PARTICIPATION OF THE IIHF and other nations at the 1976 Canada Cup, Hockey Canada agreed to participate at upcoming Olympics and World Championships. Columnist Jim Proudfoot wrote: "Nothing less than the establishment of a national team, composed mainly of university students.... There's a full turn of the wheel for you. All that remains is for Father Bauer to become that manager-coach."[1] Bauer eagerly told a friend: "I am willing to take on this project beginning right NOW."[2]

Bauer and others believed that the hockey system needed an alternative end point: the National Team. Instead of Hockey Canada handing out Sport Canada university scholarships with little foresight, its new Olympic Committee used the monies to identify a majority of the eventual players for the 1980 Winter Games in Lake Placid.[3] Improved coaching certification

---

1   Jim Proudfoot, "Editorial," *Toronto Star*, January 21, 1976, C2.

2   David Bauer, Letter to Maurice, 1979, Box 3, File 3, Bauer fonds, Basilian Archives.

3   Hockey Canada, "Minutes of the Development Committee Meeting," May 13, 1974, MG28 I 263 19, 300-6-14, Development Committee Hockey (2 of 3) 1974–1975,

programs and university hockey supported this alternative end.[4] Minister of Sport Campagnolo used her government reports on hockey to promote the National Team. The merging of thought made one reporter note, "The irony is that the committee thinking and the current emphasis on college hockey all harken back a decade to what Father Bauer was trying to accomplish and was being laughed at for even trying."[5] Questioned in his job interview about how he would manage the National Team, Bauer commented: "How can I adequately answer these questions? Surely all the answers were to be found in how we'd put together the original team."[6]

Hockey Canada ratified plans for the team with little time to prepare for the Lake Placid Games.[7] Bauer complained to family and friends at a New Year's Eve party in Winnipeg in 1977: "Can you believe that they only gave me two years to get a team ready for the 1980 Olympics? Can you imagine the gall of them asking that of me in such a short period of time?"[8] His frustration was reasonable. European countries had long been preparing for 1980. As with previous National Teams, players would choose to forego playing major junior or professional hockey, while earning only a scholarship and stipend. Of the nearly one million dollars budgeted to train and educate fifty players for possible participation in the Olympics, the federal funding agent for amateur athletes, Game Plan, was to grant $200,000, with the rest of the money coming from Hockey Canada, the Canadian Olympic Association, sponsorship, and revenue from exhibition games.[9] The money from Hockey Canada was effectively from Canada Cup revenues, totalling around $600,000.[10] Accepting funds from an Eagleson-led tournament may have felt like a deal with the devil for Bauer, but it largely financed the National Team.

LAC. The committee members were Regimbal, Hindmarch, L'Heureux, Wintermeyer, and former National Team player Bourbonnais.

4   Hockey Canada, "Development Policy Committee"; Alan Watson, *Catch On and Run with It: The Sporting Life and Times of Dr. Bob Hindmarch* (Vancouver: AJW Books, 2012), 298–99.

5   Roy MacGregor, "History Appears to be Ready to Repeat Itself—And That's Just Fine," unknown magazine, 1978, Bauer Fr. David file, St. Michael's College School Archives, 48.

6   MacGregor, "History Appears," 48.

7   D. Ramsay, "Olympic Team Plan Likely to be Ratified by Hockey Canada," *The Globe and Mail*, February 22, 1978.

8   Paul Schmalz and Steve Freiburger, interview with author, January 18, 2019.

9   Ramsay, "Olympic Team Plan."

10   Derek Holmes, interview with author, October 16, 2020.

As managing director, Bauer oversaw the organization of the program and hired others to manage and coach. He avoided coaching the team because he sought to mitigate the pressures he faced.[11] Now in his early fifties, he determined that overseeing the program produced fewer health risks and personal difficulties. The team was more properly funded than past National Teams, and his Basilian superiors approved of the repackaged role.[12]

As the new head of the Olympic Committee, Bauer explained why an alternative vision was necessary: "We found out that hockey was no longer a growth experience for our young Canadians. More and more families were encouraging their children to opt out of this experience because it was an environment that made human growth more difficult.... We had to effectively destroy the symbolism and mystique of hockey."[13] The sport's inability to uphold broader nationalistic and educational aims for those playing the game meant that youth walked away from hockey or entered into the rough junior ranks. Hockey Canada executive Derek Holmes, a former National Team player, explained this practical reality: "A boy leaves home at the age of 15 to play hockey in another city sometimes hundreds of miles away and at 20 he ends up with a set of false teeth, and if he's lucky a pro contract."[14]

Bauer drew up a long-term plan toward Lake Placid and beyond: "A four-year cycle of preparation ... [would] identify the most promising Canadian amateur hockey players ... [and] must include the best coaching appropriate to their level of development, a continuing training and conditioning program, a stress on the development of attitudes appropriate to ideals of sportsmanship and on special features of international competition."[15] Instead of promoting a one-and-done international tournament attitude, Bauer wanted

11   David Bauer, Personal Notes, October 17, 1976, Box 3, File 5, Bauer fonds, Basilian Archives.

12   Superior general Hanrahan remained a steady support, as did Bauer's local superior at St. Mark's, Father Neil Kelly, who himself was a sportsman, having played professional baseball around Vancouver. P. Wallace Platt, *Dictionary of Basilian Biography: Lives of Members of the Congregation of Priests of Saint Basil from its Origins in 1822 to 2022*, 2nd ed. (Toronto: University of Toronto Press, 2005), 320.

13   Maureen Bauer-McGahey, Notes of Unpublished Book Chapters about 1980 Olympic Hockey Team, Spring 1980, Box 3, File 1, Bauer fonds, Basilian Archives.

14   Mark Sigal, "Hockey: Canada's Collegiate Team Could Surprise," *Like It Is*, December 1979, RG29 2076, LAC, 10.

15   Hockey Canada, "Olympics 1980," Draft document, Box 1, File 6, Bauer fonds, Basilian Archives.

an all-encompassing program developing players over a four-year span as they earned a university degree. It would include summer training camps at the levels of midget, junior, and CIAU.[16] Bauer's vision meant a shift within the hockey system, but other organizations created difficulties by their demands. For instance, US college players would need to be released during part of the academic year, and junior hockey operators complained about players who chose the National Team instead of club teams.[17] Bauer encouraged junior players to determine their own career path: "a learning experience with Olympic programme vs immediate returns from ... professional careers."[18]

In addition to support from the federal government and many inside Hockey Canada, financial assistance also came from a group of businessmen in Calgary. Led by Doug Mitchell, the group wanted to establish the National Team program in Calgary.[19] In December 1978, two National teams started playing exhibition games: one touring Europe and the other at an invitational tournament in Ontario sponsored by Labatt's Brewery.[20] The Calgary committee's substantial support tilted the tables for Bauer and his program. He later admitted, "I was hooked."[21]

Bauer explained how bitterness had not gotten the best of him after the shelving of the National Team in 1970: "I always hoped somewhere along the line what we were trying to do back then would surface again.... I hoped that the philosophy would be needed again. I think we are now at that point."[22] Things had turned in Bauer's favor. Professional hockey mercenaries failed as Canadian ambassadors. The public and governments were tired of hockey's overt violence and poor role-modeling for youth. Coaching developments across the country held promise. The dissident was returning home, and Canadian hockey was seemingly realigning its values.

16   David Bauer, "Why an Olympic Team?" 1976, Box 1, File 6, Bauer fonds, Basilian Archives.

17   David Bauer, "Olympic Team Report," September 1979, MG31 E 72 35, LAC.

18   Bauer, "Olympic Team Report."

19   Mitchell was a noted sports enthusiast and later the commissioner of the Canadian Football League, and believed that the city deserved elite hockey after it had lost both its major junior team and the WHA Cowboys.

20   MacGregor, "History Appears," 48. Hockey Canada provided seed money and bursaries at CIAU institutions.

21   Jim Proudfoot, "Father Bauer Recalls 'Giant Act of Faith,'" *Toronto Star*, 1987 or 1988, Box 4, File 9, Bauer fonds, Basilian Archives.

22   MacGregor, "History Appears," 47–48.

A Philosophical Basis for the 1980 Olympic Team

As early as May 1976, Bauer led discussions around the aims of a restored National Team, and two years later articulated its objectives.[23] In addition to fielding the best amateur team possible, themes reflected his ideals of a global, values-driven form of hockey: cultivating a spirit of internationalism; connecting domestic development with overseas competition; placing human ideals ahead of victory; and celebrating the human spirit in sport. It embraced scientific training methods more systemically, yet remained rooted in humanistic hockey traditions.

A team of university-aged players would be "in tough" against the Soviets, who defeated an NHL All-Star team in the three-game Challenge Cup in 1979. Bauer admitted that "the highest priority for 1980 should not be placed on winning gold or silver medals at any cost," but on developing young people physically, mentally, and morally.[24] In light of his reading of Solzhenitsyn, he sought "a well-rounded education" for players based on western ideals of "freedom and morality … as opposed to that of the [communist] Soviet Union," which seemed inhumane in many ways. For his detractors, Bauer's plan seemed too modest or too fearful of communist thought. To counter this, he pointed to players from his 1960s National Teams: "We had over 80 players go through our system back then and, almost to a man, all are successful professionals—doctors, lawyers, teachers—today. A few, like Ken Dryden and Wayne Stephenson, are still in the NHL, but they both have something else after their careers are finished."[25] Developing better people, Bauer believed, would always enable a level of success.

Canadian hockey had made a terrible mistake in the 1970s, Bauer told a reporter. By advocating for physical violence and intimidation, the system had detracted from individual hockey skills and the game's natural excitement.[26] For Bauer, that meant "giving our young people a kind of automated response mechanism, both to those who play the game and to those who look up to hockey stars as heroes. To me, it's like what Marshall McLuhan said when he talked of the effect of the mass media on the minds of people. They lose

23   Hockey Canada, "Olympics 1980"; David Bauer, "Attachment to Olympic Team Report," September 1979, MG31 E 72 35, LAC.

24   John Dooley, "Rev. Bauer Back on the Front Lines for '80 Olympics," *The Record*, February 1979, Carmelite Sisters of St. Joseph Collection.

25   Dooley, "Rev. Bauer Back."

26   Dooley, "Rev. Bauer Back."

the ability to think and reason for themselves. They go out on the ice and do their best to play within a system that tells them to interfere with and intimidate the opponent." [27] McLuhan, who taught at the University of St. Michael's College, developed a friendship with Bauer that included dining together at the McLuhan household.[28] For McLuhan, the new media became an extension of the person; television, for instance, impacted the inner life of the person and made them more power-hungry, eager, and impatient. His insights became part of popular imagination, with phrases like, "The medium is the message." In the case of hockey, the televised version of the sport deeply changed players across the nation. It forged a model of intimidation that sunk deeply into their psyches.

Televised broadcasts could perpetuate a dominant meaning to the sport, to the detriment of other values.[29] Drawing from McLuhan, Bauer claimed that players came to accept automatically that violence—not human freedom and moral goodness—undergirded hockey and human communities. Bauer saw this in major junior hockey, where intimidation mixed with highly drafted, natural goal scorers outweighed the value of young people's enthusiasm for team play.[30] The corporate game's short-sighted philosophy blocked many young players from understanding the game at a higher level, and stunted proper human development. Despite this, Bauer declared that Canadian players still had an edge over the Russians because they still possessed a "spirit and fire" for the game. This passion was not based on domination, but on the freedom to develop one's gifts and flourish as persons and a community.

The Dangers of Technical Advancements in Hockey

Bauer's enthusiasm for coaching and strategic innovations within Canadian hockey turned to concern with what he saw as an overemphasis on scientific technique. Led by prominent hockey researcher George Larivière, the advanced training program for the new Olympic program would become

---

27   Dooley, "Rev. Bauer Back."

28   University of St. Michael's College, "Our History," accessed May 19, 2021, https://stmikes.utoronto.ca/about-us/our-history/. McLuhan joined its faculty in 1946. Lisa Bauer-Leahy, interview with author, January 17, 2019.

29   Televised hockey also minimized the draw of local senior hockey games in towns across Canada.

30   David Bauer, Notes, Box 3, File 5, Bauer fonds, Basilian Archives.

like no other in the country.[31] In the 1970s, Larivière led a CAHA committee that oversaw university research projects on skills, physiology, and academic achievement for young players.[32] Skill improvements were to match developments in sport coaching internationally. In Canada, the scientific study of sport began its professionalization in the 1960s with the establishment of the Canadian Association of Sports Sciences, helping push forward the modernization of Canada's sport system.[33]

Bauer was not averse to learning from a more technically-driven sport system, like that of the Soviet Union. For instance, at a 1960s tournament, Bauer took in an entire practice led by Tarasov.[34] The Soviet coaches quickly changed after practice to watch Bauer lead his team, the Russian coach recalled: "And there we suddenly saw our Canadian colleague repeating the drills that had been just executed by our team.... What was that?" Tarasov crowed that imitation was the highest form of flattery: "It means that from the very beginning [of our interaction with Bauer and Canadian hockey] we selected a new rational way." Bauer showed an unmistakable interest in the "rational way" of the Russians.

However, as the 1980 Olympic Team became more influenced by a scientifically-driven sport, with leaders like Larivière and a "rational planning model" promoted by Sport Canada, grave doubt crept into Bauer's thinking.[35] Reading the works of historian Christopher Dawson, Bauer understood how

31   Ramsay, "Olympic Team Plan." Larivière was a Hockey Canada director and University of Montreal professor. He had worked with the CAHA's Technical Advisory Council in the early 1970s, when he helped write the National Coaches' Certificate Program and was chair of the CAHA Research Council. Canadian Amateur Hockey Association, "Minutes of Annual Meeting," 1973, Charlottetown, PEI, Minutes file, Hockey Canada Archives, 78.

32   Canadian Amateur Hockey Association, "Minutes of Annual Meeting," May 1976, Penticton, BC, Minutes file, Hockey Canada Archives, 3.

33   J. E. Merriman, "Canadian Association of Sports Sciences: A Historical Review," *Canadian Medical Association Journal* 96, no. 19 (May 13, 1967): 1340–42. Today it is called the Canadian Society for Exercise Physiology. Canadian Society for Exercise Physiology, "Celebrating 50 Years of Science to Practice in Canada," accessed January 6, 2021, https://timeline.csep.ca/; and Donald MacIntosh and David Whitson, *The Game Planners: Transforming Canada's Sport System* (Montreal: McGill-Queen's University Press, 1990), 122.

34   This was a common practice among international coaches. Anatoly Tarasov, *The Father of Russian Hockey: Tarasov* (Glendale, CA: Griffin Publishing, 1997), 28.

35   MacIntosh and Whitson, *The Game Planners*, 7.

a system geared toward the production of trained specialists threatened the spiritual foundations of society. Dawson believed that this was the path taken with the expansion of public education in the 1960s.[36] He acknowledged that traditional forms of classical education may have become antiquated, but that education in any form—whether in the classroom or in sport—must "provide some principle of cohesion to counterbalance the centrifugal tendencies of specialization and utilitarianism."[37] Underlining spiritual values taken from antiquity and Christianity, Dawson argued that "there will never be a machine for the creation of moral values. The last word in human affairs always belongs to the spiritual power that transcends both the order of nature and the order of culture and gives human life its ultimate meaning and person."[38] This thinking lingered in Bauer's mind: how would hockey's scientific growth overshadow the moral order that holds the hockey community together?

Bauer wrote that empiricism, or the science of manipulation, needed to be balanced by the science of understanding, that is, wisdom, religion, and a philosophy of first principles.[39] This true humanism, as outlined by Maritain, explained that the manipulation of things eventually becomes the manipulation of people. Without a counterbalance to the science of manipulation, Bauer warned, spiritual values are abandoned.[40] He had experienced this in the genesis of Hockey Canada, where profits outweighed interests in human development. Bauer's critique reflected the work of physical educators at Canadian universities in the 1960s and '70s, who promoted ethical and philosophical traditions in physical education faculties despite the trend toward the science of human movement.[41]

Bauer's critique of an overly scientific approach also reflected a typed excerpt he kept from the writings of French philosopher Jacques Ellul.[42]

---

36 Christopher Dawson, *Understanding Europe* (Washington, DC: Catholic University of America Press, 1952), 15.

37 Dawson, *Understanding Europe*, 16–17.

38 Dawson, *Understanding Europe*, 205.

39 David Bauer, Teaching Notes, Box 3, File 1, Bauer fonds, Basilian Archives. See also David Bauer, Notes, Box 3, File 4, Bauer fonds, Basilian Archives. A philosophy of first principles is commonly known as metaphysics.

40 Bauer, Teaching Notes, Box 3, File 1, Bauer fonds, Basilian Archives.

41 MacIntosh and Whitson, *The Game Planners*, 133. For example, John Meagher and Earle Zeigler.

42 Jacques Ellul, *The Technological Society* (New York: Random House, 1964), 382–84. Excerpt found in Box 4, File 5, Bauer fonds, Basilian Archives.

Ellul argued that in technically driven civilization "real play and enjoyment, contact with air and water, improvisation and spontaneity all disappear." That is, the spirit of human beings is replaced when "training in sport makes of the individual an efficient piece of apparatus which is henceforth unacquainted with anything but the harsh joy of exploiting his body and winning." Bauer could see this happening before him. When specialized, technical education becomes central to human activity, Ellul argued, "harmony, joy, or the realization of a spiritual good" within sport are pushed aside and "nothing gratuitous is allowed to exist." This shift changes the human person: "[Sports'] mechanisms reach into the individual's innermost life, working a transformation of his body and its motions as a function of technique and not as a function of some traditional end foreign to technique," like friendship or peace. Technique-driven sport, for Ellul, enslaves human beings and offers distraction as the only relief. Thus, Bauer believed that this kind of approach to sport left persons feeling threatened, and extinguished their inner freedom.[43]

Years later, sport sociologists MacIntosh and Whitson would use a Weberian socio-historical critique of "rationalization" in sport to explain the expansion of the Canadian sporting system in the 1970s and '80s. They argued that scientific analysis changed both sporting structures and coaching techniques through an emphasis on efficiency and productivity.[44] The resulting new structures of control, as felt by Bauer, often gave a rational framework the sense of inevitability because efficiency and results-orientation became unrivaled values of the system. The government's allowance for the corporatization of the hockey system and sport science's drive for high-performance results would impact Bauer's 1980 Olympic team.

Bauer's Philosophical Stance Creates Tensions

Bauer felt increasingly threatened by sport scientists. Team general manager Rick Noonan recalled a meeting among sport scientists in Calgary that unnerved Bauer, who then vented concerns about his autonomy.[45] Bauer wrote that he was concerned that "Georges [Larivière] was technisizing a human art form which

---

43   David Bauer, Letter to unknown, post-1980, Box 3, File 5, Bauer fonds, Basilian Archives.

44   MacIntosh and Whitson, *The Game Planners*, 10–12.

45   Rick Noonan, interview with author, May 27, 2019.

should be a spontaneous activity of persons—not just a Sovietizied or Czech patterned copy of an already dangerous drift towards a standardized system which automatizes and therefore is alien and in fact kills the human spirit."[46] Efficient systems of production within sport change the people playing the game, thought Bauer. For example, years later Larivière placed radio transceivers in players' helmets so they could hear real-time instructions from coaches.[47] He admitted that players felt "like robots; they just did what their coach was telling them to do, instead of reacting to the game." Paid technical staff were putting the squeeze on Bauer's autonomy to direct his team.[48]

Was hockey only about execution and performance? Or, was it also a test of moral character and teamwork? According to Noonan's recollections, Bauer fought against a mentality that viewed the National Team as a science experiment: "If the team members weren't guinea pigs—and really 100% so—they can't win."[49] Thus, Bauer's mantra, "make use of technique, but let the spirit prevail," deepened in meaning, more consciously critiquing an overly scientific approach to sport. Although Bauer tried to keep Larivière on in a limited capacity, his deep reservations led Campagnolo to remove Larivière.[50]

Bauer became less willing to trust others. Hockey Canada secretary Chris Lang noted that Bauer was often inside himself, unwilling to share too much, and difficult to get to know because of it.[51] Whereas Bauer wrote that Lang lacked an "integrated overview of life" because he was willing to work so closely with Eagleson,[52] Lang countered that he shared Bauer's vision of sport and simply had a working relationship with Eagleson. In heated discussions, Bauer even accused confidant Rick Noonan of supporting Eagleson.[53] The politics within Hockey Canada made for constant deal-making, where Bauer

46   David Bauer, Letter to Barbara Bauer, March 21, 1983, Terry O'Malley Collection.

47   Karine Proulx, "George Larivière: For the Love of the Game," *Hockey Canada*, July 29, 2011, https://www.hockeycanada.ca/en-ca/news/2011-qhs-003-en.

48   MacIntosh and Whitson, *The Game Planners*, 5. This funding trend was in Hockey Canada and Sport Canada throughout the 1970s.

49   Noonan, interview.

50   Bauer, Letter to Barbara Bauer, March 21, 1983. Lang and Lefaive advocated for Bauer to the minister.

51   Chris Lang, interview with author, June 6, 2019. Noonan was likely Bauer's staunchest supporter and protector.

52   David Bauer, Notes, Box 3, File 1, Bauer fonds, Basilian Archives.

53   Kevin Primeau, interview with author, November 13, 2020.

felt that others could be against him one day and the next day protect him from encroaching dangers.[54] He acted more guarded and anxious.

Several factors left the Olympic Team at risk. Lang and others gave the impression that Bauer did not fully understand the pressures they felt from other board members—pressures that threatened the National Team's long-term survival.[55] Hockey Canada executive Derek Holmes warned Bauer that if he did not advocate for the team amongst the board members, their lukewarm support of the entire program could be swayed by others.[56] Holmes encouraged Bauer to go head-to-head with Eagleson at meetings, but felt disappointed that Bauer reacted meekly and lacked assertiveness as a board member.[57] Bauer the fierce competitor who had stood up to the game's powerbrokers was absent. Holmes encouraged him nonetheless: "Father, you've got to jump in and say things. You're legitimate." But Bauer hemmed and hawed, apparently "psychologizing" his role to Holmes, and he allowed Eagleson to bully him like the others. For instance, in a rant, Eagleson would holler, "That cocksucker. That fucking guy," and then mockingly turn and say, "Oh, sorry, Father," and laugh under his breath.[58] Eagleson intimidated from across the boardroom table, saying anything to dictate the board agenda.

Eagleson's aggressiveness gave him more power in Hockey Canada, and he effectively took control from its president, Doug Fisher.[59] At times, Eagleson's power could be circumvented by Campagnolo's assurances.[60] However, Bauer felt threatened by Eagleson's tactics: "Eagleson will stop at almost nothing to get control of the Olympic team as well as a seat on IIHF. He is consumed by an unusually inordinate ambition for power."[61] Bauer's

---

54   David Bauer, Notes, Box 3, File 5, Bauer fonds, Basilian Archives. Some Hockey Canada directors approved the 1980 Olympic team so that they could receive IIHF consent for European involvement in the Canada Cup.

55   David Bauer, Untitled Letter, "Bauer, Dave, 1971–1980 file," St. Mark's College Archives.

56   Holmes, interview. At the time, Holmes cautioned Bauer that President Fisher and Eagleson were "going to mount quite an attack ... against George's program—our Olympic program." Bauer, Untitled Letter.

57   Holmes, interview.

58   Holmes, interview. Eagleson would call out others like board member Bill Hay: "You're here because your dad Charlie started this."

59   Holmes, interview.

60   David Bauer, Notes, Fall 1980, Box 3, File 1, Bauer fonds, Basilian Archives.

61   Bauer, Untitled Letter.

anxiety about the team's survival was met in jest by the wife of Bauer devotee Terry O'Malley (at 39, O'Malley joined for his second tour with the National Team). She jokingly bought Bauer a poster that stated: "Just because you're paranoid doesn't mean they aren't out to get you."[62]

Besides the political tug-of-war within Hockey Canada, the renewed National Team faced two major obstacles. First, despite Bauer believing he had a verbal, five-year agreement for the team's future, Holmes explained at the time: "It's a matter of economics. The team costs $750,000, and if they don't put up a good showing [in Lake Placid] it's going to be hard to raise that kind of money for the team's continuation."[63] Both the private and public sectors supported the National Team as never before. More than a third of Hockey Canada's budget came from the federal government, however, and Clarence Campbell, Eagleson, and others sought a financially-viable, commercialized amateur hockey product without federal support.[64]

Second, many still questioned the validity of pitting nonprofessional Canadian players against other nations' best. Author MacGregor wrote: "It is one of the mystifying ironies of life that the future often lies like tracing paper over the past, and shadowed and blurred through the cover of those coming Olympic Games lurks the ghost of one Father David Bauer. The muffled sound from the past is booing as Bauer uses kids to defend Canada's international hockey manhood."[65] This simplified take on the National Team overlooked a change in attitude within Canadian hockey—toward better coaching, improved skills, and less goon play—that aligned with Bauer's ideals.[66] As argued by one reporter, "Father Bauer was ahead of his time, and only now are some of his hockey concepts getting the wide public attention and acceptance they deserve. This time around, I believe, his concept of an ongoing national hockey team will stick, simply because the 'victory or else'

---

62   Terry O'Malley, email message to author, March 6, 2023.

63   Sigal, "Collegiate Team Could Surprise," 14.

64   "Canada's National Hockey Team vs The U.S. Olympic Hockey Team," Pre-1980 Game Program, Bauer Fr. David box, Post-Memorial Cup file, St. Michael's College School Archives. Its budget was $1.1 million in 1979–80.

65   MacGregor, "History Appears," 48. Many other Canadian Olympic sports relied heavily on government funds.

66   Ted Blackman, "Pollock Plan: Use Soviets for TV Lure," *Toronto Star*, January 29, 1978, B1. Further, the NHL also sought engagement with international hockey as a means to secure a larger US national television contract.

curse no longer hangs over the team's head."[67] Best-on-best competition had opened the eyes of many. Bauer spoke about shifting the sport toward "a much faster, cleaner game than we play here in Canada."[68]

Bauer's pre-Olympic Speech on the Role of Hockey in Canada

In a full-length speech given to hockey coaches and players in fall 1979, Bauer presented his criticism of corporatized sport systems and scientific training.[69]

The speech began with Bauer situating hockey within a geopolitical framework. He named the "rise of war, genocide, violence and terrorism" in many countries and interpreted these as the result of "the critical denial of dignity of the human person ... in frightening proportions." This was no ordinary speech given to hockey coaches. Naming the harsh realities of international strife, Bauer drew on thinkers like Solzhenitsyn and philosopher E. R. Schumacher to make the case that "our priorities must be in place" to forge a philosophy of sport. He explained: "We must be loyal to the truth, to our friendships and we must strive to create an environment in which an athlete can continue to grow as a human person.... The reason we are in sport and coaching is not merely to learn the philosophy and techniques of the game and make professional hockey players. Rather we believe and hope we have something more to give our young people."

In the speech, Bauer argued for "the personal growth of each boy or girl," so that they may find "what is meaningful and most significant in life." Hockey involvement should not close people off to educational options. He distinguished between the business of hockey—bluntly quoting former NHL President Campbell as saying, "we're in it for the money ... and it's not my function to take care of five hundred thousand Canadian boys"—and the aims of amateur sport: "hockey should not only require the acquisition and mastering of physical skills; it should also provide information that nurtures values, that increases a player's power to create for himself a healthy way of life, be it pro or amateur."

67 Sigal, "Collegiate Team Could Surprise," 11.
68 Sigal, "Collegiate Team Could Surprise," 14.
69 David Bauer, "The Role of Hockey," 1979, Terry O'Malley Collection. Perhaps it was at a fundraising dinner for a minor hockey association or as an act of boosterism in Calgary.

Bauer was distressed that technical advancements in the training of the Olympic Team placed "know how" ahead of human values: "In the game of hockey we also can go overboard in simply learning technique and forgetting other contributions that Canadians have made in the hockey world.... Science, engineering, and technology produce know how, but 'know how' is nothing by itself. It is the means without an end.... [T]he task of education would be to stress the idea of human value, of spirit, and of how to find new meaning in our lives."[70] Then Bauer summarized his aims with his motto, "Make use of technique, but let the spirit prevail." To illustrate the point, he quoted the famed Montreal Canadiens' player Jean Béliveau: "I was taught that the stick was for passing, for taking a pass, shooting and scoring, but after observing this year's Stanley Cup series, we've turned it into an instrument of intimidation." Bauer exclaimed: "We've put 'know how' ahead of value!"

Bauer's speech posited that what was needed was "for the game of hockey [to] be motivated by the habitual vision of greatness": an idealized approach that sought excellence for individuals and communities. This was to begin with coaches: "Our role as coaches is not to make a professional athlete but to help each person we meet have a positive self-image, inner discipline, a sense of loyalty, and responsibility to themselves and society." Building character requires reflecting on life, Bauer demanded: "We must give our players a vision of the whole world, so that they can locate themselves right here and now, 'Why am I playing this sport?'" Coaches needed to consider the creative dynamism within players.

After highlighting the rise in violence in Canadian society, the speech included a lengthy quotation from Solzhenitsyn: "... we are witnessing the emergence of a whole new situation, a crisis of an unknown nature.... It is a turning point [in world history] at which the hierarchy of values to which we were dedicated all our lives ... and which causes our lives and our hearts to beat is starting to waver and perhaps collapse."[71] Bauer interpreted: "I don't want to become too serious, but ... we are in a time of critical change and with that change a questionable change in values." His audience undoubtedly found him serious, but his circumstances compelled him to speak about what values anchored society. Coaches did not coach hockey in a vacuum.

Bauer concluded his speech: "If there is one place that you and I, as coaches and players can start to remove violence from our society, it's

---

70 Bauer, "The Role of Hockey."
71 Bauer, "The Role of Hockey."

right here and now. But, if we don't see life in the larger perspective and understand what is taking place in the world we're going to get drawn in and trapped in a variety of ways." He challenged his audience's complacency. A narrow focus set on winning alone mirrored a major cultural problem: "We are living in a culture and society that is rapidly losing its sense of balance." Thus, the gathering needed to get "clear in our minds the difference between entertainment and the growth and dignity of the human person." This required coaches "to consider some of the deeper reasons *why* we are coaching, and *why* we are playing."

Bauer's speech reflects the ancient Christian tradition of the "two ways."[72] Which path should minor hockey coaches choose? The first path defines sport primarily as a form of entertainment; the other prioritizes the development of persons. Because professional hockey was so dominant, particularly with the aid of mass media, he used a dialogical style to challenge assumptions and motivations. Could hockey coaches and players name their intentions and work toward larger purposes? The audience's reaction is unknown, but it was not uncommon for some attendees to leave a Bauer talk saying, for example, "You know, I couldn't tell you much about what was said here, but it's affected me deeply."[73] Bauer's teachings were difficult for others to synthesize and articulate. Nonetheless, many were moved by his practical reasoning and presumably grappled with their own motivations within the sport.

Coaching Preparations for the Olympics

Canadian university hockey had coaches of the same ilk as Bauer. He, Noonan, and these coaches chose team members in 1978–79. In the first summer, three camps were held—in Edmonton, Toronto, and Quebec—with 120 eligible players from across Canada. During that hockey season, Bauer, Holmes, and former National Team member Lorne Davis scoured the continent for additional players.[74] A Calgary training camp began the following August for sixty-eight players and ten coaches, with many recognizable connections to

---

72   This approach is exemplified in the opening chapters of the second century text *The Didache*. Shawn J. Wilhite, *The Didache: A Commentary*, foreword by Clayton N. Jefford (Eugene, OR: Cascade Books, 2019).

73   Greg Schmalz, "Farewell Friends," *Newshound* 3, no. 4 (Spring 1989): 1–2.

74   Bauer, "Olympic Team Report." Davis later scouted for the St. Louis Blues and Edmonton Oilers.

Bauer and past National Teams: Hindmarch, Barry MacKenzie, and Marshall Johnston, who coached at the University of Denver. Four highly successful university coaches—Clare Drake, Tom Watt, Pierre Pagé, and George Kingston—would eventually coach in the NHL.[75] Drake and Watt were both given a year's leave of absence from their universities when a Canadian brewery picked up the tab on their salaries.[76] Watt, head coach of the Varsity Blues, was familiar with a longtime St. Michael's priest, Father Harry Gardner, who was a booster for the Toronto team.[77]

A young Dave King, who later coached the National Team, assisted with the earlier 1978 camps. He recalled how Drake, Watt, and Kingston were leading collegiate coaches whose insight into coaching techniques and team strategies were superior to the typical professional hockey coach.[78] For King, Bauer was more conservative in his approach to the game, yet he endorsed strong, defensive one-on-one play to control the often more talented Soviet or Czech teams. Bauer's approach required high levels of commitment and motivation among teammates. Reflecting back on his time as the National Team coach in the 1980s, King came to understand deeply why Bauer backed this kind of a philosophy: "I could sometimes think, 'This is what Father Bauer must have been thinking when he was playing the Russians.' You've got to be so good in every situation."[79]

Bauer differed from Watt and Drake because he saw the game as a series of one-on-one battles on the ice. Bauer's individualized focus, whether it was taking out a man in the corner or angling a player on the forecheck, was less attentive to large system strategies promoted by the others.[80] They would kid privately that Bauer's critiques of practices boiled down to one

75   University affiliations were Clare Drake (University of Alberta), Tom Watt (University of Toronto), Pierre Pagé (Dalhousie University), and George Kingston (University of Calgary). Drake was inducted into the Hockey Hall of Fame in 2017.

76   Tom Watt, interview with author, September 18, 2020.

77   University of Toronto Varsity Blues, "In Memorandum [sic], Fr. Harry B. Gardner," accessed May 19, 2021. https://varsityblues.ca/sports/2012/4/13/GEN_0413122903.aspx?path=. Gardner sat on many university hockey and recreation committees.

78   Dave King, interview with author, September 4, 2020.

79   King, interview.

80   Watt, interview. Although Watt and Drake were labelled as "technical coaches," Watt firmly stated: "I appreciate the technical side of hockey, but I wouldn't have ever claimed that I was a technical coach."

thing: "I want to see more one-on-one drills."[81] And Watt understood that Bauer's approach on the ice matched his philosophy off of it. He recalled Bauer critiquing the communist political system and how it restricted people's individuality. Watt drew a parallel: "When the team would meet, we had to worry about the players as individuals, not just as hockey players."[82] It was not that Bauer individualized a team game—he clearly believed in team spirit— but he coached the game as a series of one-on-one battles so as to draw out what was deep within each player.

During practices, Bauer could be seen high up in the dimly lit stands writing his thoughts in his notebook.[83] He stayed at the Basilian House in Calgary and, according to Watt, never let his concerns at the board level seep into the day-to-day operations of the team.[84] Conversations focused on hockey and the players, with two particular pieces of Bauer's coaching philosophy sticking with Watt after decades of coaching. Before an important game, Bauer had his team scrimmage at the end of practice because every hockey player likes playing the game most. After ten minutes of fun, Bauer demanded that Watt "cut them right off. Don't let them touch the puck. Leave them hungry to play tomorrow."[85] Fan the passion and do not overcomplicate the game, believed Bauer. Also, Watt never forgot that Bauer adamantly "wanted to see the team score the last goal," whether in victory or defeat. The positive energy carried over into the next game.

The coaches were part of a values-driven tradition. As player Kevin Primeau explained: "You were a better person after playing with Coach Drake and ... Father Bauer."[86] Both sought player and individual development. Another player, John Devaney, noted that both of their coaching styles were "calm, firm and direct," not loud or boisterous.[87] They were thoughtful, well-prepared, motivational coaches who encouraged self-determination and self-improvement. Primeau concluded: "If you [as a coach] turned one person off the sport or if you've damaged somebody's outlook on life ... , then

81   Watt, interview.

82   Watt, interview.

83   Wayne Skene, "The Unpaid Boys of Winter," *Toronto Star*, January 26, 1980, 12.

84   Watt, interview.

85   Watt, interview. Watt used this method the day before games, including when he helped coach a team to the 1989 Stanley Cup.

86   Primeau, interview.

87   John Devaney, interview with author, November 26, 2020.

you're a failure as a coach." Needless to say, the team's coaches were advanced thinkers who recognized that a fast, responsive, and defensively-sound game plan was necessary for the undermanned Canadians.

1980 Olympic Team Players

Nearly one thousand junior, senior, and college level players expressed initial interest in playing for the new National Team.[88] Engaging university players and coaches set up the program for Hockey Canada's planned expansion into CIAU hockey. Team captain and defenseman Randy Gregg, who was studying medicine at the University of Alberta, was joined by three other players from Drake's squad at that school. They had ties to Bauer. Forward Dave Hindmarch was the son of Bob Hindmarch. Devaney had met Bauer as a ten-year-old boy when his older brother received a US college hockey scholarship. Kevin Primeau's father was very close to his first cousin "Gentleman" Joe Primeau.[89] Jim Nill and Paul MacLean played at the University of Calgary and Dalhousie University, respectively. Tim Watters and Glenn Anderson played at US colleges. An exception to the university student roster was goaltender Bob Dupuis, who played senior hockey and was married with children. A notable tryout player was a young Mark Messier.[90] Many of the players were picked after the first round of the NHL draft and wanted to avoid extended stints in the minor leagues. Only one French-speaker made the team, which accented a longtime representational problem for the National Team program.[91]

Players received a $50 per month training allowance and $215 per month living allowance.[92] Gregg noted a different attitude when compared to NHL teams he played with later: "When you're paid a lot of money, it's a job. When you're paid $4,000 for a whole year, you're doing it because of the passion you have in the game, the commitment towards your team, and the country

88   David McDonald, "Hockey Team is Back on the Ice: Derek Holmes Optimistic," A Piece of Canadian Sport History, March 1979, http://canadiansporthistory.ca/champion-magazine/march-1979-mars/hockey-team-is-back-on-the-ice/.

89   Devaney, interview. Devaney knew a local Catholic priest, Father Bonner, who helped get Devaney's older brother to Brown University. Bonner was close to Bauer. Kevin Primeau, email message to author, January 6, 2021.

90   King, interview.

91   Noonan, interview.

92   Skene, "Unpaid Boys," 13. The few married players received a meager additional amount.

you're representing."[93] Gregg played many years for championship Edmonton Oilers teams and said that "there was something really natural and innocent about the Olympic program." They were not stars, as they packed their own hockey bags on and off the bus.

Instead of housing the players in hotel suites from August until the Olympic Games in February, Bauer accepted the gift of ATCO trailers from an oil company that were transferred from Alaska and parked behind the Calgary Corral arena.[94] This area became known as "The Rig." The trailers had suites with two beds in each room, while players ate together nearby in the grungy Stampede Pavilion social hall. The shared bedrooms, common areas, washrooms, and dining hall were set up in keeping with Bauer's design. Primeau recalled the players complaining about the living arrangements, but now believes Bauer did so to create adversity that would unite them. Primeau did not see Bauer as a throwback coach living in the past, but rather as someone who lived by what others might call "older values."[95] He called it "my best hockey experience," as friendships were forged while living in the oil rig trailers.[96] When a teammate committed a major rule infraction, Bauer preferred the team understand the value of giving the guilty player a second chance—with the team empowered to support the player.[97] What the team lacked in recognizable, world-class players, they made up for in loyalty and dedication to one another.

The youngest player on the team was Glenn Anderson, who would become its most accomplished hockey player and later play internationally in Canada Cups and world championships. Anderson was intrigued from an early age with Russian hockey and, with the support of his head coach at the University of Denver, chose the Olympic team instead of entering the NHL draft. In choosing a US college and then Bauer's team, Anderson came to realize that there were alternatives to professional hockey. According to a newspaper article, Anderson credited Bauer as having had a great impact on his life and that "he

93   Randy Gregg, interview with author, November 9, 2020. Gregg summarized: "We were just hockey players that were given the chance to play for our country in the biggest sporting experience in the world."

94   Frank Orr, "Oil Rig Is New Home for Gold Seekers," *Toronto Star*, October 5, 1979, B4.

95   Primeau, interview.

96   Primeau, interview. Primeau went on to play and coach in professional hockey for decades, including as the head coach of the Hungarian National Team.

97   Primeau, interview.

actually turned things around for me back then."[98] Anderson explained: "It's a great feeling when you got someone who can inspire you that much to keep you in for the love of the game and the passion for the game."

Players at the 1979 training camp were in better condition than typical Canadian players, and they put aside fighting and stick infractions.[99] Drake explained how Canadian players often lost their poise and vented their frustrations vocally and physically on the ice.[100] Because university hockey generally followed the amateur code of sportsmanship, the coaches promoted a similar less-violent form of play. The team was both young and small: the average player was 22 and weighed just under 170 pounds, which was 10 pounds lighter per player than the US Team.[101]

Scouting of Canadian talent occurred right up to the August training camp, when Bauer started locking in player spots to ensure he had his players' loyalty. Holmes believed a better team was possible if they extended the window for picking up top-end talent—for instance, US college goal-scorer Dave Poulin might have joined later that fall.[102] However, Bauer did not want a long selection process that could disrupt team cohesion; team loyalty lifted their shared spirit. The team was limited to twenty skaters and two goalies, but used three goalies throughout fall 1979. The Quebec league's Paul Pageau played periodically with the team alongside regulars Bob Dupuis and Ron Patterson.[103] Without a definitive top goaltender, the team was at a disadvantage compared to past National Teams, which had goalies like Seth Martin and Wayne Stephenson.

Calgary Seminars

The National Team met every couple of weeks after practice at the Basilian House along Calgary's Bow River. The players, many of whom had attended university and were older than junior players, generally warmed to these

98 Peter Cudhea, "Fond Memories," *Waterloo Chronicle*, November 30, 1994, Bauer Fr. David box, Obit file, St. Michael's College School Archives, 37–38.
99 Derek Holmes, "Report on Olympic Team," Fall 1979, MG31 E 72 35, LAC.
100 Bauer-McGahey, Notes of Unpublished Book.
101 Skene, "Unpaid Boys," 13. The average age was 21 without O'Malley.
102 Holmes, interview. Poulin played at the University of Notre Dame.
103 Frank Orr, "Medal or Not, Olympic Team Was Indeed a Worthwhile Effort," *Toronto Star*, January 6, 1980, C4. See also Allan Ryan, "Pride Spurs Canada's Hockey Team," *Toronto Star*, February 9, 1980, D1. Paul Pageau played for the Shawinigan Juniors, Bob Dupuis for the Barrie Seniors, and Ron Patterson for UBC.

Calgary seminars.[104] These sessions were the product of Bauer's work at St. Michael's and St. Mark's, which had then been fine-tuned over several weekends with his nieces and nephews.

Those family weekends, in turn, had their beginnings in tragedy. Between 1964 and 1967, three of Bauer's brothers—Frank, Bobby, and Gene—died from congenital heart disease. Dave, believing in the importance of youth mentorship, felt compelled to do something for the children of these families, especially with some teens no longer attending church.[105] His uneasiness reflected changes in Canadian society. Rural towns like Waterloo that had been strongholds of the Christian faith were changed by the urban influences stemming from economic development and activities that drew youth away from church-run events.[106]

At the family cottage on Lake Huron at Bayfield, Ontario, Bauer established an annual family weekend retreat for more than twenty teens and young adults in the early 1970s.[107] Dubbed the "State of the World" seminars, these reviewed the history of western civilization and the primary institutions of different eras.[108] Bauer explained that the ancient Greeks and Romans had politics at the center of their societies, whereas the Middle Ages chose religion. The Age of Reason placed politics and economy as central: modern people chose between Marxism, forms of socialism, and capitalism. Any one of the six primary institutions—i.e., education, religion, economics, leisure, family, and politics—could act as the hub of society and become its central institution. Nieces and nephews discussed how society and their lives changed when a different hub was chosen; their uncle admitted to the difficulty of keeping religion central in his life.[109] Time for recreation was included. Uncle

---

104 Watt, interview. He recalled coaching Varsity Blues' players who graduated in dentistry, medicine, and law.

105 Paul Schmalz and Steve Freiburger, interview with author, January 18, 2019.

106 Hugh McLeod, *The Religious Crisis of the 1960s* (Oxford, UK: Oxford University Press, 2010), 123.

107 Not all of his nieces and nephews attended. The sons of Bobby Bauer were not involved. When Bobby married in the Baptist church, he became "like a black sheep" in a devotedly Catholic family, recalled his son Bobby Jr. The family eventually reconciled, but families maintained different social circles and schedules. Bob Bauer, Jr., interview with author, June 6, 2019. Schmalz and Freiburger, interview.

108 Bauer-McGahey, interview. See also, Maureen Bauer-McGahey, Seminar Notes, June 2019, Maureen Bauer-McGahey Collection.

109 Further details about the seminars were offered in Schmalz and Freiburger, interview.

Dave played a mischievous referee in a family football game, and late nights involved drinking German-made Blue Nun wine.

In letters written to a niece in the 1970s, Bauer used the image of a central hub to reflect on what he saw happening during that decade. Galloping inflation and rising unemployment, along with the questioning of social institutions and the growth of consumerism, in part led Bauer to question economics as the dominant institution of society. A consumeristic framework was failing society, like it had duped Bauer in hockey. He claimed that the largest problem slowly unfolding was "the despiritualization of all men. . . . [Aristotle] said, 'We become what we know,' and of most men on all levels are becoming materialists . . . the fault belongs to all of us who neglect the spiritual."[110] Interpreting the chaos in his hockey life and on the world stage could make Bauer despair about the world's plight, but he elsewhere called for courage: "No, we won't set the world on fire but we can give a witness to ultimate values . . . all I do is really trust that what God has begun He will complete."[111]

In the same spirit of dialogue, Bauer hosted the Calgary seminars with his hockey players. He asked Olympic team members to talk about their lives' direction, with promptings from book reading.[112] Life was to be contemplated like a book: discussed, not simply recalled.[113] The team read and discussed works by Solzhenitsyn and Schumacher, recalled Watt, that taught about the individuality of each person and the responsibility to develop each individual.[114] Watt added that the discussion brought out the priest in Bauer. With a team of mostly students, he had a receptive audience to his philosophies, his pedagogical methods of concentric circles, and his passion for dialogue.

The players took the discussions to heart.[115] Forward Ron Davidson explained to a reporter how different nations utilized sport for political or

110   David Bauer, Letter to Barbara Bauer, February 13, 1974, Terry O'Malley Collection. Barbara Bauer spent six months in Japan as part of a reading course on Eastern religions. Together, the two read much about Confucianism and Buddhism. Marc Bauer-Maison, interview with author, January 18, 2019.

111   David Bauer, Letter to Barbara Bauer, November 24, 1974, Terry O'Malley Collection. David Bauer, Letter to Barbara Bauer, February 24, 1974, Terry O'Malley Collection.

112   Rick Noonan, interview with author, May 27, 2019.

113   Bauer-Leahy, interview.

114   Watt, interview. The reading from Solzhenitsyn was a Harvard convocation address, and everyone received a copy of *Small is Beautiful: A Study of Economics as if People Mattered* by E. F. Schumacher.

115   Watt, interview.

economic gain, and how team discussions made him reflect on the purpose of Canadian hockey.[116] Forward Kevin Maxwell had his eyes opened to different hockey alternatives. The University of North Dakota student explained: "When I first started with the program, I [wanted to] … play well in front of the scouts and see what happens. Now there's only the team.… Father just didn't want guys to get caught up with the dollar signs. I still want to play pro, but now I've seen the alternatives and I'm a better person for it. Hockey's just not all there is."[117] Years later, forward Devaney recalled Bauer leading a late-night discussion, where his point would be made but only after some time. Bauer's underlying viewpoint was clear: "hockey had brought us together, but it wasn't the reason we were there."[118]

Gregg echoed Devaney's sentiment.[119] While training in Calgary, Gregg and three other players left one evening for an Edmonton Halloween party in a beatup car and returned by daybreak. More than a year later—when Gregg was a player-coach in Japan—Bauer told Gregg that the coaches had heard about the plan through the paper-thin walls of the ATCO trailers. But they elected to say nothing. Bauer had been upset because four players risked many things when driving in late fall Alberta weather in an unreliable car. Gregg recalled Bauer's explanation: "Randy, I realize that one of the biggest things we can do for all of you being part of this Olympic program is to make you into great gentlemen, great men, who will make decisions on their own. You'll live with the consequences."[120] Bauer and the coaches prioritized the growth and autonomy of players instead of overmanaging their decision-making.

Although the team's youthful enthusiasm could be interpreted cynically as naïveté, one reporter was struck by the sincerity of the players' nationalistic convictions.[121] Another reporter noted the countercultural spirit of the team: patriotic pride, supreme togetherness, family spirit, and sacrifice.[122] The reporter noted how "corny" it all sounded. General manager Noonan

116   Ryan, "Pride Spurs," D1. He was a forward from Queen's University, enrolled in its Law program.

117   Ryan, "Pride Spurs," D1. He was a native of Penticton, BC, and a third-round pick of the Minnesota North Stars.

118   Devaney, interview. He became a chartered accountant.

119   Gregg, interview.

120   Gregg, interview. Gregg also recalled Bauer wearing his clerical clothes and showing the much taller Gregg how to properly pin his opponent against the boards.

121   Skene, "Unpaid Boys," 17.

122   Ryan, "Pride Spurs," D1.

responded by saying how the players hesitated to speak about it because "everything they say about how they feel comes across sounding so … well, strange." It was by no accident that the spirit of the team distinguished itself from the hockey portrayed on television.

Preparing for the Olympics and Beyond

Following the August camp, Coach Watt teased reporters about underestimating the team's speed, smarts, and stamina: "After Lake Placid, I might have to worry about our bandwagon tipping over from people jumping on it."[123] The team went on a European tour, where they lost 5–3 against the World Champion Soviet team, which had added superb players like Vacheslav Fetisov and Alexander Yakushev.[124] Exhibition games versus both Canadian and American NHL teams in October resulted in four wins and two losses. Bauer desperately wanted to play more North American professional teams but Eagleson, the chief negotiator, was unable to arrange it. He showed little enthusiasm for game scheduling, especially when the NHL did not wish to cooperate mid-season.[125] NHL teams discouraged top draft picks from playing in the Olympics, making even junior players fearful about displeasing their drafting team.[126]

Bauer and Bill Hay formally introduced the concept of a major university hockey structure to the directors of Hockey Canada after years of discussions. Many of them, according to Bob Pugh of the CIAU, "strongly felt … that the future of Olympic Hockey in Canada lay with the university hockey program."[127] A National University League would connect education and hockey, creating a feeder system for the long-term success of the National Team. Support was found across the country. One prominent promoter was Bobby Boucher, a former St. Michael's Major who became head coach at St. Mary's University in Halifax.[128] Hockey Canada would need

123   Ryan, "Pride Spurs," D2.

124   Sigal, "Collegiate Team Could Surprise," 12.

125   Alan Eagleson, Letter to Bauer, March 6, 1979, Box 1, File 9, Bauer fonds, Basilian Archives.

126   Robert Pugh, "National University Hockey League," October 12, 1979, MG31 E 72 35, LAC.

127   Pugh, "National University Hockey League."

128   Watt, interview. See also The Bob Boucher Hockey Assistance Fund, "About Bob Boucher," accessed October 26, 2020, https://bobboucher.wordpress.com/about/.

to raise scholarship monies, while a set of National Teams would play out of mid-sized cities like Ottawa, Halifax, Winnipeg, and Victoria.[129] A university super league became the most attractive possibility.

The National Team continued to fine-tune its game, which included advanced scientific conditioning programs, until the end of November. From December to February, they played exhibition games in Minneapolis, Moscow, Japan, and Calgary. A journalist paraphrased the US Navy's recruiting slogan: "Join Canada's Olympic hockey team—and see the world."[130] Besides the playing schedule, a lot of practice time enhanced their skills, which was unheard of in North American professional hockey.[131] A team fitness trainer boasted that the rigorous training and testing meant that the Olympic team players had more pure power than Soviet players.[132]

National Team staff found it difficult to entice and keep natural goal scorers. Both Laurie Boschman and Paul Reinhart, who went on to lengthy NHL careers, left the team to sign professional contracts shortly before the Games; the latter had Eagleson as his agent.[133] One Hockey Canada representative critiqued, "I'd say you have too many barn painters and not enough artists!"[134] Bauer continued to beat his drum about development and mixing the art of the game with the science. Questions remained about the squad's overall talent level.[135]

Bauer knew that one of his few strengths against European teams, especially the favored Soviets, was that his team was largely made up of unknown players playing an unknown system. According to Hockey Canada's

129   Holmes, interview.

130   Jim Coleman, Untitled, August 1, 1979, File 3, David Bauer fonds, Canada's Sports Hall of Fame Archives. In all, the team spent more than 75 days on the road from September to January, winning twice as many games as it lost. Skene, "Unpaid Boys," 14.

131   Howard Wenger and H. Arthur Quinney, Letter to Hockey Canada, 1979, Box 36, "Bauer, Dave, 1971–1980" file, St. Mark's College Archives. This included dry land training for improved conditioning led by the Fitness and Sport Center at the University of Alberta and Dr. Howard Wenger at the University of Calgary.

132   Skene, "Unpaid Boys," 17.

133   Orr, "Oil Rig," B4. Goalie Vincent Tremblay also signed a late pro contract with the Leafs.

134   Terry O'Malley, "Father David Bauer csb (1924–1988)—A Life in 'Quotations,'" Terry O'Malley Collection, 28.

135   Bauer, "Olympic Team Report."

Lou Lefaive at the time, "Father explicitly told Al [Eagleson] that he did not want to handle the Izvestia tournament with the Olympic team as he wanted to hold playing the Soviets until Lake Placid."[136] Eagleson forced the issue and Bauer sent nine players and a coach to play with a group of fringe NHLers at the December tournament. The Canadian team finished last among five teams and was outscored 22–5. The team's lackluster performance caught the attention of the longtime Canadian ambassador to the Soviet Union, Robert Ford. He privately demanded that Hockey Canada send its best to prestigious tournaments or "withdrawal from competitions here altogether."[137] He explained, "Without mincing words, Canada's contribution to this year's Izvestia Cup was an embarrassment.... [E]ach Soviet defeat over a Canadian team reinforces Soviet belief that their system has once again triumphed over that of Western capitalism." The hastily put together team was out of sync and further fed public frustrations about Canadian representation at international tournaments. Its failure was also seen as making a stronger case for the National Team program and its long-term viability.

Newly appointed board chair of Hockey Canada Willard "Bud" Estey, a justice of the Supreme Court of Canada, received Ford's demands at the Lake Placid Games: "The time has come to refuse to leave the selection of teams representing Canada in the hands of NHL owners whose interest in our national prestige is minimal."[138] Similar to Bauer's diplomatic concerns with the National Team throughout the 1960s, Ford exhorted Estey to develop an international hockey team for "the propagation of the best possible image for Canada in all parts of the world"—and to keep it beyond the reach of the NHL.[139]

Estey privately met NHL President John Ziegler shortly after. He detailed demands about how the NHL ought to make players available, play exhibition games against the National Team, and reimburse Hockey Canada for players developed in their program.[140] The suggestions all surely infuriated Ziegler, who wanted to support the National Team as little as possible. Estey was not

136   Lou Lefaive, Letter to Willard Estey, January 24, 1980, MG31 E 72 35, H2 (1) a, Hockey Canada—General: correspondence (file 3), LAC.

137   Eric Morse, Letter to Willard Estey, January 15, 1980, MG31 E 72 35, H2 (1) a., Hockey Canada—General: correspondence (file 3), LAC.

138   Morse, Letter to Willard Estey.

139   Morse, Letter to Willard Estey.

140   Willard Estey, "Prepared Questions for Meeting with John Ziegler," February 17, 1980, Lake Placed, NY, MG31 E 72 35, H2 (1) a, Hockey Canada General: correspondence (file 3).

easily intimidated, however. He was not a typical stern and remote Supreme Court Justice. Instead, he could be belligerent and even distasteful.[141] One board member remembered him as unafraid to speak his mind, even if a wild thought might leave listeners "bug-eyed" from the conversation: "he wasn't really confined by judicial positions."[142] Estey pushed back against the power brokers of the sport, with diplomatic support from Ford, and positioned himself to endorse Bauer's long-range plan for the National Team.

At the same time that Estey was appointed as chair of Hockey Canada, Lou Lefaive became its first full-time president. Lefaive was a key builder in the formative years of the Canadian sport system, and played an active role in the creation of the 1972 Summit Series as a director of Hockey Canada.[143] He was raised in Windsor, Ontario, by francophone parents who were devout Catholics.[144] At the age of 13, Lefaive boarded at the University of Ottawa, which enabled him to complete secondary studies in French at a Catholic institution run by the Oblate Fathers of Mary Immaculate. He played basketball and football for the University of Ottawa and later attended St. Peter's Seminary in London, Ontario. He nearly became a priest—he was ordained a deacon—but left the seminary to marry. According to his daughter, Lefaive saw sport "as an equalizer in society ... as a way of bringing people together and ... to honor God's creation."[145] With his *joie de vivre*, he promoted sport as a public good that should celebrate human living. He would serve as the first president of the Canadian Paralympic Committee.

In Lefaive, Bauer found yet another committed and religiously-formed sport leader who represented a values-driven sporting model. Bill L'Heureux studied under the Basilians in Windsor and worked with Bauer on the *Report*

141 Murray Costello, interview with author, June 3, 2019.

142 H. Ian Macdonald, interview with author, September 23, 2020.

143 "Lefaive Moves to Head Up Sport Canada," A Piece of Canadian Sport History, accessed May 19, 2021, http://canadiansporthistory.ca/champion-magazine/may-1978-mai/lefaive-moves-to-head-up-sport-canada/. Lafaive served twice as the director of Sport Canada: from 1968 to 1975, and 1978 to 1980. Upon his return to Sport Canada after four years as president of the National Sport and Recreation Centre, he wanted to improve the consultative processes with the sport community after Sport Canada had taken large steps toward high performance sport with the development of the federal government's Game Plan and the Coaching Association of Canada under Roger Jackson.

144 Louise Meagher, email message to author, May 20, 2020.

145 Meagher, email.

on *Amateur Hockey* in the late '60s; Regimbal also attended St. Peter's in London and supported Bauer on the development committee of Hockey Canada. Both were instructors and teachers, while Lefaive also lectured at Laurentian University.[146] Like Bauer, all three had seriously considered religious life and sought to influence sport through higher ideals. Inspired by their spiritual lives, they saw sport as an extension of living and a place to unite body and soul. They promoted the flourishing of the human person. In Bauer, Lefaive found someone in sync with his values, and the two remained committed to the National Team program following Lake Placid.

1980 Winter Olympics

Heading into the Games, Bauer recognized that the team lacked experience and realistically was contending for the bronze medal against three other teams.[147] Once at Lake Placid, Bauer reported that "the team was in good spirits and are comfortable at the [Olympic] Village,"[148] which was originally designed as a penitentiary and would function thusly after the Games. Bauer continued to advocate for camaraderie—for instance, leading a piano sing-along with the team.[149] While Eagleson questioned his approach, Bauer did everything possible to bar the agitator from access to the team. He protected the coaches' abilities to perform their roles and tried to avoid the limelight and political jockeying in Hockey Canada.

The team won its first two games against lesser hockey powers, but lost a crucial game to Team Finland—a contender for the bronze medal. It was particularly devastating because his team's goaltender fanned on a dump-in from the Finnish blue line. The puck trickled into the goal and the team never recovered.[150] The goal was an embarrassment. Canadian hockey fans

146   Meagher, email.

147   The Canadian Press, "Bauer's Dream Revived at Games," February 14, 1980, Carmelite Sisters of St. Joseph Collection. To beat the Soviets, they would need to catch many breaks and have superb goaltending.

148   Hockey Canada, "Minutes of Board of Directors," February 16, 1980, Lake Placid, NY, MG31 E 72 35, H2 (1) a, Hockey Canada General: correspondence (file 3), LAC.

149   Noonan, interview.

150   Bob Dupuis had earlier taken a hard shot underneath his blocker, which injured his hand and made stickhandling difficult. Players were rushing toward him and he was doubly distracted, leading to the miscue. O'Malley, email.

understood why Bauer could not get a high scoring center, but an adequate goalie should have been easier to find.[151] Elite-level goaltending was necessary for the young Canadian team, yet no one had seized the opportunity to be the starting goalie in the lead up to or at the Games in Lake Placid.[152] The cruel proof of this necessity was found in the US Team, which had superior goaltending and produced the fabled "miracle on ice."[153] The team's goaltending had been unsettled, unlike National Team's in the past. The group collected itself and handily beat the Japanese National Team coached by Bauer's friend and associate Mel Wakabayashi.[154]

To advance to the medal round, the team needed to beat the defending gold medalist Soviet Union team in the next game. The Canadians held a 3–1 lead but surrendered a goal with seconds left in the second period, which could not help but raise doubt in the players' minds as they rested during the second intermission. The team battled well in the third despite giving up two early goals and tied the game at four—but eventually lost 6–4. The golden dream was over. Anderson lamented, "I cried for two hours straight after we lost to the Russians."[155] It was the collegiate players on the American team that beat the overconfident Soviets and who inspired play-by-play person Al Michaels to produce the iconic call, "Do you believe in miracles? Yes!" It was more painful than miraculous for the National Team, who with a full lineup had consistently played well against the American squad in exhibition games and who had its players go on to play more games in the NHL.[156]

Bauer took the losses at the 1980 Games particularly hard. Upon returning to Vancouver, he lamented the Lake Placid results, especially the Finland game. Noonan recollected: "He'd be at our place and ... with a bottle

---

151   Costello, interview.

152   Primeau, interview.

153   National Team forward Primeau recalled a related coaching platitude: "You want to be a good coach, get a good goalie." Primeau, interview. Manager Noonan recalled not including UBC Thunderbird goalie Ron Patterson on the final team because there was political pressure to include the French-speaking Pageau instead. Noonan, interview.

154   Mel Wakabayashi, interview with author, July 21, 2020.

155   David Staples, "I've Always Had a Carefree Spirit," *Edmonton Journal,* January 10, 1988, https://edmontonjournal.com/sports/hockey/nhl/cult-of-hockey/this-was-glenn-anderson-hero-of-the-ice-palace-in-1988.

156   Primeau, interview.

of scotch open and he'd say, 'Put it on.' And I knew what he meant: 'Put that tape of that game on.'"[157] Bauer wrote a summary of a probing conversation with Noonan about Lake Placid, in which he questioned whether he should have coached the team himself.[158] Having three co-head coaches—Drake, Watt, and Davis—could cause some confusion; coaches disagreed sometimes on how to perform a skill or tactic and this perhaps did not give a definitive direction for the team.[159] But Bauer was open to innovation and the coaching arrangement was a step in his long-term plans: establishing at least two National Team sites after the Olympic Games with the co-coaches from western and eastern Canada.[160]

Watt and Drake were very successful varsity hockey coaches, but they were not the same kind of coach as Bauer. For him, the two coaches ran the risk of creating self-centered players concerned more about technique than spirit.[161] Bauer ideally wanted reflective players concerned about community spirit and international outreach. In addition, the hockey men had different coaching philosophies. Bauer respected each coach, but with the devastating fallout from the loss to the Finns he reviewed and lamented the minutiae of many prior decisions.

Bauer admitted "the truth" to himself that "it just would not have worked out if I had assumed the role of the bench coach—there were just too many off ice problems."[162] In his writings, he rehashed details from the loss to Finland. Should he have stayed in the dressing room during the first intermission instead of doing a radio interview? Why did the Swedish referee give so many "undeserved penalties" to the Canadians? How could the team not score more when outshooting the Finns 26–6 in the third period? It was the agony that any dedicated coach suffers, especially when the future of a team might hinge on one loss.

157 Noonan, interview.

158 Bauer, Notes, Box 3, File 1, Bauer fonds, Basilian Archives.

159 Greg Oliver, *Father Bauer and the Great Experiment: The Genesis of Canadian Olympic Hockey* (Toronto: ECW Press, 2017), 235.

160 Noonan, interview.

161 David Bauer, Letter to Barbara Bauer, November 8, 1974, Terry O'Malley Collection.

162 Bauer, Notes, Box 3, File 1, Bauer fonds, Basilian Archives.

The Future of the National Team

Because the Hockey Canada board gave Bauer a verbal promise that the program would continue up to the 1984 Olympics—and he had the support of both Chairman Estey and President Lefaive—he believed the National Team could induce the growth of university hockey and help reorganize hockey in Canada.

The National Team took time off after the Olympics and reconvened in Calgary to prepare for an invitational tournament that April.[163] Some players committed to another four years with the National Team in preparation for the 1984 Winter Games hosted in Sarajevo, Yugoslavia (now Bosnia and Herzegovina). Gregg recalled both Estey and Eagleson entering the team's dressing room three weeks prior to the Olympics and declaring, "we guarantee that if you commit to this program, we'll continue the program through the next four years to Sarajevo."[164] Gregg, Anderson, and others were excited about this prospect, which itself was a moral victory for the program.[165] Bauer thought that two-thirds of the 1980 team had a future in professional hockey, yet he wanted a "sincere alternative" where "players can finish their education and continue to be involved in the program through to 1984."[166]

A refurbished National Team program was in the works. Gone were many of the direct connections to St. Michael's and the hand-to-mouth existence that characterized the startup experiment. What had reemerged was a communal spirit within the team, where youthfulness and enthusiasm mattered despite the increased insistence on improved technical training. For Bauer, it marked the possibility of creating a different image for Canadian hockey, one that could be imitated and pursued by Canadian children from coast to coast.

---

163   A. Abel, "Father Bauer Not Disappointed, Hockey Experiment Paid Off," *The Globe and Mail,* February 22, 1980, ProQuest Historical Newspapers: The Globe and Mail, 35.

164   Gregg, interview.

165   Gregg, interview. See also O'Malley, interview.

166   Hockey Canada, "Minutes of Board," February 16, 1980.

The Reconfiguration and Conclusion
of the National Team Program

THE NATIONAL TEAM'S SIXTH-PLACE FINISH at Lake Placid was forgettable. Sport columnist Bob Hanley summarized that "the concept of the Canadian national amateur hockey team ... has probably seen its final, fated revival."[1] He disapproved of Bauer, "the man who dared most to dream," who "infect[ed] others with his beliefs and enthusiasm." Hanley thought that the near million-dollar exercise could not compete with heavily subsidized programs in US college hockey and the Soviet Union: "Father Bauer, the learned Basilian and inspirational influence, should know by now that psychology can't always beat the numbers game, and it can't always beat the financial resources of the opposition."[2]

Bauer saw things differently. The poor results indicated larger problems in Canadian hockey: too much control by the NHL, not enough cooperation amongst all parties toward nationalistic aims, and a team amassed too quickly.

---

1 Bob Hanley, "Bauer Program However Noble, Dated, Dead," *The Spectator*, May 6, 1980, 23.

2 Hanley, "Bauer Program."

A more stable, long-term organizational structure was needed. To a reporter, Bauer explained an alternative system proposed by Hockey Canada that would entice high quality U18 players into a new university super league.[3] Bauer argued that some young men and their parents wanted a less violent game of high quality, that is not driven by "total commercialization." Moms and dads could "look at our team and say, 'There's something else for my boy.'"

Even so, Bauer recognized that the National Team program needed to evolve somewhat. It was to be an "ongoing" program instead of a "team in being," explained Terry O'Malley at the time, which "means a team that's brought together for tournaments. You disperse to your regular team whether it's university or senior and are brought back together again."[4] There would be more player turnover than the former National Teams, with some players coming and going each year, but a core group would remain. Meetings discussing the future of the National Team program were slated for Spring 1980 at Ottawa and Calgary, with a final decision to be made in late June. With Estey as chair and Lefaive as president of Hockey Canada, Bauer saw a clear path toward a long-term National Team program.[5] He felt that he could not trust Eagleson, whose interests were divided as a player agent, head of the NHLPA, and friend of the NHL.[6]

At a directors' meeting held in Lake Placid, newly elected chair Estey supported a proposal to put together a University Hockey Super League within two years, which would play a weekly nationally televised game.[7] Elsewhere Estey added his goal of "pursuing the possibility of establishing

---

3 A. Abel, "Father Bauer Not Disappointed, Hockey Experiment Paid Off," *The Globe and Mail*, February 22, 1980, ProQuest Historical Newspapers: The Globe and Mail, 35.

4 Maureen Bauer-McGahey, Notes of Unpublished Book Chapters about 1980 Olympic Hockey Team, Spring 1980, Box 3, File 1, Bauer fonds, Basilian Archives.

5 Noonan recalled receiving a long-distance phone call from Estey at Lake Placid: "We've got to keep this National Team program going." He added that Noonan should not worry about Eagleson. Rick Noonan, interview with author, May 27, 2019.

6 For instance, the National Team withheld quality players from the NHL, but it also provided Eagleson with a talent pool for his player agency business. One player noted Eagleson's preferential treatment to those who planned to play in the NHL and who also needed a player agent. Randy Gregg, interview with author, November 9, 2020.

7 Hockey Canada, "Minutes of Board of Directors," February 16, 1980, Lake Placid, NY, MG31 E 72 35, H2 (1) a, Hockey Canada General: correspondence (file 3), LAC.

our current Olympic team on a permanent national team basis."[8] New board members were brought on to help achieve these aims, including three Canadian university presidents—including H. Ian Macdonald from York and Norman Wagner from Calgary—and former GM of the Montreal Canadiens, Sam Pollock.[9] Estey's appointees could guide Hockey Canada toward building up university hockey, defend professional hockey interests, and strengthen connections to the Calgary Committee—Doug Mitchell's group of Calgary businessmen trying to keep the National Team in their city.[10]

Calgary's interest in the National Team had been longstanding. It began when several members from the 1967 Canadian Hockey Foundation, such as Max Bell and Charlie Hay, joined Hockey Canada as directors. The University of Calgary was planning to build a hockey facility on its campus. In 1974, oilman D. K. "Doc" Seaman thought the city could act as Hockey Canada's headquarters in western Canada: promoting "coaching clinics, skill testing programs and the support of skilled athletes to pursue their academic careers by means of scholarships and bursaries."[11] By 1978, the university hired Roger Jackson as Dean of the Faculty of Physical Education. He leveraged his national contacts and public persona as a sport administrator and former gold medalist to strengthen the 1988 Olympic Games bid and established a human performance lab, a computerized sport system, and sport medicine center.[12] Bauer may have been advanced as a hockey coach,

8 Willard Estey, Letter to Turmel, February 16, 1980, MG31 E 72 35, H2 (1) a, Hockey Canada General: correspondence (file 3), LAC.

9 Hockey Canada, "Minutes of Board," February 16, 1980. Also selected for the board was Jean-Guy Paquet at Université Laval. Pollock had coached the Ottawa-Hull Junior Canadiens against a touring Soviet team in 1958. Todd Denault, *The Greatest Game: The Montreal Canadiens, the Red Army, and the Night that Saved Hockey* (Toronto: McClelland & Stewart, 2010), 18.

10 H. Ian Macdonald, interview with author, September 23, 2020. The Calgary Committee supported a "more direct relationship with Father Bauer" with respect to the National Team. Chris Lang, Letter to Lou Lefaive, February 27, 1980, MG31 E 72 35, H2 (1) a, Hockey Canada—General: correspondence (file 3), LAC.

11 Doc Seaman, Letter to Doug Fisher, April 9, 1974, MG28 I 263 19, 300-6-14, Development Committee Hockey (2 of 3) 1974–1975, LAC. Calgary would host hockey's Centre of Excellence, with Bill Hay actively promoting this possibility from the beginning.

12 Bruce Kidd, interview with author, June 5, 2019; University of Calgary, Faculty of Kinesiology, "About: History of Kinesiology," accessed August 27, 2020, https://kinesiology.ucalgary.ca/about/history-kinesiology.

but he was behind sport performance experts like Jackson who pushed the limits of sports science to seek gold medals for the nation.[13]

Bauer continued to question an overly technical approach to sport despite leaders like Jackson and Larivière seeing Bauer as a sport relic. There was, he wrote, a "growing threat in some quarters to adopt the model of the East Europeans. The standardized hockey player—opposite to the one developed in Major Junior hockey—seems to be coming to the fore.... It is giving oneself over to a process almost exclusively as a technical approach to the development of a player."[14] The gap between Bauer and the sport scientists was widening, as he still preached the importance of willpower, character, and spirit.

During the next few months, Hockey Canada made financial, facility, and scheduling plans for the "ongoing" National Team program. On top of a planned TV deal for university hockey and a million-dollar trust from previous international tournaments, Hockey Canada budgeted for a seven-million-dollar trust fund to cover scholarships for top varsity players in the country.[15] Outside assistance came from the Calgary Committee and Doug Mitchell, who had raised nearly $500,000 for the program.[16] The National Team would play thirty to thirty-five games per year, including many at international tournaments. Calgary would host half of the games, especially with the promise of an Olympic-sized ice surface as part of its 1988 Olympics bid.[17] Players would play for their home universities and, in effect, this would assist universities and improve Canadian university hockey. The ultimate hope, according to Lefaive, was that inter-division games across the nation would bring about a two-tiered university league that could retain

13   Kidd, interview. Jackson became the CEO of Own the Podium, the program that led Canada, at Vancouver in 2010, to its most successful haul of Olympic gold.

14   David Bauer, Notes, July 1980, Terry O'Malley Collection.

15   Estey, Letter to Lou Lefaive. The plan sought five million dollars of unclaimed Lotto Canada payments. Willard Estey, Letter to Businessmen on the Board, May 1, 1980, MG31 E 72 35, H2 (1) a, Hockey Canada General: correspondence (file 4), LAC. About 500 Canadians a year attended US colleges on hockey scholarships; this plan would entice some or most of them to attend college in Canada.

16   Hockey Canada, "Minutes of Board," February 16, 1980.

17   Hockey Canada, "Minutes of Conference Meeting," March 12, 1980, Lake Placid, NY, MG31 E 72 35, H2 (1) a, Hockey Canada General: correspondence (file 3), LAC. The arena would become the Olympic Saddledome. The NHL Flames would eventually play in it; they arrived in the city in spring 1980.

high-end talent.[18] A center for hockey research and development would build off medical research and training programs for the 1980 team. With support of board members and the University of Calgary president, the city, and the province, the National Team program looked like it might stickhandle its way around threats from Eagleson and corporate hockey.[19]

Estey's Reversal and the Shelving of the National Team

A Canadian federal election during the Lake Placid Games returned the Liberal Party to power under Prime Minister Trudeau. Newly elected Member of Parliament Gerald Regan became the minister in charge of the sport portfolio. During his youth in Nova Scotia, he played hockey and was a sports radio announcer.[20] Beginning in 1951, Regan arranged a series of spring games between local senior teams and the Boston Bruins in Atlantic Canada. He began scouting local talent for the Bruins in the early 1960s, and later met with Russian hockey leaders to setup tours across Canada.[21] These plans were brushed aside by the CAHA. Whereas former sport minister Campagnolo sided with Bauer's National Team, Regan had contacts in professional hockey and had been frustrated by amateur hockey's control over the international game.

Judge Estey showed signs of doubt in May 1980. He wrote a "delicate memo" to only three board members, including Eagleson, that $600,000 per year for overhead of Hockey Canada was high especially "without creating one single new bit of hockey talent."[22] He had determined that the 1980 Olympic Team program had done nothing exceptional in developing

18 Lou Lefaive, "Document Work-Up Sent to Doc Seaman," March 13, 1980, MG31 E 72 35, H2 (1) a, Hockey Canada General: correspondence (file 4), LAC.

19 Norman Wagner, Letter to Doc Seaman, April 28, 1980, MG31 E 72 35, H2 (1) a, Hockey Canada General: correspondence (file 4), LAC.

20 "The Hon. Gerald A. P. Regan," *The Chronicle Herald*, November 28, 2019, https://www.thechronicleherald.ca/obituaries/the-hon-gerald-a-p-regan-30418/.

21 Estey had shortlisted Regan to be on an enlarged board of Hockey Canada, but Regan declined because of the upcoming federal election. Regan's political career was darkened by sexual offense allegations in the '90s. Michael Nolan, *CTV—The Network that Means Business* (Edmonton: University of Alberta Press, 2001), 186. In 1979, Estey asked David Johnston, president of McGill, to return as a board member. Willard Estey, "Reorganization of Hockey Canada," 1979, MG31 E 72 35, LAC.

22 Willard Estey, "Hockey Canada: Alternate Plan for Existence," May 16, 1980, MG31 E 72 35, H2 (1) a, Hockey Canada General: correspondence (file 4), LAC.

hockey players in return for substantial amounts of taxpayers' money. He wondered if the board was morally obligated to consider cutting the Ottawa staff and instead direct the money to hockey scholarships. Estey's newly proposed downsizing of Hockey Canada would seriously hamper the National Team program, which would "assemble on relatively short notice" the best university hockey talent for "participation in isolated tournaments."[23] Such an ad hoc team would focus on victory instead of development, and this approach would discount past National Team successes in terms of people, international standing, and providing an alternative path for young players.[24]

Before Estey and the directors could make their final decision on the National Team at the end of June, a bombshell hit Hockey Canada: Minister Regan directly threatened its very existence. In a letter addressed to Lefaive, Regan wrote in support of the "dissolution of Hockey Canada" if a number of conditions were not met by Lefaive, Estey, and the board.[25] The letter advocated for the NHL and NHLPA to be part of planning world invitational tournaments, whereas the CAHA would lead the World Junior Championships. What remained for Hockey Canada? It would only act as "a forum" and possibly be given "a revised and reconstituted proposed Hockey Canada Board." Regan's suffocating vision would effectively terminate the National Team, especially when control of the million-dollar trust fund, which remained unsettled between Hockey Canada and the CAHA, was demanded to be resolved "within a matter of days."[26] The tersely written letter was sent to only some board members—to the exclusion of Bauer

23 Estey, "Hockey Canada: Alternate Plan."

24 A May executive board meeting did not mention Estey's new plans. Hockey Canada, "Executive Committee Meeting Minutes," May 27, 1980, MG31 E 72 35, H2 (1) a, Hockey Canada General: correspondence (file 5), LAC.

25 Gerald Regan, Letter to Lou Lefaive, June 4, 1980, MG31 E 72 35, H2 (1) a, Hockey Canada General: correspondence (file 4), LAC.

26 Eagleson and the CAHA worked out an unwritten deal that the over $1 million of 1976 Canada Cup profits would be put in a trust run by Hockey Canada, with the interest paid to the CAHA. The CAHA's new president, Murray Costello, moved to get control of the trust and withdrew from the board of Hockey Canada. The issue was settled in 1982: CAHA received the million dollars and Hockey Canada kept the interest payments. See Julie Stevens, "The Canadian Hockey Association Merger: An Analysis of Institutional Change" (PhD thesis, University of Alberta, Edmonton, 2001), ProQuest Dissertations Publishing, 63; and Regan, Letter to Lou Lefaive.

and Hay, for instance—and expedited Estey's new plan to shelve the National Team.[27]

For Estey, the underlying purpose of Minister Regan's letter was coercion: "Money carries power to direct and control."[28] To avoid this power grab, Estey believed he needed to shrink Hockey Canada's plans and protest requests from the federal government. He promoted a scaled-down Hockey Canada administrative facility in Calgary to replace the Ottawa office, with the CAHA taking charge of international hockey. Hockey Canada would act as a forum for hockey interests; a vision that went against Bauer's ongoing National Team program.

At the June 20th board meeting, held that morning at the Constellation Hotel in Toronto, Estey declared that the board needed to determine a response to Minister Regan's letter.[29] According to meeting minutes, Eagleson declared that the postponed 1980 Canada Cup and the subsequent shortfall in funds meant that the National Team program should be cancelled for the year. University of Calgary President Wagner agreed, and promoted the idea that Hockey Canada could be based in Calgary. Further, Estey reminded them that Doc Seaman, part owner of the new Calgary NHL franchise, intended three-quarters of the team's profits to go to amateur hockey development in Canada. A new professional team made getting a new arena with an Olympic sized ice surface highly probable. The move to Calgary was an easy decision for the board, but there were those unwilling to drop the ongoing National Team. Secretary-treasurer Lang offered a financial picture that made keeping the team possible. Bauer reminded the board "that he had taken on the job of the 1980 Olympic Team with the understanding that it was a five-year program to 1984." He questioned dumping players who had committed to the program long-term. The board members in attendance split their votes on the motion "THAT the national team undertake the obligation to represent

---

27 Bauer commented: "it appears the judge wants to close the Ottawa office … such a move is designed to get rid of Lou Lefaive … [who] has been a thorn in the side of Bud [Estey] and Gerald Regan.… Lou suspects [this] … is one further step in the demise of HC." David Bauer, Letter to John, Box 3, File 1, Bauer fonds, Basilian Archives.

28 Willard Estey, "Letter to Executive Committee of the Board," June 20, 1980, MG31 E 72 35, H2 (1) a, Hockey Canada General: correspondence (file 4), LAC.

29 "Board Meeting Minutes," June 20, 1980, MG31 E 72 35, H2 (1) a, Hockey Canada General: correspondence (file 5), LAC.

Canada in the 1981 World Championships to be run by the management of the national team, and blended with professionals if necessary." In favor were Bauer, Hay, Pugh, and Lefaive. Against were those with strong ties to the NHL—Pollock, Eagleson, Campbell—and U of C President Wagner. "There being a tie vote," recorded the minutes, "the Chairman, Mr. Estey, exercised his vote against the motion. DEFEATED." The National Team program and Bauer were once again dumped by Hockey Canada.

Bauer's Response to the Shelving of the National Team

Bauer was furious about the shelving of the program. Caught up in the moment, he challenged the legality of the vote.[30] He questioned whether the former NHL president, Clarence Campbell, had a right to vote. The meeting minutes wrongly included Campbell as an observer, but he had become a voting member since stepping down as the league's president.[31] Outwardly, he no longer had a conflict of interest.

A frustrated, perplexed Bauer detailed what he thought had happened on several pages of notes at the end of July. On a large tabloid-sized sheet of paper, he first mapped out different groups and persons involved in the June 20th decision—Hockey Canada, CAHA, the Calgary Committee, CIAU, etc.— and then on the left side listed those who were in competition with each other. It looked like a list of upcoming Saturday night hockey games: Lang vs. Estey, Lefaive vs. Lesaux, Eagleson and Ziegler vs. the National Team, Pollock and Campbell vs. the National Team, and, in a clear mistake about his understanding of Minister Regan, "Minister—on fence."[32] Bauer also positioned himself against the University of Calgary group with Wagner at its lead—who Bauer elsewhere claimed had "sold out to get a team at U of C."[33] In the middle of

30   David Bauer, "On June 20, 1980," Box 4, File 8, Bauer fonds, Basilian Archives.

31   Other records show that Campbell had become a voting member in 1977. "Hockey Canada Report, 1985," MG 31 E72 36, Hockey Canada—Documents: 1985 report, Appendix I: Hockey Canada Board of Directors 1969–1985, LAC.

32   David Bauer, "Mapping of Hockey Political Landscape," Summer 1980, Box 3, File 4, Bauer fonds, Basilian Archives. Bauer seemed to miss the Maritimer's old connections to the NHL and his frustration toward amateur hockey's control over Canadian negotiations in international hockey.

33   David Bauer, Notes, Box 3, File 1, Bauer fonds, Basilian Archives. Bauer added that Roger Jackson, who was so driven and demanding, seemed to be against

the spreadsheet, Bauer placed a dotted box and inside wrote, "Philosophy of the Human Person vs. Technique for Technique Sake." When the board had one of two paths to follow, it chose know-how instead of values. Beneath that central head-to-head issue, he added: "Make use of Technique, but let spirit/spontaneity prevail." For Bauer, the human spirit was being cross-checked out of hockey. His hockey alternative had been taken over by NHL interests.

Bauer wrote further about his bewilderment. His frustration focused foremost on Judge Estey, who had cast the tie-breaking vote. According to Bauer, on four public occasions that spring, Estey had told Bauer and Noonan to make plans for a continued program.[34] Bauer complained that Estey's reasoning did not add up. Neither a shortage of funds nor Estey's concern about too much government interference required ending the program.[35] A funding plan was available and Estey, later in a July meeting with the minister, would agree to some cooperation with the federal government.

In his notes, Bauer acknowledged that in sticking with Lang and Lefaive he had put himself in the crosshairs of Estey, who now wanted to downsize Hockey Canada. Estey turned to Sam Pollock, Bauer wrote, as "his great mentor and leader" and neutralized Bauer, Lang, and Lefaive "by believing the new technocrats—Roger [Jackson], George [Kingston], and Norm Wagner." Choosing between spirited hockey and the new technocrats, Bauer believed Estey did an about-face: he embraced the technocrats and found support from those with NHL connections. Bauer questioned whether Estey knew that Eagleson and Ziegler could not put together any better of a team than the 1980 Olympic Team and that his choice meant "this year's players have only one option if they wish to play competitive hockey—the NHL. Does he see all of this?" For Bauer, their urging was guided by self-interest and Estey had consented to their co-opting. Could Estey not recall the rationale for an alternative stream for Canadian hockey?

---

everyone. See also Alan Watson, *Catch On and Run with It: The Sporting Life and Times of Dr. Bob Hindmarch* (Vancouver: AJW Books, 2012), 335.

34 The four events were: Hockey Canada meeting with Calgary Committee members, a Hockey Canada executive committee meeting, an Olympic Team banquet in Calgary, and the directors' meeting at Lake Placid.

35 Estey, Letter to Doc Seaman. The Canada Cup was postponed because of the Soviet invasion of Afghanistan.

Estey Reconciles with Regan
and the Fallout from His Decisions

Judge Estey's reversal and siding with NHL interests was altered when he rectified his relationship with Minister Regan and the June 4th letter. In mid-July, Estey, Eagleson, Pollock, Bauer and possibly others met in a parliamentary cafeteria with Regan.[36] Estey charged: "the Board ... could not accept the right or entitlement of the Minister of Fitness and Amateur Sport to dissolve Hockey Canada in law or in fact." He also wrote that "the Board took exception in fact to the proposition that ... the Government of Canada had the power to dictate any rejuvenation" in hockey. Bauer agreed with Estey that Hockey Canada did not need federal funding "if it meant that HC was owned by the Minister of Sport."[37]

Estey defended the independence of the corporation, yet agreed with the minister that Hockey Canada would not operate a National Team in 1980.[38] Instead, it would host an international hockey tournament during the Christmas holidays, led by top university players interested in the 1984 Olympics.[39] Estey and Regan agreed not to fire Hockey Canada staff in Ottawa (like Lang and Lefaive) while hockey operations would occur out of Calgary.[40] What seemed to Bauer to be another about-face by Estey—determining to keep the Ottawa staff and supporting an ad hoc team of university players—left him even more confused.

Estey's flip-flop led Bauer to protest that "on the surface it looks as though EXPEDIENCY is his PRINCIPLE."[41] Instead of acting with "credibility and philosophy," Estey had made a quick decision. Such a fast move caused Bauer to comment: "this most bizarre series of events [is] apparently perpetrated and manipulated by one who sits on the highest court of the land." Estey

---

36 Willard Estey, Letter to the Board, July 15, 1980, MG31 E 72 35, H2 (1) a, Hockey Canada General: correspondence (file 4), LAC.

37 Bauer, Notes, Box 3, File 1, Bauer fonds, Basilian Archives.

38 Estey, Letter to the Board, July 15, 1980. See also, David Bauer, Notes, July 31, 1980, Box 3, File 4, Bauer fonds, Basilian Archives.

39 Estey, Letter to the Board, July 15, 1980. See also, Bauer, Notes, July 31, 1980.

40 Bauer recalled that Eagleson had "gotten up no less than six times to quit" his role in Hockey Canada over the political appointments of Lang and Lefaive. Bauer, Notes, July 31, 1980.

41 Bauer, "On June 20, 1980."

paired up with professional hockey to obstruct the growth of the hockey alternative and then decided, a month later, to endorse a university-based team. Bauer was befuddled by the reversal.[42]

It was Bauer and the players of a would-be, ongoing National Team who were most adversely affected by Estey's decisions. When the final whistle blew, Bauer was left without a National Team in the short term, and was nudged out of a leadership position. Estey's two quick turns of direction left the NHL with the most to gain: many National Team members at the time (and in the future) automatically advanced to play in the NHL; scholarships for university hockey would be set by an all-roads-lead-to-the-NHL system; the league's hegemony was expanded as Hockey Canada let Pollock take charge of its international committee; and only limited control was handed over to those running technological advancements in Calgary, which also fulfilled the commercial purposes of the NHL. Minister Regan unmistakably sided with professional hockey, and Estey agreed to the takeover of the National Team.

Bauer had become weary of the rise of sport technocrats, but it was the dominant, overly-commercialized hockey system that squeezed him and the National Team for a second time. Run down from behind by Estey and let down by Hockey Canada, Bauer surprisingly admitted in his notes that he supported a revised team under agreeable leadership.[43] Despite his frustrations and how others had treated him, he still believed in the National Team program.

Blowback over the decision also came from the Calgary Committee.[44] The committee's Doug Mitchell wrote Estey about the deception the group experienced: "Let me remind you of the commitment you personally gave to the windup banquet held in Calgary in April. At that time you confirmed the program would continue in the 1980–81 season and that the team would be based in Calgary. It was also confirmed ... at the final home game before a sellout crowd."[45] The committee had lined up three thousand season ticket

---

42 With a new Liberal government taking power under Trudeau in February 1980, the problem was not fiscal either. Val Ross, "Stress, The Business of Coping," *Macleans*, May 5, 1980, 46.

43 Bauer, Notes, July 31, 1980.

44 Bauer, Notes, July 31, 1980.

45 Douglas Mitchell, Letter to Willard Estey, September 1980, MG31 E 72 36 17, LAC. The Calgary Committee was committed, as they had previously raised $800,000 for the 1980 team.

holders for upcoming National Team home games in Calgary, while raising more than $600,000 for the team moving forward. Mitchell was dismayed to learn about the program's shelving through a "wire story out of Toronto in June." He angrily commented: "We are sure you agree this is a rather unusual manner in which to do business with your 'partners.'"[46]

Players were also upset with the dissolution of the team. For instance, forward Glenn Anderson felt betrayed by a broken promise. The future Hockey Hall of Fame player was not sold on professional hockey and was planning to return to the National Team program after Lake Placid. "Father Bauer was always saying pro hockey is not what it's cracked up to be.... He was very right. There's a lot more that goes on behind the scenes than what is put out front, in either the media's eyes or the public's eyes."[47]

In summer 1980, Bauer penned a letter of resignation to the Board of Hockey Canada because he felt he needed to act with integrity. Ending the program was "a sham" and "a play by some of the special interest constituencies now represented on the [board of directors]."[48] A frustrated Bauer added: "It seems to me that such manoeuvres, expedient as they may seem for the moment, are the moves which are hastening the ... dissolution of Western civilization and values. It remains to be seen if the present decision of HC is in the best interests of the youth of the country."[49] Lefaive and Lang did not allow Bauer to resign, leaving him feeling trapped in a hockey no-man's-land. It became clear to Bauer that "special interest constituencies [on the board] don't want me out. Don't want me in."[50] Those

---

46   Hay, Lefaive, and Lang tried to ease the situation, saying the team was "paused" for a year. Hockey Canada, "Minutes of Executive Committee," September 29, 1980, MG31 E 72 36, H2 (1) a, Hockey Canada General: correspondence (file 5), LAC; and Hockey Canada, Response Notes to Douglas Mitchell, 1980, MG31 E 72 36, LAC.

47   David Staples, "I've Always Had a Carefree Spirit," *Edmonton Journal,* January 10, 1988, https://edmontonjournal.com/sports/hockey/nhl/cult-of-hockey/this-was-glenn-anderson-hero-of-the-ice-palace-in-1988. Anderson privately shared with Bauer his disappointment when he was not asked to try out for the 1981 Team Canada roster. Bauer responded that the business of hockey was hard on those who played for the love of the game. David Bauer, Notes, Summer 1981, Box 3, File 5, Bauer fonds, Basilian Archives.

48   David Bauer, Notes, Fall 1980, Box 3, File 1, Bauer fonds, Basilian Archives.

49   Bauer, Notes, Fall 1980.

50   Bauer, Notes, July 1980.

directors who disliked Bauer wanted his involvement because of his public image, but wished to exclude his alternative approach. Further, he was not a true insider of the sport because he had a profession outside of hockey as a clergyman.[51] His authority was whittled down to his personal integrity. But he did not call a press conference to announce the problems in black and white, despite feeling like corporate hockey had taken over Hockey Canada: he declared in writing, "As of this moment, HC is the NHL. Eagleson & Ziegler—Estey. Sam [Pollock] for seasoning."[52]

Bauer's life in hockey was overthrown on June 20th. His vindication had turned into a nightmare. The redemption of his ideas were dealt a serious blow—and by a Supreme Court Justice, no less. He also lost his job. By fall 1980, Bauer began to suffer from shingles, likely caused by the stresses of that summer. He wrote of his inability to exercise because of the pain and that he alleviated some discomfort by smoking cigars. Moving on meant that he began asking his Basilian superiors about a sabbatical leave to study the Bible.[53] Upon his return to Vancouver that autumn, he described how the area's natural beauty allowed for "the release from so many pressures I experienced in the east."[54]

Bauer, Eagleson, and Hockey Canada

Because Bauer had not resigned from the Hockey Canada board and still believed in the National Team, he sometimes worked with Eagleson. The most important player agent in Canada, Eagleson set NHL policy through leading collective bargaining negotiations and continued as Hockey Canada's chief negotiator for the international game.[55] His tactics for maintaining control of hockey players' interests repulsed Bauer, who complained in private notes after Team Canada's loss at the 1981 Canada Cup: I'm "still stunned by Alan [Eagleson] being loved at end of Cup. I stated that Alan's bottom line

---

51   Macdonald, interview.

52   Bauer, Notes, Fall 1980.

53   David Bauer, Letter to Barb Bauer, September 11, 1980, Box 3, File 4, Bauer fonds, Basilian Archives. He was also offered an assistant coaching role at UBC and teaching role for a philosophy of sport course. David Bauer, Letter to Paul Burns, January 15, 1981, Box 3, File 3, Bauer fonds, Basilian Archives.

54   Bauer, Notes, Fall 1980.

55   Deidra Clayton, *Eagle: The Life and Times of R. Alan Eagleson* (Toronto: Lester & Orpen Dennys, 1982), 220.

philosophy offended lovers of hockey and [he] sees people only as in seat dollar signs."[56] However, Eagleson worked with Pollock on committees in the CAHA and Hockey Canada, and this gave him credibility as a fully competent hockey person.[57] Thus, Bauer, even with the encouragement of others in Hockey Canada, felt unable to take a tougher stance and co-opt people on the board to actualize his vision.[58]

Without an institution behind him, Bauer accepted Eagleson's authority, as did many in Canadian hockey. Reporter Russ Conway, known for his detailed work that uncovered Eagleson's exploitation of NHL players' pensions, noted that Eagleson effectively controlled Hockey Canada.[59] He pleaded guilty to several counts of fraud and was imprisoned in 1998.[60] In an interview with Conway, Holmes claimed that when board members questioned Eagleson about finances, he extolled: "Listen, I raised it. I'll tell you how we're going to spend it."[61] Directors feared retribution from standing up to Eagleson: "You might get verbally smacked and frozen out. He always had an answer whether it was adequate or not." Conway concluded that the Hockey Canada board of directors by the late 1980s either lacked deep hockey knowledge or were "mainly his close friends" and allowed him "almost autocratic rule."[62] Costello summarized: "There was no Hockey Canada, there was just Eagleson. He did whatever the hell he wanted."[63]

Perhaps most impactful on the National Team program was Eagleson's cozy relationship with NHL President John Ziegler and longtime NHL Chairperson Bill Wirtz. Eagleson could control Hockey Canada and international hockey events if he kept players' NHL salaries artificially low.[64] When some US-based, NHL team executives balked at supporting the 1976

---

56   David Bauer, Notes, 1980–1983, Box 3, File 5, Bauer fonds, Basilian Archives.

57   Hockey Canada, *The Building of a Canadian Dream* (Calgary: Hockey Canada, circa 2017), 38. Murray Costello, interview with author, June 3, 2019.

58   Derek Holmes, interview with author, October 16, 2020. Holmes knew of Bauer from his studies at St. Michael's in the late 1950s: "He was a tough guy as a hockey player and as a coach."

59   Russ Conway, *Game Misconduct: Alan Eagleson and the Corruption of Hockey* (Toronto: MacFarlane Walter & Ross, 1997), 221.

60   Conway, *Game Misconduct*, 221.

61   Conway, *Game Misconduct*, 222.

62   Conway, *Game Misconduct*, 215.

63   Costello, interview.

64   Conway, *Game Misconduct*, 273.

Canada Cup, Wirtz defended Eagleson: "What Alan has done is put the NHL in indirect control of international hockey by his own involvement—meaning we don't have a third party, Hockey Canada, in the driver's seat.... It is better to have our partner there running it than a stranger."[65] Was that "stranger" Bauer? Whatever the case, like-minded board members could block an alternative hockey path and enable the full convergence of hockey into the NHL. The game's autocratic rulers could dismiss Bauer's common-sense approach.

Reconfiguring the National Team

Bauer was made to look outdated by his opponents.[66] Corporate sport had a new partner in a scientific approach to hockey. Both considered results-driven performances to be their highest goal.

In mid-July 1980, Estey nevertheless asked Bauer to work with Pollock to duplicate the success of the US Olympic Team at Lake Placid.[67] Pollock turned down the offer because it seemed "bound by the past" and he wanted "the appearance of newness."[68] Estey knew the shift in perspective for the National Team had many challenges, beginning with "the future role and involvement of Fr. Bauer would have to be worked out."[69] In 1982, Pollock was appointed Chairman of Canada's Olympic Hockey Committee, whereas Bauer, who had been Chairman of the Olympic Program in 1981, was in 1982 given the seemingly honorific title of Vice-President of Hockey Canada.[70] Pollock had good working relationships with the CAHA, the NHL's Board

65   Conway, *Game Misconduct,* 274.

66   Donald MacIntosh and David Whitson, *The Game Planners: Transforming Canada's Sport System* (Montreal: McGill-Queen's University Press, 1990), 130–31.

67   Bauer, Notes, July 31, 1980. Estey approached Pollock to lead a committee to select a team each season.

68   Willard Estey, Letter to Executive Committee, September 29, 1980, MG31 E 72 36, H2 (1) a, Hockey Canada General: correspondence (file 5), LAC.

69   Willard Estey, Letter to Alan Eagleson and Hartland MacDougall, October 17, 1980, MG31 E 72 36, H2 (1) a, Hockey Canada General: correspondence (file 5), LAC. Inserting Pollock into the management of international hockey would "most seriously affect" Bauer. Hockey Canada, "Minutes of Executive Committee." Pollock believed a team-in-being for 1984 was "not realistic." Sam Pollock, Letter to Willard Estey, February 19, 1981, MG31 E 72 37, H2 (3), Athletic Assistance Programme 1980–1981, LAC.

70   Chris Lang, Letter to Willard Estey, October 11, 1985, MG31 E 72 36, H2 (1) b, Hockey Canada General: correspondence (file 5), LAC.

of Governors, and could massage any difficulties arising from Eagleson's personality.[71] Minus an ongoing National Team in 1980–81, the direction for Hockey Canada stayed much the same: professional hockey representation at the Canada Cup and World Championships, building up university hockey, and a trust for hockey scholarships.[72] Not as evident was Bauer's central value: the development of human persons.[73] He chaired the hockey scholarship committee and advised the National Team leading to 1984.[74]

Many issues persisted, as outlined by Bauer in a letter to a fellow Basilian.[75] Bauer was angry about the "polarization of the two sets of directors of HC since the Machiavellian tactics employed by Judge Estey—chairman of HC—to kill the team and program."[76] A disgruntled Bauer recalled that Estey "thought his divide and conquer strategy had succeeded without a flaw," but quickly realized that his power-grab with Eagleson and Ziegler could not also expel his opponents—like Hay, Pugh, and Bauer—off the board, and falsely assumed support from the Calgary Committee. One director on the board recalled later that meetings were filled with "crises and shouting matches."[77] Bauer felt pushed to the brink: "If the judge and Sammy [Pollock] attack me, I know he fears an open fight should we decide to join forces with CAHA."[78] The situation was dire, and Bauer was ready to leave Hockey Canada.

71 Paul Quarrington, *Hometown Heroes: On the Road with Canada's National Hockey Team* (Toronto: Collins, 1988), 94–95.

72 Hockey Canada, "Long Range Plan Proposal to Sam Pollock," October 17, 1980, MG31 E 72 36, H2 (1) a, Hockey Canada General: correspondence (file 5), LAC. Many of Bauer's ideals remained: excellence in international competition, skill development, and "full participation in the life of our country."

73 Some directors, like Bill Hay, continued to push for "an alternate route to the pros." Eric Duhatschek, "Hockey Institute," *Calgary Herald*, June 18, 1981, MG31 E 72 37, H2 (3), Athletic Assistance Programme 1980–1981, LAC.

74 Willard Estey, Memo to File Re Telephone Conversation with Father Bauer, June 15, 1981, MG31 E 72 37, H2 (3), Athletic Assistance Programme 1980–1981, LAC. See also Hockey Canada, "Draft—Four More Years: Hockey Canada 1981–1985," MG31 E 72 39, H2 (8) b, Olympics 1984—Financing, LAC.

75 Bauer, Letter to Paul Burns.

76 Bauer, Letter to Paul Burns.

77 Hartland MacDougall, Letter to Willard Estey, October 16, 1985, MG31 E 72 36, H2 (1) b, Hockey Canada—General (file 2), LAC.

78 Bauer, Letter to Paul Burns.

Bauer and His Uncertain Role with the National Team

The National Team, under the board leadership of Pollock, became less of a program that Bauer promoted and, in Bauer's words, more of "a channel for the NHL."[79] The hockey world was gravitating toward the ways and purposes of the league. Many believed that Bauer needed to recognize the end of amateurism. Hockey Canada's Holmes recalled speaking with Bauer about the National Team becoming a stepping-stone for players on a path to the NHL, but it was "something that Father Bauer couldn't come to grips with."[80] In this revised version, the National Team could become a hothouse for talent. Players could mature hockey skills quickly through superb training while competing nightly against top European teams. The difference was slight, but for Bauer it was not simply a matter of logistics. His concern remained philosophical: what is the purpose of hockey in Canada? To comprehend the difference required knowledge of hockey history, education, values and ethics, and international affairs. He wanted to increase youth participation and opportunities, effectively expanding players' horizons. His vision faced a complex reality; for naysayers, the difference was academic.

With the awarding of the '88 Winter Olympic Games to Calgary in 1981, an increased fervor toward the National Team was felt. Hockey Canada expanded the number of hockey scholarships at Canadian universities and promoted a university super league. It also relentlessly lobbied for North American professional hockey players' participation at the Olympics. Coach Dave King acknowledged that following Lake Placid, Hockey Canada's international committee "had a real professional hockey relevance to it."[81] Bauer hoped his supporters in Hockey Canada could regain control of the National Team before the Calgary Games, if not by 1984.[82] He wanted his alternative to resurface again.

Bauer disliked the unfairness of sham-amateurism as much as anyone, but believed professional representation at Olympic hockey did not serve the best interests of Canadian youth. Having an alternative hockey stream could bring better opportunities and equity for youth playing hockey. Bauer

79 Clancy Loranger, "Finally, Father Bauer," *The Province,* November 30, 1983, Box 2, last file, Bauer fonds, Basilian Archives, 59.

80 Holmes, interview.

81 Dave King, interview with author, September 4, 2020.

82 Bauer, Letter to Paul Burns.

stuck to his principles, speaking to a reporter: "A national team, with the Olympics as its objective, could be the focal point of a whole new program for hockey in Canada. The National Hockey League is often the right course to follow, surely. But we need another set of possibilities for boys who wish to pursue excellence in hockey and who may feel there's more to life than a huge contract."[83] Bauer's pragmatism was clear: not every child could make the professional ranks, nor would every person benefit from the experience. Men like Pollock and King, too, saw value in education and development, which could also prove beneficial for future NHL players.[84]

Rumours surfacing in the mid-1980s pointed to the acceptance of NHL players at the Olympics. Bauer thought this change would negatively impact hockey: "The role of hockey coaches at the minor level is not to turn out professionals for the National Hockey League.... Such an approach would take the joy and spontaneity out of hockey and turn youngsters away from the game."[85] He added, "The whole organization of amateur sport is to build in options for boys and girls. We don't want one-dimensional people coming out of hockey. That would diminish that person's contribution to society and to himself."

Bauer was increasingly frustrated, becoming worn down by his political defeats that left him ready to move on from hockey.[86] He penned another Hockey Canada resignation letter, but remained a board member.[87] He became like an elder statesman of the game, who could act as a counterpoint to Pollock and Eagleson.[88] He became less prominent in Hockey Canada, whereas men like Eagleson and Estey forged friendships and stayed in power.[89] Bauer wrote about his feelings elsewhere: "they make the product secular. I'm supposed to sell it—no dice.... [There is] no inspiration at present."[90]

---

83   Jim Proudfoot, "Père Bauer Was a Lot More Than a Hockey Coach," *Toronto Star*, November 11, 1988, Box 2, last file, Bauer fonds, Basilian Archives.

84   Bauer, Notes, July 31, 1980. See also, Bauer, Notes, 1980–1983.

85   Al Sokol, "Father Bauer Says Pros in Olympics Bad Deal for Youth," *Toronto Star*, February 26, 1986, Box 4, File 9, Bauer fonds, Basilian Archives, C4.

86   Noonan, interview. See also, Carmelite Sisters of St. Joseph, interview with author, January 17, 2019.

87   David Bauer, Draft of Letter to Hockey Canada, March 30, 1984, Box 4, File 9, Bauer fonds, Basilian Archives.

88   Chris Lang, interview with author, June 6, 2019. See also Noonan, interview.

89   Estey warmly received a pair of Gucci watches from Eagleson at his retirement in 1987. See Willard Estey, Letter to Alan Eagleson, January 7, 1987, MG31 E 72 36, LAC.

90   Bauer, Notes, Box 3, File 1, Bauer fonds, Basilian Archives.

The 1984 Winter Olympics

While Pollock oversaw the National Team within Hockey Canada, Dave King took over as the head coach after a lengthy run with the University of Saskatchewan Huskies.[91] He had assisted with the 1978 summer evaluation camps for the National Team, and recalled how Bauer sized him up during a lengthy conversation about hockey, philosophy, and world affairs.[92] King helped coach at the 1982 World Championships in Helsinki for head coach Marshall Johnston, and noted a similar Bauer-like philosophy in Johnston: "He was really worried about people first—performance really comes from being a good person, a motivated person."[93] King suspected that this came through Bauer: "that the spiritual man was as important as the technical hockey man." Winning in hockey required a core of character-strong people, according to King, who could mitigate challenges and support difficult personalities within the dressing room.

When King became the head coach of the National Team prior to Sarajevo, he too was in tough against some of the best players in the world. A strategist of the game, he followed Bauer's logical thinking that the National Team needed to be strong defensively. While King incorporated more complex defensive schemes, he could understand Bauer's tactical emphasis on one-on-one battles: if you review the sequence of events that lead to a goal against, there are one or more head-to-head battles that are lost.[94] Thus, King always included a one-on-one drill during practice in his decades of coaching.

In August 1983, college and junior coaches and a variety of scouts collected information on players at three on-ice evaluation camps of about 50 players hosted across the country. King explained: "The format that Father Bauer had in 1980 was to give really quality hockey players from coast-to-coast a chance to be considered."[95] The selected team played exhibition games against European and NHL teams in the fall. At Sarajevo,

---

91   He won the men's CIAU national title in 1983, prior to which he was coaching the junior National Teams.

92   King, interview.

93   King, interview.

94   King, interview.

95   King, interview; see also Hockey Canada, *Canadian Dream*, 41. Two other successful university hockey coaches—Jean Perron (Moncton) and George Kingston (Calgary)—flanked King.

it finished a disappointing fourth. The lineup included many top prospects from US and Canadian colleges, along with players from the junior ranks, and produced many future NHL players (e.g., Russ Courtnall, Patrick Flatley, James Patrick, and Carey Wilson among others), coaches (e.g., Kevin Dineen, Bruce Driver, Doug Lidster, Kirk Muller, Dave Tippett, and J. J. Daigneault), and administrators (e.g., Darren Eliot, Dave Gagner, and Vaughn Karpan).[96] Particularly noteworthy are two players: Dineen head-coached Canada's women's team to Olympic gold at the 2014 Sochi Games; and Joe Grant was mentored at the University of Toronto by Basilian Father Harry Gardner.[97]

Many players continued to head for US Colleges instead of playing in their homeland for Hockey Canada scholarships. The organization found it difficult to determine the top players at various Canadian universities and colleges, and then formulate a monitoring system of their academic enrollment.[98] Nevertheless, the organization established hockey scholarships at two dozen Canadian universities by 1983, which included about 60 scholarships for the 1982–83 season.[99] Funding came entirely from profits made at the 1981 Canada Cup.

Attracting top-end talent to Canadian university hockey programs did not happen. By 1985, Hockey Canada sizably increased its estimate for a scholarship trust; it needed up to $35 million to compete with US college hockey.[100] Estey complained about a lack of support for the National Team in terms of management, finances, and marketing. Unable to gain a foothold in the

96 Hockey Canada, *Canadian Dream*, 42. The coaches and administrators above also played in the NHL.

97 Kidd, interview. See also Jim Proudfoot, "For Aging Olympic Rearguard, NHL Isn't Ultimate in Hockey," January 6, 1984, MG31 E 72 36, H2 (1) b, Hockey Canada—General (file 2), LAC, where Grant speaks about the hockey alternative and following the ideals of his coaches, especially Tom Watt.

98 Wagner wrote to Estey about this problem. Norman Wagner, Letter to Willard Estey, May 7, 1981, MG31 E 72 37, H2 (3), Athletic Assistance Programme 1980–1981, LAC. Nonetheless, Hockey Canada continued to offer academic scholarships into the early 1990s; a practice that it had followed since its inception. Chris Lang, "Draft Report on First 16 Years," September 20, 1985, MG31 E 72 36, H2 (1) c, Hockey Canada—Documents: report (1985), LAC. See also Costello, interview.

99 Willard Estey, "Hockey Canada—International Hockey Representative," May 11, 1983, R12287 41, LAC.

100 Hockey Canada, "Hockey Canada: Hockey Scholarships," March 1, 1985, MG31 E 72 37, H2 (1) d, WZE Program memos, 1981–1985, LAC.

hockey market, Estey concluded, "Canadian college hockey is unattractive."[101] Ian Macdonald, who succeeded Estey as board chair, recalled that the idea of building up university hockey never had enough "instinctive enthusiasm" to overcome the institutional boundaries between universities. The mixed motives of universities across the country could not conjure up the needed determination.[102] Holmes charged that lesser university programs demanded equal distribution of scholarship money, which spread out resources and made unifying hockey prowess in the top dozen teams nearly impossible.[103] Overall, according to King, universities only liked hockey as an additive to the student experience and resisted a high-octane sports model as represented in the NCAA.[104] Changing Canadian university hockey could not be stomached by some. Mixed interests limited cooperation and resolve of supporters.

Bauer's Perspective on Sport Leading Up to the 1988 Winter Olympics

Prior to the Calgary Games, Hockey Canada remained a "bi-focal operation," according to Macdonald. He recalled: "the NHL was always hovering in the background and the hope was that one day it would become the basis of the Canadian Olympic team and the Canadian international team."[105] Hockey Canada saw professional players' inclusion as a matter of justice: how could the nation that forged the sport not use its best players?[106] The IOC under the presidency of Juan Antonio Samaranch was moving away from an amateurism ideal toward including best-on-best competition at the Olympic Games.[107] When the IOC gave its blessing to professional North American hockey players at the Olympics in 1986, many hoped that players would suit up in time for the Calgary Games. But NHL cooperation was less than certain since

101   Willard Estey, "Memo: The Problems," January 7, 1985, MG31 E 72 37, H2 (1) d, WZE Program memos, 1981–1985, LAC.

102   Macdonald, interview.

103   Holmes, interview.

104   King, interview.

105   Macdonald, interview.

106   The 1984 Olympic team took two American Hockey League players to Sarajevo in the hope they could play. King, interview. The two players, Don Dietrich and Mark Morrison, never played a game.

107   Don Morrow and Kevin Wamsley, *Sport in Canada: A History*, 3rd ed. (Don Mills, ON: Oxford University Press, 2013), 281.

the Winter Olympics fell right in the middle of the league's regular season. Hockey Canada continued managing the National Team in the short term with the support of the CAHA.[108]

With increased financial support, improved training and facilities, and now the potential inclusion of NHL players, the National Team had a reconfigured appearance. When asked by a reporter about comparisons between his early National Teams and the 1988 Olympic team, Proudfoot noted that Bauer was apparently "bemused by the big-time sophistication of the present operation. He understands how necessary it all is but can't help drawing comparisons with the hand-to-mouth existence his national sides endured."[109] Despite the evolution of the game, Bauer's ideals remained: players played in part for the intrinsic value of sport, self-growth, patriotic virtue, and for little money.[110] Bauer remained endeared to those early teams: "A lot of our success occurred because of our spirit, our verve. Spontaneity was the hall-mark of our hockey during those years. I don't think we can repeat an experience like that.... This team must create its own identity out of this present situation.... We must stress the team approach and develop our systems on that basis."[111] He pragmatically accepted a greater team-systems approach for a new day.

Bauer still preferred a high-skill game with spirited, artful play instead of intimidation or team-systems. During the 1987 Canada Cup, he marveled at Canadian players like Gretzky and Grant Fuhr. He told a reporter: "This Canadian team has so many skilled players it's amazing. I don't think we've ever had such a collection of gifted individuals."[112] He

---

108 The National Team received major financial support from the federal government, the Alberta-based Project 75, and the Calgary Saddledome Foundation. Hockey Canada, International Committee, "Update on the Development of Canada's National Hockey Team for the 1988 Winter Olympics. Prepared for the Honorable Otto Jelinek," April 1986, Box 3, File 7, Bauer fonds, Basilian Archives. Because the CAHA looked after the U17, U18, and World Junior levels and its expanded Program of Excellence, it helped Hockey Canada identify prospects for the Olympic Team and other national representative teams" Hockey Canada, International Committee, "Update."

109 Jim Proudfoot, "Father Bauer Recalls 'Giant Act of Faith,'" *Toronto Star*, 1987 or 1988, Box 4, File 9, Bauer fonds, Basilian Archives.

110 King, interview.

111 Greg Kostyk, "Father David Bauer: Father of the National Hockey Program," March 31, 1988, "Father David, Coach" file, St. Michael's College School Archives, 11.

112 George Gross, "Bauer Blesses Oiler Machine," *Toronto Sun*, September 8, 1987, Box 2, last file, Bauer fonds, Basilian Archives, 87.

added, "Some people might call it the … [Edmonton] Oiler Machine. But how can you call it a machine when they operate so spontaneously? The game proved that Canada's emotional and spontaneous hockey style can match or surpass the Soviet [conditioning, strength, and] stick-handling ability." Bauer noted how the Soviets had improved their physical play: "they concentrate on developing their skills along the boards, not ramming somebody through them."[113]

No other Canadian had given as much to Olympic hockey as Bauer had, and now he found himself in a limited role at Canada's first Winter Olympic Games hosted in Calgary.[114] Former National Team member Wally Kozak was a skills coach for the 1988 National Team. He remembered how those in charge of Hockey Canada "really didn't want [Bauer] but they did. And he was there … he was on the outside."[115] Bauer spoke at events leading up to the Games, promoting Olympic ideals and questioning the status quo. For instance, he told a reporter that "in a small way, hockey can improve the world," but criticized its direction: "if we say economics are the only thing that counts, which the NHL keeps saying, we're in serious trouble."[116]

Following the 1984 Los Angeles Summer Olympics, the Calgary Winter Olympics marked a fuller embrace of a corporate-driven Games. It had a large sponsorship program and a massive $309 million US television contract. Federal, provincial, and city governments also contributed upwards of half a billion dollars of venue and infrastructure support.[117] The Winter Games, which were often seen as weaker than the Summer Games, hit full stride in Calgary in terms of positive economic impact.

The financial success of the Games was not decried by Bauer, who wrote an introductory piece for a booklet promoting the Calgary Olympics. Instead, he admitted that there is nothing fundamentally wrong with the Olympics as a "money-making enterprise," or a means for glory through gold medal victories.[118] He mused that there always existed threats to the Olympic

113   Gross, "Bauer Blesses Oiler Machine," 87.
114   Wally Kozak, interview with author, September 25, 2020.
115   Gross, "Bauer Blesses Oiler Machine," 87.
116   Proudfoot, "Father Bauer Recalls."
117   Morrow and Wamsley, *Sport in Canada*, 282.
118   David Bauer, "Why Do We Have Olympic Games?" 1987, Terry O'Malley Collection, 1.

experience, such as "elitist amateurism," "commercialization," or "political exploitation of winning."[119] For him, however, the "heart of the Olympic experience" was "to compete, to do one's best and to be pushed beyond one's best by the presence of others doing their best." Finding balance and determining one's priorities were necessary not only for individuals but for movements like the Olympics. He added a warning: "The study of human kinetics [and] the application of technology have made new levels of achievement possible.... [T]he danger that I see, however, is that it is fatally easy to confuse this sort of physiological development with the full human development."[120] He explained:

> In order to understand what human development of the individual really means we must meditate profoundly on what a human person really is. We must see that person—each person—as uniquely valuable. We must see him or her also in relation to others in society, in the familiar, the local, the national and the world community. We must see the role of athletics in relations to all the other aspects of human activity, social, economic, political, intellectual, artistic and religious. We must let the spirit prevail.
>
> The ancient Olympic Games were primarily a religious festival. This is not so in the modern Olympics, and I would not want it to be so. What we do need, however, is the recognition that the holding of these Games offers something much more than an opportunity to develop bodies and hone skills. Peace, justice, love, joy—these are universal human longings that are represented in the Olympic Games. The opportunity to participate offers an athlete the chance to do what he or she does best in this full human context. If we forget the context we destroy the opportunity.[121]

Here, Bauer the philosopher situates sport within his concentric circles model, where sport can play an integral part in human society. Given sport's prominence, he believed the purposes of human development needed clarification. They required reflection for improved ways of shaping human beings within their micro and macro communities. Sport, as an arena of fostering relationships and values, was to widen and enrich opportunities for participants.

119   Bauer, "Olympic Games," 2.
120   Bauer, "Olympic Games," 3.
121   Bauer, "Olympic Games," 3.

In a speech titled, "Olympic Hockey: 'Make Use of Technique, but Let the Spirit Prevail,'" Bauer addressed a hockey audience in the face of Soviet domination of the international game. He began by openly admitting that Soviet hockey had surpassed Canadian hockey in its preparations—in both skill and conditioning—and in its strategies and tactics. However, he argued for a vital final element in hockey: "there is the element of spirit, of drive, eagerness, enthusiasm, spontaneity, and desire: this, showing itself in the course of a context, will often determine victory or defeat."[122]

Figure 8.1 Bauer discusses Canadian hockey.

Courtesy of D.K. (Doc) Seaman Hockey Resource Centre, Hockey Hall of Fame

Bauer believed that Canadians would be dissatisfied to earn victory if it meant giving up their spirit and drive. He assumed that when people reflect on sport and life, they find that winning in the short term is not really enough. Attention must be turned to "moral and spiritual issues in Canada and the

122   David Bauer, "Olympic Hockey: 'Make Use of Technique, but Let the Spirit Prevail'," Box 1, File 4, Bauer fonds, Basilian Archives.

world." A values-driven, spirit-enlivened sport "may provide a stimulus for an effort which will carry Canada and the whole world much further."[123] His focus on spirit was reflected in a note he received from Soviet coach Tarasov: "Dear David! It is great, my dear colleague, that hockey has introduced us to each other. It is great that we helped each other to experience hockey—the most intellectual, emotional game of the 20th century."[124]

The two above Olympic pieces written late in the Bauer's life underline how he wanted Canadians to reflect upon the value of sport and how it impacted participants: did it impoverish, expand, or free their human spirits? Gaining skills and abilities through participation were important, but sport should cultivate human values for youth and society.

The 1988 Olympic Team

Despite the removing of amateur restrictions for the Calgary Games, contractual and logistical issues remained for Canadians who played in the National and American hockey leagues and wanted to play in the Games. Lake Placid Olympians and NHL veterans like Tim Watters joined the team. Watters found that the 1980 experience gave him the confidence to reach the NHL, while the 1988 team was better prepared because of the well-organized programming and larger support staff.[125] King remained the full-time head coach, while managerial positions functioned under the direction of Hockey Canada. Both the CAHA and the CIAU offered cooperation.[126] The creation of the first "Centre for Excellence" in Calgary included initial projects like an international coaches' seminar and a video bank on international play.[127] The National Team had become a more finely-tuned, high-tech machine.

123 Bauer, "Make Use of Technique."

124 Anatoly Tarasov, Note to David Bauer in *ДЕТЯМ О ХОККЕЕ* by Anatoly Tarasov, 1986, Box 2, no file, Bauer fonds, Basilian Archives. The note was an inscription inside the book copy given to Bauer.

125 Joe Pelletier, "Legends of Team Canada: Tim Watters," *The Hockey History Blog* (blog), *Greatest Hockey Legends.com*, September 20, 2017. http://www.greatesthockeylegends.com/2017/09/legends-of-team-canada-tim-watters.html.

126 Hockey Canada Research Institute, "Centre of Excellence," 1984, MG31 E 72 39, H2 (8) b, Olympics 1984—Financing, LAC.

127 Hockey Canada Research Institute, "Centre of Excellence." It also included a physiotherapy/research area and computerized recordkeeping about "young potential players for the 1988 Olympic Team."

Former team captain Randy Gregg, who left his substantial NHL salary to relive his Lake Placid experience, was disappointed with his decision: "It was a completely different experience. It was basically run by the NHL," with the team acting as a feeder for the league.[128] He added elsewhere: "It turned out the organization was focused almost exclusively on winning, with absolutely no interest in the sort of character development we'd seen under Father Bauer."[129] Changes in the National Team affected the players' experience.

Gregg believed in Bauer and Drake's broader vision for international hockey. Prior to the Games, he explained to a reporter: "We have to come out of it with more than just the hockey games. It's a social and cultural experience. An understanding of different people, and why there's tensions in the world—this as well as being the best hockey players we can be."[130] Bauer spoke to the team prior to the Games. Gregg lightheartedly recalled that Bauer's speech went over the heads of his teammates.[131] They were not prepared for a bigger vision of the sport.

Playing within King's team-first and technically-strong system, the team produced an upset Izvestia tournament win in Moscow only a couple months before the Calgary Games. This buoyed the players' confidence and lifted the expectations of a nation—perhaps winning a gold medal on Canadian soil was not farfetched. But it yielded knowledge about the team and its players for upcoming competition at the Games.[132] The surprise element was conceded.

When the team arrived in Calgary after its final exhibition game, it was informed that another professional player would be joining the lineup once he returned from his NHL team's road trip. Gregg recounted how painful it was to see a third-line center replaced after he had played four years with the National Team: "you could just see the dressing room fall apart" after that decision broke the spirit of a former teammate.[133] He summarized: "you realize very well that the glue that held the players together was as important as the quality of the players."

128   Gregg, interview.
129   Charles Wilkins, *Breakaway: Hockey and the Years Beyond* (Collingdale, PA: Diane Publishing Company, 1995), 173–74.
130   J. Christie, "Gregg Defenceman with a Mission: Former Oiler Repays Olympic Team Debt," *The Globe and Mail*, October 24, 1987, E3.
131   Gregg, interview.
132   Hockey Canada, *Canadian Dream*, 56–57.
133   Gregg, interview.

The team finished a disappointing fourth place. Despite better financing and improved coordination among some hockey organizations, the team still could not defeat opposing teams like the gold medalist Soviets. Professional players had not pushed the team over the hump, while Finland won their first medal in hockey with its former NHLers, like Reijo Ruotsalainen. In a radio interview with Bauer during the 1988 Olympics, Brian Conacher rehashed the past with Bauer: "We talked about how far Canada's national hockey program had come since 1963.... And the truth was, not very far. That year's Team Canada faced many of the issues and challenges the first team had struggled with. Hockey Canada, the CAHA and the NHL were still ambivalent, uncommitted and not united about how Canada should be represented at the top level of international sport."[134]

The Final Years of the National Team

Following the Calgary Games, the space for elite amateur sport shrank even more. Just as senior hockey had become largely ill-fated a generation earlier, Hockey Canada's team ran into the problem of simply being an NHL feeder team.[135] When sprinter Ben Johnson tested positive for steroids later that year at the Seoul Summer Olympics, funding dipped for national team programming across amateur sport. Things remained a challenge for hockey's National Team.

Bauer was primarily left outside of hockey circles, but made appearances at different hockey events and was committed to Hockey Canada board meetings. Prior to the Games, Chair Ian Macdonald invited Bauer onto a long-term planning committee for Hockey Canada.[136] Specific concerns of the committee included engagement with university hockey, whereas "institutional and structural factors influencing Canadian hockey" needed careful analysis and, thought Macdonald, Bauer's background could

134 Brian Conacher, *As the Puck Turns: A Personal Journey Through the World of Hockey* (Toronto: John Wiley & Sons Canada Limited, 2007), 195.

135 Bruce Kidd, *The Struggle for Canadian Sport* (Toronto: University of Toronto Press, 1996), 270.

136 Hockey Canada, "Planning and Development Committee Report to the Board of Directors," Annual General Meeting, December 7, 1985, Box 3, File 7, Bauer fonds, Basilian Archives.

contribute significantly.[137] Bauer and Eagleson were the only two original members remaining on the board.[138]

A Hockey Canada report in 1987 argued that "the national team represents an important landmark in the development of Canadian Hockey.... The inception of the National Team has provided an infusion of innovation into the Canadian hockey landscape and has accomplished this on a scale great enough to effect the substantive changes required in Canada."[139] A scientifically-informed, internationally-concerned form of hockey began affecting domestic hockey development. The National Team, whether under Bauer's control or not, "facilitated a new approach to the game and its methods in Canada in the minds of players, coaches and spectators alike."[140] The report must have encouraged Bauer, even if it did not draw distinctions between his vision and a post-1980, hothouse reality for the hockey alternative. A different vantage point for understanding hockey continued, as Centres of Excellence sprung up in other cities and the National Team continued to bring new strategies and coaching insights back to Canada.[141] The convergence of authority in the NHL and a national drive for improved innovation, however, ran the risk of obscuring the importance of values and ethics in sport.[142]

Bauer's priority on developing persons first was still supported by others. For instance, leaders in both Hockey Canada and the CAHA agreed to central values for the National Team program in a collaborative statement for a post-Calgary team.[143] It named the sport's "intrinsic worth to the country and its youth" and how it should show "respect for the integrity of the individual and ... the game as a basic ingredient in [people's] total growth and development." The stated values even sought "a more concerted effort

---

137 Hockey Canada, "Planning and Development Committee."

138 Lang, "Draft Report." Chris Lang had also been active with the organization since its origins.

139 "Hockey Canada—'The Road Ahead', A Discussion Paper for the Board of Directors," May 12, 1987, private email attachment from Paul Carson, Vice President, Hockey Development of Hockey Canada, January 22, 2019.

140 Hockey Canada, "Planning and Development Committee."

141 Hockey Canada, *Canadian Dream*, 51. Coaching clinics included coaches from around the hockey world, and coach King created a video series to enhance innovative instruction.

142 Kozak, interview.

143 "Hockey Canada/CAHA Post-1988 Arrangement," September 3, 1987, Box 3, File 7, Bauer fonds, Basilian Archives.

toward integration of hockey development with educational development."[144] The two organizations wanted better cooperation in the International Committee.[145] Bauer, the elder statesman, attended meetings discussing the arrangement as late as the year he died.[146]

The amalgamation of these viewpoints is most evident in the longest-serving National Team coach, Dave King. King recognized that the team was doing more than just playing hockey. Players on these underdog teams developed quickly because of the intensity of the games, as they "were developing work habits, focus, resilience ... in whatever they did, should they not play pro hockey."[147] The team members crafted a team spirit: "Our national team players are really close. You can't compete like that and not forge deep, deep bonds with each other." For instance, National Teams in the 1960s and 1980s sacrificed their bodies by shot blocking because that was how they could win.[148] A patriotic passion drove players to give it their all on the ice.

King summarized the National Teams' primary ideal: "we could win through the spirit of a person, usually more than we could because of the skill. We had skilled players ... but we needed to have a team that could play together and believed together. And that's why the National Team was so special."[149] King saw his tenure with the National Team as an extension of his university coaching, where he developed people and their skills. Players were meagerly paid, but they had special goals in mind that were linked historically to Bauer.

The connection between education and the National Team had weakened considerably since 1980, but the last few teams did include several college players—such as Paul Kariya, of Japanese descent, who played at the 1994 Olympics. National Teams at the 1992 and 1994 Olympics were a mix of core team members and drop-in professionals. They picked up disgruntled NHL-caliber players like Eric Lindros and Sean Burke, while developing

144 "Hockey Canada/CAHA Post-1988 Arrangement."

145 Hockey Canada, "Minutes of the Board of Directors of Hockey Canada," September 14, 1987, Ottawa, ON, Box 4, File 7, Bauer fonds, Basilian Archives. This was especially the case as the CAHA became more powerful, with international events like the World Junior tournament and its grassroots connection to Canadian hockey culture. Hockey Canada, International Committee, "Update."

146 Hockey Canada, "Minutes of the Board of Directors of Hockey Canada," May 10, 1988, Box 4, File 8, Bauer fonds, Basilian Archives.

147 King, interview.

148 King, interview.

149 King, interview.

players like Joe Juneau and Adrian Aucoin. King coached at his third Olympic Games in 1992, winning a silver medal. Tom Renney's 1994 team came one shootout goal away from ending Canada's Olympic gold medal drought.

For Renney, becoming the head coach of the National Team fulfilled a long-term goal. He recalled meeting Bauer at a minor hockey banquet as a 12-year-old player in Cranbrook, British Columbia, where Bauer delivered a speech about the virtues of hockey and the meaning of being Canadian.[150] Renney played hockey at a US college and eventually coached the National Team for two years. In the early morning of the gold medal game in Lillehammer, he reflected on coaches like Bauer who had inspired him to coach in the National Team program. Like King, Renney felt that there was something special with the fraternity of National Team players from across the decades: "It's a golden thread to me: to play because you love your country and you love hockey. Compensation had zero to do with it."[151]

The National Team was discontinued when best-on-best competition was allowed at the 1998 Nagano Olympics. It was a sad day for Renney and King because the team played a role in bringing top level hockey into small communities across the country.[152] Just as early National Teams took playing tours throughout the nation, King recalled playing national teams from Russia and Sweden in places like Sudbury or North Bay, Ontario. The team would host a coaching clinic in conjunction with the game, while locals shared a post-game potluck dinner after seeing top-level hockey in their hometown.[153] With more Europeans playing in the NHL, there was greater interest in seeing who the next superstar from overseas might be. Each game, recalled King, was an event for the host communities.[154] People grew together, and local hockey organizations received a boost. From 1985 to 1992, the National Team played more than 225 games across Canada in more than a hundred communities.[155]

In 1994, Hockey Canada and the CAHA merged into one organization with a melded name, the Canadian Hockey Association, which, in 1998, was

150   Tom Renney, interview with author, January 10, 2022.

151   Renney, interview. He went on to coach several NHL teams.

152   King, interview. King had become the head coach of the Calgary Flames.

153   Renney, interview. Renney recalled pre- and post-game meetings with local coaches to discuss game strategies.

154   King, interview.

155   Hockey Canada, *Canadian Dream*, 56–57. Ron Robison was key in organizing the events. King, interview.

renamed Hockey Canada.[156] Hockey Canada chair Macdonald pushed for the merger, while presidents of both organizations—Bill Hay and Murray Costello—negotiated the joining of hockey institutions. Macdonald recalled Bauer's support for the merger prior to the priest's death in 1988.[157] The final Hockey Canada vote was not without contention; chair Macdonald cast the final ballot in the split vote.[158] From start to finish, collaboration was never easy in Hockey Canada. Contrasting viewpoints and motivations hamstrung pursuit of a common vision and practical plans for the sport.

Bauer's Lasting Influence On the National Team

As the National Team came to an end, so did the end-point of a distinct hockey structure within the Canadian hockey system. The team that had emerged after 1980 had many of Bauer's fingerprints on it: playing for patriotic pride; combining education and hockey; seeking a nonviolent form of hockey; playing with character; providing life opportunities to players; and experiencing a team spirit built upon the individual spirit and drive of each player. Bauer's philosophical prioritization of the development of human persons had shrunk, yet remained. The National Team had been another option for players, but as a career path, it converged with the NHL.

Bauer had taken on an impossible challenge, according to Costello: "He was literally going against the system and the NHL owners. They would say all nice things, but under their breath, you know, 'We don't need this guy around.'"[159] Ultimately, without an organization or hockey system clearly behind him, Costello summarized, "Bauer was really taking on the world by himself almost.... It was him against the establishment, if you will.... But you've got to get some openings on the other side to allow you to move into a void ... and he didn't have much of that."[160] Bauer may have competed fiercely, but his opponent had blocked outside assistance.

Bauer remained what chair Ian Macdonald termed an "insider-outsider": he participated in hockey but was not strictly a hockey person.[161] Macdonald

---

156 Stevens, "Canadian Hockey Association Merger," 1.
157 Macdonald, interview.
158 Macdonald, interview.
159 Costello, interview.
160 Costello, interview.
161 Macdonald, interview.

felt that without a solely-dedicated designation within the game, the priest-coach could not be fully trusted by insiders who earned their livelihood from the sport. Bauer could not maintain control of the National Team when the NHL aimed at eliminating player options and downplaying noncommercial motives in the sport.[162] The league held control of the hockey system, and Hockey Canada board members accepted this political and economic reality.

162 O'Malley, email.

CHAPTER NINE

Bauer's Lasting Influence

BAUER'S LONGTIME FRIEND PÈRE MURRAY DIED IN 1975, leaving Notre Dame Collegiate in Wilcox, Saskatchewan, in desperate need of reorganization. Bauer became a member of its board of regents, and was determined to ensure that the school would maintain a "spiritual, moral and religious tone" instead of becoming a "school built around the midget hockey player."[1] Bauer coaxed Barry MacKenzie and Terry O'Malley—Bauer disciples at St. Michael's, on the National Team, and in Japan—to become a school director and teacher, respectively. MacKenzie explained that he wanted students to develop more than their hockey skills: they could participate in extracurricular programming, build comaraderie, and earn an education in case professional hockey passed them by.[2] The Bauer pupil advocated for young players to strive for a US college hockey scholarship.[3]

---

1   David Bauer, Marginal Notes in "Post-Secondary Education at Notre Dame: A Review of the Past and a Plan for the Future," 1981, Box 4, File 2, Bauer fonds, Basilian Archives; and David Bauer, Notes, Box 4, File 5, Bauer fonds, Basilian Archives. Bauer rejected pleas that he become the school's president.

2   Neil Campbell, "Notre Dame Means More Than Hockey Winners," *The Globe and Mail*, December 3, 1982, 19. An intra-school hockey program began in the early 1980s, named the Father David Bauer League.

3   Campbell, "Notre Dame Means More," 19.

Not unlike St. Michael's in the 1950s, Notre Dame was a rare high school with a hockey program. Minor hockey leagues began to accuse it of breaking jurisdiction rules, as the school tried to recruit players from across the country.[4] Since it was a boarding school, each player's residential home became an issue; CAHA rules dictated that players should play close to home, and Notre Dame's wide recruitment threatened to disturb the level playing field.[5] By 1982, the CAHA established the "Notre Dame Rule," which limited the school to three inter-branch transfers.[6] Tensions with the CAHA coincided with support from Hockey Canada and the National Team. Coach King wrote in 1985 of the school's "fine tradition" with the National Team: Notre Dame was the alma mater of coaches MacKenzie and O'Malley, and players Gord Sherven, James Patrick, and Russ Courtnall.[7] King told a reporter at Wilcox, "There appears to be a strong Olympic feeling instilled in your players. No other school has contributed as Notre Dame has."[8]

To keep alive both Murray's and Bauer's vision of education and hockey, coaches distributed an inspirational quote from Pope John Paul II to players:[9]

> Every type of sport carries within itself a rich patrimony of values, which must be always kept present in order to be realized ... the proper commitment of one's own energies, the control of sensitivity, the methodical preparation, perseverance, resistance, the endurance of fatigue and wounds, the domination of one's own faculties, the

4 John Moss, Letter to Willard Estey, October 20, 1982, MG31 E 72 40, H2 (16), Notre Dame (1982–1985), LAC. The school denied these allegations.

5 John Moss, Letter to Willard Estey, Notre Dame College, December 15, 1982, MG31 E 72 40, H2 (16), Notre Dame (1982–1985), LAC.

6 If Notre Dame had included other high schools in a school-based league, recalled Costello, this could have begun a major shift in the Canadian minor hockey system. Murray Costello, interview with author, June 3, 2019.

7 Dave King, Letter to Willard Estey, January 23, 1985, MG31 E 72 40, H2 (16), Notre Dame (1982–1985), LAC. Gord Kluzak and Todd Strueby played with the National Junior Team, too. Along with dozens of alumni who became NHL players, several became NHL coaches, including Jon Cooper and Barry Trotz. See Tom Gulitti, "Eastern Final Coaches Learned Life Lessons at Same Canadian Prep School," *National Hockey League*, September 12, 2020, https://www.nhl.com/news/barry-trotz-jon-cooper-learned-life-lessons-at-athol-murray-college-of-notre-dame/c-319001964.

8 "Olympics and Notre Dame," *Newshound* 7, no. 3 (Summer 1984): 5.

9 Bauer had hand-copied the speech. David Bauer, Teaching Notes, Box 3, File 4, Bauer fonds, Basilian Archives.

sense of joy, acceptance of rules, the spirit of renunciation and solidarity, loyalty to commitment, generosity toward the winners, serenity in defeat, patience toward all.

This papal proclamation of sports' values was idealized and promoted by Bauer's disciples.

Bauer also promoted a liberal arts program at Notre Dame that could address what he called "the *real needs* of the modern world."[10] In a letter to his niece, he explained that the most human of needs too often lay outside of conventional educational concerns.[11] Schooling too often obsesses with adapting life to a technological mindset—actual human needs become minimized. Inspiration for the arts program came from readings critical of mainstream culture and that leaned toward futurist thinking. For example, his companionship with McLuhan led to a friendship with Father Pierre Babin. This French thinker believed that a technological culture reconfigured the inner lives of human beings, making them more power-hungry and impatient while upending their spiritual life.[12] At first computerization produces better possibilities in life, but users' acceptance of a new way of life reinforces a new reality.[13] An electronic age could marginalize the talent of young people.

Bauer drew upon other accessible thinkers, like futurist Alvin Toffler and philosophers Teilhard de Chardin, Martin Buber, and Søren Kierkegaard.[14]

---

10   David Bauer, Letter to Barbara Bauer, January 15, 1981, Box 3, File 3, Bauer fonds, Basilian Archives.

11   Bauer made a copy of a quote from Schumacher: "No civilization has ever devoted more time, money and energy to organized education. So much reliance is to-day being placed in the power of education just to cope with the problems thrown up by technological progress." Bauer, Notes, Box 3, File 3, Bauer fonds, Basilian Archives.

12   Pierre Babin, *The Audio-Visual Man* (Dayton, OH: Pflaum Publishing Group, 1970), 14. Babin, an Oblate of Mary Immaculate, collaborated with McLuhan.

13   Clarity for this sentence came from N. Kowalsky and R. Haluza-DeLay, "'This Is Oil Country': The Alberta Tar Sands and Jacques Ellul's Theory of Technology," *Environmental Ethics* 37, no. 1 (2015): 81.

14   Bauer also relied on the thought of Ellul, which was highlighted in Chapter 7. Alvin Toffler, *The Eco-Spasm Report* (Toronto: Bantam Books, 1975); Pierre Teilhard de Chardin, *The Divine Milieu* (New York: Harper & Row, 1960); Martin Buber, *Two Types of Faith*, trans. Norman P. Goldhawk (Syracuse, NY: Syracuse University Press, 2003); and Søren Kierkegaard, *The Present Age*, trans. Alexander Dru (London, England: Collins, 1962).

He also found support in some Basilian fathers, who committed to offering lectures in Wilcox. For example, Father Gerry McGuigan, a former economics professor, researched issues of hunger and malnutrition in Niger. He spoke about the needs of Indigenous Peoples and supported self-sustaining agricultural techniques that respected their culture.[15] He highlighted how technology must integrate with social aspects of persons.[16] The resources critiqued a technological age, the loss of ethics, and the unhinging of decision-making from human meaning. Bauer wanted students to retreat from a hectic world like ancient monastics and consider humanistic questions.[17]

With Bauer's support, Notre Dame school leaders envisioned an Institute of Human Development and Sport.[18] It would offer both a three-year Arts degree and a one-year Quest program for high school graduates and adults who sought direction in their life. Hanrahan, who had become president of St. Thomas More College in Saskatoon, took a leadership role in the endeavor.[19] The Institute's Arts program would be run as a partnership with the University of Regina, examining sport inter-disciplinarily through philosophy, history, psychology, sociology, spirituality, and so on.[20] Bauer's values-driven sport found a home in the project.[21]

Plans for a full-fledged Institute for Sport ended early, but all was not lost.[22] Modest preparations for a one-year Quest program, which included

15 "Speaker Introduction of McGuigan," 1985, Wilcox, SK, Box 1, File 3, Bauer fonds, Basilian Archives; and P. Wallace Platt, *Dictionary of Basilian Biography: Lives of Members of the Congregation of Priests of Saint Basil from its Origins in 1822 to 2022*, 2nd ed. (Toronto: University of Toronto Press, 2005), 412.

16 "Why Did You Come," *Alumni and Friends Newsletter* 8, no. 2 (Spring 1985): 1.

17 Bauer, Notes, Box 3, File 1, Bauer fonds, Basilian Archives.

18 Notre Dame Review Committee, "Post-Secondary Education at Notre Dame: A Review of the Past and a Plan for the Future," 1981, Box 4, File 2, Bauer fonds, Basilian Archives. The school had a long-standing postsecondary affiliation with St. Paul's University in Ottawa that ended around the time Père Murray died.

19 Notre Dame Review Committee, "Post-Secondary Education."

20 Louis Xhignesse, "Outline of a Proposed Notre Dame College Three-Year Arts Program," Notre Dame College, January 11, 1981, Box 4, File 2, Bauer fonds, Basilian Archives; and Notre Dame Task Force Committee, "Report of the Task Force on Post-Secondary Education at Athol Murray College of Notre Dame," Presentation, April 27, 1982, Box 4, File 2, Bauer fonds, Basilian Archives.

21 David Bauer, Notes, Box 4, File 3, Bauer fonds, Basilian Archives.

22 The Institute rested too much on the goodwill of leaders and guest instructors, and it did not have adequate financial and academic support.

community service and a work placement, were backed by the Basilian Fathers and a $30,000 grant from the provincial government in 1985.[23] Bauer spoke at a press conference: "How can we expect young people ... to be able to serve the real needs of our world when they find themselves perplexed and uncertain of what they can contribute to a society which is itself filled with confusion?"[24] The Quest program offered philosophical readings and drew inspiration from new and old sources: "It must be a solid Christian Catholic centre from which sparks must fly in all directions to light up a rather sometime dull and drab existential world around it."[25] Bauer did not want a "hippie haven" at Wilcox; attendees could orient their lives and earn college credit.[26]

Several of Bauer's nieces attended Notre Dame. Barbara led the school's religion department and Lisa enrolled in the Quest program as she prepared for the 1984 Los Angeles Summer Olympics in field hockey. In her youth, Lisa played pond hockey with her brothers, but was not allowed to play minor hockey as a girl, unlike her aunt Rita in the 1940s.[27] Uncle Dave asked if she planned to try out for the sport's national team.[28] As a woman in sport, she appreciated his encouragement and credited him with getting her to think deeply about sport. Training on the prairies, her view was expanded in preparation for the Olympics.[29]

Juggling time between Vancouver and Wilcox stretched Bauer, as did tensions within the school's board of regents and strains within the Catholic Church after the reforms of the Second Vatican Council.[30] The anxiety within

23 "Quest Program, 1983–1984," Box 4, File 4, Bauer fonds, Basilian Archives; and Kevin Corrigan, Letter to Minster Gordon Currie, May 13, 1985, I—1988— Bauer—Quest box, File 2, Basilian Archives.

24 Press Release, Box 1, File 4, Bauer fonds, Basilian Archives.

25 David Bauer, Untitled, Box 3, File 3, Bauer fonds, Basilian Archives.

26 Bauer, Untitled, Basilian Archives; David Bauer, Notes, Box 36, "Bauer, Dave 1971–1980" file, St. Mark's College Archives.

27 Larry Anstett, "New Era Unfolding for Bauer Family," *Kitchener-Waterloo Record*, July 28, 1984, C7–C8. Lisa became the University of Waterloo's all-time leading scorer and a female athlete of the year.

28 Lisa Bauer-Leahy, interview with author, January 17, 2019.

29 Bauer-Leahy, interview.

30 Bauer, Notes, Box 3, File 5, Bauer fonds, Basilian Archives. For instance, the Council's teachings about spirituality moved away from traditional devotions to the Virgin Mary and Our Lady of Fatima—Bauer held both dearly. David Bauer, Letter to Lisa Bauer, Box 3, File 1, Bauer fonds, Basilian Archives.

Bauer increased because of his concerns about societal issues of violence, substance abuse, nuclear proliferation, and a consumeristic worldview.[31] He admitted to his own anxious feelings, compounded by health fears.[32] In one note, he even felt bitter about helping others who had found greater success than he did.[33] He questioned if he had wasted his time in hockey.[34] Many supported him through his weakness. People like Hindmarch and Holowaty reminded him of young people he had positively impacted.[35] Lifelong friendships with parishioners at St. Mark's College chapel also helped ease his pain.

The Quest program at Notre Dame lasted only a few short years in the mid-1980s.[36] His work in Wilcox reveals his desire to name the challenges facing young people and to support their full development. This determined effort exemplifies why he tried to wed hockey and education. In the end, the Basilians relocated Quest to the Toronto separate (Catholic) school district, where Bauer could mentor educators and support the communication of faith in a technological age.[37]

The Father David Bauer Olympic Arena

Bauer's legacy in Canadian ice hockey was symbolically captured with the renaming of a Calgary arena. At a cost of nearly $3 million dollars, the renovated rink would support the National Team on a permanent basis in

31   Bauer, Notes, Box 3, File 5, Bauer fonds, Basilian Archives; and see also David Bauer, Letter to Barbara and Marianne, Box 3, File 4, Bauer fonds, Basilian Archives.

32   David Bauer, Notes, Box 3, File 5, Bauer fonds, Basilian Archives.

33   Bauer, Letter to Lisa, Box 4, File 5, Bauer fonds, Basilian Archives. He wrote about McLeod, Watt, Eagleson, and Hindmarch.

34   Bauer-Leahy, interview. Terry O'Malley, email message to author, March 6, 2023.

35   Bob Hindmarch, interview with author, August 17, 2018; and Bill Holowaty, interview with author, February 1, 2019.

36   Bauer never moved to Wilcox permanently, which weakened the program. Barry MacKenzie, interview with author, March 12, 2020; Bauer, Letter to Lisa, Box 4, File 5, Bauer fonds, Basilian Archives; and Bauer, Notes, Box 36, "Bauer, Dave 1971–1980" file, St. Mark's College Archives. Hanrahan thought the program would have fit better at a larger institution like St. Thomas More College at the University of Saskatchewan. Bauer, Notes, Box 3, File 1, Bauer fonds, Basilian Archives; and Jack Gallagher, interview with author, January 15, 2019.

37   O'Malley, email.

the leadup to and following the Calgary Games.[38] The minister of sport, Otto Jelinek, christened the arena "The Father David Bauer Olympic Arena." Ron Robison of Hockey Canada broke the news to Bauer: "[I] admired the work you have done with Canada's Olympic Hockey Team for many years and ... truly believe they could not have found a more appropriate name for the facility."[39]

As a board member with Hockey Canada, Bauer met with Minister Jelinek, who, like many previous ministers, sought to reduce violence in sport. Bauer wrote how Jelinek's efforts mirrored those of his religious community: "the Basilian Fathers have kept in touch with hockey for 75 years in an attempt to reduce violence."[40] The minister's anti-violence campaign put Hockey Canada in a difficult political situation, according to Judge Estey, "because of obvious difficulties" it raised in light of their work with the game's powerbrokers.[41]

Minister Jelinek led the official reopening on September 21, 1986, and many Bauer associates attended. Keeping to form, Bauer's speech explained that he wanted to "provide values that would one day help [players] become leaders in a turbulent world" in the hope that "in a small way, hockey can improve the world."[42] Jelinek's own speech likely mirrored words given at another event that same year:

> Father David Bauer stands out as a coach who has shaped the lives
> of many Canadians both on and off the rink. He has fostered
> the development of their drive, spirit and enthusiasm. We see the

---

38　Crosbie Cotton, "Rink Improves Odds for '88 Hockey Team," *Calgary Herald*, July 16, 1985, Box 4, File 9, Bauer fonds, Basilian Archives. Renovations to the older Foothills Arena provided an Olympic-sized ice surface for team practices during the Calgary Games.

39　Ron Robison, Letter to David Bauer, July 17, 1985, Box 1, File 6, Bauer fonds, Basilian Archives. Robison later became the Commissioner of the Western Hockey League (WHL), while the building became the national headquarters for Hockey Canada from 1992 to 2011, and then the head offices for the WHL. Hockey Canada, *The Building of a Canadian Dream* (Calgary, AB: Hockey Canada, circa 2017), 50–51.

40　David Bauer, Rough Draft of Letter to Sport Minister Otto Jelinek, Box 3, File 5, Bauer fonds, Basilian Archives. Mayor Ralph Klein and the Chair of the Calgary Organizing Committee, Frank King, were also present.

41　Willard Estey, Memo on Removal of Violence from Sport, June 10, 1986, MG31 E 72 36, LAC.

42　Chima McLean, "The 'Quest' for Peace and Tolerance Evident Throughout Fr. Dave's Life," Hockey Showcase: Father David Bauer Cup, March 28–30, 1996, 8.

outcome of his efforts in his many proteges who are successful, spirited public figures.... Father Bauer, you continue to be a mentor and role model for many of us. We thank you for your personal drive and determination on behalf of our future—Canada's youth.[43]

Bauer was more embarrassed than anything about the arena acknowledgement, but as former player Holowaty explained, he used his celebrity to deliver his main message: people need to think bigger than just a game inside a hockey rink.[44] For Holowaty, Bauer received much respect from an older generation because he tried to change the game toward players' needs.[45]

Father Bauer and the Drive for a Values-Driven Hockey Tradition

With the establishment of the National Team program, Bauer expanded how the Basilian tradition engaged hockey. Churches had promoted sport as a means to Christian participation in Canadian society at a time when St. Michael's entered Ontario's evolving, organized hockey system.[46]Although the Basilian Fathers withdrew the Majors from an NHL-influenced junior hockey system in 1961, they backed the National Team. It was an original venture in the spirit of Maritain: through participation in a social enterprise, people could understand themselves and promote higher ideals. It put values at the fore of the national and international stage. It tried to foster positive attitudes and promote personal development as the very purpose of the sport. It was larger than a hockey experiment and more difficult to grasp.

Holding life values and hockey together was difficult. Bauer moved outside of a safely bunkered classroom to embody Maritain's transcendent humanism at the hockey rink. It took years for other Basilians to realize the broader impact Bauer was making through his efforts, while countering the dominant sporting ethos became more difficult.[47] Bauer increasingly

---

43   Otto Jelinek, Remarks at the Launch of the Royal Canadian Mint's 1988 Olympic Hockey and Biathlon Coins, February 25, 1986, Hockey Hall of Fame, Toronto, ON, Maureen Bauer-McGahey Collection.

44   Don McLeod, interview with author, June 4, 2018; and Holowaty, interview.

45   Holowaty, interview.

46   David Marshall, *Secularizing the Faith: Canadian Protestant Clergy and the Crisis of Belief, 1850–1940* (Toronto: University of Toronto, 1992), 7.

47   McLeod, interview; and Ted Schmidt, "Fr. David Bauer Untouched by Perils

felt marginalized in many hockey circles and sometimes ostracized within his own religious community. In the midst of this isolation, he maintained friendships with like-minded coaches and former players. He also wrote about support found in Basilian confreres. Early Basilian sport figures like Carr and LeBel, along with many of his generation—Hanrahan, Garvey, Kelly, and McGuigan—gave him hope that his contribution was worthwhile, despite his becoming worn down at the end of his life.[48]

Coach Tom Watt called Bauer a "real mixture" of two worlds: "sometimes you were talking to a hockey coach and the priest came out, and then other times you thought you were talking to the priest and the coach came out."[49] Bauer was an enigma incubated by design within Basilian institutions. He was a mix of a religious priest-educator and a public hockey figure. The unsettling effect he sometimes had on others was intentional: priest-coaches wanted to promote a particular hockey-faith tradition that cut against the grain of corporate hockey. Bauer was a complete hockey person, yet was dyed in priestly clerical colors. Player Randy Gregg recalled when Bauer teasingly wore a rival team's t-shirt underneath his black clerical shirt. Gregg took a message from it: "I may be a Basilian priest, but underneath it I'm a hockey guy."[50] Those that ran the hockey system did not like how Bauer let his religious values influence his hockey decision-making. It countered their ambition to make top-flight players.

Without a large national institution directly supporting his motives, it was next to impossible for Bauer's hockey alternative to flourish in the long term. The Basilian sporting tradition was aging, and his own gravitas could carry the National Team only so far. The convergence of the hockey landscape into the NHL left little room for an alternative path.[51]

---

of Sports World," *Catholic New Times*, December 18, 1988, 16. An institution like St. Michael's struggled to adapt because lay hires typically could not critically put sport into perspective based on the strong intellectual and spiritual legacy of Carr, Bauer, etc. Ted Schmidt, *Never Neutral* (Toronto: Self-published, 2012), 116.

48   Bauer, Notes, Box 3, File 1, Bauer fonds, Basilian Archives. By the 1970s and '80s, many Basilians had also ventured into ministries outside of high schools. Neil Kelly, Letter to Lisa Bauer, December 6, 1988, Box 1, File 4, Bauer fonds, Basilian Archives, 2–3.

49   Tom Watt, interview with author, September 28, 2020.

50   Randy Gregg, interview with author, November 9, 2020.

51   Former National Team player Marshall Johnston also had a lengthy NHL management career; he reconciled himself to the reality that "things change … times change." Marshall Johnston, interview with author, August 22, 2019.

Bauer remained inspired by Pius XII's motto, "Use technique but let the spirit prevail," as a summary of Maritain's thinking. Early on, Bauer promoted technical advancements and coaching clinics across the country. However, as the 1980 National Team learned from the scientific developments in European hockey, he believed an overemphasis on technique gave way to a performance-oriented, rational form of hockey. It demoted traditional traits embedded in Canadian sport—i.e., team spirit, character, and spontaneity—and also devalued spirited effort in one-on-one battles and hard-nosed play. Thus, we can say that the ambidextrous Bauer promoted a two-sided form of player development: spirit and technique. The twinning of hockey and education, the Bauer-led seminars, and his informal late-night discussions ensured players bumped up against different thinking that could impact their human spirits. "Letting the spirit prevail" ignited the individuality of a player—ability, intelligence, decision-making, and character—and instilled a doggedness for play and skill development at the highest level.[52] This passion and drive was not about fighting and brutality à la Don Cherry. Violence in hockey begets more violence. A warlike mentality cannibalizes growth of the human spirit and the larger human community.

The motto did not die with Bauer. Head coach Pat Quinn used it at the 2002 Salt Lake City Winter Olympics, where Canadian hockey won its first Olympic gold medal in fifty years. Prior to the Games, the men's team coaches debated team strategies and asked a women's team assistant coach (and former National Team player), Wally Kozak, to join in the discussion.[53] After a look at the team's playbook, Kozak reasoned: "Are you kidding me? ... You got the best players in the world and you're going to try and tell them how to fore-check in their end.... Let them play.... They'll figure it out."[54] Quinn smiled, Kozak recalled, and said, "I think we'll let 'em figure it out." Years later, one of the coaches called to mind what he learned during his first Olympic experience: "A team becomes a team when the players take over."[55] Reflecting

52   See similar basketball examples: John R. Wooden and Steve Jamison, *The Essential Wooden: A Lifetime of Lessons on Leaders and Leadership* (New York: McGraw-Hill, 2007); Phil Jackson and Hugh Delehanty, *Eleven Rings: The Soul of Success* (New York: Penguin Press, 2013); and Nick Nurse and Michael Sokolove, *Rapture* (New York: Little, Brown and Company, 2020).

53   Wally Kozak, interview with author, September 25, 2020.

54   Kozak, interview.

55   Ken Hitchcock, "Ken Hitchcock on Team Canada's Olympic Management

further on the motto, Kozak said: "the Xs and Os don't matter as much as the spirit of the game. And you don't ever want to take the spirit of a player."[56] When coaches build a successful team, they begin to understand team spirit.

Pope Pius's motto is part of the Catholic Church's longstanding involvement in sport. Its athletic philosophy was announced at the Vatican's 2016 conference, Sport at the Service of Humanity (SSH), where 200 global political, business, faith, and sport leaders sought to unite people regardless of faith and nationality around six core principles: "compassion, respect, love, enlightenment, balance, and joy."[57] Attendee and NHL executive Pat LaFontaine described the capacity of sport to bring people together, where hockey can become part of a larger, purposeful picture about sport.[58] He added: "I think there's a spiritual part of the game.... There's the passionate side of the game.... [With] the Pope and religious leaders speaking up, and hoping hockey is following what all sports do, this is something way bigger than all of us."[59] LaFontaine's values-based, transcendently-aware perspective on hockey fits seamlessly with Bauer's incorporation of true humanism.

A year later, LaFontaine led a press conference on "an historic day" when leaders throughout the hockey world came together to declare their ethical ideals:[60]

> We believe every leader of the sport has the responsibility to inspire stakeholders in an effort to deliver a positive family hockey experience. Hockey participation offers families value beyond making an individual

Staff. Plus Penguins GM Search and the NHL Schedule COVID-19 Headache," *The Athletic Hockey Show*, February 3, 2021, podcast audio, 1:00:29.

56 Kozak, interview.

57 Ed Edmonds, "The Vatican View on Sport at the Service of Humanity," *8 Notre Dame J. Int'l & Comp. L.* 20 (2018): 23. https://scholarship.law.nd.edu/law_faculty_scholarship/1322.

58 Greg Wyshynski, "Is God a Hockey Fan? Pope Francis Sends Endorsement Letter to NHL," *Yahoo! Sports*, September 6, 2017. https://ca.sports.yahoo.com/news/god-hockey-fan-pope-francis-sends-endorsement-letter-nhl-171316335.html. LaFontaine became the VP of Hockey Development in 2014 and is a Hall of Fame inductee.

59 Wyshynski, "Is God a Hockey Fan?"

60 NHL Public Relations, "NHL, NHLPA Unveil Hockey's Declaration of Principles," *National Hockey League,* September 6, 2017. https://www.nhl.com/news/nhl-nhlpa-unveil-hockeys-declaration-of-principles/c-290869842. Since then, these Principles are particularly pointed because of hockey examples of racism and sexual harassment.

a better player or even a better athlete. The game of hockey is a powerful platform for participants to build character, foster positive values and develop important life skills. These benefits are available to all players, desirable to every family and transcend the game.

Today, guided by our common values, we jointly pledge to the following Principles.

We Believe:

1. Hockey should be an enjoyable family experience; all stakeholders—organizations, players, parents, siblings, coaches, referees, volunteers and rink operators—play a role in this effort.
2. Hockey's greatest value is the role it plays in the development of character and life skills.
3. All hockey organizations—regardless of size or level of competition—bring value to players and families in their ability to deliver a positive family experience.
4. Physical activity is important for a healthy body, mind and spirit.
5. There are significant benefits of youth participation in multiple sports.
6. Hockey programs should be age-appropriate for all players, accounting for each individual's physical, emotional and cognitive development.
7. There is great value in all forms of hockey, both on and off the ice.
8. All hockey programs should provide a safe, positive and inclusive environment for players and families regardless of race, color, religion, national origin, gender, age, disability, sexual orientation and socio-economic status. Simply put, hockey is for everyone.

We believe in our ability to improve lives and strengthen communities globally through hockey. We believe that living by these Principles will provide a healthy, balanced and enjoyable experience for all and inspire impactful service beyond the rink.

These ethical principles and the SSH share philosophical and historical links to Bauer. Their values reflect Bauer's pragmatic philosophy, as endorsed by many like-minded coaches. A historical connection lies between the Vatican and Bauer's longtime supporter in Hockey Canada, Chris Lang, who was a major organizer of the SSH and its spin-off foundation.[61] The SSH Foundation hosts events around the globe promoting the concept of a "values-driven sport" that highlights larger purposes in sport.[62]

Open to all people and focused on the developmental possibilities of sport, a values-driven tradition endorses time-tested ideals as a means to anchor sport. It bears resemblance to muscular Christian traditions of the past, but must reorient itself in today's world. For instance, while Bauer recognized the place of women in sport—especially as shown in his sisters' and nieces' involvement—his practical participation was primarily with boys and men. From the side of sport, the Declaration of Principles—supported by Hockey Canada, IIHF, NHL, NHLPA, NHL Coaches' Association, and another thirteen signees—shows a major shift in thinking and political alignment over a forty-year period, where professional leagues, at least on paper, endorsed values promoted by global religious leaders.

Drawing in part on the diffused legacy of muscular Christianity and under the inspiration of thinkers like Maritain and McLuhan, Bauer found sources for his sporting alternative that differed from progressive movements gaining strength in physical education and kinesiology departments in the 1960s and '70s.[63] He found support for his views across a spectrum from hockey purists to progressives: sport as a test in character and cooperation, a place to develop life skills, something larger than the final score, and an open environment for anyone who wants to play. If these values are not explicitly stated and kept central in sport, the brokenness of the human condition will bury and conceal them. Bauer had his own philosophical premises for these values, but shared many aims of traditional Protestant ideals that were embraced and expanded by progressive physical educators.[64]

61   Chris Lang, interview with author, June 6, 2019.

62   "Chris Lang," Lang Partnerships Network, accessed May 19, 2021, https://langpartnerships.ca/chris-lang/. See also, "Sport for Humanity Foundation Leadership and Management Team," Sport at the Service of Humanity, accessed May 19, 2021. https://sportforhumanity.com/leadership-and-management/.

63   The explicit influence of Protestant muscular Christianity was smaller by the 1950s, giving way to a values-based, progressive sport. Marshall, *Secularizing the Faith*, 131 and 8. See also, Bruce Kidd, "Muscular Christianity and Value-Centred Sport: The Legacy of Tom Brown in Canada," *Sport in Society* 16, no. 4 (2013): 410–11.

64   Sport sociology has overlooked Bauer because it generally has little interest in, and/or capacity to study, religion. See C. Shilling and P. A. Mellor, "Re-Conceptualizing Sport as a Sacred Phenomenon," *Sociology of Sport Journal* 31, no. 3 (2014): 349–76.

Bauer did not think hockey ought be Canada's civil religion. He believed hockey had a special status in the life of the country: its importance nationally and internationally grew with the appearance of the Cold War and greater interest from around the globe. The game's energy could attract millions to television sets, but Bauer held that wealth and celebrity gained on the ice could be deceptive.[65] He was unwilling to embrace the teachings of the so-called "hockey ecclesia."[66] The economic magnitude of today's sports dangerously threaten long-preserved values and personal growth. NSOs like Hockey Canada easily evolve into corporate entities that primarily manage wealth and promote their brands, potentially becoming institutions that are false images of what is held to be good by Canadians.[67]

Bauer's Impact on Canadian Hockey

Bauer sought improvements to the structures of the Canadian game. His moral critique of the Canadian hockey system impacted junior hockey and subsequently helped improve university hockey across Canada. In 2011, the Canadian Hockey League (CHL) Champions Program began offering each player a $10,000 scholarship at a Canadian university for every year played in Major Junior.[68] Jim Gregory exclaimed that scholarships earned today have Bauer "at their core."[69] Major Junior hockey recognized the need to improve the education of its players: the CHL distributes more than $8 million annually to over five hundred former players at Canadian postsecondary institutions.[70]

65   M. Andrew Holowchak and Heather L. Reid, *Aretism: An Ancient Sports Philosophy for the Modern Sports World* (Lanham, MD: Lexington Books, 2011).

66   Tom Sinclair-Faulkner, "A Puckish Look at Hockey," in *Religion and Culture in Canada*, ed. Peter Slater (Waterloo, ON: Wilfrid Laurier University Press, 2006), 397; Carmelite Sisters of St. Joseph, interview with author, January 17, 2019.

67   Kerry Gillespie, "Canada's National Sport Organizations Are Facing a Reckoning. Here's What Can Be Done to Create Change," *Toronto Star*, October 21, 2022, https://www.thestar.com/sports/amateur/2022/10/21/canadas-national-sport-organizations-are-facing-a-reckoning-heres-what-can-be-done-to-create-change.html.

68   Alexandra Mountain, "A Battle for Sanity: An Examination of the 1961 Withdrawal from the Ontario Hockey Association by the St. Michael's Majors," *Boyhood Studies* 10, no. 1 (March 2017): 108.

69   Greg Oliver, *Father Bauer and the Great Experiment: The Genesis of Canadian Olympic Hockey* (Toronto: ECW Press, 2017), ix.

70   Canadian Hockey League, "CHL Scholarship Program Investment Tops $9.6 Million in 2017–18," May 22, 2018, https://chl.ca/article/chl-scholarship-program-investment-tops-9-6-million-in-2017-18.

Many young men earn a degree, while some go onto professional hockey careers in North America or Europe.[71] Former National Team players Herb and Gerry Pinder, who were co-owners of the Western Hockey League's Regina Pats, paved the way for the program by offering scholarship funds to their players in the early 1990s.[72] Bauer was not the only one who saw that the situation was unjust; however, his work with the National Team created a visible solution that challenged old thinking in hockey.

Postsecondary scholarships for former CHL players have raised the caliber of Canadian university hockey to a level never seen before.[73] Nonetheless, some top-end talent still prefer to play hockey while earning a US college education.[74] Once a player joins a Major Junior hockey team, they are ineligible for an NCAA scholarship; only a small percentage of these junior players end up playing in the NHL. Thus, playing at a US College is a safer bet for a 17-year-old prospect who needs more time to develop and simultaneously get a college experience.[75]

Although Bauer would be pleased about the educational advancements for Major Junior players, he would still question why educational values are not on par with hockey ones. A commercially-driven mentality merely tries to make room for education, where short-term hockey interests often go ahead of long-term player interests. For instance, a 2018 study found delayed psychosocial development of Major Junior hockey players when compared to the general male college student population.[76] Pressures on the CHL are many: legal cases question minimum wage and benefit payments, anticompetitive practices for Canadian men under 20, long-term effects of repeated brain

---

71 Mountain, "A Battle for Sanity," 108. Critics question the program's quick expiration date, where players must enroll within eighteen months of their final CHL season.

72 Oliver, *Father Bauer*, 252. Improved high school and college education exists for CHL players. Online learning has helped. Terry O'Malley, interview with author, June 26, 2018.

73 Watson, *Catch On*, 229. The influx of players has altered the structure of university hockey.

74 Watson, *Catch On*, 229.

75 Bob Duff, "More Canadian Players Choosing NCAA Over Canadian Hockey League," *Featured*, July 23, 2019, https://stories.featurd.io/2019/07/23/more-canadian-players-choosing-ncaa-over-canadian-hockey-league/.

76 Alexander Sturges, "Psychosocial Development of Junior Hockey Players" (PhD dissertation, College of Physical Activity and Sport at West Virginia University, Morgantown, 2018), https://doi.org/10.33915/etd.7295.

trauma caused by fighting, and hazing rituals players experienced in the past.[77] Some lawsuits also name Hockey Canada and professional leagues. Public pressure has resulted. In 2022, allegations against Hockey Canada's executive and board, particularly because of their handling of sexual misconduct allegations against players on at least two National Junior Teams, led to the resignation of the entire board and its CEO.[78] (Former National Team coach Tom Renney was the preceding CEO when an alleged victim received a multimillion-dollar settlement—without leadership pushing hard to unearth the player-perpetrators' identities.) The culture of elite youth hockey is in distress. The CHL itself remains a commercial enterprise under threat—and yet seems in control of its hockey domain.

Many people have called for change to the Canadian hockey system, but Bauer's National Team actualized a path like no other.[79] Nothing since has matched how it challenged hockey's status quo. The NHL's readiness to kick Bauer out of his own program, and its de facto takeover of the program in 1980, reveals its all-encompassing influence on the sport. The league first and foremost looked out for its commercial interests; it shamelessly blocked and then took over its competitor. It exploited the Canadian public's demand for victory in international hockey, and then chose when and how to engage global tournaments according to its own self-interests.

Positively, the National Team program raised interest in the international game and promoted bridge-building among nations. The program's platform

77   The Canadian Press, "Lawsuit Alleges NHL, Junior Leagues Conspiring to Limit Players' Opportunities," *CBC Sports*, September 16, 2020, https://www.cbc.ca/sports/hockey/nhl/lawsuit-alleges-nhl-junior-leagues-working-together-to-limit-players-opportunities-1.5726142; Ken Campbell, "Shocking Allegations in CHL Lawsuit Detail Sexual Abuse and 'A Deviant Culture,'" *The Hockey News*, December 9, 2020, https://www.si.com/hockey/news/shocking-allegations-in-chl-lawsuit-detail-sexual-abuse-and-a-deviant-culture; and Rick Westhead, "Former Player Taught 'Craft' of Fighting at 16 Wants WHL Held Accountable, Affidavit Says," *TSN*, May 18, 2021, https://www.tsn.ca/westhead-former-player-taught-craft-of-fighting-at-16-wants-whl-held-accountable-affidavit-says-1.1641818. Issues of youth sport organizations not providing adequate compensation for elite, young adult players have arisen with the NCAA, which has led to student-athletes marketing their image for financial gain.

78   David Shoalts, "Hockey Canada C.E.O. and Board of Directors Resign Amid Controversy," *The New York Times*, October 11, 2022, https://www.nytimes.com/2022/10/11/sports/hockey/hockey-canada-board-resigns.html.

79   Ideas presented here were supported by a helpful conversation with Morris Mott. See Mott, interview.

of education and high-end hockey attracted many quality players, effectively forcing the NHL to defend its supremacy over the sport's talent pool and become involved in international hockey. The league's delayed interest in the global game showed how it also lagged behind Bauer and others who brought innovative hockey ideas to Canada. Sharing strategies and tactics with European counterparts led to sharing ideas across Canada, which eventually sprouted coaching clinics and programming through Hockey Canada and the CAHA. The nation's game has now become a global game: for instance, the NHL has incorporated more speed and less violence in its matches. These mirror European innovations. The rise of a narrow, performance orientation continues to threaten human elements like joy, team spirit, and spontaneity. All told, Bauer's critique of the Canadian hockey system anticipated future issues and changes remarkably well.

The Qualities of Bauer's Hockey Alternative for Today

Hockey continues to change. At a time when there is much uncertainty about the exact role of the sport in Canadian society, recalling Bauer's experiences and vision can help give direction. Below, the five qualities of the Basilian sporting tradition—as found in chapter 2—are recast in light of Bauer's work and writings, offering how his hockey alternative might speak to the youth hockey system today. The qualities are aspirational, but no less pragmatic for that.

First Quality: Balance

The Basilian tradition upheld sport as a way to cultivate the unity of body and soul. Priest-coaches sought to balance the physical, mental, social, moral, and spiritual needs of young players. For Bauer, this meant giving players the best opportunity to live balanced lives. In reality, what he experienced was a hockey world often pushing performance, violence, and for-profit goals instead of human development. Like many hockey supporters today, Bauer was aware of many deterrents in youth hockey: a lack of fun, costs for equipment and ice rental, registration fees, and time and schedule demands.[80] He sought balance in the sport, where coaches and parents could discuss and work toward instilling higher ideals in youth today.[81]

---

80   Ken Campbell and Jim Parcels, *Selling the Dream: How Hockey Parents and Their Kids Are Paying the Price for Our National Obsession* (Toronto: Viking, 2013).

81   Many coaches supported a player-centric vision across Canada. Primeau, interview.

Second Quality: Mentorship

For Bauer, the fundamental problem in youth hockey is that it orbits a corporate model of sport.[82] It is not hard today to see how youth hockey mirrors the adult professionalized game, even operating like a hothouse for elite talent.[83] One Bauer disciple who watched local coaches double-shift children at U9 and U11 levels exclaimed: "That's why Father Bauer imploded!"[84]

Bauer personified the Basilian ideal of coach-mentorship, decrying senseless violence and rejecting the physical and psychological dangers inherent in an overly-commercialized game.[85] He believed that hockey coaches could discredit violence in society and, in a small way, create more just communities. While professional and youth hockey have become less overtly violent on-ice and show greater awareness of mental health problems related to concussions, alcoholism, drug use, sexual misconduct, fighting, and forms of discrimination, they remain caught in these problems.

Over several decades, the NHL has improved the treatment of its adult players, but the spread of a business mindset into youth sport—an "all-in" focus on skills coaches, expensive equipment, and year-round training—makes athletes more vulnerable to abuse and harassment. It accelerates a performance mindset that can create a toxic environment for youth. In response, Bauer sought a firewall between youth and professional hockey, where coaching-mentors take charge of a hockey system based on developing people.[86] In the spirit of coaches like Bauer, Drake, and King, parents and coaches need to prioritize the values of youth hockey: first, life skills; second, hockey skills; and third, success. A spirited coach-player relationship lies at the heart of his solution.

82   See a recent work supporting this viewpoint: Sean Fitz-Gerald, *Before the Lights Go Out: A Season Inside a Game on the Brink* (Toronto: Penguin Random House, 2019).

83   Kozak, interview. See also Fitz-Gerald, *Lights Go Out*, 248.

84   Kozak, interview.

85   Even at life's end, Bauer became an adviser to a Basilian school because of its team's many memorable brawls. This player-started team was not officially part of the high school program. Lois Kalchman, "Bauer's Bound for Toronto as Crusaders Clean House," *Toronto Star*, 1987, Box 4, File 9, Bauer fonds, Basilian Archives. Several St. Michael's football team players pleaded guilty to sexual assault charges in 2020. Michele Mandel, "Witnesses Kept Quiet About Sex Assault at St. Michael's College School," *Toronto Sun*, February 4, 2021, https://torontosun.com/news/local-news/mandel-witnesses-kept-quiet-about-sex-assault-at-st-michaels-college-school-court-hears.

86   Kozak proposes a new module about ethical coaching for Hockey Canada's coaching certification. Kozak, interview.

Third Quality: Integral Development

Instead of manufacturing hockey players with a narrow purview, Bauer wanted to expand and integrate different experiences for each individual. Know-how and skill development were not enough; coaches needed to coach from their heart and model living by a moral code. If development in hockey simply means increasing hockey skills, young people receive a warped understanding of human relations and the purpose of sport. Carried to its extreme, attention becomes fixed on harvesting top-flight players to the neglect of fairness, inclusion, and the living out of sport's humanistic ideals.

Bauer argued that the central circle in sporting organizations' concentric circles of concern must be the integral development of human persons. In a handwritten 1980s speech, he explained: "If sport in any form is to serve human needs and hopes not to become just another arena of human corruption, it must be taken as a whole and related to the whole of human life."[87] He argued that coaches need to be able to discuss their approach with parents and mentor children for life on and off the ice. Instead of isolating hockey from the rest of human living, sporting experiences should be understood as "a reflection in a self-revealing mirror of [people's] growing awareness and understanding of all that is human."

Fourth Quality: Citizenship

The Basilian tradition held sport as a means to promote democratic citizenship. Bauer complained in his notes that people in hockey "play so many games that neither a coach nor a player is able to find time to communicate an overall concept of the game of ice hockey."[88] He endorsed democratic principles by promoting listening and conversations, as evidenced in his speeches, hockey documents, and discussions with coaches and players.

In the face of war and sporting violence, he aspired to draw upon the democratic ideals of his nation. Because social problems within hockey reflect larger societal issues, he believed sport could play a significant role through the development of citizens. The Declaration of Principles reflects Bauer's ideal of citizenship; however, without continued discussions about improvements to hockey and society, the document is an empty promise.

87 David Bauer, Speech Notes on His Philosophy of Sport, Box 1, File 6, Bauer fonds, Basilian Archives.

88 Bauer, Notes, Box 3, File 5, Bauer fonds, Basilian Archives.

Fifth Quality: Enjoyment

Bauer endorsed the final trait of the Basilian sporting tradition: sport as a means of joy, celebration, and spontaneity. Bauer once told a story about seeing this spirit in action: "In a large farmer's field ... a natural ice surface had formed. Two goal nets were set up and a young boy played by himself shooting and skating—JUST FOR FUN! I was touched by the scene.... For he demonstrated to me something very precious about our sporting heritage ... Have fun. Enjoy. Love your sport."[89] Advocating for this spirit in a speech to Canadian Olympic athletes, Bauer challenged them to strive their hardest and share in the glory of sporting competition.

For Bauer, hockey needed to be centered on ideals like delight, drive, excellence, and unity. He was not against owners or players making money from the sport. However, for-profit mentalities, overly rational forms of play, and tacit acceptance of violence threatened to chase the human spirit from the heart of the game. Bauer underlined elements of spirit and spontaneity because they visibly display human freedom and connect people to one another. Without this spirit of play, people live the sport according to their own self-interests and ultimately make room for violence.[90]

The five above qualities of Bauer's hockey alternative remain relevant today. The game has made many improvements, but many challenges remain. To restructure hockey around the development of young people would protect it from hockey's powerbrokers. His alternative promoted ideals of balance, personal character, and citizenship, relying on coaching-mentorships that celebrate the joy of sport. Bauer's vision remains a benchmark today, a reference point for respecting those who play the game and seek excellence in all they do.[91]

Bauer's Final Year and Posthumous Honors

At the end of his life, Bauer's family remained close to him. They had inspired his passion for sport, his curiosity about truth through reflection and debate, and his dedication to God and country. The success of the National Team required his family as much as it needed the Basilian community. His

---

89   David Bauer, Speech Notes in a Niece's Handwriting, 1987, Box 3, File 5, Bauer fonds, Basilian Archives.

90   Terry O'Malley, email message to author, March 6, 2023.

91   Renney, interview.

enthusiasm for ideals, however, became more difficult to maintain because of weakening physical and mental health. Bauer felt burnt out and his body was aging.[92] With no pension, he had limited means to secure his future as he faced retirement.[93] In the spring after the Calgary Olympics, he traveled to Rome and was photographed with his niece Lisa and Pope John Paul II in St. Peter's Square.[94] Upon Bauer's return, the Carmelite Sisters recalled his enthusiasm for the Quest Program—it was a month before he learned of his fatal illness.

When Bauer was told that he had pancreatic cancer, he quietly sought, with the support of his family members, a miraculous healing at the shrine to Our Lady of Medjugorje in then-communist Yugoslavia.[95] His piety toward the Virgin Mary remained constant throughout his life.[96] A physical healing in Medjugorje did not happen, and surgery in July was unsuccessful.[97] Because of his failing condition, his family transferred him to his brother Ray's cottage near Waterloo at summer's end.[98] As his condition worsened quickly through the fall, people from across the country pilgrimaged to Bayfield. Several former players and coaches made the trip: MacKenzie, O'Malley, Conlin, Johnston, Broderick, McDowell, Hindmarch, and others. Many Basilian Fathers and other associates paid their respects.[99] When Conlin joined other former players to see Bauer, he was already bedridden but briefly met with each person privately.[100] Even near death, he told his doctor to manage his pain medication so that he would be alert enough to witness quarrelsome family members together at his bedside.[101] He continued to try to orchestrate like a maestro in his final days.

92   In a 1986 letter, he asked his superior general for a leave of absence: "I feel I have a case of accumulated burn out syndrome." David Bauer, Letter to Bill, Box 3, File 1, Bauer fonds, Basilian Archives. He wrote about burnout a year later. David Bauer, Letter to Fr. Bert Pare, 1987, Box 1, File 3, Basilian Archives.

93   Bauer, Letter to Fr. Bert. Many Basilian educators had a teacher's retirement plan.

94   Carmelite Sisters of St. Joseph, interview.

95   Paul Burns, interview with author, August 15, 2018.

96   Bauer-Leahy, interview.

97   Bauer, Notes, Box 3, File 1, Bauer fonds, Basilian Archives.

98   He resided with the Vancouver Oblate Fathers for a short time prior to returning to Ontario. Maureen Bauer-McGahey, interview with author, June 4, 2019.

99   Those closest to him worried that the sheer number of visitors was too taxing on him. The Canadian Press, "Bauer Instilled Strong Sense of Values, Duff Says," *The Globe and Mail*, November 12, 1988, Box 2, last file, Bauer fonds, Basilian Archives.

100   Conlin, interview.

101   Bauer-McGahey, interview.

Bauer experienced a near-death vision of his family while at the Goderich general hospital. When friends and family took a 24-hour vigil, niece Maureen rushed to her uncle's room because she heard him call out.[102] Bauer had a vision of brothers Frank, Bob, and Gene, who formed a welcoming committee for their young brother. Dreams or visions of family members prior to death is not an uncommon dying experience, where people seek reconciliation with others and are encouraged to take one final step in this life.[103] In the brothers' youth, they called Dave to the Bauer front yard skating rink in Waterloo. Now they called him into a world beyond this one. Bauer died soon after, on November 9, 1988, on a grey cloudy day with wet snow falling.[104] It was a week after his 64th birthday and, fittingly, an Olympic year.

Many memorial services were held for him. At St. Mark's in Vancouver, several former players and associates gathered—including the Oilers' Gregg and Anderson.[105] Other services were held in Calgary and Wilcox. The Basilian Fathers held a special memorial service at St. Basil's in Toronto. Hanrahan preached at the Mass: "I don't think there has ever been a coach more concerned with team spirit, with developing a sense of mutual concern among his players."[106] Several former St. Michael's and National Team players spoke to reporters afterwards. Fran Huck said, "It's a sad day for Canada and a sadder day for hockey.... His presence moved people."[107] Conacher concluded that Bauer "became the man who most influenced my life."[108]

The funeral Mass and burial took place in Waterloo. One of the biblical readings included a passage from the Letter to the Colossians: "Set your minds on things that are above, not on things that are on earth" (Col 3.1–4).[109]

102   Bauer-McGahey, interview.

103   Christopher Kerr, *Death Is but a Dream* (New York: Avery, 2020).

104   Carmelite Sisters of St. Joseph, interview.

105   Gregg, interview.

106   The Canadian Press, "Bauer Instilled Strong Sense."

107   Archie McDonald, "Father Bauer Remembered," *Vancouver Sun*, November 10, 1988, Box 2, Bauer fonds, Basilian Archives, E1. Dick Duff added: "He taught people to have personal discipline in their lives, in sport and in family." The Canadian Press, "Bauer Remembered as Teacher," Box 2, Bauer fonds, Basilian Archives.

108   Trent Frayne, "It's How You Played the Game That Mattered to Father Bauer," *The Globe and Mail*, November 10, 1988, Box 4, File 9, Bauer fonds, Basilian Archives.

109   "The Mass of Christian Burial for Father David W. Bauer, November 2, 1924–November 9, 1988," Bauer Fr. David File, St. Michael's College School Archives.

The phrase captured the life of this hockey philosopher: higher ideals should guide hockey and celebrate the God-given dignity of each person. Bauer was buried in the family plot at the Mount Hope Cemetery.[110]

For years later, Bauer's trust and foundation financially supported the Quest Program that offered a religious education for teachers in separate (Catholic) schools. Many Basilian priests, family, and friends gave their assistance in loving remembrance of Bauer.[111] Niece Barbara and her husband Marc Bauer-Maison took the lead in organizing and running the program.[112]

Only a year after his passing, Bauer was inducted into the Hockey Hall of Fame. The quickness of the committee's decision spoke to his impact on the game. *The Hockey News* feature article on the 1989 Inductees spoke highly of the priest-coach: "Few have done more for the game of hockey in Canada than Father David Bauer. Yet the late Basilian priest was the first to insist excellence in sports should not be an end in itself, but a way of expressing one's service to mankind."[113] Despite the induction of Soviet coach Tarasov during his lifetime—in the early 1970s—the Hall of Fame induction committee overlooked Bauer until after his passing. Some apparently had heard and read enough of the hockey philosopher and were determined to block him from taking center stage, even briefly, at the ceremony. His Hall of Fame plaque speaks of his ideals for amateur sport, but does not explicitly describe his efforts to create an alternative stream in hockey: "Father Bauer never gave up his belief that a boy could play high calibre hockey without

110   Paul Schmalz and Steve Freiburger, interview with author, January 18, 2019. Typically, Basilian priests are laid to rest in a local Basilian plot, yet there is a not uncommon practice for priests to be buried near family. As best is known, six other Basilian Fathers were buried in their hometown with their family. Cyril Doherty, email message to author, October 6, 2020. Bauer's affection for them and their desire for a nearby grave site led to the Kitchener burial. Cyril Doherty, email message to author, September 17, 2020.

111   For example, Hockey Canada's Chris Lang co-chaired a fundraising campaign for the trust. Draft Letter from the Father David Bauer Quest Program, June 16, 1989, I—1988—Bauer—Quest box, File 10, Basilian Archives.

112   Marc Bauer-Maison, interview with author, January 18, 2019. Quest still operates today, although more modestly since the passing of Barbara in 2005.

113   "Bauer," *Hockey Hall of Fame Magazine*, 1989, Bauer Fr. David file, St. Michael's College School Archives, 41. The article quoted Marshall Johnston, who recalled Bauer sharing the writings of Solzhenitsyn as a way to explain international hockey: Bauer put the Russian writer into "a hockey perspective, to make a better player out of you."

forgoing higher education. As a lifelong builder of the hockey community, he constantly fought to raise the profile of amateur sports, and to encourage Canadians to see amateur achievement as a valid goal for elite athletes."[114] Bauer shared an induction class with Alan Eagleson, who later resigned after being convicted of fraud and embezzlement. In 1997, Bauer was inducted into the Hall of Fame's international section.[115]

Figure 9.1 Bauer at a St. Michael's sports gala hosted in his honor in 1988.

Courtesy of St. Michael's College School

Two other tributes were particularly important. At the 100th anniversary event celebrating hockey at St. Michael's College School, the likes of Frank Mahovlich, Dave Keon, Ted Lindsay, and Murray Costello directed their admiration to the late Bauer. Reporter George Gross summarized what Bauer meant to these men and himself: "Bauer instilled dignity in any discussion, whether it was sports, politics or religion.... Father Dave was the true

114 Hockey Hall of Fame, "Father David Bauer," Induction Speech, 1989, Rev. Bauer File, Seaman Hockey Resource Centre. Brother Bobby was posthumously inducted into the Hall, too, in 1996.

115 International Ice Hockey Federation, "IIHF Hall of Fame," accessed May 19, 2021, https://www.iihf.com/en/static/5114/hall-of-fame.

father of Canada's national hockey team, a hockey tutor in his own country and abroad, a man who preached dignity as a coach and, prior to that, as a player."[116] At Wilcox, Notre Dame erected a permanent tribute to Bauer in the foyer of its skating arena. Both Bauer's Order of Canada and 1964 Olympic medal for sportsmanship are on display in a large maple-leaf-shaped case. A brief description of Bauer ends with, "Make use of technique, but let the spirit prevail."[117]

Prior to the St. Michael's event, the major loop that encircles downtown Waterloo was renamed Father David Bauer Drive.[118] When a young Dave left home for St. Michael's College during the Second World War, smokestacks lined Waterloo's horizon. Today, growing industries are tech companies, like Blackberry and Google, and not far from where the Bauer family home once stood is the Perimeter Institute, a leading center for scientific research into theoretical physics. The smokestacks are nearly all gone. Scientific innovation, fueling a knowledge-based economy, has changed the city's skyline. In much the same way, Bauer witnessed major shifts in Canadian hockey, where community-based teams and muscular Christian traditions could no longer rival a commercially-consumed game that eventually embraced a more technical, rational approach. The marginalization of sporting traditions like Bauer's has not lessened the need for solutions that can alter and re-prioritize the structures of the game. If he were alive today, Bauer would certainly be waiting for his philosophy to resurface again.

116   George Gross, "Father Bauer an Inspiration," *Toronto Sun*, March 4, 2007, S10.

117   Matt Hoven, trip to Wilcox, SK, June 25, 2018.

118   Bauer Family, *Bauer (A Family History of Edgar and Bertha's Family)* (Waterloo, ON: Self-published, 2003), under "Raymond Aloysius Bauer."

EPILOGUE

Bauer believed that the impact of the National Team program was best measured by its positive impact on people. As one confrere said, Bauer engaged his young players—particularly those on the 1964 team—in an educational experience that changed their lives.[1] Every couple of years since, former National Team players, in groups of about 20 to 25, gather for a reunion in different parts of the country.[2] Men who played through the 1960s typically attend these reunions more faithfully; players from the 1964 team have been dubbed the "originals."[3] Those also from the 1980s have participated, as the players share a common bond from their experience.

Perhaps more than any other National Team, the 1964 team bought into the ideal of becoming better citizens and leaders in the nation.[4] Terry O'Malley and Barry MacKenzie grabbed onto Bauer's philosophy, following him around the country and to Japan. Both became formal educators and major leaders at Notre Dame. MacKenzie declared plainly that Bauer changed his life.[5] MacKenzie was a fiery, physical player who learned to balance his competitiveness because Bauer condemned violence. Together, MacKenzie and O'Malley promoted hockey as a means to educate and help individuals grow.[6] Both men made an impact at Notre Dame, including the coaching and mentoring of future NHLers like Wendel Clark, Russ Courtnall, and James

---

1   Jack Gallagher, "The Basilian Way of Life & Higher Education," *Toronto St. Michael's Majors: The Tradition Lives On ... The Official Magazine of the Toronto St. Michael's Majors*, 1997, 20.

2   Derek Holmes, interview with author, October 16, 2020. In the fall of 2019, the team met in St. John's, Newfoundland, where George Faulkner had grown up playing. Robin Short, "Fr. David Bauer Took a Flyer on George Faulkner, and the Move Paid Off," *The Telegram*, September 13, 2019, https://www.thetelegram.com/sports/local-sports/fr-david-bauer-took-a-flyer-on-george-faulkner-and-the-move-paid-off-352305/.

3   Holmes, interview.

4   Bob Hindmarch, interview with author, August 17, 2018.

5   Barry MacKenzie, interview with author, March 12, 2020.

6   MacKenzie, interview.

Patrick. O'Malley also went on to coach the UBC men's hockey team and the University of Regina women's team.[7]

Another original, Brian Conacher, spoke and wrote with Bauer about the problems in Canadian hockey. He criticized the narrow viewpoint of the NHL and the NHLPA. He later became the president of the NHL Alumni Association, where he quickly realized the difficulties that many poorly educated players faced in retirement.[8] Conacher later coached at Upper Canada College in Toronto, where he advocated for educating hockey players. Marshall Johnston, who went on to play, coach, and manage in the NHL, marveled at the 1964 team experience, especially the comradery sustained from being one of the first North American teams to play in the Soviet Union.[9]

Many other originals kept alive the inspiration of Bauer. Roger Bourbonnais played with the National Team through the 1968 Olympics and then turned down an NHL contract to earn his law degree; Bourbonnais' granddaughter has played for the women's National Team.[10] For Paul Conlin, a Majors transplant who practiced law in Ottawa for decades, Bauer provided "the benefit of life altering mentorship" and a space to foster lifelong friendships.[11] Like all team members, he regretted not winning an Olympic Gold medal, because the program needed a major international victory. MacKenzie added that a gold medal victory would have changed attitudes in Canada and solidified the link between hockey and education.[12]

Bauer was proud that all of the nearly one hundred players in his National Team system became successful professionals after their hockey careers.[13] Players liked the opportunities for travel, education, skill development, and avoidance of riding buses in the minor leagues, and later felt the benefits of the broader experience endorsed by Bauer.

---

7   University of Regina Cougars, "Terry O'Malley," accessed May 19, 2021, https://www.reginacougars.com/sports/womens-ice-hockey/roster/coaches/terry-o-malley/614.

8   Brian Conacher, interview with author, June 5, 2019.

9   Johnston, interview. Johnston was a teacher when the team was stationed in Winnipeg.

10   Roger Bourbonnais, interview with author, August 26, 2019.

11   Paul Conlin, interview with author, June 4, 2019.

12   MacKenzie, interview.

13   Fred Hume, "Father David Bauer," UBC Sports Hall of Fame, accessed by May 19, 2021, https://gothunderbirds.ca/honors/ubc-sports-hall-of-fame/father-david-bauer/55.

Bauer's relationships with players changed as he became the general manager of West and East National Teams. Morris Mott joined the National Team in 1965 and stayed until the team ended in 1970, after which he played a few seasons in the NHL. Amidst his playing career, Mott completed graduate studies and became a professor of Canadian history, with his research focused on early Canadian sport.[14] He lacked a personal connection with Bauer, but had a profound respect for him and the opportunities that arose from playing on the National Team.

Wally Kozak played one year for the Winnipeg-based National Team in 1968–69. Although he too had limited interaction with Bauer, he called it "the most important year of my life and it had the biggest impact even today."[15] Like others, he doubted if professional hockey would accept him after playing for the National Team: "we were ostracized because of our education, our open mindedness, and our intelligence about making decisions about what to do."[16] The philosophy of the program in part inspired Kozak to become a physical education teacher in Calgary. He worked with both the men's and women's National Teams into the 2000s.

Terry Caffery played junior hockey with the Toronto Marlboros before a persuasive Bauer recruited him to play for the National Team instead of at a US college or with the Chicago Black Hawks.[17] Playing the 1968–69 season for the Ottawa team, Caffery said it was the "best year of playing hockey" because he toured the world and still attended university. He and his brother built a successful sporting goods business, where he worked for more than 35 years.[18]

Jim Keon, who played at St. Michael's, joined the National Team, unlike his famous Maple Leaf brother, Dave.[19] Jim liked the sport but was not interested in playing professionally: "I found the hockey life numbing. I wasn't stimulated."[20] He played on the Ottawa team in 1968–69 and

14   Morris Mott, interview with author, July 15, 2020. He taught at Brandon University in Manitoba.

15   Wally Kozak, interview with author, September 25, 2020.

16   Kozak, interview.

17   Terry Caffery, interview with author, November 10, 2020. The Chicago team had drafted Caffery third overall.

18   Caffery, interview. Caffery finished his degree after playing professional hockey.

19   Jim Keon, interview with author, November 12, 2020.

20   Keon, interview.

appreciated the values enacted in the program. He also recognized Bauer's persistence when the hockey world worked against him.[21] At Dave Keon's Hall of Fame Induction in 1986, Jim's speech included the following: "Father [Bauer] said that he had never seen a more stubborn man in his life than my brother Dave." He looked at Bauer in the audience and added, "Father, you probably aren't using a mirror to shave in the morning."[22] In the 1980s, Jim Keon became a company executive and on business trips to Vancouver would pick up Bauer and drive to Rick Noonan's house for dinner. Bauer liked having a "captive audience," and talked to Keon about world events and the importance of mental health—and never about hockey.[23]

Playing for five years on the National Team—followed by several teams in the NHL and WHL—Fran Huck was able to earn his law degree.[24] Later he formed a company to support elite sport performers in their retirement, after he found the transition particularly difficult for himself.[25] Longtime National Team goaltender Ken Broderick told a reporter how he had found the transition from hockey to be a "hairy, scary experience" in his retirement, even with his two college degrees.[26] After playing a decade of professional hockey, he understood Bauer's motivation for connecting hockey to education. Most prominently, Ken Dryden worked toward his law degree as a National Team member and had a lengthy Hall of Fame playing career and life in NHL management. He has authored many books, including one about the dangers of concussions and head trauma in the sport.[27]

Those on the 1980 Olympic Team also spoke about Bauer's influence and the experience of playing within the program. Medical doctor Randy Gregg believed that Bauer knew how elitism and over-commercialization had

21   Keon, interview.

22   Keon, interview.

23   Keon, interview.

24   Edge Digital Media, "After the Applause—Edge Digital Media," YouTube, August 19, 2011, video, 7:16, https://www.youtube.com/watch?v=lFyZS9809Os.

25   Danny Gallagher, "Golden Hawk Lands in Wilcox," *Leader Post Regina*, Box 4, File 9, Bauer fonds, Basilian Archives.

26   Wayne Parrish, "Fr. Bauer's Team Wasn't for Sale," *Toronto Sun*, August 13, 1987, Box 2, last file, Bauer fonds, Basilian Archives.

27   Ken Dryden, *Game Change: The Life and Death of Steve Montador and the Future of Hockey* (Toronto: McClelland & Stewart, 2017).

warped hockey.[28] Not consumed by victory even when the program's survival depended on it, Bauer worried more about "whether you leave this program a better person, able to go into the community, to integrate, to be a good father, to be a good husband," according to Gregg.[29] He played on Edmonton Oilers teams with great players like Gretzky and Messier, yet there was only once when Gregg had his children pose for a picture with a hockey person—that individual was Bauer. Life in the NHL had shown Gregg that elite hockey players "are no better than the next person down the street, other than the fact we skate a little bit faster."[30] After seeing NHL hockey players with serious problems—alcoholics, physical abusers, those with dysfunctional families— Gregg became a physician so as to make a difference in his community and in the lives of children. Kevin Primeau, who coached for many years in Europe, believed that Bauer was most proud of the 1980 members' off-ice success as doctors, bankers, and the like.[31]

Also noteworthy is Bauer's work with UBC hockey players, as he remained an assistant coach up to the 1987–88 season.[32] Hindmarch supported his involvement and Noonan, who became the men's athletic director, continued a long friendship with Bauer that began at St. Michael's. Noonan declared, "I would be absolutely nowhere without him.... [H]e was my mentor, my teacher, and my friend."[33] The Thunderbirds alumni association honoured Bauer with a hockey scholarship in his name and a special commemorative game between the Thunderbirds and the Canuck Oldtimers in December 1983.[34] Former Maple Leafs Frank Mahovlich and Dave Keon traveled to Vancouver to play. Doug Buchanan, who had played with the 1980 National Team, arrived from Japan. Glenn Anderson and Randy Gregg attended the evening—they played the hometown NHL team the following night.

28 David Staples, "Coach's Spirit Drives Ex-Oiler Toward Goal," *Edmonton Journal*, May 23, 1993, Rev. Bauer File, Seaman Hockey Resource Centre.

29 Randy Gregg, interview with author, November 9, 2020.

30 Gregg, interview. Today, Canadian University Sports (U SPORTS) annually gives out the Randy Gregg Award to a most outstanding player who also excels in academics and community involvement.

31 Kevin Primeau, interview with author, November 13, 2020.

32 "Priest Behind Bench," May 1988, Carmelite Sisters of St. Joseph Collection; Bauer, Notes, Box 3, File 1, Bauer fonds, Basilian Archives.

33 Rick Noonan, interview with author, May 27, 2019.

34 "Thunderbird 1986 Centennial Hockey Classic, Jan. 2–5: Hockey with Spirit," Program, 1986, Box 1, File 7, Bauer fonds, Basilian Archives, 12.

Teammate Wayne Gretzky even made an appearance.[35] The event also advertised a New Years' international tournament hosted at UBC; Ken Dryden was honorary tournament chair. All proceeds went to the Father David Bauer (FDB) Hockey Scholarship fund.[36]

The Thunderbird Hockey Alumni Association's Father Bauer Golf Classic was established in the early '80s and has raised more than one million dollars for UBC hockey scholarships.[37] Noonan recalled one donor who gave annually to the fund because he had once driven Bauer home from a Thunderbirds game and exclaimed, "it's the most enlightening talk I've ever had."[38] A reporter relayed how Bauer had made a personal connection with George Gardner, a former Vancouver Canucks goaltender, whom he visited multiple times as Gardner withered during a lengthy battle with colitis.[39] A year later, after Gardner had recovered, the UBC alumni hockey players went for a beer and Bauer joined them—but he did not recognize the much heavier Gardner. When someone pointed him out to Bauer, the priest approached his table and bellowed, "My goodness, George, I thought you died!" The reporter added, "They embraced. And tears flowed as freely as the wine."[40]

Coach Dave King summed up how successful National Team members became: "hockey worked for them beyond just becoming a better hockey player."[41] Costello echoed this sentiment: "[Bauer] was trying to have you see

35   Mickey McDowell, interview with author, August 16, 2018.

36   Noonan, interview. The event was covered on the front pages of the Lower Mainland's newspapers.

37   University of British Columbia Thunderbirds, "Rick Noonan," UBC Sports Hall of Fame, accessed May 19, 2021, https://gothunderbirds.ca/honors/ubc-sports-hall-of-fame/rick-noonan/125. See also Flyn Ritchie, "Father David Bauer's Hockey Legacy Still Honoured at UBC and across Canada," Church for Vancouver, June 14, 2018, https://churchforvancouver.ca/father-david-bauers-hockey-legacy-still-honoured-at-ubc-and-across-canada/. In 2022, St. Mark's College announced the "Father David Bauer, CSB Award for Athletic Excellence," to support a varsity athlete who demonstrates sportsmanship and community engagement. Corpus Christi College, "New Award for Student Athletes Pays Tribute to Fr. David Bauer," February 3, 2022, https://corpuschristi.ca/cc-news/new-award-for-student-athletes-pays-tribute-to-fr-david-bauer-csb-olympic-hockey-coach-and-beloved-priest/.

38   Noonan, interview.

39   Greg Douglas, "Father of Canada's Olympic Hockey Dies," *Vancouver Courier*, November 13, 1988, Box 2, Bauer fonds, Basilian Archives.

40   Douglas, "Father of Canada's Olympic."

41   Dave King, interview with author, September 4, 2020.

the values in developing all sides of who you are, not just this narrow focus on hockey, as the NHL would like."[42] The success of the National Team off the ice was its most convincing effect—and the most powerful tribute to Bauer the coach and mentor.

42 Murray Costello, interview with author, June 3, 2019.

ACKNOWLEDGEMENTS

I owe thanks to many people. First to mind are the individuals whom I interviewed for this book: Father Bauer's family, friends, colleagues, and players. Several of the Bauer family shared their recollections with me, while Paul Schmalz and Steve Freiburger toured me around the Waterloo region. Meeting Bauer's only remaining sibling, Marg Laudenbach, was a special moment—especially when she has since passed away. Others shared letters and notes from their uncle, while some helped find potential photos to include in the book. National Team members told stories and connected me to their teammates. Basilian Fathers and other friends also told me about their perspectives and stories, and dusted off their decades-old newspaper clippings.

Among the many archivists and librarians who assisted in finding Bauer's notes, letters, speeches, and photos were: Michelle Sawyers (General Archives of the Basilian Fathers); Susan Millar, Paul Burns, Yujin Han, Helena Kudzia, and Kenton MacDonald-Lin (St. Mark's College Archives), Margarita Lopez and Michael De Pellegrin (St. Michael's College School Archives), Craig Campbell (D. K. (Doc) Seaman Hockey Resource Centre and Hockey Hall of Fame), Helena Deng (Canada's Sports Hall of Fame Archives), Carolyn Pinsent and Paul Carson (Hockey Canada Archives), Gerry Scheibel (Athol Murray College of Notre Dame Archives), Jim Franks (University of Alberta Research & Collections Resource Facility), Janet Sealy (Waterloo Public Library and Archives), Marnee Gamble (University of Toronto Archives), Angela Kindig (University of Notre Dame Archives), and many staff members at the Library and Archives of Canada. The Basilian Fathers helped coordinate my visits to their archives in Toronto. Particular thanks to Fathers Terry Kersch, George Smith, Andrew Leung, Jeff Thompson, and Morgan Rice. Several priests shared their stories and insights about Bauer.

Scholars and hockey writers gave important feedback in many ways. I am indebted to those who reviewed sections or the entire manuscript—whether as colleagues or friends—and engaged me in discussion: Andrew Holman, Joe Price, Andrew Meyer, Marvin Chupka, Wally Kozak, Morris Mott, Mo

Akbar, Don McLeod, CSB, Todd Denault, Kyla Madden, Gary Mossman, Mark Mercer, and others. Particular thanks to former National Team player Terry O'Malley for his thoughtful responses to each chapter of the text. Thanks to the editors and reviewers of a special issue of the *International Journal of the History of Sport* who gave critical comments and suggestions about my work on the early Basilian sporting tradition. Reviewer responses to articles published in *International Studies in Catholic Education* and *E-journal of Catholic Education in Australasia* also sharpened many ideas.

I received feedback on the project at several conferences organized by the North American Society for Sport History, Global Congress on Sport and Christianity, Hockey Conference, American Academy of Religion, International Conference on Catholic Religious Education, Christian Society for Kinesiology, Leisure, & Sport, and the Vatican's Sport for All Summit. The manuscript benefited greatly from criticisms and commentary offered by two anonymous reviewers recruited by the Catholic University of America Press. Copy editor James M. Reilly showed meticulous concern for each detail in the text, while Trevor Lipscombe, Trevor Crowell, and Brian Roach carried the project through to its completion. At the University of Alberta, I am grateful for the advice and support of M. Ann Hall and PearlAnn Reichwein, the latter of whom allowed me to guest lecture about my work in its early stages. Many thanks go to my colleagues at St. Joseph's College, who valued this project and encouraged its completion at our monthly Sprachtisch meetings. Funding through the College's STIR grant and the Peter and Doris Kule Chair in Catholic Religious Education made the project financially possible. Michelle Rochard provided invaluable editorial work on the text, index, and references. Three of my nieces—Rachel, Katarina, and Emily Hoven—reviewed and corrected every footnote. They were a bona fide hat trick!

Thanks to my parents and parent-in-laws for asking how things were progressing, even after several years of queries. To Mom, I am happy that you will look upon the final manuscript with your own eyes. To my wife, Crystal, thanks for never waivering in your belief in this project. My children have seemingly only known me as a professor writing about Father Bauer. Forgive me for those times when I had that "lost in thought" look. Writing involves a lot of thinking—and good ideas can arise at any moment.

During many stuck-at-home months in the pandemic, I wondered what Father Bauer would say about this or that chapter if he were sitting across from me. What would he say about hockey, his life, and the Canadian hockey system? I trust that his speeches, letters, and notes—along with hearing from those who knew him well—capture his plans and what he was all about. Any mistakes in this book are mine. I hope that I have accurately portrayed his life's work and ministry in hockey arenas across Canada and around the globe.

BIBLIOGRAPHY

Abel, Allen. "Father Bauer Not Disappointed, Hockey Experiment Paid Off." *The Globe and Mail*, February 22, 1980, 35. ProQuest Historical Newspapers: The Globe and Mail.

Adams, Carly. "'Queens of the Ice Lanes': The Preston Rivulettes and Women's Hockey in Canada, 1931–1940." *Sport History Review* 39, no. 1 (2008): 1–29.

Adogame, Afe, Nick J. Watson, and Andrew Parker, eds. *Global Perspectives on Sports and Christianity*. Abingdon, Oxfordshire: Routledge, 2018.

Alpert, Rebecca, and Arthur Remillard, eds. *Gods, Games and Globalization: New Perspectives on Religion and Sport*. Macon, GA: Mercer University Press, 2019.

Amis, John Matthew. "The Internal Dynamics of Strategic Change in Canadian National Sport Organizations." PhD thesis, University of Alberta, Edmonton, 1998. https://doi.org/10.7939/R33R0Q26V.

Anderson, Glenn. "Glenn Anderson: Learning How Russia Changed the Canadian Game." *CTV News*, September 28, 2012. https://www.ctvnews.ca/w5/glenn-anderson-learning-how-russia-changed-the-canadian-game-1.975721.

Anstett, Larry. "New Era Unfolding for Bauer Family." *Kitchener-Waterloo Record*, July 28, 1984.

Armour, Leslie, and Elizabeth Anne Trott. *The Faces of Reason: An Essay on Philosophy and Culture in English Canada 1850–1950*. Waterloo, ON: Wilfrid Laurier University Press, 1981.

Armstrong, Kenneth. "Father Higgins Lends Name to St. Mary's Sports Field (6 Photos)." *SooToday*, October 30, 2015. https://www.sootoday.com/local-news/father-higgins-lends-name-to-st-marys-sports-field-6-photos-184196.

Azzi, Alex. "The Current State of Professional Women's Hockey, Explained." *NBC Sports*, January 19, 2021. https://onherturf.nbcsports.com/2021/01/19/the-current-state-of-professional-womens-hockey-explained/.

Babin, Pierre. *The Audio-Visual Man*. Dayton, OH: Pflaum Publishing Group, 1970.

Bagnato, Andrew. "Superstitions Play a Key Role in All NHL (Head) Games." *The Ottawa Citizen*, March 3, 1997.

Baker, William J. *Playing with God: Religion and Modern Sport*. Cambridge, MA: Harvard University Press, 2007.

Barbieri, William A., Jr. "The Post-Secular Problematic." In *At the Limits of the Secular: Reflections on Faith and Public Life*, edited by William A. Barbieri, Jr., 129–61. Grand Rapids, MI: William. B. Eerdmans Publishing Company, 2014.

Bauer, David. "Defensive Skill First Essential to Be Winner." *Hockey Canada Magazine*, November 1962.

Bauer, David. "Puck Control is the Key to Offensive Success." *Hockey Canada Magazine*, October 1962.

Bauer, David. "Teams Must Play to Win, But Not at Any Price." *Hockey Canada Magazine*, October 1962.

Bauer, Olivier. *Hockey as Religion: The Montreal Canadiens*. Champaign, IL: Common Ground Publishing, 2011.

Bekkering, Denis J. "Of 'Lucky Loonies' and 'Golden Pucks': Canadian Hockey Relics and Civil Religiosity." *Studies in Religion/Sciences Religieuses* 44, no. 1 (2015): 59–76.

Beneteau, Marty. "The Great White Elk: A Profile of Rev. Ronald Cullen." *The Windsor Star*, November 8, 1986.

Bennett, Paul W. "Training 'Blue-Blooded' Canadian Boys: Athleticism, Muscular Christianity, and Sports in Ontario's 'Little Big Four' Schools, 1829–1930." *Journal of Sport History* 43, no. 3 (Fall 2016): 253–71.

Berglund, Bruce. *The Fastest Game in the World: Hockey and the Globalization of Sports*. Oakland: University of California Press, 2021.

Besant, Annie. *The Origins of Theosophy*. Routledge Revivals. New York: Routledge, 2015.

Blackman, Ted. "Pollock Plan: Use Soviets for TV Lure." *Toronto Star*, January 29, 1978.

Blake, Jason, and Andrew C. Holman, eds. *The Same but Different: Hockey in Quebec*. Montreal: McGill-Queen's University Press, 2017.

The Bob Boucher Hockey Assistance Fund. "About Bob Boucher." Accessed October 26, 2020. https://bobboucher.wordpress.com/about/.

Boyle, Don. "Fitsoo-San." *Scarboro Missions*, 1983–1984.

Boyle, Donald. "Promoting Hockey in Japan." *Catholic Week*, December 8, 1973.

Brown, David W. "Sport, Darwinism and Canadian Private Schooling to 1918." *Canadian Journal of the History of Sport* 16, no. 1 (May 1985): 27–37.

Buber, Martin. *Two Types of Faith*. Translated by Norman P. Goldhawk. Syracuse, NY: Syracuse University Press, 2003.

Bundgaard, Alex. *Muscle and Manliness: The Rise of Sport in American Boarding Schools*. Syracuse, NY: Syracuse University Press, 2005.

Burke, Ashley. "Investigator Hired to Look into Group Sexual Assault Allegations Involving 2003 World Junior Players." *CBC News*, September 4, 2022. https://www.cbc.ca/news/politics/independent-investigator-hired-investigate-2003-group-sexual-assault-allegations-1.6571631.

Byng, Evelyn Moreton. *Up the Stream of Time*. Toronto: Macmillan, 1945.

Campanelli, Stephen S., director. *Indian Horse*. Toronto: Elevation Pictures, 2018.

Campbell, Ken. "Shocking Allegations in CHL Lawsuit Detail Sexual Abuse and 'A Deviant Culture.'" *The Hockey News*, December 9, 2020. https://www.si.com/hockey/news/shocking-allegations-in-chl-lawsuit-detail-sexual-abuse-and-a-deviant-culture.

Campbell, Ken, and Jim Parcels. *Selling the Dream: How Hockey Parents and Their Kids Are Paying the Price for Our National Obsession*. Toronto: Viking, 2013.

Campbell, Neil. "Notre Dame Means More Than Hockey Winners." *The Globe and Mail*, December 3, 1982.

"Canada Backward in Sports, Administration is Pitiful: Rea." *The Globe and Mail*, May 13, 1969. ProQuest Historical Newspapers: The Globe and Mail.

Canada. *Parliamentary Debates*. House of Commons. September 22, 1961 (Lester Bowles Pearson, Leader of the Official Opposition). https://www.lipad.ca/full/1961/09/22/4/.

"Canadian Amateur Hockey Association's Decision on Age Limits Protested by Group in Toronto." *The Globe and Mail*, January 22, 1968.

The Canadian Baseball Hall of Fame and Museum. "Ronald Cullen." Inductees, 1996. Accessed May 19, 2021. http://baseballhalloffame.ca/blog/2009/09/17/ronald-cullen/.

Canadian Department of National Health and Welfare. *Report on Amateur Hockey in Canada by the Hockey Study Committee of the National Advisory Council on Fitness and Amateur Sport*. By William L'Heureux, David Bauer, Frank Dunlap, Max Bell, Bill Crothers, and John Meagher. Ottawa, ON: Department of National Health and Welfare, 1967.

Canadian Hockey League. "About the CHL." https://chl.ca/aboutthechl.

Canadian Hockey League. "CHL Scholarship Program Investment Tops $9.6 Million in 2017–18." May 22, 2018. https://chl.ca/article/chl-scholarship-program-investment-tops-9-6-million-iToddn-2017-18.

The Canadian Press. "15 for Fighting: QMJHL Announces Stiffer Penalties for Players who Drop the Gloves." *CBC Sports*, October 1, 2020. https://www.cbc.ca/sports/hockey/qmjhl-new-fighting-penalties-1.5745501.

The Canadian Press. "Don Cherry Calls Media Coverage of Kneeling Protests Hypocritical." *National Post*, September 28, 2017. http://nationalpost.com/pmn/sports-pmn/hockey-sports-pmn/don-cherry-calls-media-coverage-of-kneeling-protests-hypocrticial.

The Canadian Press. "Fitness Council Asks for Bill to Protect CAHA from NHL." *The Globe and Mail*, January 26, 1967.

The Canadian Press. "Juckes Reflects on Years in Amateur Hockey." *Lethbridge Herald*, May 27, 1981.

The Canadian Press. "Lawsuit Alleges NHL, Junior Leagues Conspiring to Limit Players' Opportunities." *CBC Sports*, September 16, 2020. https://www.cbc.ca/sports/hockey/nhl/lawsuit-alleges-nhl-junior-leagues-working-together-to-limit-players-opportunities-1.5726142.

Canadian Society for Exercise Physiology. "Celebrating 50 Years of Science to Practice in Canada." Accessed January 6, 2021. https://timeline.csep.ca/.

Canadian Sport School Hockey League. "National Leaders in Education Based Hockey." http://www.csshl.ca/wp-content/uploads/sites/2/2021/07/csshl-flatsheet-2021-22.pdf.

Cardinal, Will. *First Nations Hockey Players*. Edmonton: Eschia Books, 2008.

Carr, Henry. "Teaching the Catholic Religion at a Secular University." *The Basilian Teacher* 5, no. 1 (October 1960): 3–12.

Carrier, Roch. *The Hockey Sweater*. Toronto: Tundra Books, 1984.

Carter, Cyril. "Principles for an Athletic Program." *The Basilian Teacher* 2, no. 2 (November 1957): 22–24.

Casey, Liam. "Teen Guilty of Sex Assault at St. Michael's College School in Toronto Given No Time Behind Bars." *CBC News*, November 2, 2021. https://www.cbc.ca/news/canada/toronto/st-michaels-sexual-assault-sentencing-teen-1.6233740.

Cavanaugh, William. "The Invention of the Religious-Secular Distinction." In *At the Limits of the Secular: Reflections on Faith and Public Life*, edited by William A. Barbieri, Jr., 105–28. Grand Rapids, MI: William. B. Eerdmans Publishing Company, 2014.

Champion, Christian. *The Strange Demise of British Canada: The Liberals and Canadian Nationalism, 1964–1968*. Montreal: McGill-Queen's University Press, 2010.

Christie, J. "Gregg Defenceman with a Mission: Former Oiler Repays Olympic Team Debt." *The Globe and Mail*, October 24, 1987.

Clarke, Brian P., and Stuart Macdonald. *Leaving Christianity: Changing Allegiances in Canada Since 1945*. Montreal: McGill-Queen's University Press, 2017.

Clarke, Mary. "Here's Why the Pope Endorsed the NHL's Declaration of Principles Initiative." *SB Nation*, September 7, 2017. https://www.sbnation.com/nhl/2017/9/7/16267474/nhl-pope-endorsement-declaration-of-principles-the-vatican-pat-lafontaine.

Clayton, Deidra. *Eagle: The Life and Times of R. Alan Eagleson*. Toronto: Lester & Orpen Dennys, 1982.

Coakley, Jay. *Sports in Society: Issues and Controversies*. 7th ed. New York: McGraw-Hill, 2001.

Cohen, Tom. "Three Hockey Enforcers Die Young in Four Months, Raising Questions." *CNN*, September 1, 2011. http://www.cnn.com/2011/SPORT/09/01/nhl.enforcers.deaths/index.html?hpt=hp_c1.

Coleman, Jim. "Canadian National Team Deserves Some Support." *Edmonton Journal*, October 22, 1965.

Coleman, Jim. "Editorial." *The Whig-Standard,* June 3, 1975.

Conacher, Brian. *As the Puck Turns: A Personal Journey Through the World of Hockey.* Toronto: John Wiley & Sons Canada Limited, 2007.

Conacher, Brian. *Hockey in Canada: The Way It Is!* New York: Poseidon Press, 1993.

Conlin, Paul. "The Cold War and Canadian Nationalism on Ice: Federal Government Involvement in International Hockey during the 1960's." *Sport History Review* 25, no. 2 (1994): 50–68.

Conway, Russ. *Game Misconduct: Alan Eagleson and the Corruption of Hockey.* Toronto: MacFarlane Walter & Ross, 1997.

Corpus Christi College. "New Award for Student Athletes Pays Tribute to Fr. David Bauer." Corpus Christi News. February 3, 2022. https://corpuschristi.ca/cc-news/new-award-for-student-athletes-pays-tribute-to-fr-david-bauer-csb-olympic-hockey-coach-and-beloved-priest/.

Cosentino, Frank. *Holy Hockey! The Story of Canada's Flying Fathers.* Toronto: Burnstown Publishing House, 2018.

Cullen, Ron. "Discussion." *The Basilian Teacher* 1, no. 8 (January 1957): 18–19.

Dawson, Christopher. *Understanding Europe.* Washington, DC: Catholic University of America Press, 1952.

DeLuca, Nick. "Christianity and Ice Hockey in Canada: The Role of Violence." In *Gods, Games and Globalization: New Perspectives on Religion and Sport,* edited by Rebecca Alpert and Arthur Remillard, 288–304. Macon, GA: Mercer University Press, 2019.

Denault, Todd. *The Greatest Game: The Montreal Canadiens, the Red Army, and the Night that Saved Hockey.* Toronto: McClelland & Stewart, 2010.

Desjardins, Marcel. "Un Souhait du P. Bauer: Voir le Hockey Fleurir au Canada." *La Presse,* October 4, 1965, 40.

Dicastery for Laity Family and Life. *Giving the Best of Yourself: A Document About the Christian Perspective on Sport and the Human Person.* Vatican City: Dicastery for Laity, Family and Life, June 1, 2018. Giving the best of yourself - 060118 ING - Dare il meglio di sé - web.pdf (laityfamilylife.va).

Dillon, Michele. *Postsecular Catholicism.* New York: Oxford University Press, 2018.

Dowbiggin, Bruce. *The Meaning of Puck: How Hockey Explains Modern Canada.* Markham, ON: Red Deer Press, 2011.

Dryden, Ken. *The Game.* New York: Wiley, 1983.

Dryden, Ken. *Game Change: The Life and Death of Steve Montador and the Future of Hockey.* Toronto: McClelland & Stewart, 2017.

Dryden, Murray. *Playing the Shots at Both Ends.* Toronto: McGraw-Hill Ryerson, 1972.

Duff, Bob. "More Canadian Players Choosing NCAA Over Canadian Hockey League." *Featured,* July 23, 2019. https://stories.featurd.io/2019/07/23/more-canadian-players-choosing-ncaa-over-canadian-hockey-league/.

Dunn, Robert, and Christopher Stevenson. "The Paradox of the Church Hockey League." *International Review of the Sociology of Sport* 33, no. 2 (1998): 131–41.

Eagleson, Alan, and Scott Young. *Powerplay: The Memoirs of Hockey Czar Alan Eagleson.* Toronto: McClelland & Stewart, 1991.

Eagleson, R. Alan. "Sport is Big Business and Hockey is a Sport." *The Empire Club of Canada Addresses,* January 29, 1970. http://speeches.empireclub.org/61279/data.

Edge Digital Media. "After the Applause—Edge Digital Media." YouTube. August 19, 2011. Video, 7:16. https://www.youtube.com/watch?v=lFyZS9809Os.

Edmonds, Ed. "The Vatican View on Sport at the Service of Humanity." *8 Notre Dame J. Int'l & Comp. L. 20* (2018): 20–34. https://scholarship.law.nd.edu/law_faculty_scholarship/1322.

Edwards, Jonathon. "Recruiting and Retaining Canadian Minor Hockey Players by Local Youth Club Hockey Organizations, Canada's Governing Hockey Organizations, Major Junior, and Intercollegiate Hockey Organizations: Exploring Canada's Elite Level Hockey Development System." Doctoral thesis, University of Alberta, Faculty of Physical Education and Recreation, 2012.

English, John. *Shadow of Heaven: The Life of Lester Pearson, Volume 1: 1897–1948.* London: Random House UK, 1994.

Enright, James. "Hockey—Its History at C.C." *The Basilian Teacher* 3, no. 3 (Dec 1958): 61–63.

Farrell, Arthur. *Hockey: Canada's Royal Winter Game.* Montreal: C. R. Corneil, 1899.

Ferguson, Bob. "Federal Intervention in Hockey Needed." *Ottawa Citizen,* May 28, 1968.

Fisher, Douglas. "A Hockey Series That Challenged Canadians' View of Themselves," *International Perspectives,* November/December (1972): 13–20.

Fitkin, Ed. *The Gashouse Gang of Hockey.* Toronto: W. M. Baxter Publishing Company, 1951.

Fitz-Gerald, Sean. "20 Questions with Don Cherry: On His Move to Rogers, Criticizing P. K. Subban and Autograph Requests from Exotic Dancers." *National Post,* July 6, 2015. http://nationalpost.com/sports/hockey/nhl/20-questions-with-don-cherry-on-his-move-to-rogers-criticizing-p-k-subban-and-autograph-requests-from-exotic-dancers.

Fitz-Gerald, Sean. *Before the Lights Go Out: A Season Inside a Game on the Brink.* Toronto: Penguin Random House, 2019.

Fitz-Gerald, Sean. "Hockey Canada Faces Uncertainty as Registration Numbers Plummet." *The Athletic,* November 27, 2020. https://theathletic.com/2222532/2020/11/27/hockey-canada-faces-uncertainty-as-registration-numbers-plummet/.

Flahiff, George. "Toward a Theology of Sport." *The Basilian Teacher* 4, no. 5 (February 1960): 123–32.

Foster, Susan, and Carl Brewer. *The Power of Two: Carl Brewer's Battle with Hockey's Power*

Brokers. Toronto: Key Porter Books, 2007.

Gallagher, D. A., J. W. Evans, and W. Sweet. "Maritain, Jacques." In *New Catholic Encyclopedia*, vol. 9, 2nd edition, 177–80. Detroit: Gale, 2003.

Gallagher, Jack. "The Basilian Way of Life & Higher Education." *Toronto St. Michael's Majors: The Tradition Lives On … The Official Magazine of the Toronto St. Michael's Majors*, 1997.

Garvey, Edward. "Philosophy of Sport." *The Basilian Teacher* 3, no. 7 (April 1959): 184–87.

Gibbons, Tom. "Challenging the Secular Bias in the Sociology of Sport." In *Global Perspectives on Sports and Christianity*, edited by Afe Adogame, Nick J. Watson, and Andrew Parker, 13–28. Abingdon, Oxfordshire: Routledge, 2018.

Gillespie, Kerry. "Canada's National Sport Organizations Are Facing a Reckoning. Here's What Can Be Done to Create Change." *Toronto Star*, October 21, 2022. https://www.thestar.com/sports/amateur/2022/10/21/canadas-national-sport-organizations-are-facing-a-reckoning-heres-what-can-be-done-to-create-change.html.

Goldstein, Jordan. "Building Canadian National Identity within the State and through Ice Hockey: A Political Analysis of the Donation of the Stanley Cup, 1888–1893." PhD diss., The University of Western Ontario, London, 2015.

Gorman, Jack. *Père Murray and the Hounds*. Winnipeg: Hignell Printing, 1977.

Gorman, Patrick. "Debating and Hockey: Either, Neither-Both?" *The Basilian Teacher* 3, no. 6 (March 1959): 163–65.

Government of Canada. *Report by the Committee on International Hockey to Iona Campagnolo*. By S. L. Buckwold, A. Caouette, B. Holliday, R. Lasalle, and S. Leggatt. Ottawa: Government of Canada, 1977.

Government of Canada. *Report of the Task Force on Sport for Canadians*. Ottawa: Queen's Printer, 1969.

Government of Canada. *A Status Report on the Canadian Hockey Review*. By J. J. Urie and L. E. Began. Ottawa: Government of Canada, 1979.

Griffin, Ron, and Michael Hayden. "Transformations and Consequences: The Basilians in France and North America." *Historical Studies* 82 (2016): 7–20.

Gross, George. "Father Bauer an Inspiration." *Toronto Sun*, March 4, 2007.

Gross, George. "Father Dave Friend to All." *Toronto Sun*, November 11, 1988.

Gulitti, Tom. "Eastern Final Coaches Learned Life Lessons at Same Canadian Prep School." *National Hockey League*, September 12, 2020. https://www.nhl.com/news/barry-trotz-jon-cooper-learned-life-lessons-at-athol-murray-college-of-notre-dame/c-319001964.

Guttmann, Allen, and Lee Thompson. *Japanese Sports: A History*. Honolulu: University of Hawai'i Press, 2001.

Hanley, Bob. "Bauer Program However Noble, Dated, Dead." *The Spectator*, May 6,

1980.

Hanrahan, James. *The Basilian Fathers (1822–1972)*. Toronto: The Basilian Press, 1973.

Hardy, Stephen, and Andrew C. Holman. *Hockey: A Global History*. Champaign: University of Illinois Press, 2018.

Hardy, Stephen, and Andrew Holman. "Periodizing Hockey History: One Approach." In *Now is the Winter: Thinking About Hockey*, edited by Jamie Dopp and Richard Harrison, 19–36. Hamilton, ON: Wolsak and Wynn Publishers Limited, 2009.

Harper, Stephen. *A Great Game*. Toronto: Simon & Schuster, 2013.

Harvey, Jean. "Sport and the Quebec Clergy, 1930–1960." In *Not Just a Game: Essays in Canadian Sport Sociology*, edited by Jean Harvey and Hart Cantelon. Ottawa: University of Ottawa Press, 1988.

Hellemans, Staf. "Is There a Future for Catholic Social Teaching after the Waning of Ultramontane Mass Catholicism?" In *Catholic Social Thought: Twilight or Renaissance?*, edited by Jonathan S. Boswell, Francis P. McHugh, and Johan Verstraeten, 13–32. Leuven: Peeters Publishers, 2000.

Higgins, Albert Lee. "Hold That Line." *The Basilian Teacher* 2, no. 1 (October 1957): 20–22.

Higgins, Albert Lee. "Restoring Right Order in Athletics." *The Basilian* 2, no. 3 (March 1936): 49–50.

Higgins, Michael, and Peter Kavanagh. *Suffer the Children unto Me: An Open Inquiry into the Clerical Sex Abuse Scandal*. Toronto: Novalis, 2010.

Hitchcock, Ken. "Ken Hitchcock on Team Canada's Olympic Management Staff. Plus Penguins GM Search and the NHL Schedule COVID-19 Headache." *The Athletic Hockey Show*. February 3, 2021. Podcast audio, 1:00:29.

Hockey Canada. "Answers to Questions Asked by Hockey Parents." https://www.hockeycanada.ca/en-ca/hockey-programs/parents/faq.

Hockey Canada. *The Building of a Canadian Dream*. Calgary: Hockey Canada, circa 2017.

Hockey Canada. "Guide to Female Hockey in Canada." 2018. https://cdn.hockeycanada.ca/hockey-canada/Hockey-Programs/Female/Downloads/female_hockey_guide_e.pdf.

Hockey Canada. "History of the Hockey Canada Skills Academy (HCSA) Program." https://www.hockeycanada.ca/en-ca/hockey-programs/schools/hcsa.

Hockey Canada. "Hockey Canada, Bauer Hockey Extend Equipment, Grow-The-Game Partnership." May 18, 2018. https://www.hockeycanada.ca/en-ca/news/partners-bauer-signs-for-8-more-years.

Hockey Canada. "Hockey Canada Playing Rules, 2020–2021." May 2020. http://rulebook.hockeycanada.ca/english/introduction/.

Hockey Ministries International. *Breakaway: Hockey New Testament* (English Standard

Version). Montreal: Canadian Bible Society, 2016.

Hogan, Brian. "Ivory Tower and Grass Roots: The Intellectual Life and Social Action of Congregation of St. Basil, Archdiocese of Toronto, 1930–1960." In *Catholics at the "Gathering Place": Historical Essays on the Archdiocese of Toronto, 1841–1991*, edited by Mark George McGowan and Brian P. Clarke, 255–74. Toronto: Canadian Catholic Historical Association, 1993.

Holman, Andrew. "The Canadian Hockey Player Problem: Cultural Reckoning and National Identities in American Collegiate Sport, 1947–80." *Canadian Historical Review* 88, no. 3 (2007): 439–68.

Holman, Andrew. *A Hotly Contested Affair: Hockey in Canada*. Toronto: University of Toronto Press, 2020.

Holowchak, M. Andrew, and Heather L. Reid. *Aretism: An Ancient Sports Philosophy for the Modern Sports World*. Lanham, MD: Lexington Books, 2011.

The Holy See. "Address of His Holiness Pope Francis to Participants in the International Ice Hockey Federation." September 27, 2019. http://www.laityfamilylife.va/content/dam/laityfamilylife/Documenti/sport/eng/magisterium/Francis/Address%20of%20His%20Holiness%20Pope%20Francis%20to%20the%20Participants%20in%20the%20International%20Ice%20Hockey%20Federation%20-%20Clementine%20Hall%2027.

The Holy See. "Address to the National Scientific Congress on Italian Sport." November 8, 1952. https://w2.vatican.va/content/pius-xii/it/speeches/1952/documents/hf_p-xii_spe_19521108_gran-cuore.html.

The Holy See. "Discorso Di Sua Santità Pio PP. XII Ai Dirigenti E Agli Associati Del Centro Sportivo Italiano." October 9, 1955. https://www.vatican.va/content/pius-xii/it/speeches/1955/documents/hf_p-xii_spe_19551009_centro-sportivo-italiano.html.

The Holy See. "Message of His Holiness Pope Pius XII to Catholic Athletes Participating in the Melbourne Olympic Games." October 24, 1956. https://w2.vatican.va/content/pius-xii/fr/messages/pont-messages/documents/hf_p-xii_mes_19561024_atleti-olimpiadi.html.

Holy See Press Office. "Giving Yourself the Best of Yourself: A Document on the Christian Perspective on Sport and the Human Person, from the Dicastery for Laity, Family and Life." Summary of Bulletin. June 1, 2018. https://press.vatican.va/content/salastampa/en/bollettino/pubblico/2018/06/01/180601b.html.

"The Hon. Gerald A. P. Regan." Obituaries, *The Chronicle Herald*, November 28, 2019. https://www.thechronicleherald.ca/obituaries/the-hon-gerald-a-p-regan-30418/.

Horton, Lori, and Tim Griggs. *In Loving Memory: A Tribute to Tim Horton*. Toronto: ECW Press, 1997.

Hoven, Matt. "Nonviolence and Catholic School Sport: Recommendations for

Supporting Mission as Drawn from a Historical Case Study." *International Studies in Catholic Education*, published online (February 1, 2023): 1–13.

Hoven, Matt. "'A Powerful Sporting Tradition among Canadian Basilians': Early Twentieth-Century Catholic Priest-Coaches at St. Michael's College." *International Journal of the History of Sport* 39, no. 4 (2022): 366–84.

Hoven, Matt. "Practices for Sport-Coach Mentorship: A Historical Case Study for Coaches in Catholic Schools Today." *E-journal of Catholic Education in Australasia*, 2023.

Hoven, Matt. "Re-Characterizing Confidence Because of Religious and Personal Rituals in Sport: Findings from a Qualitative Study of 15-Year-Old Student-Athletes." *Sport in Society* 22, no. 2 (2019): 296–310. https://doi.org/10.1080/17430437.2017.136058.

Howell, Colin. *Blood, Sweat, and Cheers: Sport and the Making of Modern Canada*. Toronto: University of Toronto Press, 2001.

Howitt, Chuck. "Bauer Seeks Bankruptcy Protection." *Waterloo Region Record*, February 24, 2009.

Hughes, Thomas. *Tom Brown's School Days*. New York: Macmillan Publishers, 1857.

Hume, Fred. "Father David Bauer." UBC Sports Hall of Fame. Accessed May 19, 2021. https://gothunderbirds.ca/honors/ubc-sports-hall-of-fame/father-david-bauer/55.

International Ice Hockey Federation. "IIHF Hall of Fame." Accessed May 19, 2021. https://www.iihf.com/en/static/5114/hall-of-fame.

Jackson, Phil, and Hugh Delehanty. *Eleven Rings: The Soul of Success*. New York: Penguin Press, 2013.

Johnson, Henry F. *A Brief History of Canadian Education*. Toronto: McGraw-Hill, 1968.

Johnson, Paul. "The Lost Ideals of Youth." *New York Times Magazine*, March 25, 1984. https://www.nytimes.com/1984/03/25/magazine/the-lost-ideals-of-youth.html.

Kardas, Raymond. "The Popes on Sport." Master's thesis, McGill University, Montreal, May 1992.

Kennedy, Brian. "Confronting a Compelling Other: The Summit Series and the Nostalgic (Trans)Formation of Canadian Identity." In *Canada's Game: Hockey and Identity*, edited by Andrew C. Holman, 44–62. Montreal: McGill-Queen's University Press, 2009.

Kennedy, Sheldon, and James Grainger. *Why I Didn't Say Anything: The Sheldon Kennedy Story*. Toronto: Insomniac Press, 2006.

Kennedy, Terrence. "I Was Warned It Would Be Different." *Scarboro Missions*, 1964.

Kenny, Nuala. *Still Unhealed: Treating the Pathology in the Clergy Abuse Crisis*. Toronto: Novalis, 2020.

Kerr, Christopher. *Death Is but a Dream*. New York: Avery, 2020.

Kessler, Karl. *Three Storeys High, A Hundred Stories Deep: 189 Mary Street*. Kitchener, ON: Pandora Printshop, 2005.

Kidd, Bruce. "Muscular Christianity and Value-Centred Sport: The Legacy of Tom Brown in Canada." *Sport in Society* 16, no. 4 (2013): 405–15. https://doi.org/10.1080/17430437.2013.785752.

Kidd, Bruce. *The Struggle for Canadian Sport*. Toronto: University of Toronto Press, 1996.

Kidd, Bruce, and John MacFarlane. *The Death of Hockey*. Toronto: New Press, 1972.

Kierkegaard, Søren. *The Present Age*. Translated by Alexander Dru. London, UK: Collins, 1962.

Kimelman, Adam. "Pope Francis Extols Declaration of Principles." *National Hockey League*, September 6, 2017. https://www.nhl.com/news/pope-francis-extols-nhl-declaration-of-principles/c-290876704.

Klein, Christa. "Jesuits and Boyhood in Victorian New York." *U.S. Catholic Historian* 7, no. 4 (1988): 375–91.

Klein, Christa. "The Jesuits and Catholic Boyhood in Nineteenth-Century New York City: A Study of St. John's College and the College of St. Francis Xavier, 1846–1912." PhD diss., University of Pennsylvania, Philadelphia, 1976.

Knowles, Steve. "Canadian College Hockey." In *Total Hockey*, edited by Dan Diamond, 417–24. Kansas City, MO: Andrews McMeel Publishing, 1998.

Kowalsky, N., and R. Haluza-DeLay. "'This Is Oil Country': The Alberta Tar Sands and Jacques Ellul's Theory of Technology." *Environmental Ethics* 37, no. 1 (2015): 75–97.

Kurtz, Morris. "A History of the 1972 Canada-USSR Ice Hockey Series." PhD thesis, The Pennsylvania State University, State College, 1981. ProQuest Dissertations Publishing.

L'Heureux, Bill. *Hockey for Boys*. Chicago: Follett Publishing Company, 1962.

"L'Heureux, Willard Joseph." Donohue Funeral Home, Obituary. Accessed May 19, 2021. https://donohuefuneralhome.ca/tribute/details/4138/Willard-L-Heureux/obituary.html.

Lamphier, Gary. "Values that Sustained Influential Educator Worth Remembering Today." *Edmonton Journal*, July 10, 2010.

Lang Partnerships Network. "Chris Lang." Accessed May 19, 2021. https://langpartnerships.ca/chris-lang/.

Lautens, Gary, interviewer. "Violence in Sports." Heritage, CBC production, March 12, 1967.

Lavelle, Michael. "Values in Coaching." *The Basilian Teacher* 8, no. 5 (February 1964): 250–54.

Lemoyne, Jacques. "L'Équipe Nationale de l'Est Remporte Deux Victoires et Apprend Une Leçon!" *La Liberté et Le Patriote*, December 21, 1967, 4.

Lemoyne, Jacques. "Le Père Bauer Croit que l'Idéal Olympique Doit Nous Inciter à

Continuer!' *La Liberté et Le Patriote*, September 4, 1964.

Lightman, Alan. "The Role of the Public Intellectual." MIT. https://web.mit.edu/comm-forum/legacy/papers/lightman.html.

Lixey, Kevin. "Sport in the Magisterium of Pius XII." In *Sport and Christianity: A Sign of the Times in the Light of Faith*, edited by Kevin Lixey, Christoph Huenthal, Dietmar Mieth, and Norbert Muller, 104–20. Washington, DC: Catholic University of America Press, 2012.

Lonn, George. *Faces of Canada*. Toronto: Pitt Publishing, 1976.

Looby, A. R. "Are Extra-Curricular Activities Compatible with the Basic Aim of Education? [Pro]." *The Basilian Teacher* 1, no. 7 (December 1956): 12, 14, and 18.

Lorenz, Stacy, and Geraint B. Osborne. "'Talk About Strenuous Hockey': Violence, Manhood, and the 1907 Ottawa Silver Seven-Montreal Wanderer Rivalry." *Journal of Canadian Studies* 40, no. 1 (2006): 125–56.

Ludwig, Jack. *Hockey Night in Moscow*. Toronto: McClelland & Stewart, 1972.

Lynch, M. S. "The Place of Athletics in Our Schools." *The Basilian* 1, no. 1 (March 1935): 13–14.

MacGregor, Roy. "After Decades of Silence, Swift Current and Hockey Community Face Invisible Damage of Child Abuse." *The Globe and Mail,* January 1, 2016. https://www.theglobeandmail.com/news/national/swift-current-faces-the-invisible-damage-of-child-abuse/article27985598/.

MacGregor, Roy. *A Loonie for Luck*. Toronto: McClelland and Stewart, 2002.

MacIntosh, D., and M. Hawes. *Sport and Canadian Diplomacy*. Montreal: McGill-Queen's University Press, 1994.

MacIntosh, Donald, and David Whitson. *The Game Planners: Transforming Canada's Sport System*. Montreal: McGill-Queen's University Press, 1990.

MacSkimming, Roy. *Cold War: The Amazing Canada-Soviet Hockey Series of 1972*. Vancouver, BC: Greystone Books, 2012.

Madden, J. F. "Are Extra-Curricular Activities Compatible with the Basic Aim of Education? [Con]." *The Basilian Teacher* 1, no. 7 (December 1956): 13, 15, 18.

Mahovlich, Ted. *The Big M: The Frank Mahovlich Story*. Toronto: HarperCollins Publishers, 1999.

Mandel, Michele. "Witnesses Kept Quiet About Sex Assault at St. Michael's College School, Court Hears." *Toronto Sun*, February 4, 2021. https://torontosun.com/news/local-news/mandel-witnesses-kept-quiet-about-sex-assault-at-st-michaels-college-school-court-hears.

Maritain, Jacques. *An Introduction to Philosophy*. Translated by E. I. Watkin. New York: Sheed & Ward, 2005.

Maritain, Jacques. *The Twilight of Civilization*. Translated by Lionel Landry. New York: Sheed & Ward, 1944.

Marks, Don. *Playing the White Man's Games*. Winnipeg: J. Gordon Shillingford

Publishing, 2014.

Marshall, David. *Secularizing the Faith: Canadian Protestant Clergy and the Crisis of Belief, 1850–1940.* Toronto: University of Toronto, 1992.

Masterman, Chris. "Bauers Limited Made Batting, Twine and Padding." *Waterloo Region Record,* March 1, 2008.

McCarthy, D. "Discussion." *The Basilian Teacher* 1, no. 8 (January 1957): 5–7.

McCorkell, Edmund J. *Henry Carr—Revolutionary.* Toronto: Griffin House, 1969.

McDonald, David. "Hockey Team is Back on the Ice: Derek Holmes Optimistic." *A Piece of Canadian Sport History,* March 1979. http://canadiansporthistory.ca/champion-magazine/march-1979-mars/hockey-team-is-back-on-the-ice/.

McFadden, Scot. "An Investigation of the Relative Effectiveness of Two Types of Imagery Rehearsal Applied to Enhance Skilled Athletic Performance." PhD thesis, University of Toronto, Toronto, 1982.

McGowan, Mark. "Toronto's English-Speaking Catholics, Immigration, and the Making of a Canadian Catholic Identity, 1900–1930." In *Creed and Culture: The Place of English-Speaking Catholics in Canadian Society, 1750–1930,* edited by Terrence Murphy and Gerald J. Stortz, 204–45. Montreal: McGill-Queen's University Press, 1993.

McGowan, Mark. *The Waning of the Green: Catholics, the Irish, and Identity in Toronto, 1887–1922.* Montreal: McGill-Queen's University Press, 1999.

McKee, Taylor, and Janice Forsyth. "Witnessing Painful Pasts: Understanding Images of Sports at Canadian Indian Residential Schools." *Journal of Sport History* 46, no. 2 (2019): 175–88.

McLaughlin, Kenneth, and Sharon Jaeger. *Waterloo: An Illustrated History, 1857–2007.* Waterloo, ON: City of Waterloo, 2007.

McLean, Chima. "Father Bauer's Reputation Makes Event 'A Natural.'" Hockey Showcase: Father David Bauer Cup, March 28–30, 1996.

McLean, Chima. "The 'Quest' for Peace and Tolerance Evident Throughout Fr. Dave's Life." Hockey Showcase: Father David Bauer Cup, March 28–30, 1996.

McLeod, Hugh. "Muscular Christianity: American and European." In *Secularization and Religious Innovation in the North Atlantic World,* edited by Hugh McLeod and David Hempton, 195–210. Oxford, UK: Oxford Scholarship Online, 2017.

McLeod, Hugh. *The Religious Crisis of the 1960s.* Oxford, UK: Oxford University Press, 2010.

McMahon, P. T. "Carmelite Spirituality." In *New Catholic Encyclopedia,* vol. 3, 2nd ed., 130–40. Detroit: Gale, 2003.

McParland, Kelly. *The Lives of Conn Smythe.* Toronto: McClelland & Stewart, 2011.

Merriman, J. E. "Canadian Association of Sports Sciences: A Historical Review." *Canadian Medical Association Journal* 96, no. 19 (May 13, 1967): 1340–42.

Messier, Denis. "Sport Choc." *La Tribune: Sherbrooke*, May 8, 1967, 11.

Metcalfe, Alan. *Canada Learns to Play.* Toronto: McClelland and Stewart, 1987.

Metcalfe, Alan. "The Role of Religious Institutions in the Growth of Organized Sport in Toronto, Canada, 1919–1939." In *Proceedings of the IX International HISP Congress: Sport and Religion*, edited by Instituto Nacional Dos Desportos, 227–31. Lisboa, Portugal: Instituto Nacional Dos Desportos, 1981.

Meyer, Andrew R. "Muscular Christian Themes in Contemporary American Sport: A Case Study." *The Journal of the Christian Society for Kinesiology and Leisure Studies* 2, no. 1 (2012): 15–32.

Middleton, J. E., and Fred Landon. *The Province of Ontario: A History, 1615–1927*, vol. 4. Toronto: The Dominion Publishing Company, 1927.

Mills, Dennis. "Hockey at St. Michael's." *Toronto St. Michael's Majors: The Tradition Lives On ... The Official Magazine of the Toronto St. Michael's Majors*, 1997.

Molnar, Dale. "Supreme Court Denies Basilian Fathers Appeal to Sexual Abuse Lawsuit." *CBC News,* April 30, 2020. https://www.cbc.ca/news/canada/windsor/catholic-church-sex-abuse-father-hodgson-marshall-talach-beckett-macleod-mcmahon-1.5551156.

Montagna, Alberto. "Sparate Goal!" Translated by J. Rent. *Citta Nuova* 8, no. 4 (February 25, 1964): 4–7.

Moran, Robert. "Apostolic Hockey." *Scarboro Missions,* 1966.

Moran, Robert T., Phillip R. Harris, and Sarah V. Morgan. *Managing Cultural Differences: Global Leadership Strategies for the 21st Century*, 7th ed. Burlington, MA: Butterworth-Heinemann, 2007.

Morrow, Don. "Sport and Physical Education in Schools and Universities." In *A Concise History of Sport in Canada*, edited by Don Morrow, Mary Keyes, Wayne Simpson, Frank Cosentino, and Ron Lappage, 69–87. Toronto: Oxford University Press Canada, 1989.

Morrow, Don, and Kevin Wamsley. *Sport in Canada: A History*, 3rd ed. Don Mills, ON: Oxford University Press, 2013.

Mortimore, G. E. "Polite Revolt against the Tycoons." *The Globe and Mail*, March 15, 1963.

Mortimore, G. E. "What's Happened to Hockey? Violent World of Elastic Morals." *The Globe and Mail*, March 14, 1963.

Mossman, Gary. *Lloyd Percival: Coach and Visionary.* Woodstock, ON: Seraphim Editions, 2013.

Mountain, Alexandra. "A Battle for Sanity: An Examination of the 1961 Withdrawal from the Ontario Hockey Association by the St. Michael's Majors." *Boyhood Studies* 10, no. 1 (March 2017): 101–16.

Murphy, Dan. "Everything You Need to Know About the NCAA's NIL Debate." ESPN, September 1, 2021. https://www.espn.com/college-sports/story/_/id/31086019/everything-need-know-ncaa-nil-debate.

Murphy, Stanley. "The Assumption Lecture League." *The Basilian* 1, no. 2 (April 1935): 27–28.

NHL.com. "NHL Lady Byng Memorial Trophy Winners." *National Hockey League*, September 11, 2020. http://www.nhl.com/ice/page.htm?id=24938.

"N.H.L. Given 'Bodycheck' By Anglicans." *Montreal Star*, September 11, 1952, 55.

NHL Public Relations. "NHL, NHLPA Unveil Hockey's Declaration of Principles." *National Hockey League*, September 6, 2017. https://www.nhl.com/news/nhl-nhlpa-unveil-hockeys-declaration-of-principles/c-290869842.

Nolan, Michael. *CTV—The Network that Means Business*. Edmonton, AB: University of Alberta Press, 2001.

Norbert, Ruth. "Academic Standards in Our High Schools." *The Basilian Teacher* 3, no. 1 (October 1958): 3–12.

Nurse, Nick, and Michael Sokolove. *Rapture*. New York: Little, Brown and Company, 2020.

O'Brien, Andy. "How College Hockey Can Come Back." *Weekend Magazine* 12, no. 3 (1962): 34–35.

"Offre-t-on Notre Équipe Nationale de Hockey en Sacrifice?" *La Liberté et Le Patriote*, December, 18, 1968, 5.

Ogden, Josh, and Jonathon R. Edwards. "Are Canadian Stakeholders Resting on Their Laurels? A Comparative Study of the Athlete Pathway Through the Swedish and Canadian Male Ice Hockey Systems." *Journal of Sport Management* 30 (2016): 312–28.

Oliver, Greg. *Father Bauer and the Great Experiment: The Genesis of Canadian Olympic Hockey*. Toronto: ECW Press, 2017.

"Olympics and Notre Dame." *Newshound* 7, no. 3 (Summer 1984): 5.

The Order of Canada. "1967 Creating a National Order." Accessed October 4, 2018. https://www.orderofcanada50.ca/1967.

Orr, Frank, "Medal or Not, Olympic Team Was Indeed a Worthwhile Effort." *Toronto Star*, January 6, 1980.

Orr, Frank. "Oil Rig Is New Home for Gold Seekers." *Toronto Star*, October 5, 1979.

Ozanian, Mike, and Kurt Badenhausen. "NHL Team Values 2020: Hockey's First Decline in Two Decades." *Forbes*, December 9, 2020. https://www.forbes.com/sites/mikeozanian/2020/12/09/nhl-team-values-2020-hockeys-first-decline-in-two-decades/?sh=594ab17370dd.

Pearce, Joseph. *Solzhenitsyn: A Soul in Exile*. Grand Rapids, MI: Baker Books, 2001.

Pearson, Lester B. *The Memoirs of the Rt. Hon. Lester B. Pearson, Volume Two: 1948–57*. Toronto: University of Toronto Press, Scholarly Publishing Division, 2015.

Pelletier, Joe. "Legends of Team Canada: Tim Watters." *The Hockey History Blog* (blog). Greatest Hockey Legends.com. September 20, 2017. http://www.greatesthockeylegends.com/2017/09/legends-of-team-canada-tim-watters.html.

"Le Père Bauer Doit Bien Se Demander ce qui Lui Arrive." *Le Petit Journal,* June 30, 1968.

Phelan, Gerald. "The End of Education and Extra-Curricular Activities." *The Basilian Teacher* 1, no. 8 (January 1957): 3–4.

A Piece of Canadian Sport History. "Lefaive Moves to Head Up Sport Canada." Accessed May 19, 2021. http://canadiansporthistory.ca/champion-magazine/may-1978-mai/lefaive-moves-to-head-up-sport-canada/.

Platt, P. Wallace. *Dictionary of Basilian Biography: Lives of Members of the Congregation of Priests of Saint Basil from its Origins in 1822 to 2002, 2nd ed.* Toronto: University of Toronto Press, 2005.

Platt, P. Wallace. *Gentle Eminence: A Life of Cardinal Flahiff.* Montreal: McGill-Queen's University Press, 1999.

Poulton, J. Alexander. *A History of Hockey in Canada.* Edmonton: Overtime Books, 2010.

Proudfoot, Jim. "Editorial." *Toronto Star,* January 21, 1976.

Proulx, Karine. "Georges Larivière: For the Love of the Game." *Hockey Canada,* July 29, 2011. https://www.hockeycanada.ca/en-ca/news/2011-qhs-003-en.

Putney, Clifford. *Muscular Christianity: Manhood and Sports in Protestant America, 1880–1920.* Cambridge, MA: Harvard University Press, 2003.

Quarrington, Paul. *Hometown Heroes: On the Road with Canada's National Hockey Team.* Toronto: Collins, 1988.

Raftis, Ambrose, J. "Christopher Dawson, Pioneer Historian of Unity." *The Basilian Teacher* 6, no. 1 (October 1961): 9–22.

Ramsay, D. "Olympic Team Plan Likely to be Ratified by Hockey Canada." *The Globe and Mail,* February 22, 1978.

Ramsay, Donald. "Team Canada Loses on the Ice—and Then off It." *The Globe and Mail,* May 7, 1977.

Rappeport, Rhoda. *Fred Shero: A Kaleidoscopic View of the Philadelphia Flyers' Coach.* New York: St. Martin's Press, 1977.

Riehl, Spencer, Ryan Snelgrove, and Jonathon Edwards. "Mechanisms of Institutional Maintenance in Minor Hockey." *Journal of Sport Management* 33, no. 2 (2019): 93–105.

Ritchie, Flyn. "Father David Bauer's Hockey Legacy Still Honoured at UBC and across Canada." *Church for Vancouver,* June 14, 2018. https://churchforvancouver.ca/father-david-bauers-hockey-legacy-still-honoured-at-ubc-and-across-canada/.

Robidoux, Michael A. "Imagining a Canadian Identity through Sport: A Historical Interpretation of Lacrosse and Hockey." *Journal of American Folklore* 115, no. 456 (Spring 2002): 209–26.

Robidoux, Michael A. *Men at Play: A Working Understanding of Professional Hockey.* Montreal: McGill-Queen's University Press, 2001.

Robidoux, Michael A. *Stickhandling Through the Margins: First Nations Hockey in Canada*. Toronto: University of Toronto Press, 2012.

Rose, Ainsley B. "An Historical Account of Canada's Participation in International Ice Hockey, 1948–1970." Master's thesis, University of Western Ontario, London, 1976.

Rowell, Marg, Ed Devitt, and Pat McKegney. *Welcome to Waterloo*. Waterloo, ON: Waterloo Printing, 1982.

Ryan, Allan. "Pride Spurs Canada's Hockey Team." *Toronto Star*, February 9, 1980.

Ryan, Dennis P., and Kevin B. Wamsley. "The Fighting Irish of Toronto: Sport and Irish Catholic Identity at St. Michael's College, 1906–1916." In *Emigrant Players: Sport and the Irish Diaspora*, edited by P. Darby and D. Hassan, 163–81. Abingdon, Oxfordshire: Routledge, 2008.

Sasakamoose, Fred. *Call Me Indian*. Toronto: Viking, 2021.

Schmalz, Greg. "Farewell Friends." *Newshound* 3, no. 4 (Spring 1989): 1–2.

Schmidt, Ted. "Fr. David Bauer Untouched by Perils of Sports World." *Catholic New Times*, December 18, 1988.

Schmidt, Ted. *Never Neutral*. Toronto: Self-published, 2012.

Scholes, J., and R. Sassower. *Religion and Sports in American Culture*. New York: Routledge, 2014.

Schwade, A., and P. F. O'Donoghue. "The Catholic Church in Japan." *The New Catholic Encyclopedia*, vol. 7, 2nd ed., 736–44. Detroit: Thomson/Gale, 2003.

Seravalli, Frank. "Jagr Sticks with His Faith." *Philadelphia Enquirer*, May 3, 2012. https://www.inquirer.com/philly/sports/flyers/20120503_Jagr_sticks_with_his_faith.html.

Shannon, Anne Park, and Lana Okerlund. *Finding Japan: Early Canadian Encounters with Asia*. Vancouver: Heritage, 2012.

Shea, Kevin, Larry Colle, and Paul Patskou. *St. Michael's College: 100 Years of Pucks and Prayers*. Bolton, ON: Fenn Publishing Company Limited, 2008.

Sherwood, Harriet. "Unsealing of Vatican Archives Will Finally Reveal Truth about 'Hitler's Pope.'" *The Guardian*, March 1, 2020. https://www.theguardian.com/world/2020/mar/01/unsealing-vatican-archive-reveal-hitler-truth-pope-pius-xii.

Shilling, C., and P. A. Mellor. "Re-Conceptualizing Sport as a Sacred Phenomenon." *Sociology of Sport Journal* 31, no. 3 (2014): 349–76.

Shoalts, David. "Hockey Canada C.E.O. and Board of Directors Resign Amid Controversy." *The New York Times*, October 11, 2022. https://www.nytimes.com/2022/10/11/sports/hockey/hockey-canada-board-resigns.html.

Short, Robin. "Fr. David Bauer Took a Flyer on George Faulkner, and the Move Paid Off." *The Telegram*, September 13, 2019. https://www.thetelegram.com/sports/local-sports/fr-david-bauer-took-a-flyer-on-george-faulkner-and-the-move-paid-off-352305/.

Shriver, Sargent. "The Moral Force of Sport." *Sports Illustrated Vault*, June 3, 1963. https://www.si.com/vault/1963/06/03/594230/the-moral-force-of-sport.

Simmons, Steve. "Racism in Hockey—the Story that Never Ends." *Toronto Sun*, January 24, 2022. https://torontosun.com/sports/hockey/simmons-racism-in-hockey-the-story-that-never-ends.

Simons, Paula. "Paula Simons: The Oilers and the City that Loves Them Gear Up for Glory." *Edmonton Journal*, April 12, 2017. https://edmontonjournal.com/sports/hockey/nhl/edmonton-oilers/paula-simons-8.

Simpson, J. "Stars Fly in Hockey in Japan, Has Flavor of Canada." *The Globe and Mail*, February 26, 1979.

Simpson, Wayne. "Hockey." In *A Concise History of Sport in Canada*, edited by Don Morrow, Mary Keyes, Wayne Simpson, Frank Cosentino, and Ron Lappage, 169–229. Toronto: Oxford University Press, 1989.

Sinclair-Faulkner, Tom. "A Puckish Look at Hockey." In *Religion and Culture in Canada*, edited by Peter Slater, 383–406. Waterloo, ON: Wilfrid Laurier University Press, 2006.

Skene, Wayne. "The Unpaid Boys of Winter." *Toronto Star*, January 26, 1980.

Smith, Gary. *Ice War Diplomat*. Madeira Park, BC: Douglas & McIntyre, 2022.

Smith, Zachary Taylor, and Steven Waller. "Surveying the Landscape of Theories and Frameworks Used in the Study of Sport and Religion: An Interdisciplinary Approach." *Journal of the Christian Society for Kinesiology, Leisure and Sports Studies* 6, no. 1 (2018): 1–19.

Smythe, Conn. *If You Can't Beat 'Em in the Alley*. Toronto: McClelland & Stewart, 1981.

Soares, John. "Our Way of Life against Theirs: Ice Hockey and the Cold War." In *Diplomatic Games: Sport, Statecraft, and International Relations Since 1945*, edited by Heather L. Dichter and Andrew L. Johns, 251–96. Lexington, KY: University Press of Kentucky, 2014.

Sport at the Service of Humanity. "2016 Conference Highlights." Accessed May 19, 2021. http://sportforhumanity.com/2016-conference-highlights/.

Sport at the Service of Humanity. "Sport for Humanity Foundation Leadership and Management Team." Leadership and Management. Accessed May 19, 2021. https://sportforhumanity.com/leadership-and-management/.

Stanton, Raymond. "Bauer's Plant Grows Tenfold in 40 Years." *Kitchener-Waterloo Record*, July 27, 1957.

Staples, David. "I've Always Had a Carefree Spirit." *Edmonton Journal*, January 10, 1988. https://edmontonjournal.com/sports/hockey/nhl/cult-of-hockey/this-was-glenn-anderson-hero-of-the-ice-palace-in-1988.

Steiss, Adam. "IIHF Meets the Pope." *International Ice Hockey Federation*, September 27, 2019. https://www.iihf.com/en/news/14971/iihf-meets-the-pope.

Stevens, Julie. "The Canadian Hockey Association Merger: An Analysis of Institutional Change." PhD thesis, University of Alberta, Edmonton, 2001. ProQuest Dissertations Publishing.

Stevens, Julie. "Conn Smythe: The Complexity and Contradiction of a Hockey Entrepreneur." *Sport in Society* 23, no. 9 (2020): 1468–79.

Sturges, Alexander John. "Psychosocial Development of Junior Hockey Players." PhD diss., College of Physical Activity and Sport Sciences at West Virginia University, Morgantown, 2018. https://doi.org/10.33915/etd.7295.

Sweeney, Ed. "Junior Hockey and the Memorial Cup." In *Total Hockey: The Official Encyclopedia of the National Hockey League*, edited by Dan Diamond, James Duplacey, Ralph Dinger, Igor Kuperman, and Eric Zweig. Kansas City, MO: Andrews McMeel Publishing, 2000.

Szto, Courtney. *Changing on the Fly: Hockey through the Voices of South Asian Canadians.* New Brunswick, NJ: Rutgers University Press, 2020.

Tarasov, Anatoly. *The Father of Russian Hockey: Tarasov.* Glendale, CA: Griffin Publishing, 1997.

Tarasov, Anatoly. *Road to Olympus.* Glendale, CA: Griffin Publishing, 1969.

Taylor, Charles. *The Secular Age.* Cambridge, MA: Belknap Press of Harvard University Press, 2007.

Taylor, James A. "What's Hockey Doing to Your Boy?" *United Church Observer*, February 15, 1969.

Te Hiwi, Braden, and Janice Forsyth. "'A Rink at This School Is Almost as Essential as a Classroom': Hockey and Discipline at Pelican Lake Indian Residential School, 1945–1951." *Canadian Journal of History* 52, no. 1 (Spring/Summer 2017): 80–108.

Teilhard de Chardin, Pierre. *The Divine Milieu.* New York: Harper & Row, 1960.

Thiessen, Joel. *The Meaning of Sunday: The Practice of Belief in a Secular Age.* Montreal: McGill-Queen's University Press, 2015.

Titley, Brian, and Kas Mazurek. "Back to the Basics? Forward to the Fundamentals?" In *Canadian Education: Historical Themes and Contemporary Issues*, edited by Brian Titley, 111–25. Calgary: Detselig Enterprises, 1990.

Todd, Joe, and Jonathan Edwards. "Understanding Parental Support in Elite Sport: A Phenomenological Approach to Exploring Midget Triple A Hockey in the Canadian Maritimes." *Sport in Society* 24, no. 9 (2021), 1590–1608.

Toffler, Alvin. *The Eco-Spasm Report.* Toronto: Bantam Books, 1975.

Trothen, Tracy J. "Hockey: A Divine Sport?—Canada's National Sport in Relation to Embodiment, Community and Hope." *Studies in Religion* 35, no. 2 (2006): 291–305.

Truth and Reconciliation Commission of Canada (TRC). "Document I: Excerpts from *The Survivors Speak: A Report of the Truth and Reconciliation Commission of Canada* (2015)." In *Hockey: Challenging Canada's Game*, edited by Jenny Ellison and Jennifer Anderson, 77–84. Ottawa, ON: University of Ottawa Press, 2018.

Underwood, Colleen. "Alberta's Hockey Super League Gains Momentum from Players Looking for Elite Stream." *CBC News*, February 26, 2019. https://www.cbc.ca/news/canada/calgary/alberta-hockey-super-league-1.5033314.

Underwood, John. "The True Crisis." *Sports Illustrated Vault*, May 20, 1963. https://www.si.com/vault/1963/05/20/593620/the-true-crisis.

University of British Columbia Thunderbirds. "Rick Noonan." UBC Sports Hall of Fame. Accessed May 19, 2021. https://gothunderbirds.ca/honors/ubc-sports-hall-of-fame/rick-noonan/125.

University of Calgary, Faculty of Kinesiology. "About: History of Kinesiology." Accessed August 27, 2020. https://kinesiology.ucalgary.ca/about/history-kinesiology.

University of Regina Cougars. "Terry O'Malley." Women's Hockey, Roster & Coaching Staff. Accessed May 19, 2021. https://www.reginacougars.com/sports/womens-ice-hockey/roster/coaches/terry-o-malley/614.

University of St. Michael's College. "Our History." Accessed May 19, 2021. https://stmikes.utoronto.ca/about-us/our-history/.

University of Toronto Alumni. "Lester B. Pearson." News & Stories, Featured Alumni. November 28, 2013. https://alumni.utoronto.ca/news-and-stories/featured-alumni/lester-b-pearson.

University of Toronto Varsity Blues. "In Memorandum, Fr. Harry B. Gardner." Accessed May 19, 2021. https://varsityblues.ca/sports/2012/4/13/GEN_0413122903.aspx?path=.

Valentine, John and Brandon Toal, "The Rocket, the Riot, and the Revolution: Hockey in French Canada," *Canadian Ethnic Studies Journal* 53, no. 3 (2021): 241–60.

Valley, Mike, and Justin Goldman. *The Power Within: Discovering the Path to Elite Goaltending*. Scotts Valley, CA: CreateSpace Independent Publishing Platform, 2013.

Vanysacker, Dries. "The Attitude of the Holy See toward Sport during the Interwar Period (1919–39)." *Catholic Historical Review* 101, no. 4 (2015): 794–808.

Vaz, Edmund. *The Professionalization of Young Hockey Players*. Lincoln: University of Nebraska Press, 1982.

Wagamese, Richard. *Indian Horse: A Novel*. Vancouver, BC: Douglas & McIntyre, 2012.

Wallner, John. "Athletics and Academics: St. Michael's College Withdrawal from Ontario Hockey Association Junior A Competition." Master's thesis, Carleton University, Ottawa, 1990.

Waterloo Public Library. *Waterloo 150: Profiles from the Past, Faces of the Future*. Waterloo, ON: Waterloo Public Library, 2007.

Watson, Alan. *Catch On and Run with It: The Sporting Life and Times of Dr. Bob Hindmarch*. Vancouver: AJW Books, 2012.

Westhead, Rick. "Former Player Taught 'Craft' of Fighting at 16 Wants WHL Held Accountable, Affidavit Says." *TSN*, May 18, 2021. https://www.tsn.ca/westhead-former-player-taught-craft-of-fighting-at-16-wants-whl-held-accountable-affidavit-says-1.1641818.

Westhead, Rick. "For One Hockey Family, Impact of Alleged Abuse at a Top Canadian Prep School Lingers." *TSN*, December 22, 2021. https://www.tsn.ca/for-one-hockey-family-impact-of-alleged-abuse-at-a-top-canadian-prep-school-lingers-1.1738106.

"Why Did You Come?" *Alumni and Friends Newsletter* 8, no. 2 (Spring 1985): 1.

Wilhite, Shawn J., and Clayton N. Jefford. *The Didache: A Commentary*. Eugene, OR: Cascade Books, 2019.

Wilkins, Charles. *Breakaway: Hockey and the Years Beyond*. Collingdale, PA: Diane Publishing Company, 1995.

Wise, S. F., and Douglas Fisher. *Canada's Sporting Heroes*. Don Mills, ON: General Publishing Company, 1974.

Wooden, John R., and Steve Jamison. *The Essential Wooden: A Lifetime of Lessons on Leaders and Leadership*. New York: McGraw-Hill, 2007.

Wyshynski, Greg. "Is God a Hockey Fan? Pope Francis Sends Endorsement Letter to NHL." *Yahoo! Sports*, September 6, 2017. https://ca.sports.yahoo.com/news/god-hockey-fan-pope-francis-sends-endorsement-letter-nhl-171316335.html.

Young, Scott. *100 Years of Dropping the Puck: History of the OHA*. Toronto: McClelland & Stewart, 1989.

Young, Scott. "Editorial." *Toronto Telegram*, February 20, 1970.

Young, Scott. *War on Ice: Canada in International Hockey*. Toronto: McClelland & Stewart, 1976.

List of All Archival Sources

Athol Murray College of Notre Dame Archives, Wilcox, Saskatchewan.
Canada's Sports Hall of Fame Archives, Calgary, Alberta.
Carmelite Sisters of St. Joseph Collection, St. Agatha, Ontario.
D. K. (Doc) Seaman Hockey Resource Centre and Hockey Hall of Fame, Toronto, Ontario.
General Archives of the Basilian Fathers (Basilian Archives), Toronto, Ontario.
Hockey Canada Archives, Calgary, Alberta.
Library and Archives of Canada (LAC), Ottawa, Ontario.
Marc Bauer-Maison Collection, Stratford, Ontario.
Maureen Bauer-McGahey Collection, Perth, Ontario.
Paul Schmalz Collection., Goderich, Ontario.
Terry O'Malley Collection, Regina, Saskatchewan.

St. Mark's College Archives, Vancouver, British Columbia.

St. Michael's College School Archives, Toronto, Ontario.

University of Alberta Research & Collections Resource Facility (RCRF), Edmonton, Alberta.

University of Toronto Archives (and Records Management Services), Toronto, Ontario.

Waterloo Public Library (and Archives), Waterloo, Ontario.

Basilian Archives, Other Archives, & Collections

Anderson, Andy. "Sidelights by Andy." *The Houston Press,* April 12, 1944. Basilian Archives. Box 1, File 6, Lowrey fonds.

Anderson, Neville R. "Father James Austen Whelihan, C.S.B." *The Pastoral Reporter,* Diocese of Calgary, 1986. Basilian Archives. Box 1, File 1, Whelihan fonds.

"Back in the Spotlight: Father David Bauer, c.s.b." Pepsi-Cola International Hockey Classic for the Father David Bauer Cup, December 1–5, 1982. Basilian Archives. Box 2, Bauer fonds.

Bauer, David. "Attachment to Olympic Team Report." September 1979. LAC. MG31 E 72 35.

"Bauer, David." Canada's Sports Hall of Fame Archives. File 45, David Bauer fonds.

Bauer, David. Draft of Letter to Hockey Canada. March 30, 1984. Basilian Archives. Box 4, File 9, Bauer fonds.

Bauer, David. "Fr. Bauer Notes and Letters." Terry O'Malley Collection.

Bauer, David. Letter to Allyn. January 29, 1974. Basilian Archives. Box 1, File 6, Bauer fonds.

Bauer, David. Letter to Barb Bauer. September 11, 1980. Basilian Archives. Box 3, File 4, Bauer fonds.

Bauer, David. Letter to Barbara and Marianne. Undated. Basilian Archives. Box 3, File 4, Bauer fonds.

Bauer, David. Letter to Barbara Bauer. Basilian Archives. Box 3, File 3, Bauer fonds.

Bauer, David. Letter to Barbara Bauer. Late June 1971. Terry O'Malley Collection.

Bauer, David. Letter to Barbara Bauer. August 26, 1971. Terry O'Malley Collection.

Bauer, David. Letter to Barbara Bauer. October 2, 1972. Terry O'Malley Collection.

Bauer, David. Letter to Barbara Bauer. February 13, 1974. Terry O'Malley Collection.

Bauer, David. Letter to Barbara Bauer. February 19, 1974. Terry O'Malley Collection.

Bauer, David. Letter to Barbara Bauer. February 20, 1974. Terry O'Malley Collection.

Bauer, David. Letter to Barbara Bauer. February 24, 1974. Terry O'Malley Collection.

Bauer, David. Letter to Barbara Bauer. May 1974. Basilian Archives. Box 3, File 3, Bauer fonds.

Bauer, David. Letter to Barbara Bauer. November 8, 1974. Terry O'Malley Collection.

Bauer, David. Letter to Barbara Bauer. November 12, 1974. Terry O'Malley Collection.

Bauer, David. Letter to Barbara Bauer. November 24, 1974. Terry O'Malley Collection.

Bauer, David. Letter to Barbara Bauer. December 1974. Terry O'Malley Collection.

Bauer, David. Letter to Barbara Bauer. January 10–17, 1975. Terry O'Malley Collection.

Bauer, David. Letter to Barbara Bauer. April 18, 1975. Terry O'Malley Collection.

Bauer, David. Letter to Barbara Bauer. January 15, 1981. Basilian Archives. Box 3, File 3, Bauer fonds.

Bauer, David. Letter to Barbara Bauer. March 21, 1983. Terry O'Malley Collection.

Bauer, David. Letter to Bill. Basilian Archives. Box 3, File 1, Bauer fonds.

Bauer, David. Letter to Duncan McLarty. September 14, 1962. Basilian Archives. Box 5, File 1, Bauer fonds.

Bauer, David. Letter to Fr. Bert Pare. 1987. Basilian Archives. Box 1, File 3, Bauer fonds.

Bauer, David. Letter to John. Basilian Archives. Box 3, File 1, Bauer fonds.

Bauer, David. Letter to Karl Scheibock. October 17, 1963. Basilian Archives. Box 5, File 13, Bauer fonds.

Bauer, David. Letter to Lisa Bauer. Basilian Archives. Box 3, File 1, Bauer fonds.

Bauer, David. Letter to Lisa Bauer. Basilian Archives. Box 4, File 5, Bauer fonds.

Bauer, David. Letter to Maurice. 1979. Basilian Archives. Box 3, File 3, Bauer fonds.

Bauer, David. Letter to Paul Burns. January 15, 1981. Basilian Archives. Box 3, File 3, Bauer fonds.

Bauer, David. Letter to Père Murray. February 1971. Athol Murray College of Notre Dame Archives.

Bauer, David. Letter to Red Kelly, MP. June 24, 1963. Basilian Archives. Box 5, File 1, Bauer fonds.

Bauer, David. Letter to *Sports Illustrated*. June 28, 1963. Basilian Archives. Box 5, File 1, Bauer fonds.

Bauer, David. Letter to Unknown. Circa 1981. Basilian Archives. Box 3, File 3, Bauer fonds.

Bauer, David. Letter to Unknown. Post-1980. Basilian Archives. Box 3, File 5, Bauer fonds.

Bauer, David. "Mapping of Hockey Political Landscape." Summer 1980. Basilian Archives. Box 3, File 4, Bauer fonds.

Bauer, David. Marginal Notes in "Post-Secondary Education at Notre Dame: A Review of the Past and a Plan for the Future." 1981. Basilian Archives. Box 4, File 2, Bauer fonds.

Bauer, David. Mislabeled Introduction of *Report to Munro*. Circa 1973. Seaman Hockey Resource Centre. Rev. Bauer File.

Bauer, David. Notes. 1980–1983. Basilian Archives. Box 3, File 5, Bauer fonds.

Bauer, David. Notes. Basilian Archives. Box 3, File 1, Bauer fonds.

Bauer, David. Notes. Basilian Archives. Box 3, File 3, Bauer fonds.

Bauer, David. Notes. Basilian Archives. Box 3, File 4, Bauer fonds.

Bauer, David. Notes. Basilian Archives. Box 3, File 5, Bauer fonds.

Bauer, David. Notes. Basilian Archives. Box 4, File 3, Bauer fonds.

Bauer, David. Notes. Basilian Archives. Box 4, File 5, Bauer fonds.

Bauer, David. Notes. Fall 1980. Basilian Archives. Box 3, File 1, Bauer fonds.

Bauer, David. Notes. July 1980. Terry O'Malley Collection.

Bauer, David. Notes. July 31, 1980. Basilian Archives. Box 3, File 4, Bauer fonds.

Bauer, David. Notes. October 17, 1976. Basilian Archives. Box 3, File 5, Bauer fonds.

Bauer, David. Notes. Summer 1981. Basilian Archives. Box 3, File 5, Bauer fonds.

Bauer, David. "Olympic Hockey: 'Make Use of Technique, but Let the Spirit Prevail.'"
Basilian Archives. Box 1, File 4, Bauer fonds.

Bauer, David. "Olympic Team Report." September 1979. LAC. MG31 E 72 35.

Bauer, David. "On June 20, 1980." Basilian Archives. Box 4, File 8, Bauer fonds.

Bauer, David. *Report to Munro*. 1971. Marc Bauer-Maison Collection.

Bauer, David. "The Role of Hockey." 1979. Terry O'Malley Collection.

Bauer, David. Rough Draft of Letter to Sport Minister Otto Jelinek. Basilian Archives.
Box 3, File 5, Bauer fonds.

Bauer, David. Speech Notes. October 22, 1973. Basilian Archives. Box 3, File 3,
Bauer fonds.

Bauer, David. Speech Notes. 1985. Basilian Archives. Box 3, File 6, Bauer fonds.

Bauer, David. Speech Notes in a Niece's Handwriting. 1987. Basilian Archives. Box
3, File 5, Bauer fonds.

Bauer, David. Speech Notes on His Philosophy of Sport. Basilian Archives. Box 1,
File 6, Bauer fonds.

Bauer, David. Teaching Notes. Basilian Archives. Box 3, File 1, Bauer fonds.

Bauer, David. Teaching Notes. Basilian Archives. Box 3, File 4, Bauer fonds.

Bauer, David. "To State My Position." Basilian Archives. Box 1, File 6, Bauer fonds.

Bauer, David. Untitled. Basilian Archives. Box 3, File 3, Bauer fonds.

Bauer, David. "Why Do We Have Olympic Games?" 1987. Terry O'Malley Collection.

Bauer, David. "Why an Olympic Team?" 1976. Basilian Archives. Box 1, File 6, Bauer fonds.

Bauer, David, and James Hanrahan. "Canada's Future in World Hockey: A Private
and Confidential Survey for the Information of the Recipient Only." 1966.
Hockey Canada Archives. Hockey Canada Library (3).

Bauer, David, and James Hanrahan. "Paper Submitted to the Task Force on Sport."
Summer 1968. Basilian Archives. Box 1, File 8, Bauer fonds.

Bauer, David, James Hanrahan, and Brian Conacher. "The Hockey Canada
Corporation and Education." Presentation to the Education Committee
of Hockey Canada Corporation, May 14, 1969. LAC. MG28 I 151 24, A18,
Hockey Canada–70, 1969–1970.

Bauer Family. *Bauer (A Family History of Edgar and Bertha's Family)*. Waterloo, ON: Self-published, 2003. Private Bauer family records owned by Paul Schmalz.

Bauer-McGahey, Maureen. Notes of Unpublished Book Chapters about 1980 Olympic Hockey Team. Spring 1980. Basilian Archives. Box 3, File 1, Bauer fonds.

Bauer-McGahey, Maureen. Seminar Notes. June 2019. Maureen Bauer-McGahey Collection.

"Bauer, Robert Theodore Joseph." University of Toronto Archives. A73-0026/022(21), Alumni Filed Records.

Beddoes, Dick. "No Nation Is an Island." *The Globe and Mail*, August 31, 1964. Canada's Sports Hall of Fame Archives. File 1, David Bauer fonds.

"Board Meeting Minutes." June 20, 1980. LAC. MG31 E 72 35, H2 (1) a, Hockey Canada General: correspondence (file 5).

"Canada's National Hockey Team: A History." Canada's Sports Hall of Fame Archives. File 37, David Bauer fonds.

Canada's Sports Hall of Fame Archives. File 38, David Bauer fonds.

Canadian Amateur Hockey Association. "Annual Meeting 1974, (Meeting of Board of Directors)." May 24, 1974. Winnipeg, MB. Hockey Canada Archives. Meeting Minutes File.

Canadian Amateur Hockey Association. "Minutes of Annual Meeting." 1968. Calgary, AB. Hockey Canada Archives. Minutes File.

Canadian Amateur Hockey Association. "Minutes of Annual Meeting." 1973. Charlottetown, PEI. Hockey Canada Archives. Minutes File.

Canadian Amateur Hockey Association. "Minutes of Annual Meeting." May 1976. Penticton, BC. Hockey Canada Archives. Minutes File.

Canadian Amateur Hockey Association. "Minutes of Board of Directors Meeting." January 26–27, 1975. Toronto, ON. Hockey Canada Archives. Minutes File.

Canadian Amateur Hockey Association. "Minutes of Semi-Annual Meeting." February 12–13, 1972. Ottawa, ON. Hockey Canada Archives. Minutes File.

Canadian Amateur Hockey Association. Unsigned Letter to the Czechoslovak Ice Hockey Section. January 7, 1960. LAC. MG28 I 151 4, Japanese and European Tours of Canada file, 1959–1960.

Canadian Department of National Health and Welfare. *Federal Government Hockey Study Report, Amateur Hockey in Canada, a Blueprint for the 70s and Beyond*. By John Meagher. Ottawa: Department of National Health and Welfare, 1971. Hockey Canada Archives. Hockey Canada Library (3) file.

Canadian Department of National Health and Welfare. *Final Report: Report on Amateur Hockey in Canada by the Hockey Study Committee of the National Advisory Council on Fitness and Amateur Sport*. By William L'Heureux, David Bauer, Frank Dunlap, Max Bell, Bill Crothers, and John Meagher. Ottawa, ON: Department of National Health and Welfare, 1968. LAC. MG28 I 263 18, 300-6-6, Federal Government Position on Hockey (2 of 2).

The Canadian Press. "Bauer Instilled Strong Sense of Values, Duff Says." *The Globe and Mail,* November 12, 1988. Basilian Archives. Box 2, last file, Bauer fonds.

The Canadian Press. "Bauer Remembered as Teacher." Basilian Archives. Box 2, Bauer fonds.

The Canadian Press. "Bauer's Dream Revived at Games." February 14, 1980. Carmelite Sisters of St. Joseph Collection.

The Canadian Press. "Father Bauer on Fitness Council." March 6, 1964. Basilian Archives. Box 2, last file, Bauer fonds.

The Canadian Press. "Special Gold Medal for Father Bauer; Players Stay Away." February 19, 1964. Canada's Sports Hall of Fame Archives. David Bauer file.

"Capt. 'Bob' Lowrey Wins M. C." Basilian Archives. Box 1, File 6, Lowrey fonds.

CBC Sports. "Flying Dutchmen Play Hockey for Canada." CBC Sports Digital Archives, January 5, 1956. https://www.cbc.ca/player/play/1466890691.

Coleman, Jim. Untitled. August 1, 1979. Canada's Sports Hall of Fame Archives. File 3, David Bauer fonds.

Conlin, Paul. "Brief Presented to Parliamentary Committee on International Hockey." October 5, 1977. Ottawa, ON. Basilian Archives. Box 3, File 1, Bauer fonds.

Corrigan, Kevin. Letter to Minster Gordon Currie. May 13, 1985. Basilian Archives. I—1988—Bauer—Quest box, File 2.

Cotton, Crosbie. "Rink Improves Odds for '88 Hockey Team." *Calgary Herald,* July 16, 1985. Basilian Archives. Box 4, File 9, Bauer fonds.

Department of External Affairs to the Parliamentary Committee on International Hockey. "Appendix D, A Report by the Canadian Embassy in Vienna." In Brief submitted to the Parliamentary Committee on International Hockey. By the Department, Senator S. L. Buckwold. September 22, 1977. LAC. RG29 2077.

Dooley, John. "Rev. Bauer Back on the Front Lines for '80 Olympics." *The Record,* February 1979. Carmelite Sisters of St. Joseph Collection.

Douglas, Greg. "Father of Canada's Olympic Hockey Dies." *Vancouver Courier,* November 13, 1988. Basilian Archives. Box 2, Bauer fonds.

Draft Letter from the Father David Bauer Quest Program. June 16, 1989. Basilian Archives. I—1988—Bauer—Quest box, File 10.

Duhatschek, Eric. "Hockey Institute." *Calgary Herald,* June 18, 1981. LAC. MG31 E 72 37, H2 (3), Athletic Assistance Programme 1980–1981.

Eagleson, Alan. Letter to Bauer. March 6, 1979. Basilian Archives. Box 1, File 9, Bauer fonds.

"Edgar J. Bauer, Industrialist, Dies." 1959. Paul Schmalz Collection.

"Editorial—Father David Bauer." *Toronto Star,* November 12, 1988. Seaman Hockey Resource Centre. Rev. Bauer File.

Ellul, Jacques. *The Technological Society.* New York: Random House, 1964. Found in Basilian Archives. Box 4, File 5, Bauer fonds.

Estey, Willard. "Hockey Canada: Alternate Plan for Existence." May 16, 1980. LAC. MG31 E 72 35, H2 (1) a, Hockey Canada General: correspondence (file 4).

Estey, Willard. "Hockey Canada—International Hockey Representative." May 11, 1983. LAC. R12287 41.

Estey, Willard. Letter to Alan Eagleson. January 7, 1987. LAC. MG31 E 72 36.

Estey, Willard. Letter to Alan Eagleson and Hartland MacDougall. October 17, 1980. LAC. MG31 E 72 36, H2 (1) a, Hockey Canada General: correspondence (file 5).

Estey, Willard. Letter to the Board. July 15, 1980. LAC. MG31 E 72 35, H2 (1) a, Hockey Canada General: correspondence (file 4).

Estey, Willard. Letter to Businessmen on the Board. May 1, 1980. LAC. MG31 E 72 35, H2 (1) a, Hockey Canada General: correspondence (file 4).

Estey, Willard. Letter to Doc Seaman. July 22, 1980. LAC. MG31 E 72 35, H2 (1) a, Hockey Canada General: correspondence (file 5).

Estey, Willard. Letter to Executive Committee. September 29, 1980. LAC. MG31 E 72 36, H2 (1) a, Hockey Canada General: correspondence (file 5).

Estey, Willard. Letter to Executive Committee of the Board. June 20, 1980. LAC. MG31 E 72 35, H2 (1) a, Hockey Canada General: correspondence (file 4).

Estey, Willard. Letter to Lou Lefaive. February 21, 1980. LAC. MG31 E 72 35, H2 (1) a, Hockey Canada General: correspondence (file 3).

Estey, Willard. Letter to Turmel. February 16, 1980. LAC. MG31 E 72 35, H2 (1) a, Hockey Canada General: correspondence (file 3).

Estey, Willard. Memo on Removal of Violence from Sport. June 10, 1986. LAC. MG31 E 72 36.

Estey, Willard. Memo: The Problems. January 7, 1985. LAC. MG31 E 72 37, H2 (1) d, WZE Program memos, 1981–1985.

Estey, Willard. Memo to File Re Telephone Conversation with Father Bauer. June 15, 1981. LAC. MG31 E 72 37, H2 (3), Athletic Assistance Programme 1980–1981.

Estey, Willard. "Prepared Questions for Meeting with John Ziegler." February 17, 1980. Lake Placid, NY. LAC. MG31 E 72 35, H2 (1) a, Hockey Canada General: correspondence (file 3).

Estey, Willard. "Reorganization of Hockey Canada." 1979. LAC. MG31 E 72 35.

"Father Bauer Hadn't Heard." *The Globe and Mail,* December 12, 1974. Seaman Hockey Resource Centre. Rev. Bauer File.

"Father James Whelihan, 1902–1986." Basilian Archives. Box 1, File 1, Whelihan fonds.

"Father Robert Emmett Lowrey." 1941. Basilian Archives. Box 1, File 6, Lowrey fonds.

Fisher, Doug. To Maurice Regimbal. May 20, 1975. LAC. MG28 I 263 19, 300-6-14 Development Committee Hockey (1 of 3) 1974–1975.

Fisher, Douglas, and Chris Lang. Memo to Maurice Regimbal, Chair of Education Committee. May 26, 1969. LAC. MG28 I 151 24, A18 Hockey Canada–70, 1969–1970.

Frayne, Trent. "It's How You Played the Game That Mattered to Father Bauer." *The Globe and Mail*, November 10, 1988. Basilian Archives. Box 4, File 9, Bauer fonds.

Gallagher, Danny. "Golden Hawk Lands in Wilcox." *Leader Post Regina*. Basilian Archives. Box 4, File 9, Bauer fonds.

The Globe and Mail. March 27, 1973. Canada's Sports Hall of Fame Archives. File 27, David Bauer fonds.

Griffiths, Phyllis. "Father Bauer: He Molded a Dream." *The Telegram*, February 11, 1964. Canada's Sports Hall of Fame Archives. David Bauer File.

Gross, George. "Bauer Blesses Oiler Machine." *Toronto Sun*, September 8, 1987. Basilian Archives. Box 2, last file, Bauer fonds.

Gross, George. "Eagle, Bobby, Agree to Disagree?" *Toronto Sun*, September 14, 1979. Canada's Sports Hall of Fame Archives. File 7, David Bauer fonds.

Hargreaves, Jack. Letter to Gordon Juckes. September 11, 1967. LAC—CAHA Fond—A18. Canadian National Hockey Foundation, MG28 I 151 24.

Hockey Canada. "Annual Report, 1969–70." Hockey Canada Archives. Annual Reports File.

Hockey Canada. "Directors Meeting." April 28, 1975. LAC. MG28 I 263 19, 300-6-24 Hockey Canada Annual Meeting 1975.

Hockey Canada. "Draft—Four More Years: Hockey Canada 1981–1985." LAC. MG31 E 72 39, H2 (8) b, Olympics 1984—Financing.

Hockey Canada. "Executive Committee Meeting Minutes." May 27, 1980. LAC. MG31 E 72 35, H2 (1) a, Hockey Canada General: correspondence (file 5).

Hockey Canada. "Hockey Canada: Hockey Scholarships." March 1, 1985. LAC. MG31 E 72 37, H2 (1) d, WZE Program memos, 1981–1985.

Hockey Canada. "Long Range Plan Proposal to Sam Pollock." October 17, 1980. LAC. MG31 E 72 36, H2 (1) a, Hockey Canada General: correspondence (file 5).

Hockey Canada. "Minutes of Board of Directors." February 16, 1980. Lake Placid, NY. LAC. MG31 E 72 35, H2 (1) a, Hockey Canada General: correspondence (file 3).

Hockey Canada. "Minutes of the Board of Directors of Hockey Canada." May 10, 1987. Basilian Archives. Box 4, File 8, Bauer fonds.

Hockey Canada. "Minutes of the Board of Directors of Hockey Canada." September 14, 1987. Ottawa, ON. Basilian Archives. Box 4, File 7, Bauer fonds.

Hockey Canada. "Minutes of Conference Meeting." March 12, 1980. Lake Placid, NY. LAC. MG31 E 72 35, H2 (1) a, Hockey Canada General: correspondence (file 3).

Hockey Canada. "Minutes of the Development Committee Meeting." May 13, 1974. LAC. MG28 I 263 19, 300-6-14, Development Committee Hockey (2 of 3) 1974–1975.

Hockey Canada. "Minutes of the Development Policy Committee." September 29, 1970. LAC. MG28 I 263 6, 400-9 Hockey Canada–1969/70.

Hockey Canada. "Minutes of Executive Committee." September 29, 1980. LAC. MG31 E 72 36, H2 (1) a, Hockey Canada General: correspondence (file 5).

Hockey Canada. "Newsletter 1, no. 1." 1971. LAC. MG28 I 151 24, A15, Fitness and Amateur Sport Directorate–72.

Hockey Canada. "Newsletter 1, no. 2." 1970. LAC. MG28 I 151 25, A18, Hockey Canada–72.

Hockey Canada. "Olympics 1980." Draft document. Basilian Archives. Box 1, File 6, Bauer fonds.

Hockey Canada. "Planning and Development Committee Report to the Board of Directors." Annual General Meeting. December 7, 1985. Basilian Archives. Box 3, File 7, Bauer fonds.

Hockey Canada. "President's Report: Board of Directors Meeting." June 17, 1971. LAC. MG28 I 151 25, A18, Hockey Canada–72.

Hockey Canada. "Report on Former Bursary Programme." June 1981. LAC. MG31 E 72 37, H2 (3), Athletic Assistance Programme 1980–1981.

Hockey Canada. Response Notes to Douglas Mitchell. 1980. LAC. MG31 E 72 36.

Hockey Canada. "A Summary." February 17, 1970. LAC. MG28 I 151 24, A18, Hockey Canada–70, 1969–1970.

Hockey Canada. "Verbatim Minutes of the Board Meeting." Toronto, ON: February 18, 1970. LAC. MG28 I 263 9.

"Hockey Canada and the Canadian Amateur Hockey Association." Circa 1978. Sudbury, ON: Laurentian University Press. Hockey Canada Archives. Hockey Canada Library (2).

"Hockey Canada/CAHA Post-1988 Arrangement." September 3, 1987. Basilian Archives. Box 3, File 7, Bauer fonds.

Hockey Canada, International Committee. "Update on the Development of Canada's National Hockey Team for the 1988 Winter Olympics. Prepared for The Honorable Otto Jelinek." April 1986. Basilian Archives. Box 3, File 7, Bauer fonds.

Hockey Canada Olympic Committee. Untitled. Summer 1977. Basilian Archives. Box 3, File 1, Bauer fonds.

"Hockey Canada Report, 1985." LAC. MG 31 E72 36, Hockey Canada—Documents: 1985 report, Appendix I: Hockey Canada Board of Directors 1969–1985.

Hockey Canada Research Institute. "Centre of Excellence." LAC. MG31 E 72 39, H2 (8) b, Olympics 1984—Financing. 1984.

Hockey Committee. "Final Report to the National Advisory Council on Fitness and Amateur Sport." February 26, 1968. LAC. MG28 I 263 18, 300-6-11, Canadian Amateur Hockey Association, 1968–1974.

Hockey Hall of Fame. "Father David Bauer." Induction Speech, 1989. Seaman Hockey Resource Centre. Rev. Bauer File.

"Hockey in Deep Trouble, Government Report Says." *Toronto Star*, May 9, 1979. LAC. RG29 2074.

"Hockey—Second Bauer." *Time Magazine*, December 27, 1963. Canada's Sports Hall of Fame Archives. File 44, David Bauer fonds.

Holmes, Derek. "Report on Olympic Team." Fall 1979. LAC. MG31 E 72 35.

Hopwood, W. J., Jr. Letter to Gordon Juckes. June 12, 1968. LAC. MG28 I 263 18, 300-6-11, Canadian Amateur Hockey Association, 1968–1974.

Howitt, Eaton. "Ahearne: He Must Have Had a Nightmare." *The Toronto Telegram*, October 1, 1970. LAC. MG28 I 151 25, A18, Hockey Canada–71.

Huck, Rita. "Dear Dad." In *Bauer (A Family History of Edgar and Bertha's Family)*. Waterloo, ON: Self-published, 2003. Private Bauer family records owned by Paul Schmalz.

Hunter, Paul. "Wanted Less Mayhem in International Hockey." *Toronto Star*, November 10, 1988. Basilian Archives. Box 2, last file, Bauer fonds.

Jackson, Roger, to Doug Fisher. "Hockey Institute." April 17, 1973. LAC. MG28 I 263 18, 300-6-6 Federal Government Position on Hockey (1 of 2).

"James Austin Whelihan." *The Basilian Newsletter* 19, November 28, 1986. Basilian Archives. Box 1, File 1, Whelihan fonds.

Jelinek, Otto. Remarks at the Launch of the Royal Canadian Mint's 1988 Olympic Hockey and Biathlon Coins. February 25, 1986. Hockey Hall of Fame, Toronto, ON. Maureen Bauer-McGahey Collection.

Johnson, Dan. Letter to Fr. Bauer. January 13, 1969. Basilian Archives. Box 1, File 8, Bauer fonds.

Jones, Terry. "Coronary Prevented Hardy from Opposing Hockey Czar." *Edmonton Journal*, December 20, 1969. University of Alberta RCRF. 83-48-378.

Journal News Services. "Swedes Demanding Ahearne's Resignation." *Edmonton Journal*, January 5, 1970. University of Alberta RCRF. 83-48-378.

Kalchman, Lois. "Bauer's Bound for Toronto as Crusaders Clean House." *Toronto Star*. 1987. Basilian Archives. Box 4, File 9, Bauer fonds.

Kaplan, Bill. "Boys at St. Thomas Bid Farewell to Father Lowrey—He's Off to the War." *Houston Press*, November 11, 1941. Basilian Archives. Box 1, File 6, Lowrey fonds.

Kelly, Neil. Letter to Lisa Bauer. December 6, 1988. Basilian Archives. Box 1, File 4, Bauer fonds.

King, Andrew. *Athol Murray, Recordings of Murray.* Wilcox, SK: Athol Murray College of Notre Dame, 2004.

King, Dave. Letter to Willard Estey. January 23, 1985. LAC. MG31 E 72 40, H2 (16) Notre Dame (1982–1985).

Koch, Henry. "R. A. Bauer Buys All Bauer Stock." *Kitchener-Waterloo Record,* June 6, 1972. Waterloo Public Library. Business Binder, Bauer Ltd.

Lang, Chris. "Draft Report on First 16 Years." September 20, 1985. LAC. MG31 E 72 36, H2 (1) c, Hockey Canada—Documents: report (1985).

Lang, Chris. Letter to Lou Lefaive. February 27, 1980. LAC. MG31 E 72 35, H2 (1) a, Hockey Canada—General: correspondence (file 3).

Lang, Chris. Letter to Willard Estey. October 11, 1985. LAC. MG31 E 72 36, H2 (1) b, Hockey Canada General: correspondence (file 5).

"Last Will and Testament of Bauer." January 17, 1989. Basilian Archives. I—1988— Bauer—Quest box, File 1.

Lawson, Isobel. "Father David Bauer." *Waterloo Chronicle,* November 30, 1988. Seaman Hockey Resource Centre. Rev. Bauer File.

Layzell, Denny. "Personality of the Week: Father Jim Whelihan." Basilian Archives. Box 1, File 2, Whelihan fonds.

Lebel, E. C. "Overview of Lebel." Basilian Archives. I. 1986 VIII 11. Box 4, File 1, Lebel, E. C. fonds.

Lefaive, Lou. "Document Work-Up Sent to Doc Seaman." March 13, 1980. LAC. MG31 E 72 35, H2 (1) a, Hockey Canada General: correspondence (file 4).

Lefaive, Lou. Letter to Mr. L. A. D. Stephens. January 9, 1969. LAC. MG28 I 263 18, File 300-6-8 Hockey—General, 1969–1975.

Lefaive, Lou. Letter to Willard Estey. January 24, 1980. LAC. MG31 E 72 35, H2 (1) a Hockey Canada—General: correspondence (file 3).

Loranger, Clancy. "Finally, Father Bauer . . ." *The Province,* November 30, 1983. Basilian Archives. Box 2, last file, Bauer fonds.

Lowrey, Robert. Letter to McCorkell. August 29, 1944. Basilian Archives. Box 1, File 1, Lowrey fonds.

Lowrey, Robert. Letter to Robert Scollard for *Basilian Annals.* April 25, 1945. Basilian Archives. Box 1, File 1, Lowrey fonds.

"Lowrey—That's a Hockey Name." *Detroit News,* December 24, 1934. Basilian Archives. Box 1, File 6, Lowrey fonds.

M & M Systems Research Ltd. "Report: The Organizational Development of Hockey Canada." Hockey Canada Archives. Hockey Canada Library (11), 1974–75, part I.

MacDougall, Hartland. Letter to Willard Estey. October 16, 1985. LAC. MG31 E 72 36, H2 (1) b, Hockey Canada—General (file 2).

Martin, Ken. "Confidential Letter to CAHA Board." February 25, 1970. LAC. MG28 I 151 25, A18, Hockey Canada–70.

Mastromatteo, Mike. "Fr. Bauer Believed in Fair Play." *Catholic Register*, November 26, 1988. Basilian Archives. Box 2, last file, Bauer fonds.

McCool, Frank. "The Morning After." Basilian Archives. Box 1, File 1, Whelihan fonds.

McDonald, Archie. "Father Bauer Remembered." *Vancouver Sun*, November 10, 1988. Basilian Archives. Box 2, Bauer fonds.

McLaughlin, Cathy. "Father Whelihan Gets Order of Canada." *Western Catholic Reporter*, January 6, 1986. Basilian Archives. Box 1, File 1, Whelihan fonds.

"Military Cross Awarded to Canadian Catholic Chaplain." November 10, 1945. Basilian Archives. Box 1, File 6, Lowrey fonds.

Mitchell, Douglas. Letter to Willard Estey. September 1980. LAC. MG31 E 72 36 17.

Morse, Eric. Letter to Willard Estey. January 15, 1980. LAC. MG31 E 72 35, H2 (1) a Hockey Canada—General: correspondence (file 3).

Moss, John. Letter to Willard Estey. October 20, 1982. LAC. MG31 E 72 40, H2 (16) Notre Dame (1982–1985).

Moss, John. Letter to Willard Estey. Notre Dame College, December 15, 1982. LAC. MG31 E 72 40. H2 (16) Notre Dame (1982–1985).

"New Agreement Is Reached; N.H.L. Gets Under Way Nov. 2." September 13, 1941. University of Alberta RCRF. 83-48-377.

News Communique. "Father David Bauer Olympic Arena Sod Turning Ceremony." July 15, 1985. Basilian Archives. Box 4, File 8, Bauer fonds.

Notre Dame Review Committee. "Post-Secondary Education at Notre Dame: A Review of the Past and a Plan for the Future." 1981. Basilian Archives. Box 4, File 2, Bauer fonds.

Notre Dame Task Force Committee. "Report of the Task Force on Post-Secondary Education at Athol Murray College of Notre Dame." Presentation, April 27, 1982. Basilian Archives. Box 4, File 2, Bauer fonds.

O'Malley, Terry. "Father David Bauer and the National Team Hockey Experiment: 1963–1980, A Personal Recollection." 2001. Terry O'Malley Collection.

O'Malley, Terry. "Father David Bauer csb (1924–1988)—A Life in 'Quotations.'" Terry O'Malley Collection.

Orban, William A. R. "Report on the Research and Educational Aspects of Hockey in the USSR and CSSR." December 18, 1969. LAC. MG28 I 151 24, A18, Hockey Canada—70, 1969–1970.

Parrish, Wayne. "Fr. Bauer's Team Wasn't for Sale." *Toronto Sun*, August 13, 1987. Basilian Archives. Box 2, last file, Bauer fonds.

Parsley, Al. "Dr. Hardy Forthright in Ideas of Changing Trends in Hockey Set-Up." 1940. University of Alberta RCRF. 83-48-377.

Pennington, Bob. "A National Experiment—On Ice." *Toronto Telegram*, December 29, 1967. University of Toronto Archives. "Bauer, David William," Alumni Files Record.

Pollock, Sam. Letter to Willard Estey. February 19, 1981. LAC. MG31 E 72 37, H2 (3), Athletic Assistance Programme 1980–1981.

Prashaw, Rick. "Russians' Timing Was a Surprise." *Toronto Star*, September 1, 1972. Canada's Sports Hall of Fame Archives. File 15, David Bauer fonds.

Press Release. Basilian Archives. Box 1, File 4, Bauer fonds.

"Priest Behind Bench." May 1988. Carmelite Sisters of St. Joseph Collection.

Private Bauer Family Records. Paul Schmalz Collection.

Proudfoot, Jim. "Father Bauer Recalls 'Giant Act of Faith.'" *Toronto Star*, 1987 or 1988. Basilian Archives. Box 4, File 9, Bauer fonds.

Proudfoot, Jim. "For Aging Olympic Rearguard, NHL Isn't Ultimate in Hockey." January 6, 1984. LAC. MG31 E 72 36, H2 (1) b, Hockey Canada—General (file 2).

Proudfoot, Jim. "Père Bauer Was a Lot More Than a Hockey Coach." *Toronto Star*, November 11, 1988. Basilian Archives. Box 2, last file, Bauer fonds.

Pugh, Robert. "National University Hockey League." October 12, 1979. LAC. MG31 E 72 35.

"Quest Program, 1983–1984." Basilian Archives. Box 4, File 4, Bauer fonds.

Regan, Gerald. Letter to Lou Lefaive. June 4, 1980. LAC. MG31 E 72 35, H2 (1) a, Hockey Canada General: correspondence (file 4).

Regimbal, Maurice. Letter to Development Committee. November 5, 1973. LAC. MG28 I 263 18, 300-6-1, "Future Role of Hockey Canada, 1969–1974."

Regimbal, Maurice. To James Hanrahan. February 28, 1974. LAC. MG28 I 263 19, 300-6-14, Development Committee Hockey.

Reidford, James. "NHL Map of Canada." Basilian Archives. Box 1, File 6, Bauer fonds.

Roberts, Bill. "'More Room for Our Boys,' Asks Father Lowrey of New Year." 1941. Basilian Archives. Box 1, File 6, Lowrey fonds.

Robison, Ron. Letter to David Bauer. July 17, 1985. Basilian Archives. Box 1, File 6, Bauer fonds.

Ronnenberg, Ernie. "Dynamic Father Dave Bauer is Hockey's Gentleman Coach." *Kitchener-Waterloo Record*, December 23, 1978. Waterloo Public Library. Biographies of Prominent Waterloo Residents, Bauer, David.

Rosenburg, Dan. "Roach Joins Ice Nationals." February 1, 1968. LAC—CAHA Fond—A18. Canadian National Hockey Foundation, MG28 I 151 24.

Ross, Val. "Stress, The Business of Coping," *Macleans*, May 5, 1980, 46–52.

Schuler, Dick. "Veteran Team Builder Sees Solution for the Stamps." *Calgary Herald*, 1985. Basilian Archives. Box 1, File 2, Whelihan fonds.

Seaman, Doc. Letter to Doug Fisher. April 9, 1974. LAC. MG28 I 263 19, 300-6-14, Development Committee Hockey (2 of 3) 1974–1975.

Sigal, Mark. "Hockey: Canada's Collegiate Team Could Surprise." *Like It Is*, December 1979. LAC. RG29 2076.

Slade, Daryl. "'Dean' of City Coaches Dies in Toronto at 84." *Calgary Herald*, 1986. Basilian Archives. Box 1, File 1, Whelihan fonds.

Sokol, Al. "Father Bauer Says Pros in Olympics Bad Deal for Youth." *Toronto Star*, February 26, 1986. Basilian Archives. Box 4, File 9, Bauer fonds.

"Speaker Introduction of McGuigan." 1985. Wilcox, SK. Basilian Archives. Box 1, File 3, Bauer fonds.

"Special Honours to Lucan Native." *Time-Advocate*, December 18, 1985. Basilian Archives. Box 1, File 1, Whelihan fonds.

Staples, David. "Coach's Spirit Drives Ex-Oiler Toward Goal." *Edmonton Journal*, May 23, 1993. Seaman Hockey Resource Centre. Rev. Bauer File.

Tarasov, Anatoly. Note to David Bauer in *ДЕТЯМ О ХОККЕЕ* by Anatoly Tarasov. 1986. Basilian Archives. Box 2, no file, Bauer fonds.

"Thoughts for Tuesday Meeting—Task Force." LAC—CAHA Fond—A18. Canadian National Hockey Foundation, MG28 I 151 25, A19, Federal Task Force on Sport for Canadians.

"Thunderbird 1986 Centennial Hockey Classic, Jan. 2–5: Hockey with Spirit." Program, 1986. Basilian Archives. Box 1, File 7, Bauer fonds.

University of New Brunswick Libraries. "L'Heureux, Willard Joseph." Pomp and Circumstance, 1967 Fredericton Convocation. Accessed September 25, 2019. https://graduations.lib.unb.ca/award/17971.

University of Toronto, Students' Administrative Council. *Torontonensis, 1939*. University of Toronto Archives and Records Management Services.

"Van Vliet Still Upset." 1964. Seaman Hockey Resource Centre. Rev. Bauer File.

Wagner, Norman. Letter to Doc Seaman. April 28, 1980. LAC. MG31 E 72 35, H2 (1) a, Hockey Canada General: correspondence (file 4).

Wagner, Norman. Letter to Willard Estey. May 7, 1981. LAC. MG31 E 72 37, H2 (3), Athletic Assistance Programme 1980–1981.

Walker, John. "Old Rules Labelled 'A Charade.'" *Edmonton Journal*, January 6, 1970. University of Alberta RCRF. 83-48-378.

Xhignesse, Louis. "Outline of a Proposed Notre Dame College Three-Year Arts Program." Notre Dame College, January 11, 1981. Basilian Archives. Box 4, File 2, Bauer fonds.

Young, Leighton F. Letter to Robert Lowrey. January 30, 1974. Basilian Archives. Box 1, File 5, Lowrey fonds.

Zeisberger, Mike. "Fr. David Bauer." *Toronto Sun*, November 10, 1988. Basilian Archives. Box 2, last file, Bauer fonds.

St. Michael's College School Archives & Yearbooks and
St. Mark's College Archives

Alviano, Ray. "Friend Remembers Bauer as a Caring Individual." November 15, 1988. St. Michael's College School Archives. Bauer Fr. David box, Obit file.

Artiss, Laurie. Newspaper Editorial. August 16, 1967. St. Mark's College Archives. Box 7, Carr—Correspondence and Misc. file.

Bauer, Dave. "Hockey's Special Position." 1973. St. Mark's College Archives. Box 36, "Bauer, Dave 1971–1980" file, Accession number 2014-2.

Bauer, David. Letter to Fr. Eugene Lebel. Spring 1968. St. Mark's College Archives. Box 7, Carr-Correspondence and Misc. file.

Bauer, David. Letter to Fr. Hanrahan. 1968. St. Mark's College Archives. Box 36, "Bauer, Dave 1971–1980" file.

Bauer, David. Letter to James Hanrahan. Late October 1973. St. Mark's College Archives. Box 36, "Bauer, Dave 1971–1980" file, Accession number 2014-2.

Bauer, David. Letter to James Hanrahan. July 1975. St. Mark's College Archives. Box 36, "Bauer, Dave 1971–1980" file, Accession number 2014-2.

Bauer, David. Notes. St. Mark's College Archives. Box 36, "Bauer, Dave 1971–1980" file.

Bauer, David. "Position Paper: Hockey Canada Development Committee." 1973. St. Mark's College Archives. Box 36, "Bauer, Dave 1971–1980" file, Accession number 2014-2.

Bauer, Dave. Speech Given at Hockey Canada Meeting. April 25, 1975. St. Mark's College Archives. "Bauer, Dave, 1971–1980" file.

Bauer, Dave. Speech to the Board of Hockey Canada. April 26, 1975. St. Mark's College Archives. Box 36, "Bauer, Dave 1971–1980" file, Accession number 2014-2.

Bauer, David. Untitled Letter. St. Mark's College Archives. "Bauer, Dave, 1971–1980" file.

Bennett, Jack. "Richardson Stresses Importance of Nats." *Winnipeg Free Press*, September 14, 1967. St. Mark's College Archives. Box 7, Carr—Correspondence and Misc. file.

CAHA/Hockey Canada/Fed. Govt. Meeting Agenda. July 2, 1975. St. Mark's College Archives. Box 36, "Bauer, Dave 1971–1980" file, Accession number 2014-2.

"Canada's National Hockey Team vs The U.S. Olympic Hockey Team." Pre-1980 Game Program. St. Michael's College School Archives. Bauer Fr. David box, Post-Memorial Cup file.

Carr, Henry. "Speech at the Inaugural Dinner, the Blessing and Official Opening." September 9, 1958. Vancouver. St. Mark's College Archives. Box 7, Henry Carr—Heart of the Matter file.

Christie, James. "Father Bauer Honored." *The Globe and Mail,* 1988. St. Michael's College School Archives. Bauer Fr. David box, SMCS memorial file.

Conaway, Tom. "Bauer Remembered as Feisty, Caring." *Record Newspaper,* November 15, 1988. St. Michael's College School Archives. Bauer Fr. David box, Obit file.

Cudhea, Peter. "Fond Memories." *Waterloo Chronicle,* November 30, 1994. St. Michael's College School Archives. Bauer Fr. David box, Obit file.

Dulmage, John. "Noble and Renewed." *Windsor Star,* February 24, 1978. St. Mark's College Archives. Box 36, "Bauer, Dave, 1971–1980" file.

Editorial Staff. "Who Won?" *Ubyssey,* February 11, 1964. St. Mark's College Archives. Box 50, "Research on Fr. Bauer" file.

"Father Matthew P. Sheedy, CSB." St. Michael's College School Archives. Fr. Sheedy File.

Fisher, Matthew. "Hockey History." *The Sunday Sun,* May 13, 2001. St. Michael's College School Archives. Bauer Fr. David box, SMCS Memorial file.

Fotheringham, Al. "UBC Coach Works to Restore Classic Ideal." *UBC Alumni Chronicle,* Winter 1963. St. Mark's College Archives. Box 37, "Research on Fr. Bauer" file.

Gibbons, Dennis. "St. Mike's 1961 Memorial Cup Champs Honoured 50 Years Later." May 29, 2011. St. Michael's College School Archives. The Majors 1960–61 file.

"Hockey Canada and International Play." July 1974. St. Mark's College Archives. Box 36, "Bauer, Dave 1971–1980" file, Accession number 2014-2.

Hockey Hall of Fame Magazine. "Bauer." 1989. St. Michael's College School Archives. Bauer Fr. David file.

"In Memoriam: Father David W. Bauer, CSB." St. Michael's College School Archives. Bauer Fr. David file.

Juckes, Gordon. Letter and Attachment to Douglas Fisher. June 20, 1975. St. Mark's College Archives. Box 36, "Bauer, Dave 1971–1980" file, Accession number 2014-2.

Kostyk, Greg. "Father David Bauer: Father of the National Hockey Program." March 31, 1988. St. Michael's College School Archives. "Father David, Coach" file.

MacGregor, Roy. "History Appears to be Ready to Repeat Itself—And That's Just Fine." Unknown magazine, 1978: 47–48. St. Michael's College School Archives. Bauer Fr. David file.

"The Mass of Christian Burial for Father David W. Bauer. November 2, 1924–November 9, 1988." St. Michael's College School Archives. Bauer Fr. David file.

Matheson, Jack. "Editorial." *Winnipeg Tribune,* September 14, 1967. St. Mark's College Archives. Box 7, Carr—Correspondence and Misc. file.

McCorkell, E. J. "In Memoriam H. S. Bellisle." In *Yearbook of St. Michael's College 1939.* St. Michael's College School Online Archives. https://www.stmichaelscollegeschool.com/about-us/history-and-archives/archives.

Morganson, Bunny. "Hang on to Your Seats." *Evening Telegram*, March 14, 1945. St. Michael's College School Archives. Bauer Fr. David file.

O'Brien, Andy. "Toronto's St. Michael's Has Sent 40 to the National Hockey League." In *Weekend Magazine* 8, no. 52 (1958). St. Michael's College School Archives. Bauer Fr. David box, 1965 and success of SMCS file.

O'Brien, Thomas. "Father David Bauer, C.S.B." 1999. St. Michael's College School Archives. "Bauer, Fr. David—Coach" box.

O'Brien, William. "St. Mike's Alumni Inducted into the Hockey Hall of Fame: Father David Bauer, csb." August 1996. St. Michael's College School Archives. Bauer Fr. David box, SMCS Memorial file.

Obodiac, Stan. "Father Bauer Man of the Hour." 1961. St. Michael's College School Archives. Bauer Fr. David file.

Osborne, Robert F. "Letter to Father Garvey." December 4, 1962. St. Mark's College Archives. Box 7, Carr—Correspondence and Misc. file.

St. Louis, Douglas J. "In Remembrance." *Catholic Register,* June 10, 1996. St. Michael's College School Archives. Fr. David Bauer box.

St. Michael's College School. *Calendar of St. Michael's College, For the Year 1905–1906.* St. Michael's College School Online Archives. https://archive.org/details/stmccalendar190506stmiuoft/page/n1/mode/2up?view=theater&q=calendar.

St. Michael's College School. *Hockey Yearbook 1961.* St. Michael's College School Online Archives. https://archive.org/details/stmcshockeyyearbook00testuoft/mode/2up?view=theater&q=hockey+yearbook+1961.

St. Michael's College School. *The Thurible 1942.* St. Michael's College School Online Archives. https://archive.org/details/stmcsthurible1942testuoft/mode/2up?view=theater&q=thurible+1942.

St. Michael's College School. *The Thurible 1944.* St. Michael's College School Online Archives. https://archive.org/details/stmcsthurible1944testuoft/mode/2up?view=theater&q=thurible+1944.

St. Michael's College School. *The Tower 1959.* St. Michael's College School Online Archives. https://archive.org/details/stmcstower1959testuoft/mode/2up?view=theater&q=tower+yearbook+1959.

St. Michael's College School. *Yearbook of St. Michael's College 1910.* St. Michael's College School Online Archives. https://archive.org/details/stmyearbookofstmich1910testuoft/mode/2up?view=theater&q=yearbook+1910.

St. Michael's College School. *Yearbook of St. Michael's College 1911.* St. Michael's College School Online Archives. https://archive.org/details/stmyearbookofstmich1911testuoft/mode/2up?view=theater&q=yearbook+1911.

St. Michael's College School. *Yearbook of St. Michael's College 1912.* St. Michael's College School Online Archives. https://archive.org/details/stmyearbookofstmich1912testuoft/mode/2up?view=theater&q=yearbook+1912.

St. Michael's College School. *Yearbook of St. Michael's College 1914*. St. Michael's College School Online Archives. https://archive.org/details/stmyearbookofstmich1914testuoft/mode/2up?view=theater&q=yearbook+1914.

St. Michael's College School. *Yearbook of St. Michael's College 1915*. St. Michael's College School Online Archives. https://archive.org/details/stmyearbookofstmich1915testuoft/page/n4/mode/2up?view=theater&q=yearbook+1915.

St. Michael's College School. *Yearbook of St. Michael's College 1921*. St. Michael's College School Online Archives. https://archive.org/details/stmyearbookofstmich-1921stmiuoft/mode/2up?view=theater&q=yearbook+1921.

St. Michael's College School. *Yearbook of St. Michael's College 1929*. St. Michael's College School Online Archives. https://archive.org/details/stmyearbookofstmich1929testuoft/mode/2up?view=theater&q=yearbook+1929.

St. Michael's College School. *Yearbook of St. Michael's College 1930*. St. Michael's College School Online Archives. https://archive.org/stream/stmyearbookofstmich1930testuoft/stmyearbookofstmich1930testuoft_djvu.txt.

Wenger, Howard, and H. Arthur Quinney. Letter to Hockey Canada. 1979. St. Mark's College Archives. Box 36, "Bauer, Dave, 1971–1980" file.

Wintermeyer, John J. Letter to Marc Lalonde, Minister of Health and Welfare. April 3, 1975. St. Mark's College Archives. Box 36, "Bauer, Dave 1971–1980" file, Accession number 2014-2.

Interviews & Emails:

Bauer, Bob, Jr. Interview with author. June 6, 2019.

Bauer-Leahy, Lisa. Interview with author. January 17, 2019.

Bauer-Maison, Marc. Interview with author. January 18, 2019.

Bauer-McGahey, Maureen. Interview with author. June 4, 2019.

Bourbonnais, Roger. Interview with author. August 26, 2019.

Burns, Paul. Interview with author. August 15, 2018.

Caffery, Terry. Interview with author. November 10, 2020.

Carmelite Sisters of St. Joseph. Email message to author. November 9, 2018.

Carmelite Sisters of St. Joseph. Interview with author. January 17, 2019.

Conacher, Brian. Interview with author. June 5, 2019.

Conlin, Paul. Interview with author. June 4, 2019.

Costello, Murray. Interview with author. June 3, 2019.

Denault, Todd. Interview with author. June 13, 2019.

Devaney, John. Interview with author. November 26, 2020.

Doherty, Cyril. Email message to author. September 17, 2020.

Doherty, Cyril. Email message to author. October 6, 2020.

Edwards, Jonathon. Interview with author. December 8, 2021.

Elliot, Devon, Curator at John P. Metras Sports Museum, University of Western Ontario Sports Hall of Fame. Email message to author. September 24, 2019.

Gallagher, Jack. Interview with author. January 15, 2019.

Gregg, Randy. Interview with author. November 9, 2020.

Hibbert, Neil. Interview with author. January 16, 2019.

Hindmarch, Bob. Interview with author. August 17, 2018.

"Hockey Canada—'The Road Ahead', A Discussion Paper for the Board of Directors." May 12, 1987. Private email attachment from Paul Carson, Vice President, Hockey Development of Hockey Canada. January 22, 2019.

Holmes, Derek. Interview with author. October 16, 2020.

Holowaty, Bill. Interview with author. February 1, 2019.

Hoven, Matt. Trip to Wilcox, SK. June 25, 2018.

Johnston, Marshall. Interview with author. August 22, 2019.

Keon, Jim. Interview with author. November 12, 2020.

Kidd, Bruce. Interview with author. June 5, 2019.

Kindig, Angela, Assistant Archivist at University of Notre Dame Archives. Email message to author. April 3, 2019.

King, Dave. Interview with author. September 4, 2020.

Kozak, Wally. Interview with author. September 25, 2020.

L'Heureux, Bill, Jr. Interview with author. September 18, 2019.

Lang, Chris. Interview with author. June 6, 2019.

Laudenbach, Margaret. Interview with author. January 18, 2019.

Macdonald, H. Ian. Interview with author. September 23, 2020.

MacKenzie, Barry. Interview with author. March 12, 2020.

McDowell, Mickey. Interview with author. August 16, 2018.

McLeod, Don. Interview with author. June 4, 2018.

Meagher, Louise. Email message to author. May 20, 2020.

Moran, Bobby. Interview with author. July 25, 2020.

Mott, Morris. Interview with author. July 15, 2020.

Nicholson, Bob. Email message to author. December 1, 2020.

Noonan, Rick. Interview with author. May 27, 2019.

O'Malley, Terry. Email message to author. March 6, 2023.

O'Malley, Terry. Interview with author. June 26, 2018.

O'Toole, Tom. Interview with author. January 15, 2019.

Primeau, Kevin. Email message to author. January 6, 2021.

Primeau, Kevin. Interview with author. November 13, 2020.

Regimbal, Gisele. Interview with author. March 4, 2020.

"Region of Waterloo Hall of Fame Induction Report on Father David Bauer." Private email attachment from Stacey McLennan. December 19, 2018.

Renney, Tom. Interview with author. January 10, 2022.

Sawyers, Michelle, Archivist at Basilian Archives. Email message to author. April 1, 2019.

Schmalz, Paul. Email message to author. April 25, 2019.

Schmalz, Paul, and Steve Freiburger. Interview with author. January 18, 2019.

Schmidt, Ted. Interview with author. November 16, 2020.

Wakabayashi, Mel. Interview with author. July 21, 2020.

Watt, Tom. Interview with author. September 18, 2020.

INDEX

"Professor Hoven has presented us with a detailed textbook on significant parts of the history of post-war Canadian hockey. He has also provided us with a carefully crafted, detailed, and finely balanced insight to the unique role played by Father Bauer as well as his hockey philosophy and his formative influence on the lives of a number of young players, both on and off the ice."

— *Dr. H. Ian Macdonald, president emeritus,*
York University, and former chair of Hockey Canada

"In *Hockey Priest*, Matt Hoven makes a persuasive case for the compatibility of sports and religion, in this case Canadian hockey and the Catholic tradition exemplified by Priest-Coach David Bauer. The perils and pleasures of Bauer's lifelong commitment to infuse spirituality into this sport are lovingly chronicled in this compelling biography."

— *Rebecca T. Alpert,*
professor of religion emerita, Temple University

"Father Bauer came to Japan at the invitation of Mr. Yoshiaki Tsutsumi, president of the Japanese Ice Hockey Federation. Father Bauer gave us an abundance of advice and introduced excellent Canadian players to Japanese hockey to raise our game to an international level. Thanks to his guidance I served as a director and vice president of the IIHF for 34 years."

— *Shoichi Tomita,*
former vice president of the International Ice Hockey Federation

"An excellent book on the life of Father David Bauer, a Basilian priest, who had a positive and lasting influence on the development of Canadian ice hockey. The book chronicles Bauer's success as a manager and hockey coach at St. Michael's College School in Toronto, who moved on to found and develop the Canadian National Team program. His emphasis on skill and technique, as well as the development of the whole person, had a profound effect on hockey at the amateur and elite levels. Father Bauer had a positive influence on all those fortunate enough to be involved under his guidance."

— *Dave Chambers,*
retired professor, School of Kinesiology and Health Science,
York University, Toronto Former University,
Junior A, Team Canada Junior, NHL head and assistant coach

Hockey Priest